Odyssey of a Philippine Scout

Fighting, Escaping, and Evading the Japanese, 1941–1944

by Arthur Kendal Whitehead

THE ABERJONA PRESS
Bedford, Pennsylvania

Developmental Editor: Keith E. Bonn
Production: Patricia K. Bonn
Cartographer: Tom Houlihan and Keith E. Bonn
Printer: Mercersburg Printing

The Aberjona Press is an imprint of Aegis Consulting Group, Inc.,
Bedford, Pennsylvania 15522

Printed in the United States of America
13 12 11 10 09 08 07 06 5 4 3 2 1

ISBN 10: 0-9717650-4-9
ISBN 13: 978-0-9717650-4-7

Cover:
Photos of the author, at center and lower right, from the author's collection.
Other photos from American Historical Collection, Ateneo de Manila University, Quezon City, Philippines.

Editor's Note: Special thanks to Colonel John Olson, USA (Ret.), 57th Infantry Regiment (PS); Captain Steven Myers, USN (Ret.); Lieutenant Colonel Louis A. DiMarco, USA (Ret.), Department of Military History, USA Command and General Staff College, Fort Leavenworth, Kansas; Lieutenant Colonel Hugh Foster, USA (Ret.); and Lieutenant Colonel Mark Reardon, USA, USA Center for Military History, for their invaluable assistance in the creation of this work.

To

World War II soldiers, especially those
of the 26th Cavalry Regiment (Philippine Scouts)

the Whitehead family, for their loving support

and

Keith E. Bonn, 1956–2005, who embraced
history with the highest standards

Contents

Foreword

Where do we get such men?

This question, asked about Navy Reserve fighter pilots in the Korean War and made famous in James Michener's *Bridges at Toko-Ri,* should be asked with the same hushed awe about Arthur Kendal Whitehead in World War II . . . and his spiritual successors in every American war since.

As this book is published American soldiers, for the second time in 60 years, are again engaged in a global war against ruthless enemies who are bent on the destruction of our people and our way of life. Our volunteer soldiers, sailors, airmen, and marines are well trained, well led, and competent. They are committed to their missions and devoted in their sense of duty.

Small groups of American advisors and instructors are helping Iraqis build an army and national police force to defend their country and their distinct and diverse people from ruthless domestic and foreign-bred terrorists and insurgents. The future of Iraq and the Middle East (as well as the security of countries far from those borders) hinges on the success that these small advisory groups will have in forming a modern and effective military capable of providing for their own internal defense and domestic development. Babylonian and Assyrian history has proved the Iraqi a formidable soldier if, like those from any army, he is well trained and confident in his leaders.

The US Army has an innate ability to develop unconventional warriors who live with, fight with, and lead indigenous combat forces. Probably our most celebrated example is of the alliance between the *Montagnards* or "Mountain People" of Vietnam and the 5th Special Forces Group during our Southeast Asian conflict. Armed, trained, and led by Special Forces NCOs, the *Montagnards* were dedicated, savage fighters fiercely loyal to the men who helped them defend their way of life from the Communist Vietnamese.

There are other, much more recent examples of intensive, intimate American leadership of allied soldiers from alien cultures, fighting in a common cause. One such example is Colonel Jim Coffman. To this point in the Global War on Terrorism, he has garnered the highest decoration awarded to a Special Forces soldier. Colonel Coffman, 51, earned the Distinguished Service Cross for his role in leading Iraqi Special Police commandos through a desperate five-and-one-half-hour battle against insurgents trying to overrun an Iraqi police station in Mosul.

How do we make such leaders? Where do we get such men who can at once win the confidence of warriors from a dramatically different culture *and* maintain their integrity, values, and beliefs? What traits are we looking for to select, educate, train, and develop our best unconventional warfare soldiers? How do we ensure they embody the "Warrior Ethos" as soldiers and citizens? Do they have unwavering moral compasses and the sense of right, whether as leaders of conventional formations, as a prisoner of war or active evader, as a guerrilla himself, or as an instructor for a fledgling Army?

Odyssey of a Philippine Scout describes precisely that *kind* of soldier. Long before the first green beret was awarded to a Special Forces soldier, even before the term "special forces" was coined, there were Americans who trained and led soldiers from radically different cultures, while earning their confidence and willing cooperation through a manifest respect for their customs and solidarity in their cause.

Arthur Kendal Whitehead chronicles his formative days as just such a leader as an officer of the US Army's Philippine Scouts. Specifically, he writes of his tenure as a horse cavalry platoon leader in the exotic Philippines in 1941. The reader will note not only parallels with the situations in Iraq and Afghanistan today, but will also recognize the timeless process of armies everywhere in building a soldier's sense of duty, regimental pride, *esprit de corps,* camaraderie, and, in the best examples, the bonds forged between officers, NCOs, and soldiers.

In December 1941 the Imperial Japanese Army invaded the Philippines and immediately pressed the American and Philippine Army defenders back toward the Bataan Peninsula. In combat with the last United States Army cavalry unit to fight mounted, Whitehead was left for dead, alone, and armed only with a .45-caliber pistol.

The Japanese demanded that Lieutenant General Jonathan Wainwright order all American troops in the Philippines to surrender. Faced with the moral dilemma of surrendering or being declared a deserter and, worse, exposing all of his American comrades already in captivity to slaughter, Whitehead also fully recognized the dangers concomitant to resigning himself to the care of the Japanese. Nevertheless, after having already gone to enormous exertions to evade the enemy's clutches, Whitehead reluctantly obeyed his orders and surrendered. His superiors then reminded him that having followed his orders, it was now his duty to escape . . . and he made good on that guidance at his first opportunity.

He was determined to get back into the war as best he could, either as a guerrilla or, as he decided later, to evade and escape to Australia. His odyssey took two years.

Whitehead's story is one of amazing tenacity, initiative, patience, and ingenuity. His story is not so much a combat story as it is one of piercing insight and finding the limits of human endurance. He learned and exercised a panoply of warrior skills: expertise with weapons; escape; evasion; navigation; survival; medicine; hunting; seamanship and rigging; meteorology; most of all, rapport-building and "people skills."

Whitehead had to learn to navigate around relentless Japanese land and maritime patrols; hostile Filipinos; and the endless dangers posed by nature herself. To his surprise, he discovered the depth of Japan's extensive networks of spies (many infiltrated before the war) and informers. He also learned about Filipino hospitality and courage. When he found comfortable, hospitable refuge (knowing he could sit out the duration away from the concerns of war and occupation), what drove him to continue, to plan for a formidable ocean crossing to rejoin American forces?

While luck and providence proved his strongest allies, the student warrior will recognize that God also helps him who helps himself. In reading Arthur Kendal Whitehead's candid personal chronicles, I hope and pray that today's American prospective soldiers will recognize some of his best traits in themselves.

After reading *Odyssey of a Philippine Scout*—and the citations of decorations awarded to Americans in today's headlines—I am certain that America will always find such men.

David J. Liwanag
Lieutenant Colonel, Special Forces
United States Army
Fort Benning, Georgia
Veteran's Day, 2005

Lieutenant Colonel David J. Liwanag, a Filipino-American, enlisted in the Texas National Guard's 36th Airborne Brigade in 1979 and later served as a scout in Company G (Ranger) (Long Range Reconnaissance Patrol). He is a 1982 Distinguished Military Graduate of Texas A&M University. He has served in an exceptionally extensive variety of conventional and special operations assignments in the United States, Korea, and Japan, commanding four Special Forces A detachments and serving as the operations officer for two Special Forces battalions. As such, he has participated in exercises and operations throughout Asia, Europe, North Africa, the Middle East, the Caribbean, and Australia. He has also served as the commanding officer of the US Army Parachute Team, the "Golden Knights." A qualified Ranger, Master Parachutist, Military Freefall Jump Master as well as a Green Beret, he also holds the coveted "President's Hundred" tab. He is a veteran of Operations UPHOLD DEMOCRACY in Haiti and IRAQI FREEDOM. Today, he commands the United States Army Marksmanship Unit at Fort Benning, Georgia. The son of a Special Forces veteran of combat special operations in the Korean and Vietnam wars, LTC Liwanag's paternal grandparents hail from communities on Luzon.

Introduction

This is an account of my experiences as a young cavalry officer in the Philippine Islands during the World War II years, 1941–43. It is a period of my life on which I look back with a mixed feeling of awe and fascination, often wondering by what criteria the Almighty chooses between those who will survive and those who will not.

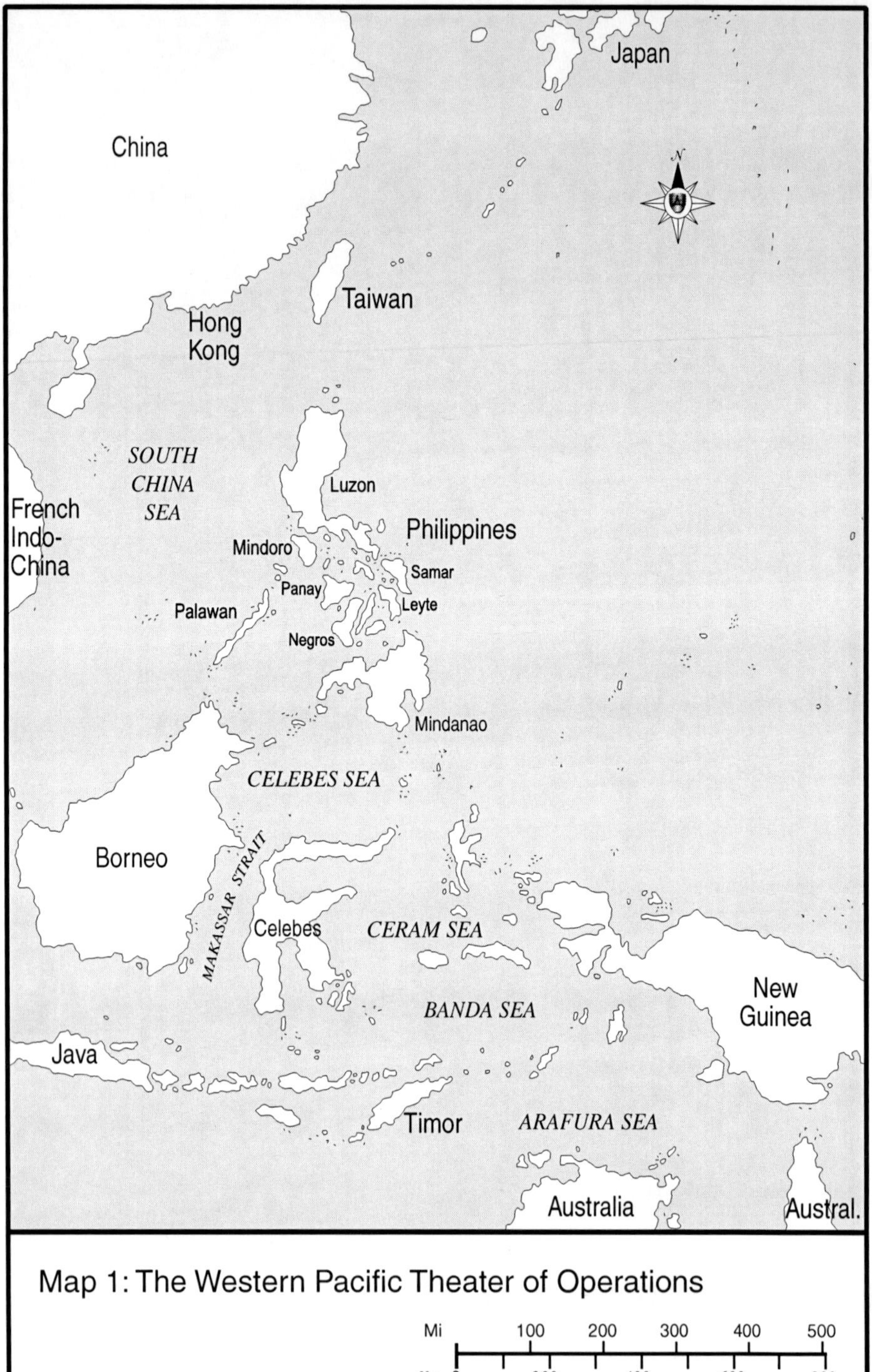

Map 1: The Western Pacific Theater of Operations

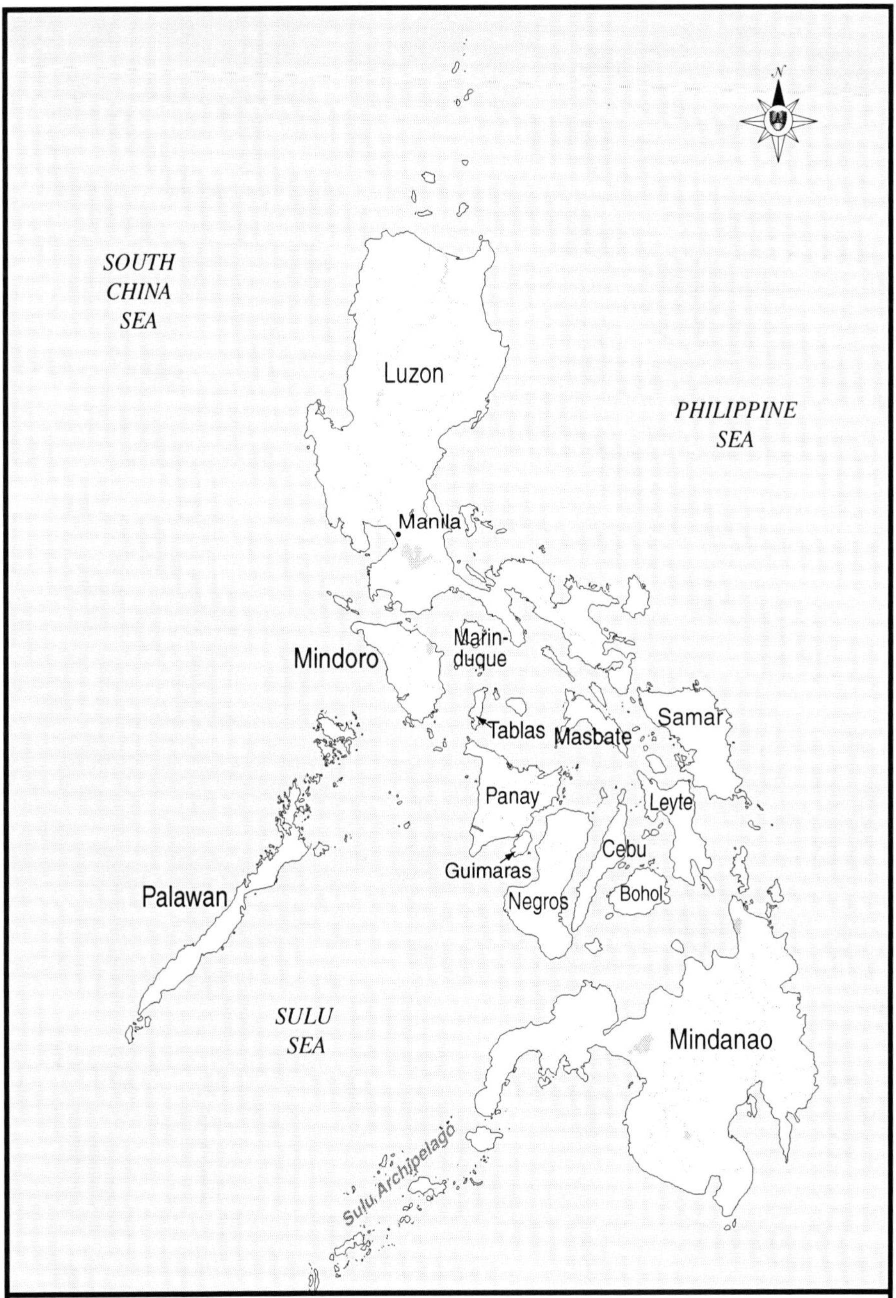

Map 2: Overview of the Philippines

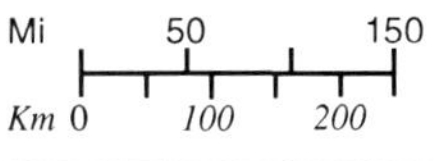

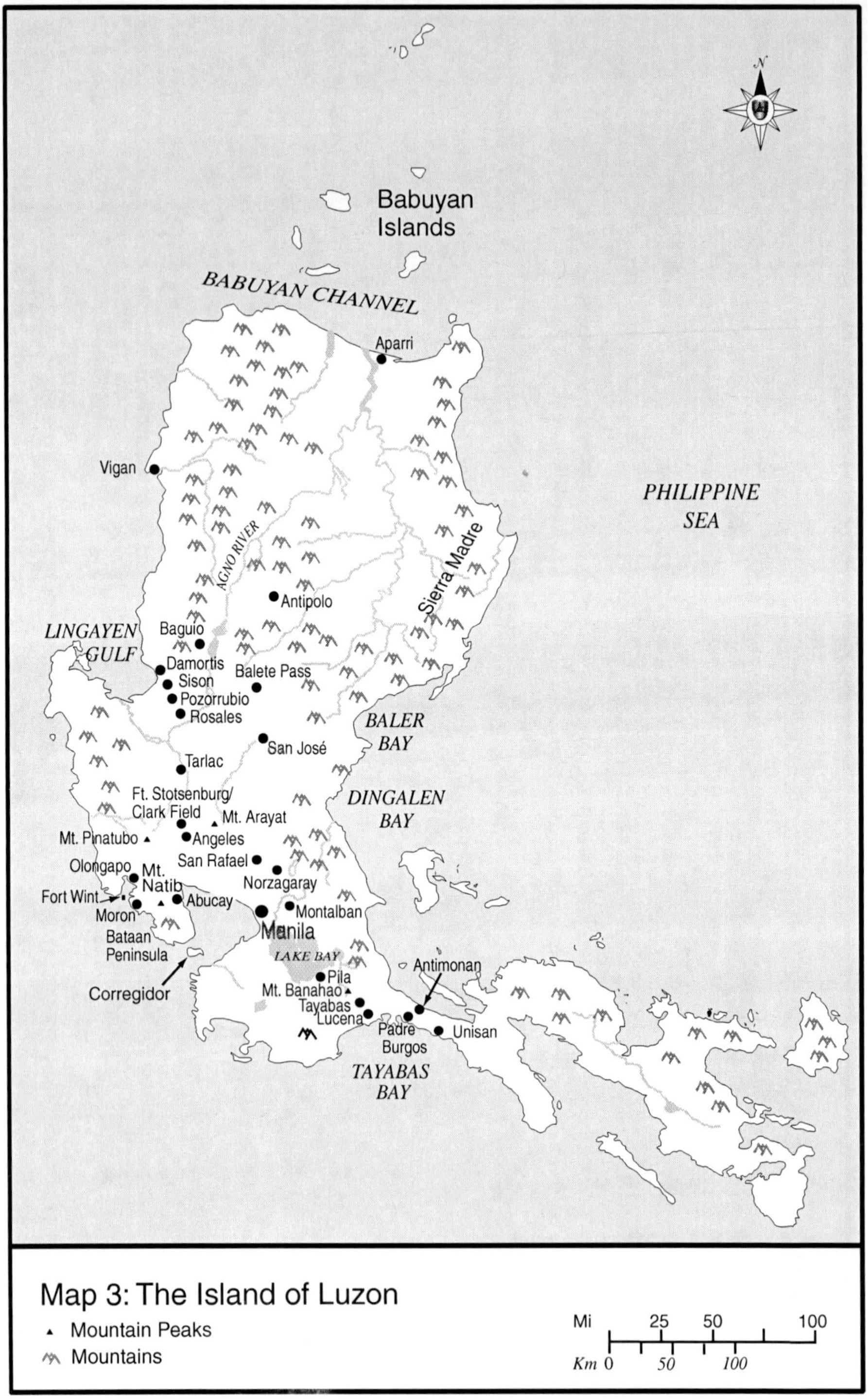

Map 3: The Island of Luzon

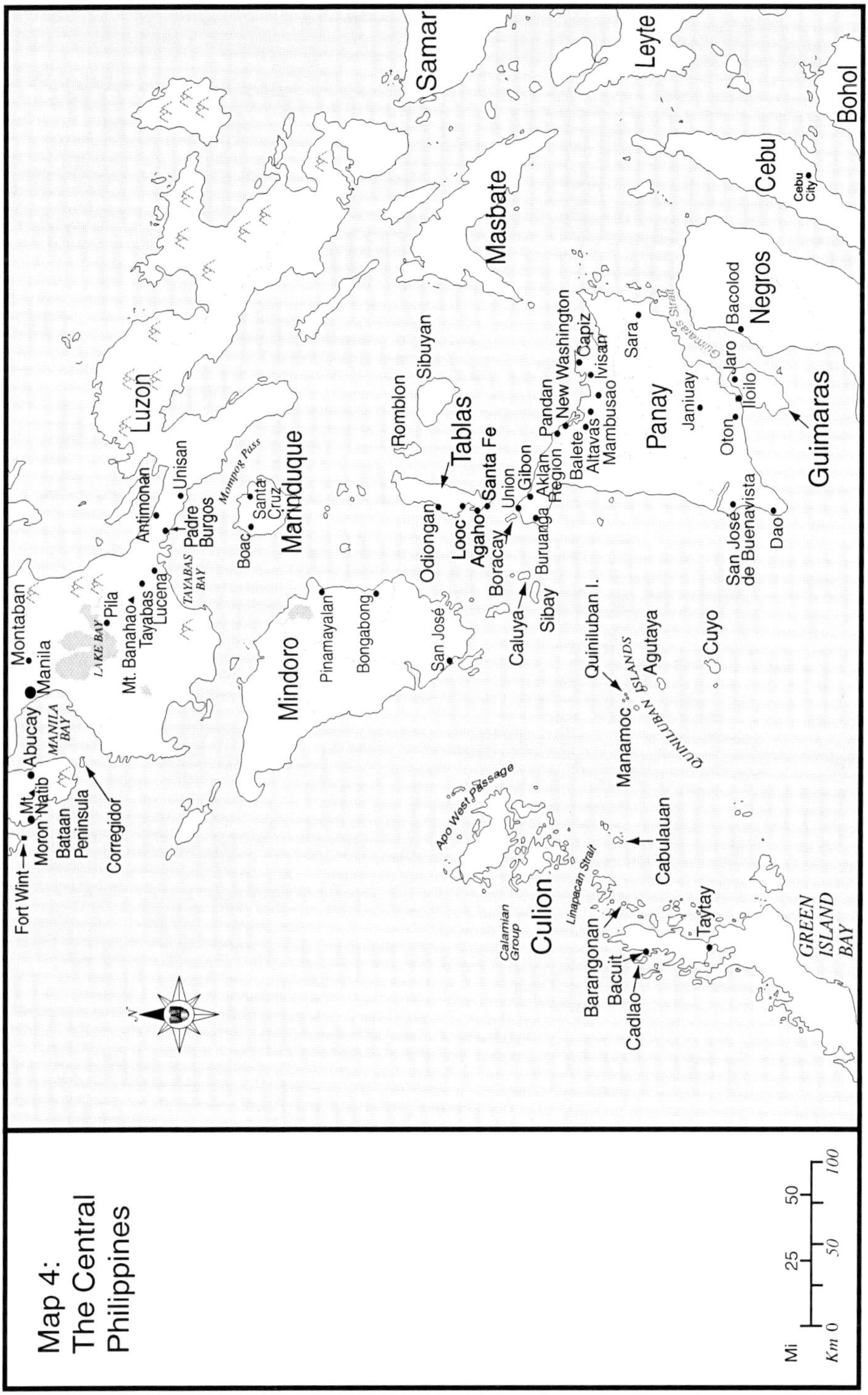

Map 4:
The Central
Philippines
Mi 0 25 50
Km 0 50 100
N
Luzon
Samar
Leyte
Bohol
Cebu
Cebu City
Masbate
Sibuyan
Romblon
Tablas
Marinduque
Mindoro
Panay
Negros
Guimaras
Fort Wint
Moron
Mt. Natib
Abucay
Bataan Peninsula
Corregidor
MANILA BAY
Manila
Montaban
LAKE BAY
Pila
Mt. Banahao
Tayabas
Lucena
TAYABAS BAY
Antimonan
Padre Burgos
Unisan
Mompog Pass
Boac
Santa Cruz
Pinamayalan
Bongabong
San José
Odiongan
Looc
Agaho
Santa Fe
Boracay
Union
Gibon
Caluya
Sibay
Buruanga
Aklan Region
Pandan
Balete
New Washington
Altavas
Capiz
Mambusao
Ivisan
Sara
Janiuay
Jaro
Bacolod
Iloilo
Oton
San José de Buenavista
Dao
Guimaras Strait
Quiniluban I.
Agutaya
Cuyo
Manamoc
QUINILUBAN ISLANDS
Apo West Passage
Cabulauan
Linapacan Strait
Calamian Group
Culion
Barangonan
Bacuit
Cadlao
Taytay
GREEN ISLAND BAY

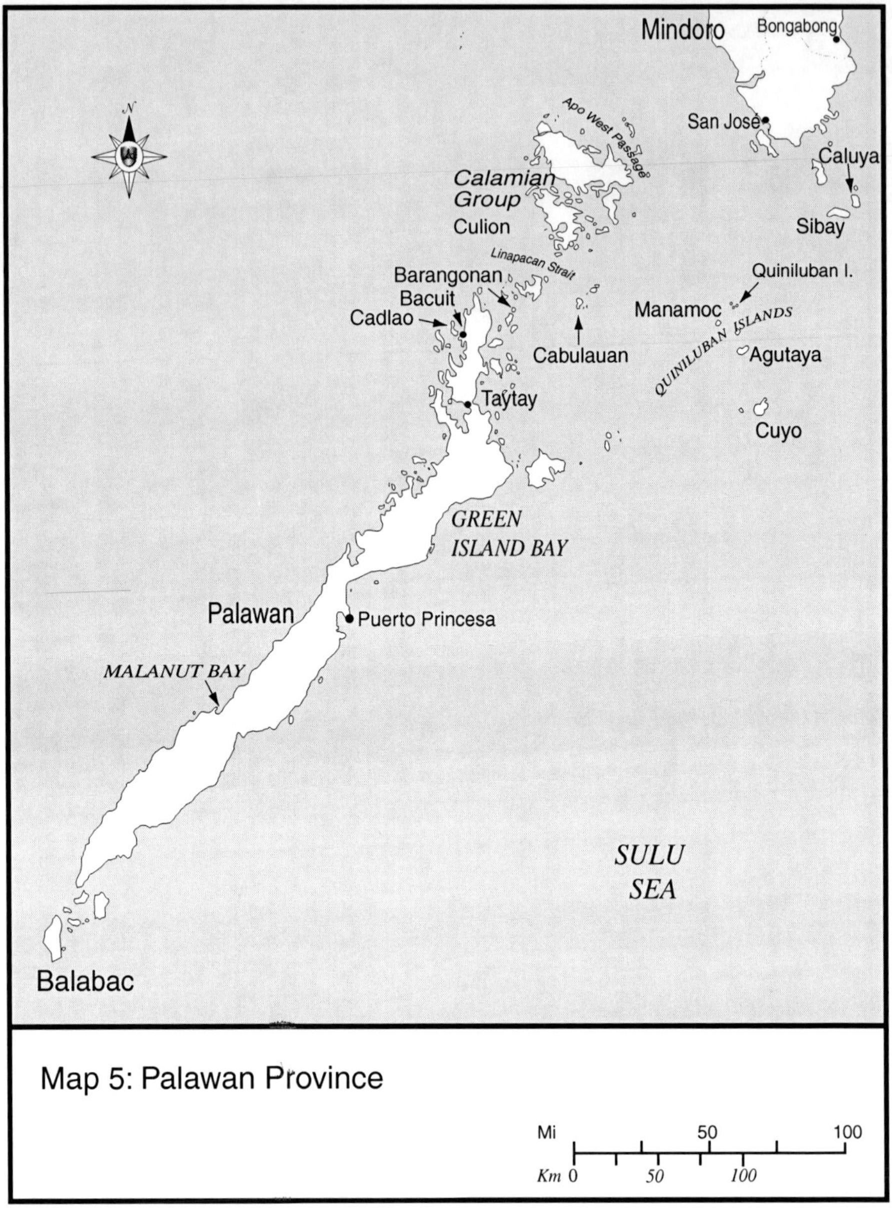

Map 5: Palawan Province

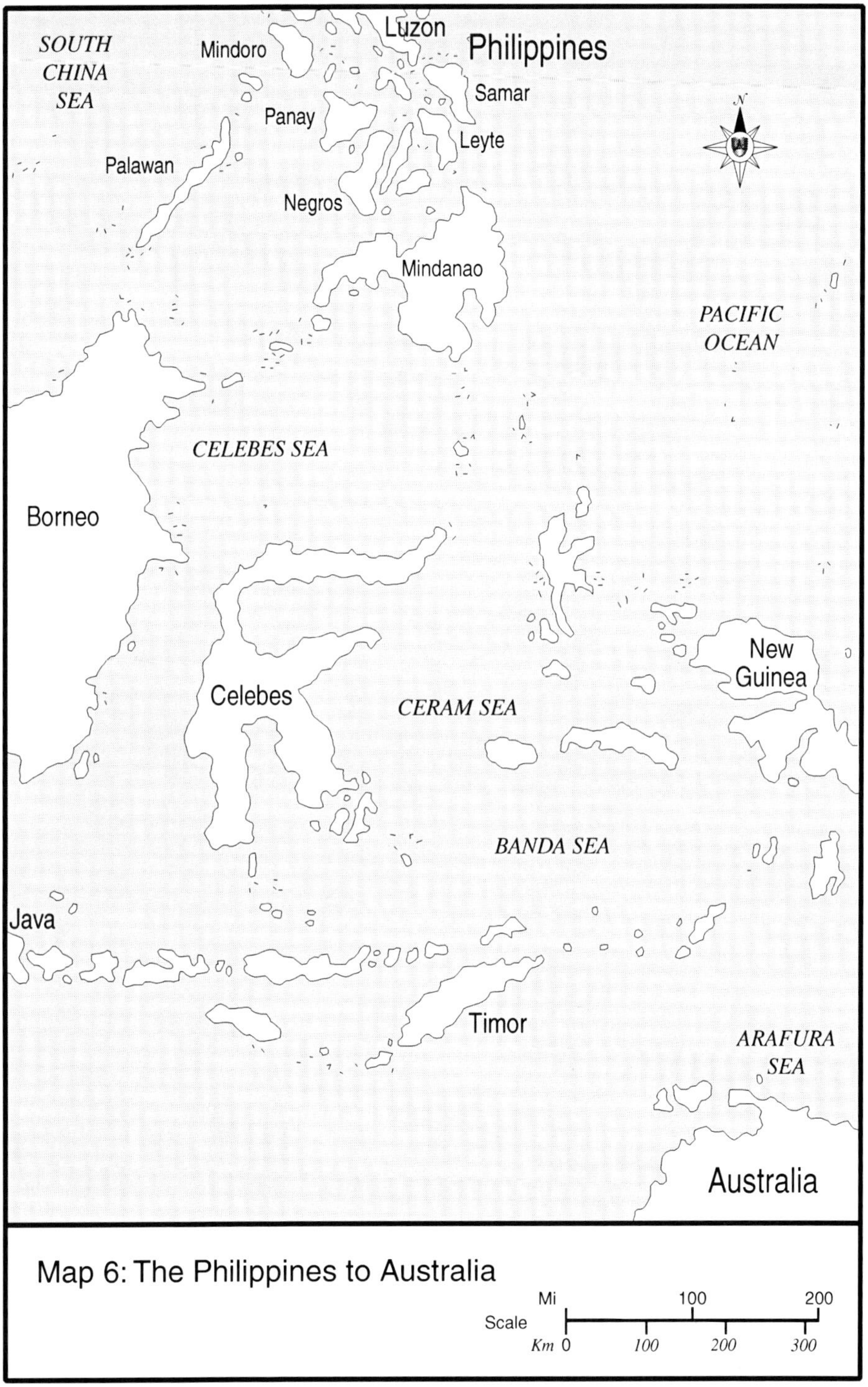

Map 6: The Philippines to Australia

Part One

BEFORE THE WAR

Chapter 1

In the last winter of the uneasy peace that still lingered in the Pacific, on 24 January 1941, I sailed from San Francisco harbor on the US Army Transport *Ulysses S. Grant.* As my friends and relatives waved goodbye on the weather-worn pier and disappeared from sight, I had little thought of how much I would miss them and my American way of life in the years to come.

At the moment, I was looking westward, excited at the thought of the new experiences that lay ahead. We were heading for the Philippine Islands. I was coming from a year and a half of duty with the 8th Cavalry Regiment, stationed at Fort Bliss, Texas. My orders assigned me to the United States Department of the Philippines.

We sailed west by south across the broad expanse of the Pacific. Leaving Honolulu, the sea became ever calmer; the cloudless sky a paler blue and the heat daily more intense.

Watching the little green flying fish skimming over the surface of the ocean that were frightened by the passing of our ship, the schools of porpoise playing about the bow, and the sighting of an occasional whale never failed to fascinate me. Card and checker tournaments, reading, excellent meals, and duty with the troops aboard made the time pass quickly and enjoyably. Neptune, the old man of the sea, came aboard to greet us and present certificates of passage to the neophytes as we crossed the International Date Line.

Guam was our first taste of the Orient and the tropics. The sight of the blue-green sea, the colorful coral formations; the brilliant white sandy beaches bordered by graceful coconut palms; and the squally weather with small, low, misty clouds blown hither and yon pouring out sheets of water, was our initiation. One moment, a torrential rain would drench us; the next, we would be dried by a sun beating down with fierceness unknown to temperate zones.

We went ashore by lighter, landing on a rickety wooden pier on the western side of an island near a small native settlement. There, for the first time, I saw

---

**Nipa* is a large palm common to the Philippines and Australia, having long leaves often used for thatching. [Ed.]

the *nipa* shacks;* the dense tropical vegetation; the plodding *carabao* pulling crudely built two-wheeled carts over muddy, rutted roads; the small native ponies; carefree, grinning, naked, brown children; and attractive women dressed in long, colorful skirts and *pina*-cloth blouses, with their latest offspring on a hip or a basket of laundry balanced on their head. Underfoot and everywhere were squawking chickens and squealing pigs. We spent the afternoon on Guam.

On the morning of 19 February, Samar, the first of the Philippine Islands to be sighted, gradually came into view to the southwest. Ahead, Luzon Island slowly rose out to the horizon. At first it was a tiny, shimmering, dark spot where the sea met the sky, gradually growing into a great mass of mountains, skirted by tiny strips of white beaches; it finally emerged into well-defined trees and native shelters. A small and charming red-and-white lighthouse guarded the rocky promontory nearest the ship. As we rounded the southern tip of Luzon, the green hills of Samar Island to the south appeared to be at arm's length from the rail of the ship.

That night the stars stood out with a brilliance that made them appear as great lamps hanging from a dark purple canopy. There was no wind. The sea was as level as a pond and resembled a dark, oily morass. The prow of our ship threw out great phosphorescent waves, lighting its way between the landmasses that loomed on either side.

Here and there small fires flickered on the hillsides. I wondered what kind of man had made those fires and what life on these islands would be like. Little did I think that in less than a year, I would be crossing this same stretch of water in a native dugout, barely escaping capture by the Japanese.

Chapter 2

It was 0700 hours on 20 February 1941, 27 days out of San Francisco, when the *Grant,* now dubbed "The Tub," crawled on a northeasterly course through the straits of the south channel into Manila Bay. The sun stood in the east, a blazing ball over the mist-shrouded city of Manila. To the north, Corregidor Island rose out of the sea, resembling the hulk of a mammoth ship. Beyond was the blue-green haze of the mountains of the Bataan Peninsula. To the south were the little islands of Carabao and El Fraile, and beyond stretched the winding coastline of the bay, a white thread of sandy beach bordered by palm groves and jungle.

The great harbor of Manila was dead calm, shimmering under the glare and awful heat of the sun. Native fish traps crowded the shallows, stretching their long arms far out into the bay to guide the schools of unwary fish to their doom. Small canoe-like boats make of hollowed logs were being lazily paddled between these traps.

It was the beginning of the hot dry season on the island of Luzon. Even at that early hour, perspiration trickled down my face and back.

Two pursuit planes buzzed our ship.* The wife of one of the pilots, standing beside me, nearly went overboard waving.

Before docking, the *Grant* stopped to take aboard a group of Americans and Philippine Scouts to process the new arrivals before landing. This was the first I had seen of the Scouts, little brown men, well-proportioned and alert, cutting fine figures in their starched khakis and highly-polished brass and boots. To my joy, I was assigned to the 26th Cavalry Regiment (Philippine Scouts).† The 26th Cavalry was stationed at Fort Stotsenburg, Pampanga Province, to the north of Manila.‡

The Philippine Scouts comprised a unique organization of the United States Regular Army. The Scouts included cavalry, infantry, artillery, engineers, and some support units, and were stationed only in the Philippine Islands. They were officered primarily by Americans; enlisted personnel were entirely Filipinos. As a US Army outfit, they were entirely distinct from the units of the Philippine Army, which was comprised entirely of Filipinos, with some American advisors.

---

*"Pursuit planes" was the official term for fighter aircraft in the US Army Air Corps, and was abbreviated with the prefix "P" in the model nomenclature, that is, P-35, P-40, and so forth. This designation was dropped in favor of "F" for "fighter" when the Air Force became a separate service after WWII. [Ed.]

†Hereafter abbreviated, per US Army convention, to "(PS)."

‡Fort Stotsenburg was named for John H. Stotsenburg, Colonel of US Volunteers and Captain in the Regular Army. Born on November 24, 1858, he was an 1881 graduate of the United States Military Academy at West Point. Colonel Stotsenburg was killed in action on 23 April 1898 while leading his regiment in battle at Quingua, Philippines.

Nearing the docks, the sprawling city of Manila became discernible through a haze of heat, dirt, and smoke. The docks were crowded with ocean-going vessels flying flags of nearly every maritime nation in the world.

As the *Grant* came alongside Pier #7, an Army band set up a terrific blare of military music. The dock was crowded with happy, waving well-wishers: officers in white uniforms and their ladies in colorful, light dresses with soft, broad-brimmed hats. Gaiety was the order of the day. Many waved little American flags, shouting in ecstasy at the sight of old friends. The band also met the joyous occasion with popular tunes of the day.

Two officers of the 26th came aboard to greet me. Major Thorpe would be my host for the first week at Fort Stotsenburg. I would live in his home. Captain Blanning would be my troop commander.

Major Thorpe and I pushed our way through the crowded dock to his station wagon and headed for the Army-Navy Club. Suddenly, we were in the midst of the confusion and dangers of Manila traffic. The streets were crowded with over-aged, broken-down "jalopies," most in the taxi business. With horns blaring and throttles pressed to the floor, the Filipinos transformed these old crates into demons in armor.

For every automobile, there were at least half a dozen *Calesa* wagons, two-wheeled rigs like rickshaws, but pulled by a pony instead of a man hitched between the shafts. The *Calesa* pony, usually a stallion, was about twelve hands high and inherently as mean as a witch. They were a menace to pedestrians, kicking and biting anyone within reach. Undoubtedly their resentment of the human race stemmed from their association with the *Calesa* driver. When he wasn't yanking on the pony's mouth to slow him down, he was beating on his posterior to speed him up.

Everyone drove on the wrong side of the street. Pedestrians darted in and out of traffic with as little regard for their necks as they had for the traffic rules. Intersection crossings were a *melée.* A traffic cop's life was a short one. I was relieved when we finally reached the Army-Navy Club.

With its white-pillared entranceway shaded by great trees and cooled by a fresh breeze blowing off the bay, the Army-Navy Club was a pleasant contrast to the hot and crowded streets and noise of the Manila traffic. Before entering the club, we stopped a moment to examine the pearls offered by a colorful group of bare-footed Moros, dressed in baggy, brightly-colored, silk pantaloons and red fezzes.

The interior of the club was refreshingly cool with its high ceilings, many fans, and the breeze blowing in from the bay through the spacious rooms. We crossed the lobby into the great ballroom filled with officers and their ladies, greeting old friends and meeting new ones. General Wainwright was at the head of the receiving line. He did not appear as lean and tough as when I had seen him a year and a half before on maneuvers in Texas. This was the welcoming party, the *Bienvenida*, given for new arrivals to the Philippines.

We left before the party was over because Major Thorpe wanted to get an early start to Fort Stotsenburg, which was more than 50 miles north of Manila.

Once again we were in heavy traffic, which made getting out of the city an ordeal. Going north into the country the traffic thinned, but dogs, chickens, pigs, *carabaos,* and naked brown children kept our driver braking, swerving, and even, at times, forcing him to stop. The road was narrow and full of potholes. We were traveling over the flat, central plain of Luzon Island, winding through rice paddies and crowded, odorous *barrios.*

The Filipinos waved and often called out to us as we passed.

"Don't let this show of friendliness fool you," Major Thorpe said. This was the first he had spoken since leaving the Army-Navy Club except to swear at his driver. "These are the *Taos,* the sharecroppers who till the land. They appear sincerely friendly, but in the end, they do what their landowners tell them. Our presence is resented by the hierarchy of the bureaucracy, made up mostly of the well-to-do. They seem to go out of their way to persecute the Americans."

"One thing you must remember," he emphasized, looking at me in all seriousness. "If ever you have an accident off a US installation, no matter how serious, keep going. Report it to the first Constabulary Post or US installation you come to. Once you get into a Filipino jail, it takes an act of Congress to get you out. Worse than Mexico."

I never forgot that advice.

The Philippine Constabulary was a paramilitary organization established in 1901 as a national police force in the wake of the Philippine Insurrection. Months later, members of the Constabulary helped me escape from the Japanese.

Chapter 3

Nearing Fort Stotsenburg, the Zambales Mountains loomed upward to the west, a shaded mass of deep green, silhouetted by the setting sun. It had taken two hours to drive the 50 miles from Manila.

Entering the post was like coming onto an oasis of freshness, cleanliness, and serenity, a welcome sight after the long sea voyage and the heat and dirt of the day. The great rectangular parade grounds of the 26th Cavalry came into view, still green from the rains of the southwest monsoon. They were bordered by huge tropical trees reaching as high as 50 feet into the air.

To the south of the parade ground was the line of the 26th Cavalry troop barracks: large, square, one-story wooden structures painted gray, standing on four-foot high stilts. Their roofs were of unpainted corrugated iron. Each barracks had a wide porch facing the parade ground. Large, wooden windows, hinged at the top and propped open with poles, provided ventilation.

To the north, across the parade ground, was the line of officers' quarters and the officers' mess. These also were square, one-story buildings on stilts, but painted green with red iron roofs, their long screened porches also facing the parade ground. To the west were the post headquarters, the theater, and the Post Exchange; to the east, the post hospital and more quarters.

Mrs. Thorpe and her two young daughters were waiting on the porch of their quarters as we arrived. I received a gracious and hospitable welcome. I shall never forget Mrs. Thorpe's warm "Welcome to Fort Stotsenburg, Lieutenant Whitehead. We are happy to have you with us."

It was the custom in the 26th Cavalry and throughout the Philippine Department that a newly-arrived officer, whether alone or with his family, spends the first few days as a guest in the household of another officer.

The rooms of the Thorpes' quarters were large, with high ceilings and walls made of thin *papier-mâché*-like wood. Strands of seashells hung in the doorways in place of conventional doors. There was little privacy, but Mrs. Thorpe assured me that the sacrifice was well worth the comfort of an unobstructed breeze. Although all the windows and outside exits were screened, little lizards were everywhere. They kept croaking "Gecko," which is what they were called. "They are much more satisfactory than flyswatters," Mrs. Thorpe explained, "and more efficient, too."

A houseboy, immaculate in his white uniform, awaited me in my room. My bags had been brought in and opened; a clean uniform was laid out on the bed.

I waited a long while in the shower for the water to run warm; finally I gave up, and bathed in cool water. It took a few days for me to realize that it was considered unnecessary to heat the bath water in this climate.

At dinner I was introduced to a delicious tropical fruit, the native papaya. It would be a long while before I would have a drink of fresh cow's milk again.

Besides the houseboy, the household included an *amah* (nurse) for the youngsters, a *lavandera* (laundress), and a cook. Each of these worked for 10, 15, or 20 *pesos* a month and their food. A *peso* was worth 50 cents.

The next morning, I reported to regimental headquarters of the 26th. Captain Fleeger, the regimental adjutant, officially informed me that I was assigned to Troop E. He took me around the headquarters to meet members of the regimental staff. I was surprised to find that my regimental commander was Colonel Clinton Pierce, with whom I had served at Fort Bliss.

The colonel remembered me, but there was little warmth in his greeting. He and I had not been on the best of terms in the States. Pierce was a *Kappa Sig,* and I was a *Sigma Chi.* There was no doubt in my mind which was the better fraternity, but I had not been able to convince him.

I started down the line of barracks to find Troop E. Little clumps of ferns skirted the roots of the huge trees that lined the walk; here and there dainty orchids, not larger than a man's thumb, grew out of their trunks. The rich green of the dew-drenched parade grounds glistened in the sunlight. What a contrast this was to the Texas desert that I had left behind.

Now and then a Scout passed, all polished, starched, and shiny. A smart salute and a brisk "Good morning, sir," was the usual greeting.

As I turned into Troop E barracks, my shirt was already damp from sweat.

Entering the orderly room, the first sergeant reported with gusto, "First Sergeant Amagable reporting, sir. I welcome the lieutenant to E Troop." I think he had been waiting for me. As all good first sergeants I had known, he had a noticeable paunch.

"Sir, the troop commander will see you." Sergeant Amagable had just come out of Captain Blanning's little office and was holding the swinging door for me.

I walked in briskly, halted, stood at attention, and reported, "Lieutenant Whitehead reporting for duty, sir." Captain Blanning returned my salute, stood up and shook hands.

"It's good to have you with us, Whitehead. Have a seat."

The captain was tall and lean. He had a hard, quizzical look; his eyes were slightly bloodshot; his voice had a nasal rasp. He offered me a cigarette and lit one for himself. He drew the tobacco smoke deep into his lungs; a quarter of an inch of the cigarette disappeared. The smoke steamed out of his mouth and long nose as he talked.

"You've just come into the best troop in the regiment." Blanning smiled as he used this cliché. "As you probably have heard, the regiment is scheduled to receive a batch of recruits that will bring it to full strength. For the past several months we have been training and preparing ourselves for their arrival. We're pretty well set to go now, but there's still a lot of work ahead of us."

"We have about an hour before regimental officers' call. Let's have a look around." Blanning burst through the swinging door at a fast walk, and I followed him. I noticed his singular, rolling gait, which was more typical of a sailor than a cavalryman. He led me on a whirlwind tour through the sleeping quarters, mess hall, kitchen, and supply room. Everything looked immaculate; morale seemed excellent. Especially noticeable was the high regard shown by the men toward their captain.

"Now to the stables," Blanning said in a relieved tone. "You'll meet Praeger there. The troop just got in from horse exercise."

Lieutenant Praeger, the other officer in the troop, was a big Kansas farm boy and proud of it. I took to him at once, as I had to Blanning.

At the stables, the captain's pace slowed noticeably. Working down the picket line, he examined every animal, calling each by name, reviewing to me their good and bad points, checking saddle sores, rope burns, skins, kicks, and anything else.

At one end of the picket line, Blanning's orderly was carefully and warily grooming two beautiful and spirited geldings, each over 16 hands. They looked to be thoroughbreds. I was informed they were part of a recently-arrived shipment of remounts. Blanning had chosen these two for himself.

At another part of the line was picketed the remainder of the troop's remounts. Among them, a little sorrel mare, barely 15 hands, caught my eye. I asked to have her led out. Her teeth showed her to be three or four years old; her legs were as clean as a ballet dancer's; her coat was as soft a silk. There was not a blemish on her. This beautiful little filly looked to be a thoroughbred and proved to be one. Her upper lip was tattooed.

Captain Blanning noticed my interest. "She's a pretty pony. You have a good eye. Would you like to try her?"

"Yes, sir, very much," I answered, and from then on she was mine.

When I returned to Major Thorpe's quarters, a Chinese tailor was waiting for me on the porch. He had come at the major's request to measure me for uniforms and civilian clothes suitable for the tropics. He took for granted that I would also need special tailoring for everything else I wore, even down to cloth watchstraps. When I found out how unbelievably reasonable the services of this Chinese from Hong Kong Street were, I gave him a generous order.

Not many days after my arrival, word came that my automobile had been unloaded and was ready to be picked up at a certain dock in Manila.

At 0600 hours, I caught the little train from the Quartermaster area for the town of Dau. There I transferred to the main train going south to Manila.

In the coolness and freshness of the morning, I suddenly became aware of the beauty of the Luzon plain, which I had completely missed on the trip north a few days earlier. The bright greenness of the rice paddies shimmering in the morning sun; little brown barrios scattered here and there; the *Taos* in their G-strings and cone-shaped straw hats following their plodding *carabaos* in the rice fields all formed a picture-book scene of the peaceful Philippine countryside that always remained with me.

The dirt, heat, and swarms of humanity rushing about at the Manila railroad station brought me back to reality.

At a street corner I stopped, watching the scrambled traffic, dreading to go out into it. I had an address where my car was to be picked up but, so far, I had found no one who could tell me where it was.

A *Calesa* finally stopped in front of me.

"Where you go?" the driver yelled.

"You speak English?" I yelled back.

"Sure," he answered.

"I want to go . . . " and read him the address.

"I know. Come." He patted the seat beside him.

Reluctantly, I pulled myself into the rickety cart. I was not at all sure that this was the right thing to do. The *Calesa* rode like an old-time buckboard. At each traffic stop when the cop gave the "go" signal, that was the start of a race between the *Calesas* to the next stop signal, a block or more away. There was great excitement among the drivers during these trials, taunting each other, threatening, cursing, and at times even using whips on each other. It was a mad scramble. I prayed that I would get out of it in one piece.

In this fashion we seemed to ride around the city time after time, finally arriving back very near to where we had started.

"There." The driver pointed. It did not look right, but I wanted no more of that *Calesa.* I stiffly dismounted and paid the driver the exorbitant amount he asked without complaint, grateful to be rid of him.

The *Calesa* driver proved to be right. My car was there. The next test was my skill as a driver on the left side of the road.

I arrived back at Stotsenburg unscathed and grateful, with a much greater respect for Major Thorpe's driver. I was thankful that the major had not been my passenger.

I had the next few days free. I spent the time making duty calls and getting acquainted with the officers of the regiment and their families. Early on I had noticed that anyone who had lived in the islands for any length of time had a tendency toward sitting; the expenditure of energy in any way was frowned upon.

Toward the end of the week, I was assigned large and spacious quarters, much the same as the Thorpes', which I was to share with two other bachelors of the 26th Cavalry.

We had a dining room, living room, three bedrooms, and porches with comfortable, informal, rattan furniture. My personal houseboy, Santiago, was an older man, 35 or 45, who had served officers at Fort Stotsenburg for more than 20 years. I paid him 15 *pesos* a month, provided him with his food and a place to sleep when he chose not to return to his *barrio* for the night. He was honest, loyal, and dependable, and served me the entire ten months I was at Fort Stotsenburg. We also had a cook and a *lavendera* to do the washing. Our groceries came from the commissary, except for fresh fruit and some vegetables that were purchased from local markets.

Chapter 4

In February 1941, the 26th Cavalry was composed of three squadrons—two rifle squadrons and a headquarters. Headquarters Squadron consisted of Headquarters and Service Troop and Machine Gun Troop. Headquarters and Service Troop was made up of Regimental Headquarters, a Communications Platoon, plus troop headquarters. Machine Gun Troop comprised a platoon of .50-calibers and two platoons of .30-caliber heavy machine guns, plus troop headquarters.

The rifle squadrons consisted of two rifle troops each, A and B in the first, E and F in the second. A rifle troop was composed of two rifle platoons and a light-machine-gun platoon, plus troop headquarters. Most units were understrength. There were no squadron headquarters. Troop F, detached, was stationed at Nichols Field, south of Manila.

My first impression of the Philippine Scout was his alertness, courtesy, and his excellent appearance. In the months that followed, I found he could ride, shoot well, and take of himself, his weapons, and his mount in the field. These men were in the Army because they liked it. They were professional soldiers. Many of the older non-commissioned officers excelled in troop tactics. A Scout had to have a high school education and be able to speak, read, and write English to qualify for enlistment. The base pay for a private was 18 *pesos*—nine US dollars—per month.

My duty consisted of horse exercise and participation in troop problems, as well as becoming acquainted with the troop's administration, mess, supply, and stables. Newcomers to the regiment were required to do a voluminous amount of reading and complete several reconnaissance rides in and about the post.

Among other facts I learned that the Philippine Archipelago consists of 7,083 islands extending from the Sulu Archipelago in the south to the Bantan Islands in the north, a distance of approximately 1,150 miles. Its western shores are washed by the South China Sea; its eastern shores by the Philippine Sea. Only 462 of these islands are more than a mile square in area. The majority of the 17 million Filipinos in 1941 were located on the islands of Luzon in the north, Mindanao in the south, and the Visayan group in between.

There are five distinct languages and more than 80 dialects in the islands. *Tagalog,* the language of the central Luzon plain, is the national language.

On the island of Luzon, the Filipinos are divided racially into three groups, Negrito, Indonesian, and Malay. Originally, there were the Negritos, small black people with flat noses and kinky hair, some standing barely five feet in height, with the women even shorter. These are considered the aborigines. Then, the Indonesians came, slim men of medium height with high cheekbones. They may have come in prehistoric times by land, when it is believed the Philippines Islands may have been connected to the Asian mainland. These people drove the Negritos from the plains into the mountains. In turn, the Indonesians were driven from the same areas by a later Malayan invasion. The Malays are the ancestors of the lowland Filipino today.

By 1250 AD, the Malays of Sumatra had been converted to Islam. Pushing north, they reached as far as Manila Bay when the Spaniards arrived in the 16th century.

The Spaniards brought Roman Catholicism to the Filipinos, and this was the faith of the great majority of Filipino Christians. The Americans brought education to the masses and improved their health and living standards.

Before World War II, the Philippine Islands were a commonwealth under American sovereignty, with a republican form of government. Spanish systems of governing, politics, land-owning, and carrying on business, however, were still firmly rooted in the Filipino mind.

There was little love lost between the majority of Americans and Filipinos. Many of the politicians and members of the younger generation resented the presence of Americans in their country. A proud and independent people, they had revolted against the foreign rule of the Spanish in the latter part of the 19th century. The revolt was stifled, however, by the establishment of the American regime in 1898, as a result of the war with Spain. The policy of the government of the United States was to gradually increase autonomy for the Philippine Islands. They were granted commonwealth status in 1935 and promised independence by 1946. As time went on, though, the Filipinos were becoming more and more impatient to be free. Consequently, they were more and more resentful of the American presence.

Between the years 1898 and 1935, the US government assumed the obligation of defending the islands. During that period, the United States maintained a garrison of about 10,000 troops in the islands, half of whom were Philippine Scouts. Prior to 1935, little effort had been made to establish a Philippine defense force; this became one of the first priorities of the new commonwealth. The fledgling government requested that the United States aid in accomplishing this task.

General Douglas MacArthur was sent to the islands as military advisor to aid in this endeavor. Although he had retired from the US Army in 1937, a year after Filipino President Quezon appointed him Field Marshal of the Philippine Army, in 1941 MacArthur was recalled to active duty. A ground force of ten infantry divisions, a small air force, and a navy consisting primarily of motor torpedo boats made up the main part of the initial organization. Training of these units, which began in 1937, met with innumerable obstacles.

By 1941, the Philippine defense establishment was still little more than a paper organization. This was a known fact among American military personnel and it was of some concern.

The power of the Japanese military machine was becoming more and more evident and menacing. While a possibility, few really believed that the Japanese on their little islands to the north ever would have the audacity to attack the

United States. Yet, from my imposed studies, an old contingency war plan called "ORANGE" stuck in my mind. In essence it dictated that in the event of a successful invasion of Luzon Island, there was to be a withdrawal of as many forces as possible into the Bataan Peninsula, where the terrain favored a strong defense.

The reading finally finished, I was free to start the reconnaissance rides. My studies, while interesting, had been confining and had gradually become a bore. I was anxious to see what this new world outside was like.

Mellandres, my newly-assigned orderly from Troop E, proved to be a fine companion and excellent guide. Also, the thoroughbred assigned as my mount proved to be well trained and fine gaited. Astride this animal, in the clear sunny days of March, it was like getting out of prison. With Mellandres at my side, talkative and full of strange and wonderful tales, our rides were both pleasurable and instructive.

Fort Stotsenburg was an army post hidden in the southern foothills of the Zambales Mountains. The cavalry was stationed on the lower post; the upper post hosted field artillery units, including the 86th and 88th Field Artillery Regiments (PS) and the Philippine Division's 23rd and 24th Field Artillery Regiments.

To the north is the Bamban River valley, a broad, deep wash, covered with boulders and clumps of small trees. A clear stream trickled down the center of the valley, barely running at this time of year. From the looks of the huge polished boulders and the washed banks, though, there was little doubt that at times it was a raging torrent.

Our next ride was south of the post; first, past a line of a dozen or so small shops along a dingy back road. This was Hong Kong Street, where the Chinese tailor who had taken my measurements had his shop. There, concessions run by Chinese and East Indian merchants included the sale of almost every imaginable Oriental item. As we rode past, Mellandres remarked, "Sir, these people sometimes do not tell you everything as it is when they try to sell. You must be very careful when you buy. Many times they will ask more when they see you are new."

I had traded in Mexico and stood advised. I then mentioned that the uniforms and suits the Chinese tailor had made for me seemed to be of good quality as well as being reasonable.

Mellandres smiled broadly, exposing two gold teeth. "Did he give a *Cumshaw?*

I was at a loss as to what *Cumshaw* was and asked him to explain.

"It is a present. It is the way of the Chinese to show gratefulness and to thank you for your purchase."

Mellandres could tell from my expression that I had not received a gift.

"You will receive one yet when he finds what he thinks you will like." A few days later I found a beautiful Chinese vase on the porch of my quarters.

As we continued our ride farther south we came to the barrio of Sapang Bato, where many of our Filipino sergeants lived with their families. It was a crowded area with shacks of bamboo and *nipa* palm with the usual swarms of dogs, pigs, chickens, and little bronze-colored children as bare as the day they were born.

The children recognized Mellandres at once and crowded around his horse in an obvious show of affection. I was a stranger and they wanted to know who I was.

We had caused a commotion that brought several women to the open windows of their little huts. Motioning toward one of them, Mellandres said, "That's the wife of Sergeant Durango."

I smiled and nodded in the woman's direction, embarrassed because I had no idea who Sergeant Durango might be. Before we could leave, I was introduced to all the wives and families in the *barrio.* I was overwhelmed by the show of friendliness and hospitality. It made me determined to make a concerted effort to learn the names of the men of Troop E, and how to pronounce them properly.

The ride I enjoyed most was west into the Zambales, a mountain range that ran north and south and separated the central plain of Luzon from its western coast.

We left the post and followed a trail that passed through an area of rolling hills covered with *cogan* grass, a high, single-bladed plant resembling sugar cane. As the path became steeper, the foliage became denser, and suddenly we found ourselves in the middle of a tropical jungle.

I stopped my horse and gazed in wonderment. Great trees a hundred feet high, with massive, gnarled, grotesquely-shaped trunks grew at random. Vegetation of all colors, shapes, and sizes enveloped us. Long vines ran from the ground into the tops of the trees as though strung for trapeze work. High up, a dense canopy formed by the upper branches of the gigantic trees blocked out the sun as if to shade and protect the entanglement of nature below.

There were birds of many colors and sizes with as many calls and songs. I recognized parakeets and canaries and jungle cocks that resembled our domestic bantams. Groups of monkeys chattered out of sight overhead. It was with an awesome feeling as I viewed this tropical strangeness for the first time.

About an hour's ride deeper into the mountains, we passed a band of Negritos, the small black people of the forest. This was the first time I had seen these aborigines. They were on the side of a hill, less than a hundred yards away and marching single file along a narrow trail. In the lead were several men armed with bows, arrows, and bolos.* Their tiny bodies, naked except for a loincloth, were finely shaped and black as ebony. Women and children walked behind; the females wore only a sarong-like cloth tied around their hips; their children were completely naked. All their worldly possessions, along with their latest offspring, were stuffed into rattan baskets and carried on the backs of the women. Closing up the rear were more males, traveling light, but well armed.

---

*The bolo is a long, heavy, knife, often used as a machete. It is usually maintained with a razor sharpness. [Ed.]

Mellandres shouted a greeting to them, which they returned smiling and waving. They appeared happy and healthy without a worry in the world.

Mellandres called them Balugas. He told me that they built shelters here and there where they did some cultivating, but much preferred a nomadic life, taking their living from the jungle, resting in the open where darkness found them. They lived mostly on wild roots, fruits of the forest, fish, frogs, snails, reptiles, and birds brought down by their arrows. Occasionally a deer or wild boar would fall prey to their weapons. These are truly children of the forest, the original inhabitants of the islands.

On that ride, Mellandres told a story about Captain Blanning that I have not forgotten. On a march in this same jungle, riding along a path at the head of Troop E, suddenly Blanning was confronted by a huge python that had lowered itself from a branch above. The head of the python was on a level with him and not far ahead. Barely able to hold his horse that had become frantic at the sight of the snake, Captain Blanning managed to draw his pistol and apparently, without taking aim, put a bullet through the head of the snake. Reduced to a squirming mass, the python dropped onto the floor of the jungle. The column had halted. Word of what had happened quickly spread rearward. Officers and non-coms rode forward to see the sight and congratulate Blanning. He immediately became the hero of the regiment and a friend forever of the local Negritos, who feasted on the snake for days.

Beyond Clark Field, an Army Air Corps base east of Fort Stotsenburg, was the little town of Angeles. It was rather non-descript except for one thing—Tinio's Place. This combination bar and store was located on the second floor above Tinio's living quarters. The commercial area was a long room with shelves from floor to ceiling, laden with myriad items unique to the Philippines. Included were bolo knives of every description; items of *pina*-cloth, from beautiful little hand-embroidered dollies, to blouses, skirts, and shawls; and hand-carved items of finely-grained tropical hardwoods, ranging from wooden hairpins to great canopied double beds. The bar itself took only one small corner of the room. Its main attraction was the fact that one could buy a large demi-john of Philippine rum selling for 14 *pesos* (seven US dollars).

My last ride was to Clark Field, one of three main airfields on the island of Luzon and the only one that could accommodate heavy bombers. Stationed there was a composite group consisting of pursuit, bombardment, and observation planes. The buildings of the field—hangars, shops, barracks, and offices—were concentrated in a small area to the south of the exceedingly long hard-topped runway. The area was flat, except for a few hills to the north.

Mellandres remarked on how unmilitary the American airmen appeared in comparison to the Scouts. I agreed, and even then could not help thinking how little thought seemed to be given to the need for security measures. Here was an important American installation with practically no ground security. Civilians were allowed to roam nearly anywhere with no apparent restrictions.

During the first days of March 1941, initial increments of an expected 1,100 recruits began to arrive at Fort Stotsenburg. They would eventually bring both the artillery and cavalry units on the post up to authorized strengths. In the 26th Cavalry, two new rifle troops and two squadron headquarters would be activated and all other units brought to full strength. The new troops became C in the 1st Squadron and G in the 2nd. The authorized strength of a rifle troop was about 85 men.

The two existing troops of each squadron were required to furnish cadre for the newly-activated troop, a squadron headquarters, and to fill some requirements at regimental level.

The relaxed life came to a sudden end. Training of the recruits began with vigor. Training now started at 0700 hours, continuing until 1600 hours in the afternoon. The day began with dismounted, close-order drill, then equitation, mounted drill, grooming the horses, and maintaining equipment, all at the stables. In the afternoons, there were classes for the new soldiers on basic military subjects.

Some of the new men did not have an understanding of basic English. This lowering of standards only complicated training. Men from different parts of the islands spoke different dialects, often not understood by the instructor who, to get the substance of his subject across, had to be assisted by an interpreter. When an instructor had to resort to the native language or dialect, my only clue to what was being taught was an occasional word in English, such as "machine gun," for which they had no substitute. These occasional English words came abruptly between staccato bursts of the native tongue.

The hot season was nearing its peak. By midmorning, an exercise outside, especially, if in an area where there was no air circulation, was like being in a steam bath. While the sun is normally 93 million miles away from most places on earth this time of year, at Fort Stotsenburg it was generally conceded to be sitting just a few feet overhead.

In addition to the sorrel mare, I had inherited three partially trained polo ponies left by an officer who had departed Troop E prior to my arrival.

Turning out for polo practice after a hot day's work often became a chore, but I enjoyed it and was determined to make trained ponies out of my green string.

What I did consider a chore was dressing for and attending the many functions and receptions held at the club. One time the party would be for new arrivals, the next, for those departing; then a general would decide it was time for his party. Everyone was required to be present at these functions, wearing tropical dress uniforms: a monkey jacket with bow tie (white mess uniform), a rig of little comfort in that climate.

I well remember one occasion that took place at the club during the month of March. It was customary to invite the leader of the Pinatuba Negritos, King Tomás, with a few of his hand-picked tribesmen, to a celebration held two to three times a year to bind ties of friendship. The name *Pinatuba* was taken from a prominent peak in the Zambales Mountains. Shortly before dark on the evening set for the event, a large group of us were gathered outside the club on the tennis courts.

Across the parade ground approaching in single file marched the Balugas led by King Tomás, a short black man strutting along as though he ruled the world. He carried a spear and was dressed in a long, outdated and oversized khaki blouse and G-string, an old campaign hat on his head. Behind him trailed four or five of his braves carrying bows and arrows, and behind them several women of different ages, naked from the waist up, some carrying young children on their hips.

The men strode along proudly with their heads high; the women approached giggling, between shy glances at the onlookers. As they neared the tennis courts, they were met by the post adjutant who escorted them inside the club to be greeted by the general. After a short while they filed back out of the club onto the tennis courts where there was to be an exhibition of their dancing. As they came under the floodlights of the cement courts, the struggle the men had to appear confident and at ease became very evident. This was not the case with the women. They made no attempt to hide their shyness, giggling and whispering amongst themselves.

After a moment a few of the women carrying string instruments, which might be called "coconut ukuleles," took positions on one side of the court, sat down cross-legged, and began to tune their instruments. The remainder of the group formed a circle in the center of the court.

When the dance was finally begun, it consisted of a series of jerks and hops executed to the tune of a monotonous strum, strum, strum of the string instruments, accompanied by an almost toneless chant. This primitive ritual went on for five or ten minutes, when the dancers and sound effects suddenly stopped. There were a few embarrassing moments until the audience realized it was over and began to applaud.

There followed a hunting dance by the men with their arrows. This varied little from the first dance except there were no women in it. A flower dance was then performed by the women that varied little from the first two except there were no men.

After the flower dance, the Balugas filed back into the club to demonstrate their skill as archers. Against the western end of the dance hall, bales of hay had been stacked. Cloth bull's eyes were pinned to each of them. The firing line was 60 to 70 feet back from the target. Behind this line, the contestants were preparing for the match, one getting the range, another tinkering with his bowstring and a third selecting a straight arrow. It was interesting to watch the seriousness with which they went about this preparation.

Each contestant was allowed five arrows; the three best scorers would shoot five more for first place. There was no time limit. A signal was given to start. There was a good deal of slow moving precision as each contestant carefully fitted his arrow to the bowstring; an equal amount of attention was given to positioning himself into a good stance. At last each warrior carefully pulled the arrow back, paused a moment before its release, then allowed the projectile to swish through the air and drive itself deep into the hay-bale target. It entered with such force that it quivered for a few moments before becoming motionless. The accuracy of these aborigines with their crude weapons was amazing. Few arrows struck outside the bull's-eye, which was ten inches in diameter.

After several ties and shoot-offs, a winner was finally selected and solemnly presented with a fine bolo. It was easy to understand that with the stealth these people possessed and their accuracy with the bow, why they had little trouble surviving in the forest.

After the formal contest, several officers in the group pinned *peso* notes on the target for a free-for-all shoot, enjoyed by both the contestants and the spectators. To end the evening festivities, the post commander presented King Tomás with several bags of hulled rice, trinkets, and a large bolt of colored cloth.

Thus was maintained the alliance between the United States and the Pinatuba Negritos.

Chapter 5

For some time now, American intelligence was aware that the Japanese were infiltrating the Philippine Islands to gather information about the islands and its people. There was evidence they were mapping, charting, locating, and organizing individuals and groups who were, or could be persuaded to become, loyal to the Japanese in the event of hostilities.

In an effort to stop this infiltration, or at least reduce it, American and Filipino forces conducted aerial, off-shore, and ground patrols. The 26th Cavalry was responsible for patrolling the coastline of the province of Zambales from Olongapo north to the town of Santa Cruz, a distance of 75 miles.

There were many beaches and coves along the western coast of Zambales Province on which it would be comparatively easy to land small craft unobserved during the hours of darkness; discharge personnel and equipment; and be off again before the light of day.

A likely assumption was that this infiltration was being accomplished using small, native sailboats that rendezvoused off-shore at night with either submarines or fast, small, surface craft from the coast of China. The native sailboats would then land personnel and equipment at isolated points along the coastline—a comparatively simple operation at night—their size and low silhouette making them difficult to spot.

To accomplish the mission assigned to our regiment, a detachment of about 40 men was stationed in a camp on Subic Bay, just north of the US Naval Station at Olongapo. The detachment was made up of a platoon of scout cars for road patrols and a platoon of horse reinforced with light machine guns for off-road work. In addition, there were administrative personnel to run the mess, stables, and supply.

These detachments were rotated on a monthly basis. I was detailed to take command of one on 1 April.

Our motor convoy departed Fort Stotsenburg early that morning. We traveled south through the dusty, hot plain covered with paddies and canals, and teeming with life. Turning west, climbing into the foothills of the Cabusilan Mountains, all of a sudden we were in a jungle.

Great trees of the rain forest bordered the road, enclosing everything in deep, cool shade. Tiny wild orchids grew in profusion out of the tree trunks. A wild cock would occasionally strut across the road ahead of us, flying off amidst his din of cackling, while the parakeets and monkeys in the treetops chattered and screeched. All this sounded like bedlam in the forest.

Out of the cool foothills we again emerged into the heat and dust through dirty little *nipa* town of Olongapo, past the naval base, and north along the waterfront road to our camp.

Subic Bay stretched out windless, blue, and hot to Fort Wint and beyond to the South China Sea. Fort Wint was a coast artillery post on a tiny island in the middle of the bay. The north and south shores of the bay were bordered by jungle. To the northwest, a conical mountain pushed its peak high into the sky.

Our camp straddled the dusty corduroy road that ran along the Zambales coast. To the west on the sandy shore were two lines of pyramidal tents, each big enough for about one squad. To the east of the road against the rain forest were the stables and a small firing range and training area. It was not an inspiring sight.

The first few days were spent in getting the camp and equipment into shape and checking the required watcher stations. These were observation posts along the seacoast between the towns of Olongapo and Santa Cruz to the north. They were manned on a 24-hour-a-day basis. The town mayors and *barrio tenientes* (lieutenants) along the coast submitted daily reports on any unusual activities to these observation posts. This information was picked up by a scout car patrol on its daily run along the coast and was radioed to our regimental headquarters.

The scout car platoon was made up of older men, well trained in their duties. Most of the time, they manned the observation posts and made the daily patrol the length of the coast. This allowed Troop E men, then consisting of about 90 percent recruits, to train. Sergeant Masanguay, my platoon sergeant, was in charge of this training.

The stables east of the road were crude, made of a *nipa* shelter with a line stretched beneath. Adjoining were a shed for forage and a large bullpen for equitation training. Beyond it was a 1,000-inch firing range.

Our camp on the opposite side of the road was on the flat, sandy beach next to the water. The two rows of tents faced the platoon street. Except for a mess tent and another for supplies, these tents provided shelter for the men. At the eastern end was a wall tent for me, and a fly under which I had my meals. My ration was basically out of cans, augmented by anything edible the mess sergeant could purchase from the local market. A truck came twice a week from Stotsenburg with food, fodder, and other needed supplies.

After the first week, we had gotten into the routine of our business. The coastline for which the 26th Cavalry was responsible had been checked to my satisfaction with the exception of an area directly northwest of camp. This area was mountainous, roadless, and practically uninhabited. I decided the best way and probably only way, to look this area over was to follow the shoreline by boat.

With three Scouts who professed to be sailors and a sailing *banca* with flotation capabilities similar to a half-opened pea pod, we started out. The *banca* was 15 feet long, cut from a log with outriggers on each side. It had a small mainsail and jib. Once loaded, it had all of five inches freeboard.

At the beginning, we had a brisk breeze from the southwest that skimmed us along at a fine clip. In no time, we were approaching the entrance to the bay. In back of us, our camp had become no more than a row of tiny specks; ahead, in the distance, was the great blue-green expanse of the South China Sea.

We found that section of the peninsula in question to be as wild and uninhabited as reported. There was no sign of human life until midmorning when we sighted movement ashore. Even with my binoculars, I was unable to determine the identity of what appeared to be a group of men in a deep cove. If they proved to be Japanese, there was no doubt in my mind that they would be armed and we would be sitting ducks. We had no choice, though, and we had to go in for a closer look. Fortunately our apprehension was short-lived; the group proved to be local Filipino woodcutters.

As we headed into the open sea, the wind started to play out. By noon, we were paddling toward a small island for a lunch break. The heat was terrific. I had put on shorts for the day and had failed to take along a hat. I was sorely regretting my errors. The intensity of the tropical sun reflected off the motionless water was unbelievable. As we came ashore, I dropped over the side of the boat into the water. Had I not done this, I believe I would have lost consciousness.

The clear, completely still water surrounding the little island covered a beautiful garden of coral. The soldiers called the coral formations "flowers." There were flowers of bright blood red, old-fashioned pink, varied shades of green and blue and pastels of these colors; their textures ranged from that of the finest lacework to that of heavily-tooled leather. Some of the coral flowers were as small as a man's hand, while others had grown into huge formations with diameters as wide as our boats were long, with shapes ranging from beautifully symmetrical designs to the most grotesque figures imaginable.

In the center of this tiny rock-covered island were a few lonely coconut trees and a weatherworn stone building, once used as a lighthouse. We found a shady spot where we could sit comfortably and have our lunch and a *siesta.*

I felt no hurry, as we were more than half the distance to our destination, and the soldiers had assured me that the wind would start to blow again soon.

"The noonday calm is the habit of the wind this time of year," they told me in their accented English.

I had become quite conscious of wind during the morning. As I lay squinting after waking, to my surprise, I noticed small flurries of ripples on the water, moving toward the south. I did not believe what I saw. I checked this several times until I was sure I was not dreaming. Even then I threw out the idea as being impossible. However, it was not long before these little puffs moving south had grown into quite a steady blow, rippling the surface of the sea as far as one could see.

I woke the soldiers to show them what I had discovered. None of them appeared surprised. They said they knew it would be that way.

"It is the custom of the wind this time of year." I felt duped.

It had not occurred to me to check the habits of the winds or the weather. I was vaguely aware that there were two seasons in the islands: that of the northeast monsoon and that of the southwest. I do not believe that at the time I had connected the monsoons with the winds.

"How are we going to sail north when the wind is coming from that direction?" I asked the soldiers.

We would spend the rest of the afternoon zigzagging into the wind. They made the motion of going back and forth with their hands.

"Would we be able to reach the first *barrio* to the north before dark?" I asked.

"Oh, yes sir," I was assured.

We started out, slowly at first, but with increasing momentum as the wind grew stronger. We did surprisingly well at the beginning, tacking almost into shore and then out from land until we could hardly see the beaches. As the wind became stronger, so did the sea, and it was not long before we were shipping in more water than we could bail out. There appeared to be a fair chance of our being swamped. The soldiers were discussing the problem with looks of apprehension as they watched the sea become rougher.

It was not long, however, until the period of hesitancy came to an end. We had already reefed the sail down to half its size and were all leaning out onto the windward outrigger supports. The mast was creaking and straining; the sail was tight as a drum. We were making no headway.

The trough of a larger-than-usual wave caught us sideways; it was easy to see what was coming, but there was little to be done. The wave broke over us, filling the boat nearly full of water. The buoyancy of the wooden bottom and the presence of mind of the two soldiers, who jumped overboard, to take their weight out of the boat, saved us from completely swamping. The man at the tiller yelled, "Let the sail down." I let it drop with a thud. In a moment the tiller man had a paddle out, working to get the bow of the boat into the wind. He motioned to me to start bailing, which I went at with a strong will.

A series of small waves after the large one gave us the chance we needed. In a few seconds, the boat was headed into the wind. The soldiers overboard were working like madmen, swishing out great sheets of water with the help of coconut shells. I was working as frantically inside the boat. With the weight mostly in the rear and the bow into the wind, no more water was coming in.

In a few minutes we had enough water bailed to allow for a breather. The two recruits crawled aboard. Exhausted, we sat there and had a good laugh, congratulating ourselves on our luck.

We paddled the rest of the way. There were only two paddles but it was just as well. After five or ten minutes one needed a rest, and with four of us on two reliefs, we made good time even against a rough sea.

At last we came to a break in the coastline. As we rounded a point, a small bay came into view. Its waters were calm, protected from the north by a strip of land running out into the sea. It was a great relief to be in calm water again. We had been struggling for five hours against the wind and the sea.

As we approached the shore we passed several *bancas* from which a group of individuals was diving. These naked divers were as black as Africans, whom at first I thought they were. The soldiers explained that the coal black color was caused by the sun. They were diving for shellfish that clung to the rocks on the bottom of the bay. The length of time they were able to stay under water with nothing but clamps on their noses was remarkable.

With my feet once again on solid ground, I swore I would never get into another *banca.* Wet and stinging from the sunburn, I was miserable. One of the soldiers went to find the *barrio teniente.* I had met him a few days before on a scout car patrol. He could not have been more helpful, taking us to his home, feeding us, and finding a truck to haul our boat and us back to camp.

The next few days I was *hors de combat*; blisters the size of the palm of my hand rose on my sunburned knees.

One morning, Sergeant Masanguay was instructing the recruits in firing the pistol. As I walked up to the group, he was about to demonstrate how to shoot from the standing position.

He turned to me, saluted and said, "Maybe the lieutenant would show us how to shoot the pistol?"

For a moment I thought he was trying put me on the spot. I was still not sure I understood these people.

"I'll tell you what, sergeant, let's both demonstrate. I'll challenge you to a little match. We'll fire five rounds each, slow fire, from both the 15 and 25 yard lines."

"As you wish," he replied with a broad smile exuding confidence. He had the reputation of being a good shot.

The target up and the distance paced off, we flipped for first shot. Masanguay would shoot first. This was at 15 yards. With his thumb, he deftly flipped his holster cover open and as in one motion withdrew his well-cared-for pistol. With a click, a clip was inserted into the grip and the slide pulled back and quickly released.

He was ready to fire, steady, calm, and confident. There was absolute silence. The new recruits idolized their sergeant, and I'm sure they hoped he would beat the young, white foreigner who was an impersonal, not-to-well understood part of their new life in the Army.

Masanguay breathed deeply, raised his pistol, and squeezed off a shot. There was no sign of it on the target. A murmur rose from the recruits; then silence again.

The second shot was fired in the same manner. No mark on the white of the target. A third, fourth and fifth. Still no mark that could be seen. His shots had all looked good. My heart sank. Then, when I saw his target close up, it sank further. All five rounds were in a small group in the center of the black.

Maybe I had a chance. This was 15 yards. With not all the calmness and confidence that Masanguay had displayed, I stepped up to the firing line. My first three shots were in the black. I could feel the pressure. I was not holding as steady on the fourth shot; it cut into the white on the edge of the black. Holding my fifth shot was a struggle. It also cut the edge of the black.

Masanguay's shooting was better but our scores were even.

It was my turn to shoot first at 25 yards. I had settled down by now. With a good position, I slowly squeezed off five shots. They all felt good. There was no sign of the white outside the black bull's-eye being broken. A close look at the target showed my shooting was better this time.

It was Masanguay's turn to be nervous, but he was not a bit. At least he showed no sign of it. In fact, he looked more confident than ever. I wondered at him. His first three shots were completely in the black. Preparing for his fourth, I noticed he took a longer breath than usual and his arm wavered slightly. He brought the pistol down to rest for a moment. Up again and he fired. It was a bull's-eye but broke the white. His fifth shot did the same.

Again we were even. We congratulated each other on the good shooting and I turned to go.

"Sir, would you like to take a few shots at 50 yards?"

Fifty yards? I didn't remember ever having shot at that distance.

After a moment's thought I said, "Why not?"

As I came on the firing line, the target looked a great distance away, the black just a pinpoint.

I held on what I could see, nonetheless, and squeezed off five shots in slow succession. Two were in the black, three outside.

Masanguay stepped up to take his turn. With care and precision, he fitted the pistol into his right hand. Then he slowly extended his right arm, took a deep breath, let out part of it and, in a series of rapid shots which sounded more like a machine gun than a single shot pistol, fired his five rounds. Four of his five shots were in the black. I could not believe it. It was an amazing and unforgettable demonstration. I often thought of his shootings, and many times dreamt of out-shooting him at 50 yards.

In the early mornings and evenings, the sound of roosters crowing came from the forest a hundred or so yards to the east of our camp. Since seeing the wild chickens on my first ride into the Zambales, I had wanted to try a hunt for them. It so happened that I had brought a shotgun with me to Subic Bay.

One evening, I set out for the forest to try my luck. Not far inside I flushed a cock. He was startled and started cackling loudly, as if to warn all creatures nearby of my presence. He ran a short distance, and then took off in a flutter of wings and cackles, alighting on a branch far ahead. On first seeing him, I had raised my gun, but immediately realized he was out of range.

I started to stalk him, sure to have roast chicken for dinner the following night. With great care, I approached the cock, sneaking from tree to tree. Each time I looked out from behind a tree, he had his eyes on me. Finally, nearly within range, getting ready to shoot, the sound of fluttering wings with increased cackling again filled the forest and he was away once more. Several times until it became too dark to see I approached him, each time getting nearly within range, only to have him fly off at the last moment.

Often in the evenings that followed I returned to the forest, always hopeful that I could outsmart this wily creature. He seemed to know the exact range of my gun. Cackling on the ground when disturbed at his evening meal, he would run a short distance, and then fly to a low-hanging branch. There, he would sit watching me, cackling raucously, challenging me to play the same old game at which he consistently came out the winner.

To this point, there had been little time to work the sorrel mare Blanning had assigned me. I had brought her to the Subic Bay camp in the hope I would have more time for her. Barely 15 hands, but with the heart and fire of a thoroughbred, she was a handful to ride. Unspoiled, though green, she was by nature a little shifty and nervous. At first she was difficult, but after a few initial "set-tos," she settled down and started to respond to her training. Seldom was it necessary to use spurs or whip on her. Much of my spare time at Subic Bay was spent worksing with her. Each day she gained more confidence and her responses to my signals improved. Her nervousness was leaving. She proved to have beautiful gaits and she had speed. She was a joy to work with and gradually becoming a delight to ride.

Periodic reports on our activities were required to be delivered personally to the commanding officer of Fort Wint. These reports were marked "SECRET' and sealed in a series of envelopes, an impressive looking package. Inquiring of regiment how I was to get out to the fort, the adjutant's answer was, "Get someone to paddle you out."

This I did, often arriving with a newly starched and pressed uniform that was wet and mussed. The commander at Wint depended upon the Navy for water transportation and was reluctant to include me. Despite this, I enjoyed the visits, which gave me a chance to talk to Americans.

Occasionally I went to the ship's store on the naval base for required items. One time there, I met up with a group of young PBY pilots. The PBYs were Navy amphibious planes that, at the time, were part of the air patrols overwatching offshore activities in certain parts of the islands.* They invited me along on a patrol, and I readily accepted. The patrol turned out to be an all-day flight of two planes over the islands of Palawan, Mindanao, Mindoro, and the Visayas (Bohol, Cebu, Leyte, Masbate, Negros, Panay, and Samar). It is one thing to study a map, but

*The PBY "Catalina" (the nomenclature stands for Patrol Bomber, manufacturer code "Y," which indicated the Consolidated Aircraft Corporation) was a twin-engine amphibian that first entered service with the US Navy in 1936. At its optimal cruising speed of 117 mph, it had a maximum cruising range of about 2,500 miles. At the time of publication, there are a few Catalinas still flying today, and some are used in fighting forest fires. [Ed.]

quite another to get a bird's-eye view of the Philippine Archipelago. As a result, for the first time, I was able fully to grasp the enormity of our task in adequately patrolling approximately 600,000 square miles of jungle-covered islands and trackless sea.

Though exciting and enlightening to me, it was boring to the pilots, who had flown the route time after time. To ease their boredom, the pilots spent much of their time flying side by side seeing which one had enough nerve and skill to tick the other's wing tips without jarring a wing loose. I had enough of that game after watching it the first time, and decided that one PBY patrol was enough.

Soon it would be time for my detachment to return to Stotsenburg. Since my first rides into the Zambales Mountains, I had heard tales of an old trail which led from Fort Stotsenburg into the Zambales and west over one of its highest peaks, Mount Pinatuba, down into the province of Zambales to the coast of the South China Sea. It had been many years since any member of the 26th had ridden that trail. The older Scouts who had made the ride spoke of its rigors and difficulties with pride. Their tales had whetted my desire to see for myself and I was determined some day to make the trip. Several of the older Scouts who knew the trail produced sketches for me as their memories served. No sketch was like another, but there was agreement on three points: the beginning was Fort Stotsenburg, the end at a small *barrio* on the coast of the South China Sea, and the fact that the trail swung around the southern slope of Mount Pinatuba.

Several times, from the Stotsenburg end, I had looked for the trail without success. During my stay on Subic Bay, however, I was confident that I could find my way back to Fort Stotsenburg.

My detachment was to be relieved on 1 May by another from the 26th Cavalry. I had permission to return the mounted portion of my command to the fort by way of the Pinatuba Trail. The remainder would return by truck under the command of Sergeant Masanguay. He was not happy about missing the ride.

The trail proved to be sketchy. Most of the time it was necessary to move cross-country by compass bearing, sometimes pushing our way through heavy growths of *cogan* grass, winding through the dense jungle, often leading the horses over rocky areas or places where the trail was unduly steep or narrow.

Nightfall of the first day caught us on the steep slopes of Pinatuba. We had difficulty finding suitable level places for man and horse to rest.

The morning of the next day proved to be more of the same. I was beginning to wonder if we were going to be able to make the crossing. Only occasionally did we see signs of a trail. It obviously had not been used for years; it was all but obliterated by the growth of the jungle. A shortage of water compounded our problems. The last water that the horses had was early the previous afternoon when crossing a small stream. Our canteens had all been emptied the night before. I hated the thought of turning back. Besides the disappointment of not being able to complete the hike, I knew I would never live it down.

We were in dire need of bolos to cut our way through the jungle overgrowth, but had not even one. By noon, leading our horses, we finally came to the crest of the southern slope of Mount Pinatuba. All of a sudden, the jungle opened up and we ran onto a well-marked trail. Apparently it had been used by the Negritos up to that point, but for some reason, no further.

Mounted, we moved down the trail with good speed and it was not long before we came to a stream. Horses and men were dry as a bone. It was amazing what that drink of cool, clear water did for our spirits and those of the horses.

The rest of the way was easy; we arrived at Stotsenburg by dusk. There had been no mishaps, and, like the older Scouts who had made the ride before, the young men could talk with pride of its rigors and difficulties.

I thanked my stars that I had resisted the temptation to turn back that morning.

Chapter 6

I had not been back at Stotsenburg long before I found I was to leave again with a surveying detail to the Bataan Peninsula. The commander of the Philippine Department had ordered a reconnaissance of the Mount Natib area of the peninsula. The 26th Cavalry got the job.

Americans knew little of this area. Our regiment's mission was to select defensive positions in the area and map and cut trails to these positions. The trail, which was reported to lie between the town of Moron on the western coast and the Hacienda Abucay on the eastern coast, was to be scouted and, if necessary, reestablished.

The detail consisted of two parties, one to go in from the east, the other from the west. I was to be part of the west party.

Lieutenant Colonel Dodd commanded the west detachment. I was the only other officer. We had about a dozen Scouts with us, armed primarily with bolos.

In Moron we learned that the trail to the Hacienda Abucay, if any, was known only to a few mountain men who made their living cutting *bahuka* (rattan) used to manufacture furniture. No guides were available at the time, so Colonel Dodd gave me the job of finding the trail.

Two Scouts and I started in an easterly direction into the mountains, following a trail when one went east, bushwhacking when necessary to maintain direction toward the base of Natib Mountain. Each of us had taken only light packs with two days' rations, a raincoat, and a light blanket.

On the morning of the third day, still searching for the trail, we became completely lost. The forest was nearly impenetrable; the floor a tangle of vines, ferns, and great roots. In places, it was necessary to cut our way through to make any progress. Even though I had a compass, our location in the maze of tropical growth was nearly impossible to determine. We had no food left. By noon hunger was getting to us. At the suggestion of the Scouts, we uncovered a few snails in a nearby stream. These boiled with wild green mangoes in our canteen cups were our first meal of the day.

During the afternoon we moved in a northeasterly direction still hoping to find the trail, the existence of which I was beginning to doubt. By nightfall I was still uncertain about our location. The evening meal was the same as at noon, but augmented with young *bahuka* shoots. A lean-to of *bahuka* and tree branches covered with our raincoats was our shelter for another night.

Breakfast was a re-run of the previous meal, which left me feeling I had eaten nothing. About mid-morning the faint sound of chopping was heard. It turned out to be a *bahuka* cutter. He assured us that there was an old trail not far away, which, if followed to the east many miles, would bring us to Abucay. Moron was only a few miles to the west. Our false start days before had cost us a lot of time.

Back-tracking to the west, we ran into our party by mid-afternoon. It had grown some with local *cargadors* (native porters) from the Moron area. A guide had been found who knew the trail across Mount Natib to Abucay.

I had experienced my first practical lesson in survival in the jungle and was happy it had not lasted longer. I gorged myself for several meals after rejoining the party. While there had been hordes of mosquitoes on the mountain, there was little concern about coming down with malaria. We had taken quinine regularly for days before leaving Stotsenburg. The ringing in my ears was a constant reminder of this. My only apprehension was drinking water directly from the streams. We had been warned time and again never to drink water outside American installations without it first being purified. It would have been simple enough to have boiled the water we drank, or to have put iodine in it. When we did find a clear stream, though, we were usually so hot and thirsty that to wait even a moment before drinking seemed out of the question. At any rate, it turned out we had no bad effects.

The rain, and consequently the muddiness of the trail, increased daily as we approached the heights of Natib. Soon the trail nearly disappeared, being gradually covered by the thick jungle growth, from disuse. The woodcutters seldom had to come this far to find *bahuka;* thus the trail was rarely used. As we neared the top, we had to cut and blaze a new trail in places where the old one had completely disappeared. Cutting through the thick growths was tedious, hot, and tiring work. It was accomplished by one man working at a time, hacking away with his bolo for all he was worth for a few minutes, then, relieved by a second man and by a third and so on until everyone had had a turn. It did not take long for a man to become soaked through with perspiration.

Ten days after leaving Moron, we made contact with the party working in from the east.

That group had experienced much the same problems as we with the muddy and overgrown trail as it approached the heights of Mount Natib. Lieutenant Colonel Clayton was in command of the east party that, like ours, had a young lieutenant and about dozen Scouts.

Natib is an extinct volcano. Towards the top, its sides are extremely steep, impassable in places even to a man on foot. On the northern slope, down where the terrain started to level off, a base camp was established. Makeshift shelters for sleeping, cooking, and messing were erected. Canvas flies, as difficult as they had been to pack in, proved well worth the trouble. If not for them, we would have been soaked most of the time. The rains were becoming stronger daily.

We released our *cargadors* from the Moron area. All supplies now came from the eastern coast, a dump having been established at Hacienda Abucay. Supplies were carried from the *hacienda* into the mountains by local Negritos. They appeared the same as those in the Zambales Mountains, the males weighing about 70 pounds with well-proportioned bodies. They seemed always to have a smile on their faces, constantly joking with one another or with the Scouts, some of whom understood their dialect. They seemed not to have a care in the world, leading a hand-to-mouth existence, eating what the forest offered, sleeping where they found themselves at nightfall.

The steep trails were becoming nearly impassable with the deep, slippery mud. Our smooth-soled cavalry boots made traveling on them slow and difficult. A few falls during the day were accepted as routine. The Negritos, however, barefoot and dressed only in a G-string, took the rain and mud in their stride. These little men could carry loads up the trails, which weighed as much as 50 pounds. Their pay was a *peso* a day and the leftovers from the Scouts' mess.

I had brought my shotgun along in the hope of finding wild chickens. When the Negritos saw the gun they immediately suggested a pig hunt. I accepted, and on an evening soon thereafter we trailed off to a nearby canyon.

The Negritos were armed with bows and arrows. Three Negritos and I were placed on the sides of a canyon, a short distance above a clearing in the bottom. The chief made signs to me to be quiet, stay put, and watch. The remaining eight Negritos of the party filed off toward the mouth of the canyon. They would go ahead a half mile or so, form a line and make a drive back toward us.

Soon we could hear the beaters approaching, making all kinds of strange noises. The Negrito who was squatted beside me became as intense and excited as a young bird dog on its first hunt. He pointed down in the canyon floor where he hoped a pig would be passing, and then fit an arrow to his bow, barely able to sit still in his excitement.

We watched and watched, but no pig showed. The beaters were nearly on us. I slipped the safety on my gun on and sat back to relax. At that moment two pigs streaked across the sandy, open patch we had been watching, ducked into the dense cover surrounding it and were gone. The Negrito by my side pointed to my gun and shook his head. I pointed to his bow and shook my head. We had both been surprised, as apparently had the two hunters across the canyon. No arrows had been released.

The beaters were not too happy with us, but they philosophically shrugged off their disappointment, inferring that maybe next time we would get a pig. It was dusk and we were done for the day. Maybe tomorrow we would try again.

With the rains came leaches, brown, slimy suckers which made their way into our boots and up our legs. They took our blood, but could not be felt doing it. A periodic inspection was the only way to detect their presence.

We worked seven days a week to get out of the miserable environment of the mountainous rain forest as soon as possible. The high point of each day came in the evening just before dinner. Colonel Clayton had brought along a good supply of bourbon. Having cleaned up after the day's hot work, we four officers seated ourselves around the mess table to sip bourbon and water and listen to World War I stories told by the two old colonels. "Old Derby Dodd" as the lieutenants affectionately referred to him, was famous for actions in several prominent battles in World War I as a young captain with his machine gun company. Colonel

Clayton's stories were about his experiences in parts of eastern Russia and the Near East, just after the formal conclusion of the war elsewhere.

Days spent scouting, trail-cutting, and mapping, our reconnaissance was coming to an end. We had been in the mountains for a month and it was good to get back to Stotsenburg.

Repeatedly, the question came to mind during the month: was this just a training exercise, or was higher headquarters seriously preparing Bataan for Plan ORANGE?

Chapter 7

It was June already. To be out of the wet, hot jungles of Bataan, back to the comparatively cool freshness of Stotsenburg was a welcome change.

The dependents of American servicemen had been ordered home. Several of us took a few days' leave to go to Manila, to see the first boatload off and do the town.

Manila was a weekend habit with many of the lieutenants of the 26th Cavalry. My first introduction to the city had left me with little desire to return. The stories floating around the club of the forays there, however, whet my appetite for another look.

There were two places to stay in Manila, the Army-Navy Club and the Manila Hotel. Many preferred the more modern conveniences of the Manila Hotel and its feminine clientele, but the Army-Navy Club had more atmosphere, so this time I chose to stay there. The Moros in their colorful regalia were near the entrance selling pearls.

Two of us had a large, high-ceilinged room on the second floor. The plumbing and furnishings were old-fashioned, yet grand. The air-conditioning amounted to a great fan overhead and a breeze off Manila Bay.

Manila was known as the "Pearl of the Orient," the beautiful, expansive, sunny capital of the Philippine Archipelago. It was the seat of centralized government, the administrative capital, chief port, and cultural center of the nation. It was also the center of vice, crime, and debauchery—and I was there to see it all.

The *Despidida* was as gala event as the *Bienvenida.* We bought flowers and saw the boat off. The real difference was the sadness as the boat left the dock.

In many ways, downtown Manila was like any large city in the United States. Along the *Escolta* were fashionable shops displaying wearing apparel as *chic* as anywhere in the world. This area of the city had a definite western atmosphere. Along its sidewalks trod representatives of the nations of the world, a polyglot and interesting group to see. The traffic in the streets was another thing, however. The taxis with horns blaring, their throttles open, streaking past; the *Calesa* carts with their frantic ponies and wild drivers; the great, overloaded buses lumbering along, their drivers unmindful of anything else, left little doubt that one was in Manila.

There were other parts of the city that were much more Oriental; they were overcrowded, with filth and poverty glaring from every corner.

There was not a city in the world, however, that would not have been proud to have a Dewey Boulevard. There was an enviable serenity about the grounds surrounding the old Walled City. Outside the city was Fort McKinley, an Army post with more soldierly-looking Scouts.

I watched a cock fight for the first time and a battle in a ring between two native stallions, and visited the great pavilion where the game of *jaialai* was played. I liked this best. One could have dinner while watching the games, placing bets as he saw fit.

There was a little White Russian hole-in-the-wall establishment called "The Balalaika" where one could dance far into the night. Another restaurant was a little French restaurant where the food was the best in the city. Also, there was the Polo Club where one might see and sometimes talk to a beautiful, dark-eyed *mestiza,* more often than not chaperoned, or order a *shandygaff,* a drink much less interesting than the name implies.*

At the end of my leave in Manila my first impression had changed radically, I left feeling it was a beautiful, convivial city. On the way back, the giant mangoes were ripe, hanging from great trees on the roadside. Several times we stopped to pick and eat a few in the shade of the mango trees. Nevertheless, once again, the freshness of Stotsenburg was a welcome sight. I had had my fill of the city and was ready to get back to work.

Slipping and falling on the muddy trails of Bataan had made me well aware of the inadequacy of cavalry boots for dismounted operations in the jungle. On my return from Manila, I purchased a pair of enlisted men's three-buckle boots and had them modified by sewing heavy-duty zippers up the front from the instep to the top. Also, I had four leather cleats nailed crosswise on the soles. The zippers made the boots quicker to put on; the cleats should make walking the muddy trails easier.

Until now I had tucked the few items I carried in the field into a pocket of my bedroll. This resulted in my gear becoming scattered when sleeping, and difficult to gather together when moving out in the darkness. To remedy this, I had a tailor sew a canvas bag three feet long with round ends a foot in diameter. It zippered shut with little trouble. In it I carried a complete change of clothing, some first aid items, a flashlight, two extra magazines of .45-caliber ammunition, a carton of cigarettes, and a quart of bourbon. The bag was rolled up in my bedding roll, making a single compact package.

There were only two officers in the troop now, Captain Blanning and me. Lieutenant Praeger had been transferred to take command of the newly-activated Troop C. I was the only full-time officer, as Blanning spent much of his time as acting squadron commander.

*A "Shandygaff" was lager beer mixed with lemonade, ginger ale, or other sweet beverage. [Ed.]

The new recruits had completed their first three months of their initial training and were starting into their advanced phase. There was a marked difference in them. They were starting to look and act like soldiers.

The training schedule varied from day to day. Because of the rains, a troop commander had the flexibility to choose between indoor and outdoor training.

The day usually started with a period of dismounted drill: first close order, next extended, then to the stables to groom the horses and saddle up. Mounted drill came next, again in both close and extended orders. This was more difficult than the dismounted work. There were still some horses that had not yet fully settled down and gave their riders a precarious time. Seldom a day passed without a runaway or a few falls. Each day, though, there was improvement and the new men seemed eager to learn.

Once a year the officers of the 26th Cavalry ate in their troop's mess. This was on the 4th of July. At 1130 hours, 4 July 1941, Captain Blanning and I walked into the orderly room of Troop E. We were decked out in our best white dress uniforms, our brass gleaming. Sergeant Amagable met us with not a little formality, showing us into Captain Blanning's office. A soldier brought in a tray with three water tumblers and a bottle of rum. The sergeant poured the tumblers full.

Raising his glass, the First Sergeant toasted, "Long live America."

"Long live America," Blanning and I repeated back to him. We touched glasses and quaffed down a good portion of the rum. The troop commander then raised his glass, "*Mabuhay Ang Filipinos*" (Long Live the Philippines).

The First Sergeant, in a low voice said, "*Marami Salamat*" (Thank you very much).

The mess hall was decorated with red, white, and blue strips of crepe paper in a manner that would have done justice to any American midwest 4th of July picnic. The Scouts, immaculate in their starched khaki uniforms, sat at attention as we entered. Captain Blanning intoned a short prayer. The main dish was steaming rice piled high on great platters down the center of the tables. The cooks had provided vegetables and meat dishes to eat with the rice, along with a variety of tropical fruits. This was my first experience with rice as the main dish. I thought it very good.

When the meal was finished, the First Sergeant said something to Captain Blanning. Blanning stood up. The undertone of conversation stopped. The men put their eating utensils down and sat up; their eyes were glued on their troop commander. There was absolute silence. Again it was obvious that this group of men thought the world of their captain. Blanning's talk was short and to the point. He complimented the troop on its excellent training record to date and warned of harder work to come. And he predicted that the troop would come out ahead in the regimental training tests later on in the year.

The month of July—with the rains and the long hours of training—seemed to grind by very slowly. My main enjoyment was at the end of the day, turning out with the polo team.

Chapter 8

In the latter part of July, the regiment was ordered to reconnoiter portions of the eastern coast of Luzon in the vicinity of Dingalen and Baler Bays. The mission was to gather information on which to base contingency plans for the defense of this area in the event of Japanese landings. Specifically, the regiment was to select and map defensive and delaying positions. If necessary, we were to cut trails needed for their utilization. This was another of several indications of the growing concern over the Japanese threat.

Our only map showed very little detail of the area. This was another example, like Bataan, of the lack of topographical information that American forces had of the more isolated parts of Luzon Island.

The detachment from the regiment, commanded by Lieutenant Colonel Clayton, was made up of two groups, one to reconnoiter the Dingalen Bay area; the other, the area of Baler Bay to the north. I was part of the detail going to Dingalen Bay. Captain Blanning commanded.

Our party left Stotsenburg during the first days of August. It consisted of a rifle platoon of older men, plus necessary mess, supply, and stable personnel, all from Troop E. For some reason, two scout cars from regiment were included. The animals were ported in large trucks designed for that purpose. The convoy also included additional trucks for supplies and transport of the men, as well as a sedan for the officers.

The muddy, ill-maintained road became impassable as we climbed into the Sierra Madres. We stopped at an old sawmill. A base camp was established. Supplies had to be packed from the sawmill to the coast, either by mule or *cargador*.

The following day, the remainder of the distance over the mountains was covered by horseback. The trail led through dripping jungle, so muddy that the horses often went down for lack of footing. Many of the swollen streams were fordable, but to get across the Dingatin River we were forced to use a crude ferry, found to be in service only after running down the operator and haggling over the momentarily inflated price.

After a miserably long day, we arrived at the coast long after dark, wet to the skin, tired, and hungry. That night the animals were fed oats carried on the saddles; there were cold rations for the men. Some deserted shacks gave us shelter from the rain for the remainder of the night.

Morning brought a respite from the downpour, at least enough to let us get a start at drying out. An initial supply of food and fodder was brought in by pack mule. By day's end, more supplies arrived, along with tents. Camp was pitched quickly and began functioning, and our work begun.

Most of the reconnaissance was accomplished by small patrols on foot. The horses were used primarily for examination of the shoreline. Plausible positions for beach defenses were selected, as were successive delaying positions inland. These were plotted and connected by trails, some existing, some having to be cut. Game trails and those used by the local Negritos were used when possible.

Although there were signs in many places of Negritos living in the area, seldom were any seen. They were as shy as wild animals. Only once during the month's stay did I run into one.

This happened one evening when I was hunting for wild fowl on a lonely trail. All of a sudden, a Negrito was standing in front of me, 50 or so yards away. He stood motionless, watching me more from curiosity than any show of fear or desire to do me harm. He was a third taller than the little men I had seen in the Zambales and on Bataan, alert and, as usual, well proportioned, armed with a bow and a few arrows.

I waved at him and shouted a greeting that I had learned from the Negritos on Bataan. He made no move nor did he change the expression on his face. I repeated my greeting more slowly this time, trying to pronounce and enunciate the strange words exactly as they had been taught me. Still, I received no response. In a moment, he turned and glided into the cover of the forest.

On another evening's hunt I sighted a beautiful stag. His antlers were many-pointed and were shaped much the same as our whitetail deer. He could have been standing for some time watching me, but the moment he caught my eye he was gone.

The wild fowl were scarce. The few I did see played the same game as those I had pursued at Subic Bay. Once in a while, a long or lucky shot would bag one, but as they usually proved to be as tough as shoe leather, I finally gave up hunting them.

The cleats I had put on the soles of my boots after Bataan had proven very practical on the muddy trails. Many considered doing the same, but usually gave the idea up, due to the horseman's age-old apprehension of having a foot caught in a stirrup and being dragged. I disregarded any such thought.

Finally our job was completed. It had been an interesting month, even though we had reached such a state of sogginess that one wondered if he would ever dry out. We had learned a great deal about survival in the rainforest.

Chapter 9

The rainy season was at its peak upon our return to Fort Stotsenburg. The air was so thick with moisture that it seemed it could be sliced with a bolo. The great trees in front of the quarters never ceased to drip. While away, my car had been parked beneath one of these trees, completely closed. On first opening a door, a blast of musty air struck my face. The inside felt like a hothouse. Mushrooms were growing out of the upholstery in uninhibited profusion. I had thought to leave a light on in my clothes closet, but never did I suspect that anything like this would happen to my car.

I had no more than become reacquainted with my sorrel mare when Captain Blanning told me to get ready to go to Baguio for a week. I was to be the instructor of a non-commissioned officer's course in demolitions. There would be between 15 and 20 non-coms, two or three selected from each of the six rifle troops.

I had taken some training in demolitions, but had forgotten most of it. For the next few days, I was hard at work reviewing available manuals on the subject, outlining a course of instruction, and assembling the necessary equipment and supplies. Our training area was located in an old mine. We would live in tents. There was no time to inspect the area before moving in and as a result, much of our preparation was guesswork.

A second cook from Troop E with a few assistants made up the mess detachment that would accompany us. A week's supply of rice, a few canned items, and a fund to purchase fresh produce from the local market took care of our food. A demolitions sergeant from regimental headquarters was responsible for the explosives, caps, fuses, and so on.

We had three trucks and a sedan in our convoy. The thrill I had felt last April upon leaving Fort Stotsenburg for Subic Bay, for my first independent command, was missing. Instead of a beautiful sunny day, the sky was pouring out water.

We crawled out of the post past Clark Field and headed north on Highway #3. By afternoon we were winding up the Kennon Road into the mountains. As we gained altitude, the feel of the cool, clear, mountain air in our lungs was exhilarating. The sight of pine trees brought back memories of the western United States, where I had been brought up.

Baguio was the summer capital of the Philippines. During the hot season, the diplomats, high government officials, and the well-to-do migrated there. There was also the American military post, Camp John Hay, where American officers stationed in the hot lowlands could vacation with their families.

The commander of Camp Hay provided a guide to the mine site. We would be under his jurisdiction while in Baguio. It was a pleasant place, clean, with wooden platforms and frames for the pyramidal tents and mock-ups of bridges, vehicles, and houses built to be destroyed. By nightfall, our tents were pitched and the mess was in operation. As at Subic Bay, I ate alone, which was the custom.

Training began the next day. Our explosives were small, rectangular-shaped blocks, solid and comparatively stable. The training was more a series of mathematical problems than of actual detonations. The Scouts proved quite adept in calculating loads and their types, and in positioning the explosives to most efficiently demolish specific structures. These non-coms were alert and intelligent, all having completed at least a high school education. I was hard pressed to stay ahead of them as instructor.

In the evenings, I had the opportunity to visit the little city of Baguio and Camp John Hay. Baguio was clean, with neat little shops mostly full of souvenirs, mainly crudely-carved wooden figures. Its sidewalks teemed with well-dressed Europeans and Igorots. This was the first time I had seen these mountain people, descendants of the early Indonesian invasion of the Philippines. In contrast to the Malays of the lowlands, their complexions are lighter, their cheekbones are more pronounced, and their eyes appear to be slightly slanted. They were heavier set and more muscular than the Malays. They were garbed in G-strings and carried spears, except for a local chief, who had added a cast-off set of black tails and a top hat as a symbol of his office. They were purportedly headhunters, and from their appearance, this was not hard to believe.

On the streets and in the marketplace, I noticed dogs on leashes offered for sale. They were a poor-looking lot, but seemed to be in demand and apparently brought a good price. When I inquired what they were used for, the answer was, "To eat, of course."

The Igorot, like some American Indians, considered a dog a delicacy. Its preparation in the Philippines, however, differed from that of the American plains. The Igorots would first fatten a dog by overfeeding and allowing it not exercise. When fattened to the satisfaction of the owner, the animal would be given nothing to eat for a period of 24 hours. When its stomach was shrunk to nothing and its system cleaned out, the dog would be allowed to gorge itself on freshly cooked rice. As the dog stuffed down its last mouthful, it was quickly dispatched and put on a spit to roast, insides and all. The resulting succulent morsel of meat, with the steaming rice permeated with the flavor of the dog, was a delicacy no true Igorot could resist.

Outside the little city on the steep mountainsides, I first saw the rice terraces. They were ingenious, yet simple and logical. With a dearth of flat places on the valley floors on which to plant, terraces had been dug on the mountainsides. They were really a series of individual, narrow basins, leveled to maintain an even water depth, surrounded by small dikes, and interconnected to allow the overflow of one basin to drain into the one below. In the wet season, the basins filled with water and were planted in the same manner as the rice paddies in the valley. These basins became dry and parched in the dry season, as did the paddies below.

Camp John Hay was another gem of a post, lush and well kept, with quarters, barracks, and administration buildings of similar construction to those a Stotsenburg. Its golf course was second to none on the island. It had a well-stocked commissary and exchange, and a more-than-adequate officers' club. The facilities for visitors were as good as any in the area and a good deal more reasonably priced for American officers, one of the compensations for the low pay of service personnel at the time. One thing that stands out in my mind about my visits to Camp Hay was the appearance of the waiters in the dining room of the officers' club. Here were the counterparts of the wild-looking, headhunting Igorots roaming the Baguio area, wearing starched white jackets; underneath was a G-string, and their legs were bare and they were bare-footed.

The Scouts performed excellently throughout the week. At the end, all were qualified in the use of the explosives at hand. In an emergency, they would be capable of the destruction of foreseeable military targets, either in daylight or in darkness.

I was amazed how my energy had returned after a few days in the cool, clear, mountain air of Baguio. I had little desire to return to the heat and humidity of the lowlands.

Chapter 10

Each time away from Stotsenburg made me appreciate more the luxury that was ours: the spacious quarters, the excellent meals in our small mess for three bachelors; and our houseboys who, with the *lavendera* and cook, meticulously looked after each of us.

The rains were letting up; the monsoon was changing. The air was becoming less humid and cooler, and the skies were clearing. This allowed more training outside. The recruits who had arrived in March had now completed their advanced individual training and had been accepted as privates into their units. Officers had been arriving regularly from the United States, bringing the units up to authorized strengths.

A typical day in garrison started with a short session of dismounted close-order drill. While the bulk of the troop was "saddling up" and "packing out," the officers and senior non-coms would attend a "chalk talk," usually given by Captain Blanning. He would outline the tactical problem to be practiced that day, sometimes at the squad or platoon levels, but sometimes as a whole troop. He had as much enthusiasm for this type of training as he had for his stables. His enthusiasm was contagious, usually resulting in a morning of intense competition between the units of the troop.

After the chalk talk, the troop would march to the training area to execute on the ground that had been taught in the classroom.

After each tactical exercise, the moment that clean up in the stables was finished, officers and non-coms of the troop would return to the classroom for a critique of the morning's problem. Everyone had a chance to get in a word. Often the arguments became heated, but they were always interesting and instructive.

Seldom was anyone excused from standing stables. With the damp heat and long hours of training, soft feet and saddle sores were increasingly becoming a problem. Dismounting and leading animals for the last half-mile or so before arriving at the stables was common practice after a hot morning's workout. This brought the animals into the stable area nearly cooled off. After packs and saddles were removed, the still warm backs were massaged until dry to get the blood circulating. After grooming, every animal was carefully inspected for bruises, sores, and faulty shoeing. Stable personnel treated minor ailments. The regimental veterinarian was called in for major problems. Then blankets had to be dried and brushed, bits washed, and tack cleaned and soaped.

Loading animals onto motor transports was a weekly exercise. Taking units with full loads over jumps up to three feet in height became a daily requirement.

The afternoons were usually spent in the classroom. Twice a week junior officers were required to attend special classes: one to study *Tagalog,* the Philippine national language; the other on Japanese army tactics, organization, and equipment. When time allowed, a group of us turned out for polo practice, hoping to have a viable team by December when we would start playing teams from the Manila area.

In October, the troop spent a week on the mounted pistol range. The range consisted of ten man-sized silhouettes, positioned to the left and right of the rider at varied distances. It required the rider to control his mount at the gallop, while firing and changing magazines in his .45-caliber pistol.

All animals, both pack and riding, were taken to the range and picketed as close to the firing as possible. This was to accustom them to the sound of firing and let them see the show. Often, the first time around for a remount and a recruit would look like a rodeo. The animal, unaccustomed to firing from his back, would start pitching at the sound of the first shot. The man, surprised by the horse's action, would usually drop his pistol to grab the reins or the saddle.

Off they would go, the pistol loaded and cocked, flopping on the end of a lanyard hanging from the man's shoulder. If the horse persisted in pitching, the man's corporal would have to gallop alongside, grabbing the remount's headstall to stop the fracas. If the remount continued his unruliness, an older rider would take him around the course with a quirt to teach him some manners.

The Scouts proved to be good shots with both pistol and rifle. This was not only borne out by their scores, but by comments of older officers, who compared them with training Americans stateside. This skill was usually attributed to the phlegmatic temperament of the average Filipino.

As the weather cooled, woolen shirts replaced the khaki worn during the hot season. Otherwise the uniform remained the same the year around: khaki breaches, boots, and the campaign hat, which was exchanged for a World War I-style steel helmet in the field. The Scout wore an ammunition belt with suspenders on which was attached his first-aid packet, a pouch holding two magazines of .45-caliber ammunition, and his pistol holster. Each man had a third magazine in his pistol. The rifle ammunition pouches on his belt were filled with eight-round clips for the M-1 rifle. Rifle ammunition was ball, except for one clip of armor-piercing and one of tracer. The gas mask hung on his left side.

Scouts rode the standard US Army McClellan saddle. His bridle was the standard military bit and "bridoon" (the bit is the steel part of a bridle inserted in the mouth of a horse and the bridoon is a light military bridle) that requires a double headstall and two sets of reins. In the field, a leather halter was worn beneath the bridle, a halter shank of hemp rope snapped to the halter ring, the free end passed over the animal's neck and tied in a knot similar to a hangman's. A nosebag was strapped on the pommel of the saddle with a feeding of oats and a raincoat. The cantle roll—made up of a woolen blanket, mosquito bar, and shelter half—was strapped behind the saddle. The cantle bags carried a set of horseshoes and nails, a grooming kit, tent pegs and ropes, a mess kit, emergency rations, toilet articles, a towel, and anything else a trooper could cram into them. On the outside of the near cantle bag was strapped his canteen cover with canteen and cup. The boot for his rifle hung on the near side beneath the skirt at an angle; the rifle was inserted muzzle first with the butt up and forward.

Strenuous day-long tactical exercises and long day and night marches were becoming commonplace. Conditioning of men and animals was the highest priority. We no longer moved out of garrison without full field equipment, including live ammunition, emergency rations, steel helmets, and gas masks. Alerts came often, both day and night. We were preparing for what appeared to be an inevitable war with Japan.

Post life had changed noticeably since my arrival in February. The dependents had long since departed. The only American women on the post were the few nurses who staffed our small hospital. The atmosphere after duty hours became more austere and formal as time went on. Dress white uniforms were required after retreat. The club had lost its relaxed, friendly atmosphere.

More cavalry officers were arriving from the United States. Some remained with the regiment, others were sent to train Philippine Army units being mobilized on the various islands.

A federalized National Guard antiaircraft unit from New Mexico arrived and took up its positions with its 90mm guns around Fort Stotsenburg and Clark Field.

A battalion of light tanks, the 192nd, arrived from the States and set up camp to the east of the post. We were introduced to the tanks by a short orientation on their capabilities and limitations and a short ride. The main armament of these tanks was a 37mm gun that looked more like a large gauge shotgun than an antitank weapon. These M3 light tanks were called "Stuarts" after the general of Civil War fame. I'm sure he would have agreed with my feelings at the time: that of the two, a horse would be preferable in combat.

About the same time, a few self-propelled, 75mm guns arrived at Stotsenburg. We did not see much of these, but it appeared they would be more useful against enemy armor than our light tanks.

Several B-17 bombers arrived at Clark Field. They had island-hopped in a roundabout way from the western coast of the United States. One of the pilots came to live in our quarters. During training exercises, their favorite trick was to dump large paper sacks of flour on us when they could catch us in a "march column" in the open.

One time on an overnight bivouac into the Zambales Mountains, we were visited by a band of Negritos. Our evening meal was finished and we were sitting around smoking and talking, when at dusk, the Negritos appeared downstream approaching our camp. As they came closer, we could see that they were sticking frogs and moving rocks in search of snails. When a snail was found, it was sucked from its shell and devoured alive. The frogs were dismembered while still alive and eaten raw. As they passed through our camp, the Negritos generously offered a piece of still-quivering frog or a raw snail still crawling, after being extracted from its shell.

As was their custom, they asked the mess sergeant for a handout. He furnished them with the leftovers from the evening meal. These were placed on large leaves. Squatting around the pile of rice and viands, the Balugas daintily fed themselves without crowding or pushing. Everyone got a share, the mothers feeding the young children.

These people never ceased to intrigue me. Their physical systems were the same as ours, yet here they were living by choice, a wild, hand-to-mouth, nomadic existence, little different from their forebears for the past millennia. There was little evidence of stress in their lives; they appeared healthy, happy, and carefree. Maybe they had the answer, but I had no desire to join them.

Marching into Fort Stotsenburg one night from an exercise in the Zambales, we were watching the searchlights of the New Mexico antiaircraft unit trying to locate high-flying aircraft. All at once, several beams seemed to lock onto a single plane. For a moment it could be seen flying horizontally, when suddenly it dived. As the plane gathered speed, it started to spin, staying all the while in the beam of the searchlights. In a moment it was over. A flare of light was seen, then, the faint sound of an explosion. Apparently, the pilot had been unable to see his instruments because of the glare of the searchlights. Enlisted personnel of the antiaircraft unit, 28 years old and older, were being sent home due to some quirk in the law. These were mostly the experienced men. Whether this had anything to do with the incident, I never found out for sure.

For a month and a half prior to the outbreak of the war, a platoon, with a squad of light machine guns attached, stood parachute watch from a half-hour before dawn to one hour afterward.

In the latter part of October, the regiment initiated tests for the rifle platoons. One phase, the reduction of a roadblock, especially impressed me. The S-3 (operations and training officer) and I carried on a running battle of wits. It was a great day for me when I could put one over on him. He had set up a roadblock where a dusty road entered a line of woods. The platoons approached the roadblock along this road and were fired upon as they entered an open field in front of it.

As I came forward to the point to have a look, a civilian truck came down the road, crossed the field in front of us and drove through the roadblock. As it went along, a great cloud of dust formed behind it and hung there in the still, morning air. It was minutes before the dust had settled.

The solution to the problem was to lay down a base of fire and conduct either a mounted or dismounted flank attack. As a joke on the S-3, I decided on another tactic. I mounted my platoon and closed it up in a column of twos, out of sight of the roadblock. As the next truck came by, we moved in close behind, concealed by the swirl of dust. As we passed through the block, my first squad attacked to the right with pistols, while the second squad did the same to the left. We took out the roadblock by using this tactic, which completely surprised the defenders.

I was disqualified for employing an unrealistic maneuver. It was the S-3's day, yet the reason this has stuck in my mind is that two months later, the Japs routed the regiment with a surprise attack, using a similar tactic.

One morning, General King, the post commander, assembled all the officers at Fort Stotsenburg in the Officers' Club. He had invited Tomás, king of the Pinatuba Negritos, and some of his lieutenants, to attend a ceremony. King Tomás, dressed in a G-string, his old khaki blouse, and campaign hat, stood next to General King, erect and with posture as regal as any European king dressed in satins. Nearby were his lieutenants, clad also only in G-strings, carrying their bows and arrows, looking just as important as their king. Facing them were the officers of the post, lined up as the audience.

General King, in a short speech, reviewed the friendship and trust that existed between Americans and the Negritos of the Zambales Mountains, and expressed his desire to strengthen this by becoming blood brother to the king of the Pinatuba Negritos. Allowing time for the interpreter to translate for the Negritos, Tomás delivered a short speech, which in the translation conveyed much the same thoughts as those of General King.

King Tomás and General King then stepped forward, each baring an arm. General King's aide stepped up and slashed the general's and the Baluga king's lower arms, deep enough to allow the blood to flow freely. Their arms were then bound together with the wounds touching each other, allowing their blood to mix. The aide then declared them blood brothers. This was translated to the Negritos. They expressed satisfaction with grunts and by simultaneous forward motions of their right arms holding bow and arrows. The Negritos seemed very impressed with the ceremony. Being realists, they were at least just as impressed with the presents of rice, trinkets and colored cloth awarded them after the ceremony.

About this time, I was promoted to first lieutenant. My base pay was raised from $125 a month to about $168. Soon after my promotion, the regimental adjutant called me to his office and offered me command of the Scout Car Platoon in Headquarters Troop. Why was I being given such a choice? This bothered me. Why was I not just transferred without any talk? At any rate, I expressed a desire to stay with the horses and that is where it ended. I often wondered if I had made a good decision.

In November, I was transferred to Troop A. This was a sad time for me. I felt I had become a part of Troop E. For the past eight months, I had trained with them and believed that I had developed a mutual feeling of trust and respect with the officers and men of the troop. I hated to think of leaving them, especially my platoon and Sergeant Masanguay, to whom I had become attached.

The Troop A commander had gone to the S-3 job at regiment some time before. A captain was due in from the States who was earmarked to take his place, but had been delayed. I was to take command of the troop until the arrival of the new captain.

Initial inspections revealed that standards of discipline and training were not up to those of Troop E. Some of the troop's weapons were rusty and dirty; equipment in general was not up to par. Stable management needed a re-shuffle and got it. It took a few weeks of working night and day before things were up to snuff. My efforts won me no popularity. In fact, I was sure I was looked upon as a tyrant.

Troop A animals were black. There was not a really fine animal in the troop. Looking for a new mount, I finally selected a horse that no one else wanted. His name was Crow Flight, large and strong with a good back and legs, but with a disposition like a Manila *Calesa* pony. He was hard to bridle, constantly throwing his head; he jigged instead of walked; when put into a gallop, he usually took the bit and was off at a dead run for the farthest horizon. I liked to ride, and decided to try to teach him some manners. In the process, I found he could jump.

In the latter part of November, the post had a horse show. I decided to enter Crow Flight in the open jumping event. Others before me had jumped him in shows, but had been unable to hold him on course. I was up early on the morning of the show, working Crow Flight in circles, figure eights, and stops, hoping to calm him down for the competition. I held him on course the first time around and managed to qualify for the finals. His excitement, caused by the presence of the onlookers, the other horses, as well as the wait for a second turn at the jumps, was just too much for him. When my turn came, I aimed Crow Flight at the first jump and loosened the reins. He took off like a bolt, nearly leaving me behind. We stayed on course, but his speed was such that instead of going over the ins and outs, we went through them. The last jump I let him have his head, knowing too many jumps had been knocked down to qualify. In all my life, I never made such a jump. At nearly a dead run, Crow Flight took off yards before the jump, seeming to flow up and over and on, soaring through the air as if on wings. Atop of him, with a breeze in my face, I found myself looking over the somewhat amazed crowd that was watching his antics. We came down with a thump, but the horse gathered himself and was off for the next province with the bit firmly in his teeth. I finally circled him to a stop. The next day he showed a little lameness in his front legs, but other than that, nothing, and he was ready to go in a couple of days.

For the past months, polo practice had continued several afternoons a week and on weekends. The regiment was developing a pretty fair team.

On Sunday afternoon, 7 December 1941, the Fort Stotsenburg polo team had its first game of the season with the Manila Polo Club. The game was held at

Stotsenburg. A large group had come up from Manila to root for their team and attend the annual party held at the Officers' Club after the game. I was to play the number one position, which I liked best. The Manila team had the older, more experienced players, but our initial dash set them back at first. As the game progressed, however, their better sticking and teamwork won the day.

The great thing for me that day was the performance of my little sorrel mare. She played like an old-timer. Her heart was in the game, her eye on the ball, and her mind on my signals. Her speed was uncanny. I had started her as a green pony nine months before on my arrival in the regiment. Being then somewhat shifty and nervous, it was questionable whether she would ever settle down.

The party after the game lasted well into the early morning. The girls who had come up from Manila put new life into the club. Troop A had scheduled a march to the north to leave barracks at 0100 hours. The first time I thought to glance at my watch and to my horror there was only enough time before the march to get to my quarters, change, and report to the troop.

At 0100 hours, 8 December 1941, Troop A left stables to march to an area between Capas and Camp O'Donnel, Tarlac, 15 miles to the north.

Part Two
THE JAPANESE INVADE

Chapter 11

At 0900 hours, 8 December 1941. Troop A was in bivouac 15 miles north of Fort Stotsenburg. The troop had arrived in the bivouac area soon after daylight. Animals had been groomed and equipment cleaned at a leisurely pace. After breakfast, all but the picket-line guards were resting.

I was dozing off when a car drove up and stopped with a skidding of wheels. I heard the door slam, then some rushing around and excited voices. Looking out of my tent, I saw the troop commander and a newly-arrived officer from the regiment talking excitedly, but could not hear what they were saying.

The troop was soon assembled.

"The United States has declared a state-of-war with Japan," Captain Kramer announced to the assembled troop. "This morning, the Japanese attacked Pearl Harbor in the Hawaiian Islands."

I looked at the faces of the men. A few of the older Scouts showed some emotion; to the younger ones, the news appeared to have little meaning, perhaps because they were still half asleep after their night march.

The news was not a surprise. It had been expected for months, but it was still hard to believe that it had really happened. My feeling at the time was that at last there would be a chance to actually test our training; that we would probably have a time of it for awhile, but that eventually the United States would bring in sufficient strength to hold the Philippines. Looking back, remembering the look of apprehension on the courier's face that morning, I wonder if he knew better than most of us what we were up against. He had two more weeks to live.

Troop A now had orders to join the regiment in the Bamban River Valley after dark, or before, if enemy planes were not overhead. The 26th Cavalry had left Fort Stotsenburg at dawn. Weapons were loaded, steel helmets covered with mud, and air scouts were posted. Tents and canvas flies were taken down. The kitchen truck was camouflaged, and the horses were dispersed in depressions.

The troop was bivouacked in the rolling foothill country east of the Zambales Mountains. Rice paddies, now harvested and dry, covered the low, level areas; *cogan* grass grew in abundance on the hills. Small streams that wound down into the valley were bordered with dense clumps of bamboo. Here and there, a *nipa* shack stood on a hillside.

Our light machine guns were set up on the hilltops surrounding our position with riflemen around them acting as air scouts. Our main concern was the possibility of low-flying aircraft approaching from the west where the Zambales Mountains would conceal them up to the last moment.

At about 1230 hours, the warning signal "Airplanes" came in from our observation post. The barely audible drone of heavy-motored aircraft sounded in the north. Two groups of planes came in sight, flying in perfect formation at an altitude of 15,000 to 20,000 feet, their silver bodies glittering in the sun.

At first we hoped these were our aircraft, but as they passed overhead there was no mistaking the round blotches of red on the underside of the wings. There were 54 of them, twin-engine, medium bombers, flying in two formations of 27 each, heading south toward Fort Stotsenburg and Clark Field. We watched them disappear in the mist.

The heavy "crump" of exploding bombs, mixed with an occasional faint rattling of machine-gun fire, soon came from the south.

It was not long before all 54 planes returned in the same perfect formation, heading north, their mission apparently completed. Clouds of black smoke were rising over Clark Field. High above this smoke, small dots of planes performed acrobatics. Three of these slowly became discernible as they maneuvered north toward the troop area. Two had grown into similar-looking silhouettes, different in pattern from the third, which was in the lead. The single plane in front looped and twisted and dove through every antic imaginable, but was unable to shake its pursuers. The stutter of machine-gun fire could be heard as the dogfight came closer. Tiny wisps of smoke from tracer bullets were visible around the little plane in front. At each swoop the two pursuing planes were closer to their prey.

Suddenly, the maneuvering of the leading plane stopped. A trace of black smoke came from its tail. It became lifeless as it drifted into an aimless glide toward the mountains, the trail of smoke gradually thickening. The pursuit continued; the attacking aircraft alternating in pumping bullets into the wounded plane until it crashed into a hillside in a great ball of black smoke. A sudden turn at the last moment had revealed that the little plane in front was one of our P-40s. The pursuing planes were Japanese Zeros.

By this time, the black smoke rising over Clark Field had become a giant cloud. The realization that we were at war began to take hold. It also began to dawn on us that it was not going to be an easy war, if the Japs could get away with such things as we had just witnessed. There was little doubt that there were a good many dead Americans and Filipinos down there where we lived, and a good chance some were our friends.

The troop had gathered on a hill to watch the Clark Field debacle. Our observation posts sounded another warning. Two Zeros, flying low and fast, were sighted to the north following the highway, which was only a mile or so to the east. They were gone in a moment, but their presence had caused a mad scramble for cover.

The troop began to saddle at about 1500 hours. Even though there had been groups of two or three enemy fighters in the air off and on throughout the afternoon, the troop commander had decided to march before dark. We would use the highway from Tarlac to Mabalakat (about 6 miles north of Angeles). The highway was paved, bordered by dirt shoulders. Beyond the shoulders, there were ditches or barbed wire fences. The ditches were deep and boggy, impossible to get a horse out of once he got into it. Our salvation was dispersion along the road.

The troop experienced several air alerts during the march, which slowed us up considerably. Jap pilots undoubtedly saw our column, but evidently it was not their day to harass horse cavalry.

Crossing the Bamban, we watered our horses, then widely dispersed up and down the river. The troop turned off the highway at Mabalakat around dusk, onto the back road leading to Fort Stotsenburg.

Groups of ordnance personnel, newly arrived from the States, with heavy maintenance equipment, were dispersed under the trees along the sides of the road. The men appeared bewildered. Further on, we passed 90mm antiaircraft guns dug in and sandbagged.

Seeing American troops in helmets, carrying gas masks, and with ammunition ready to fire was something new. Instead of the usual bantering remarks about the cavalry, there was a quiet seriousness and a look of deep concern on their faces. The shock of the Clark Field disaster had gotten to them. Their vehicles were camouflaged and foxholes had been dug. For these men, things had changed drastically since the day before. In contrast, the cavalry was used to its war kit; as soon as we had mounted up that afternoon, the men were as jaunty as ever.

As the troop neared Fort Stotsenburg, we veered off on the old road to the north, down into the Bamban Valley and up the river to a bivouac area, where the rest of the regiment had moved that morning. It must have been around 2200 hours when we arrived. The more vulnerable kitchen truck had waited until after dark to come in, and arrived several hours later. All that the horses got that night was unsaddling and a bag of oats. I was asleep on my raincoat before supper was ready.

The Bamban River Valley, north of Fort Stotsenburg, is a broad, deep gulch, as much as three miles wide in places, with extremely high banks. The rocky bottom is largely covered with a thick, low scrub, broken here and there by groups of tall tropical trees. The scrub is high enough to give good concealment to the horses. At that time of year, a shallow, swift river ran through the valley.

On the morning of 9 December, the regiment moved down the river a mile or so, into a more thickly-vegetated area that provided better concealment. There were a few fighters in the sky that morning. At a distance, it was difficult to tell the difference between the Japanese fighters and our P-40s. Often, planes would be directly overhead before we knew whose they were. I can remember that at that time it was not clear in my mind just how effective bombing and strafing were, nor what was the best protection against them. With stories rampant about the terrible destruction done to Clark Field, there was a great deal of apprehension concerning the potency of the Japanese Air Force.

In the latter part of the morning, I rode into the post with a few others from the troop, to gather up odds and ends of equipment that might be needed later on.

On the way, we passed groups of officers and men from Clark Field who had taken refuge in the Bamban River Valley. They had fled from Clark during the attack the previous day, without provisions, equipment, or proper clothing. Few had slept the night before. Never had I seen more miserable-looking men. Several times we stopped to listen to what they had to say about the attack on Clark Field. In one group, I ran across a lieutenant whom I had known in school. His disheveled appearance was so unlike him that he was hardly recognizable. Instead of taking a commission in the cavalry, he had joined the Air Corps to become a flyboy. He looked at my horse and shook his head and said, "I guess I should have stayed with the horses."

In another group, a burly sergeant said, "We drove the bastards off in the morning and made them drop their bombs in the mountains to the north to get away from our pursuit planes; then, damned if the dirty sonsabitches didn't sneak back while we were refueling and having noon chow. We were in the mess hall when all hell broke loose. The bullets came in like a swarm of bees. Some men never moved, just slumped over. Others stood up and then fell. Those of us who could, ran outside in all directions. The blasts from the bombs made the earth shake. I was sure I was a goner."

The consensus was that several hundred American had been killed or wounded. The main runway, shops, and hangers had been made almost useless. Most of the planes had been destroyed, yet it was reported that not a dummy plane had been attacked. It was evident that the Japs had an efficient intelligence system. Fort Stotsenburg had also been both bombed and strafed the previous day, but the damage was nothing compared to that described at Clark Field.

By afternoon the general feeling in the regiment was that we were as ready as we could be for anything that would come. The 26th Cavalry, minus two troops, was dispersed along the Bamban, over an area of a mile or so in length. Troop G had been sent by truck to the eastern coast of Luzon, into the Baler and Dingalen Bay areas. Troop F was still in Manila.

Every precaution had been taken against surprise from air attack; being in a valley made it easy for enemy planes to be on us without warning. Orders were to remain motionless when enemy planes were overhead. Horses were watered by squads. No more than a squad at a time filled its mess kits from the kitchen truck, and then returned to their bivouac areas to eat. As the days passed, more and more dependence was placed on the squad leaders and the seconds in command of squads. The squad leader had to know the whereabouts of his men and his platoon sergeant, night and day.

By the morning of 10 December, Air Corps personnel from Clark Field were coming to our mess to eat. Many had not had a square meal since noon two days before. They had no idea where their units were. Reportedly, Clark Field was still deserted.

On the afternoon of the 10th, the 26th Cavalry was ordered to deploy into the hills northeast of Clark Field to defeat an expected paratroop landing on the runways. The regiment was dispersed along the northern edge of the runways, under concealment. Its mission was to ride out in the event of an enemy landing and break up the Japs before they could become organized. The operation would be supported by our machine guns already in good positions.

By darkness, no paratroopers had arrived, but we had a good look at Clark Field. Destroyed planes, shot up and burned, were strewn along the runways. The runways were full of craters. Most of the nearby buildings had burned to the ground; enemy strafing had been so intense that those left standing looked like sieves.

Just before dark, the 1st Squadron, reinforced with a number of the newly-arrived 75mm guns mounted on half-tracks, combed the area east of Fort Stotsenburg and Clark Field, again searching for Japanese paratroopers. They found none. On a patrol into the town of Dau that night, I watched the artillery that had been stationed at Fort Stotsenburg filing through on its way out. The long 155mm guns were very impressive.*

We stayed on alert throughout the night. Later, it was thought that the suspected Japanese paratroopers were our own airmen jumping from crippled planes.

We were awakened by the sound of antiaircraft fire on the morning of 11 December. In the dim light, we could see Japanese bombers passing overhead at 10,000 to 15,000 feet; they seemed bothered very little by the fire.† From this day on, we saw very few of our planes in the air; the Japs had it pretty much their own way. During the morning, more enemy bombers passed overhead within range of our antiaircraft guns, but the fire proved as ineffective as it had from the first.

A couple of us went over to kid the gunners, asking them when they were going to learn to shoot. Again, we were told that most of their old gunners had returned recently to the United States as a result of a War Department order. Untrained recruits reportedly were doing the shooting.

In the afternoon, the 26th Cavalry left the Bamban, moving to a new bivouac area in the woods near Taconda Hill, a mile and a half south of Fort Stotsenburg. Just before dark, three Japanese fighters located our new position and appeared to be conducting photo reconnaissance. Then they strafed the entire area. Troop

---

*The 86th Field Artillery Regiment (PS), one of two artillery regiments stationed at Fort Stotsenburg, was equipped with M1918 155mm field guns. Known to the gunners at the time as "GPFs" ("Grande Portée Fillioux," or long-range guns designed by M. Fillioux, the French ordnance inventor), these guns were the heaviest field artillery pieces available to the Fil-American forces in 1941/42. They could accurately fire 95 pound projectiles to a range of 18,371 meters, or approximately 11.4 miles. [Ed.]

†The 3-inch guns used by the 200th Coast Artillery Regiment had a maximum vertical range of 27,000 feet. [Ed.]

A was well sprayed, but sustained no casualties. As soon as the troop had bivouacked, the men had dug slit trenches or foxholes. These had to be deep enough for a man to get his head one foot below ground level. Some of the Scouts had built up the sides of their holes with the trunks of banana trees. The pithy nature of this tree had an amazing ability to slow a bullet.

For the first time, I noticed tracers from our .30-caliber light machine guns ricocheting off the sides of the strafing Zeros. Japanese air superiority was a constant concern, but we were learning to live with it.

To put out air scouts in the daytime had become as standard as digging slit trenches. Every man in the troop was alert for the sound of planes. Talking was subdued. Men even walked quietly. It became habit to know where the nearest trench or depression was. When the air signal was sounded, the scramble for the trenches reminded one of the old game of musical chairs.

For a bomb to get a man lying in a depression, it had to land practically on top of him. The only protection from intense strafing lay in being deep in the ground. It was found that the best protection for the horses was to have them tied in a riverbed or some other depression well covered with foliage from above and well dispersed. I do not recall the troop ever being surprised by Jap planes.

It was the beginning of the dry season, so it was possible for everyone to sleep on the ground with comparative comfort. The white mosquito bars were dipped in coffee, making them less conspicuous from the air when spread over our bedrolls.

On the night of 11 December, we first noticed fires blazing on several isolated hills surrounding Fort Stotsenburg. It was rumored that these were being set by Jap sympathizers as a guide for night bombing attacks.

The following morning, the 1st Squadron held officers' call in the regimental headquarters building at Fort Stotsenburg. A few of us went in early to have a look around. The appearance of the post had changed considerably. Foxholes and slit trenches had been dug everywhere. Machine guns, with Scouts lolling beside them, were in position to deliver antiaircraft fire. A battery of 2.95-inch mountain guns was emplaced at the western end of the parade ground.*

Hong Kong Street and the Post Exchange were crowded. Men were shopping for little last-minute necessities. Some were sending radiograms home. Our quarters were just as we had left them. I wrote a note to my houseboy, Santiago, to take my belongings into the *barrio* where he lived. I remember thinking there was no hurry about it, and possibly it would not be necessary at all.

Two Jap pilots who had been shot down during the first days of the war were brought in that morning. They looked tough, with their bristly, black mustaches and close-cropped hair. Someone said that a German pilot also had been shot down in a nearby *barrio*.† We heard that King Tomás's Negritos had captured two

*The Philippine Division's 23rd Field Artillery Battalion (PS) was equipped with 2.95-inch mountain guns. These were ancient weapons (purchased between 1899 and 1904), designed and built by the British firm of Vickers-Maxim. [Ed.]

†No German pilots were involved in the attack on the Philippines. [Ed.]

more Jap pilots in the Zambales Mountains and had presented the post commander with their heads stuck on spears.

By mid-morning officers of the 1st Squadron were assembled on the porch of the headquarters building of the 26th Cavalry. The meeting had no more than started when the faint "crump" of bombs exploding could be heard from the direction of Clark Field. As the seconds passed, the sound of heavy motors grew louder. There was little doubt the Japanese bombers were heading our way. Officers' call ended abruptly as we made for the trenches and foxholes.

Scattered clouds were not more than 3,000 feet high. The roar of the heavy motors overhead was nearly on us before the planes came into view above the clouds. They seemed to approach very slowly, great hulks suspended in the sky, releasing their bombs as they came. We could see the bombs in the racks, then perceive them being released and dropping. In moments, the ground vibrated with heavy explosions. Several times I had the uncomfortable feeling that a bomb was heading right into my foxhole. Our machine guns did a lot of firing, but seemed to have little effect. The great planes circled to the south still dropping their bombs, and disappeared into the mist.

Word came that Clark Field had taken another good pasting. One bomb landed on an antiaircraft gun, blowing the gun and crew into a thousand pieces. A bomb in back of regimental headquarters had hit a jeep squarely. The driver was about ten feet away, in a hole, unhurt. In the 26th Cavalry Regiment's area, the bombing wrecked two of the barracks, two stables, and the motor pool. Horses of the regiment remaining on post had been grouped together in Machine Gun Troop stables. One bomb killed 12 of them. I learned later that one of them was my little sorrel mare. My car, parked in back of the back of the stables, had been hit and practically demolished.

Returning to the bivouac area, we found that it, too, had been hard hit. Troop A had gotten off relatively lightly, losing only two horses and one man slightly wounded. The horses were in my platoon and I knew them. One had part of his lungs exposed by a piece of shrapnel; he was standing, his legs spread apart, wild-eyed, gasping for breath. The other was hit in the flank, exposing some of the intestines and a broken leg bone. He looked dazed. These were the first horses I had seen wounded. It was a pitiful sight. There was only one thing to do. I was getting ready to shoot the first one when the regimental veterinarian came by.

"Let me do that," he said, glancing sadly at the pair.

About this time a detachment of our regiment's scout cars departed to reinforce a Philippine Army division fighting in the Cagayan Valley in northern Luzon.

On the afternoon of 12 December, the regiment was ordered to a forest midway between Fort Stotsenburg and Angeles. Getting there required crossing a considerable amount of open ground. Japanese aerial reconnaissance undoubtedly had us spotted and, from all indications over the past two days, were out to get us.

To minimize exposure, the regiment crossed the open area, several miles in length, one troop at a time. Several troops moved out before us, including one that had been strafed, and made it without casualties. We conducted the moves with speed, dispersion, and by now, the knowledge that once a Zero was in its dive, an alert man on horseback, could gallop clear of the strike area. It was with a little bravado and daring that Troop A took its turn at the crossing. Moving fast and well dispersed, the troop made it across without loss. Had the Japs come after us with two planes abreast, however, we would have had a hard time surviving.

The regiment stayed in the woods between Stotsenburg and Angeles for one or two days. Rifles and pistols had been carried loaded and locked from the first; while camped in these woods, occasionally, a man would accidentally discharge his piece. It was difficult to make the men conscious of the fact that their guns were always loaded. We spent a day or so resting, checking equipment, and watching Japanese planes pass overhead, wondering where they were from and where they would attack.

Chapter 12

At nightfall on 13 or 14 December, the regiment started toward Angeles, marching through it, then turning north on Highway #3 to the town of Bamban, where we went into bivouac.

We remained there for two or three days. Troop headquarters was a *nipa* shack next to the highway. The troop was bivouacked to the rear, in a coconut grove. Most of the *barrio*-folk had taken to the hills, but they came down during the day to visit and sell their produce. Among them was a barber, who kept busy in the troop area during the whole stay. For many, this would be the last haircut for a long time; for some, it would be their last, ever.

Somewhere, we acquired a radio and listened to Manila screaming about air raids and enemy landings in northern and southern Luzon. At the time, we were not too perturbed over the news. In fact, I believe everyone wanted to finally meet the Japs, and thought in the back of his mind that they would not be too hard to beat them. It was generally conceded that things would not get too rough before the United States would send help. The news of Pearl Harbor was still just so many words.

One night there, my platoon was detailed to guard General Wainwright's headquarters, which was nearby in the Bamban Sugar Central.* During the evening, the general came outside and spoke a few words. He was dressed in trousers, and looked pale and tired. The vim and dash that had been so noticeable two years before, on the Balmorhea maneuvers in Texas, had gone. Then, he was brown and hard and in excellent humor.

I was surprised to run into Captain Blanning, now a major. He had been transferred to Wainwright's headquarters. We had a long talk. That was the last time I saw him.†

I believe it was at this point that Troop F joined the regiment, having marched up from Manila. The 26th Cavalry Regiment was now operating nearly complete, except Troop G and the scout cars that had been sent north.

The men gradually became accustomed to carrying their weapons loaded. The bombing and strafing no longer excited them as they had at first. They were eager to fire at the planes, but were not allowed to, for fear of giving away our position.

At nightfall on 16 December, the regiment continued marching to the north. We made camp during the next day near the town of Capas, Tarlac. At dark, we were marching north again, on Highway #3. Sometime during the night, we reached the town of Gerona. Throughout 18 December, the regiment was

*One of many such sugar mills in the Philippines at the time. [Ed.]

†Major James C. Blanning served as I Corps Headquarters Commandant. He died of malnutrition and exposure at the hands of his Japanese captors in January 1945. [Ed.]

bivouacked in a coconut grove west of the town. There was little chance of getting any rest, as enemy planes threatened attack throughout the day.

Again at nightfall, the regiment hit the road. At about 0330 hours the next morning, we arrived in Rosales, Pangasinan (the province that encloses Lingayen Gulf). Some of the men had fallen asleep in the saddle on that night march. Trotting for five minutes, and then walking five, for periods of 50 minutes out of each hour, became quite monotonous, especially in the deep darkness, when all there was to hold one's attention was the tail of the horse in front, and the rhythmic clump, clump, clump of horses' hooves. The last ten minutes of each hour were a relief, when the troop dismounted and led the horses.

We camped near Rosales for two and a half days. Japanese planes were nearly always overhead. The sight of American planes was a thing of the past. It was at this time that security elements around the regimental bivouac area were considerably strengthened because of reports coming from the north that the Japs were pushing south from Aparri and Vigan, where they had made landings a week before.

Up to this time, supply had been no problem. Everything came from Fort Stotsenburg, with supplies being brought up by truck at night to avoid attack from the air. The regiment's trucks dumped off hay and grain on the road near the troop area, and from there, the fodder was hauled by hand to the animals. The mess sergeant picked up the troop's food at the same place and transferred it to the kitchen truck.

The surviving animals were in good condition. The cool night marches agreed with them. Enemy planes overhead during daylight had not disturbed their rest, as it had the men's.

By 21 December, our farriers had caught up with all required shoeing. The men were also well rested from the march north, and their morale was high. By now, the effects on us of enemy's air superiority had receded. Traveling at night did not give the Japs much of chance to bother us on the march; in bivouac during daylight, we were well dispersed and concealed with in foxholes or slit trenches. We knew that even if the Japs discovered us, the damage could not be too great.

About this time, General Wainwright moved his headquarters to the town of Santo Tomás (about 20 miles southeast of Rosales).

On the morning of 21 December, I had a shave and a bath in a bucket, with hot water and soap. It would be the last for nearly two months. In the middle of the morning, rumors started spreading that something was afoot. At noon, orders came to be ready to move in half an hour.

Troop C was dismounted; its horse equipment was put into oat sacks and loaded on trucks, and its animals were turned over to Troops A and B. Troop C personnel were then loaded on trucks and sent to a town north of Baguio, presumably to help stop the Japanese advance to the south. Each rifle squadron now had only two troops. Machine Gun Troop was still intact.

By 1430 hours, the regiment was marching west. No one had a noon meal that day. Toward what were we marching?

At the junction of Highway #3 we turned north. Thanks to Japanese air superiority, apprehension about being in the opened flared. Luckily, we managed to get through the afternoon without trouble. Before dark, the regiment bivouacked in a coconut grove in the vicinity of Pozorrubio, Pangasinan. We had marched about 20 miles that afternoon. The animals of the 1st Squadron had to be watered from a single well, with collapsible buckets carried on the saddles. It took several hours. In the absence of supply trucks, the animals were fed grain from that which was carried on the saddles. There was enough grass around to keep them going. Again, the men had nothing to eat.

We rolled up in our raincoats, close to the picket line, in readiness to pull out on a moment's notice. When the supply trucks arrived after midnight, we got up to spread hay and refill the grain bags. The kitchen truck had nothing ready to eat, so we went back to sleep.

"Saddle-up" came long before dawn on 22 December. In a short time, we were formed on the highway, ready to move out. Troop C horses were left in the bivouac area.

Daybreak found the regiment marching northwest through rolling country, toward the town of Sison. The morning was cloudy, ideal for marching, being cool and giving us protection against observation by hostile planes. We marched in a strung-out formation on both sides of the paved road that was hemmed in by barbed-wire fences. The 2nd Squadron was leading, with Troop E as advance guard.

Soon after daylight, a lone plane came "hightailing it" down the column. It happened so fast, we barely had time to get off the road and dismount. Many of us were still standing when it zoomed overhead. The plane was one of our P-40s, the first seen since the dogfights over Clark Field. Though it lasted only a moment, the sight of the little plane caused a feeling of exaltation. A cheer went up along the column. It was a wonderful boost to morale, after days of seeing only Jap planes.

At mid-morning, the regiment reached the junction where the Kennon Road branches off toward Baguio, and Highway #3 turns west toward the town of Rosario. We continued on Highway #3.

The sky was starting to clear. Japanese planes were high overhead, but apparently had not yet recognized the regiment. We halted and got off the road to rest. A company of light tanks passed through us, on toward Rosario. During the rest period, several Filipinos brought us young coconuts to eat. Soon, the regiment again was marching toward Rosario.

We had not been told what we were moving forward to meet, but there was little doubt that we were riding into some type of action. No one seemed overly concerned, however. Empty bellies, lack of sleep, and the humdrum of marching had lulled us into thinking only of the moment at hand.

The sound of heavy explosions occasionally drifted in from the northwest, in the direction of Lingayen Gulf. In the same direction, planes were seen diving out of sight, then climbing again. They were too far away for us to hear their motors.

At about 1100 hours, we entered the town of Rosario. Filipinos alongside the road made Winston Churchill's "V" sign, yelling "*mubahay*" ("good luck"), or "*veectoree.*" At the halt, they were soon knocking down green coconuts for us to eat. These were refreshing, but did little to stay the hunger that was boring into our innards. A Scout brought me a big green Philippine orange, pithy and soggy. I carefully peeled and ate the whole thing, chewing the pulp for every bit of moisture and nourishment I could get out of it.

The day had turned hot after the clouds burned off. We were unable to find any decent drinking water in Rosario. The crews of the light tank company, whom we had overtaken, were especially in need of water as they had done most of their marching through the morning with hatches closed.

New orders were distributed after a regimental meeting of squadron and troop commanders. Shortly after noon, we mounted up and moved out toward the town of Damortis to the west.

The order of march in the regiment changed, and 1st Squadron, with an attached heavy machine gun platoon, took over the lead. The order of march in the 1st Squadron was Troop B, the Heavy Machine Gun Platoon, then Troop A. Scout cars were dispersed along the column. Regimental headquarters had gone forward with the tanks. Just outside Rosario, the Japs started dive-bombing and strafing our column. They hit the head of the column hardest. When planes approached, the Scouts widened the interval between horses as much as possible, and every effort was made to get them into any kind of depression. The riders dismounted and laid down.

The scout cars stopped and engaged the aircraft with their .50-caliber machine guns. While I never saw a hit, their fire seemed to make the Japs pull out of their dives at a greater altitude than usual, at least limiting their effectiveness.

The mounted elements did no firing; it was their job to keep moving. Platoon commanders had been instructed to use their judgment when to disperse for air attacks. At times, it took a good deal of loud persuasion to keep the platoon from dispersing without orders, upon sighting approaching planes. It was necessary to watch each plane carefully, and just before one started to dive at your specific area, give the signal to disperse, and be out of the way before a plane started to fire, or release a bomb. It also took a fair amount of leadership to get the platoon back onto the road after each attack. One bomb, which I judged to be a 50-pounder, landed within 50 or 75 feet of me. My horse was standing in a ditch, with his head and saddle above ground level. Luckily, the bomb drove deep into the soft earth before exploding, causing the fragments to fly at a high angle.

The Japanese technique of strafing and dive-bombing was different from ours. Our pilots lined up on a target a good distance away, then came in at top speed. The Japs held their planes momentarily in place high above the target, maneuvering them into position, then started a glide toward the target, appearing to cut their engines until their dive was nearly completed. This slowness helped us to survive. As we moved on, the road became more and more littered with debris and bomb craters. Only twice did our column pass dead men or horses. Once, where a bomb had landed squarely in the middle of a cut for the road, there laid a dead Scout and two dead horses. The corpse had been covered with his raincoat. Another time, a dazed and wounded Scout was sitting beside the road, his dead horse nearby.

It was hard work going down the road as we did; dispersing, dismounting, throwing ourselves onto the ground, mounting, assembling back on the road, and moving on. As time wore on, the tendency became greater and greater to disperse at the first sight of a plane, and it became progressively more difficult to assemble after an attack.

One incident on this march stayed with me. After a quick dash off the road, the platoon was assembling to continue the march. I noticed my platoon sergeant was missing. Looking down off the road, I saw him dismounted, struggling to get his horse out of a *carabao* wallow. The horse was up to his belly in the wallow and could not move. I rode over with the idea of trying to help, knowing full well that it would take a good while to get the horse out. I had gone so far as to send a nearby civilian after some planks, when I looked around, and saw the platoon on the road, waiting. Suddenly I realized there was something more important than a horse in distress. I quickly dismounted a private, leaving him to take care of the mired horse, mounted the sergeant, and moved on.

About 1230 hours, the road passed over a ridge, from which Lingayen Gulf could be seen in the distance. The gulf was jammed with Japanese ships. The scene brought a full realization of the reason for the recent forced marches. This was the first I had known that the Japs were attempting a landing, so close, in such force. There was time for no more than a fleeting glance; a messenger, hurrying back from the regimental forward command post, brought instructions for the troop to move up "on the double!"

Marching in order with 1st Platoon leading, then 2nd Platoon, and with the Light Machine Gun Platoon following, we moved west toward the Gulf at a fast trot. For the first time, I felt a little excited, but it is difficult to feel too much with an empty stomach and all the moisture having been sweat out of one's body. The troop commander and 1st Platoon leader were riding at the head of the troop and wasting no time. My 2nd Platoon and the Light Machine Gun Platoon had dropped behind, due to air attacks. I had turned my platoon over to the platoon sergeant and was riding in the rear of the Light Machine Gun Platoon, to ensure that everyone moved forward. My platoon sergeant was having considerable trouble assembling the 2nd Platoon back on the road after each attack. A good many of the younger men recruited last March were still not too well disciplined.

Chapter 13

About 1330 hours, I arrived at the regimental command post. It consisted of a scout car with radio and a few staff officers standing nearby. There was no sign of the remainder of Troop A. The squadron adjutant told me to join the troop that had gone into position on a ridge to the northwest, and to hurry.

I signaled the two platoons to follow me and set out at a gallop. The troop commander was three or four hundred yards to the northwest. I spotted him high up on the ridge. As soon as he saw us, he signaled for the platoons to fight on foot and assemble on him. The 1st Platoon had left its horses mobile (one horse holder to every four horses), so I did the same.

In the bottom of the valley where the troop dismounted was a rice paddy that had been recently harvested. It was now a hard, broken field, covered with rice stubble. A streambed ran down the center of the field, which had a growth of *cogan* grass in it ten feet high. Clumps of small, heavily-vegetated trees flanked the outer edges of the rice field. The horses were dispersed along the streambed in the *cogan* grass and beneath these trees.

The two platoons assembled, dismounted, in a column of troopers, and moved up the ridge to the troop commander's location. A few of the men had taken their canteens off their saddles and secured them to their belts. Those who did not sorely regretted it. All of us were tired, hungry, and especially hot; only a few realized what was happening. Enemy planes were overhead, but at the moment were not attacking the troop.

The 1st Platoon was already in position along the crest of the ridge. The guns of the Light Machine Gun Platoon were quickly positioned on its flanks.

The company commander ordered me to send a squad of mounted riflemen from my platoon to the high ground about three-quarters of a mile to the northeast, to cover any hostile attempt to get around our right flank. I assigned my platoon sergeant to supervise the effort. He was to let me know when he first sighted the enemy. I took a man from the squad as messenger. My orderly stayed with the horses.

The remaining squad of my platoon, with two heavy machine guns attached, was to occupy a ridge running back from the right flank of the 1st Platoon's position. This ridge allowed a good field of fire for several hundred yards to its front.

After emplacing the machine guns and assigning positions for the riflemen, I returned to the main ridge to have a better look at the ground.

The main ridge, running north and south, parallel to the shore of Lingayen Gulf, overlooked the gulf and the town of Damortis. The ridge was several hundred yards long, forming a cut for the highway on the south and petering out into a gully on the north. A short distance form the north end of this ridge, a narrower ridge of about the same elevation ran east, perpendicular to it. It was on this ridge that I had positioned the remaining rifle squad of the 2nd Platoon and the two heavy machine guns.

Looking west from the main ridge, the shoreline of the Gulf was about one and one half miles away. From the shore, the land ran level for about three-quarters of a mile. From the plain to the 1st Platoon's position, there was a gradual rise of billowing hills covered mostly with *cogan* grass. Lingayen Gulf was choked with Japanese warships and transports. There was a heavy haze in the air; the sun was already low enough in the west to make it difficult to see in that direction. We watched the Japanese landing barges bringing men and supplies ashore, but we had no weapons to reach them.

On the Rosario-Damortis highway to the south of Troop A's position, there was reportedly a company of 17 American light tanks. To the rear of the tanks, the remaining scout cars of regimental headquarters were strung out, using their .50-caliber machine guns for antiaircraft fire. One car served as the regimental command post.

The Japanese dive-bombers were busy at this time, trying to hit something along the road. I guessed it was our tanks and/or scout cars. Somewhere on our left was Troop B, but I was never able to locate it. I saw no evidence that the 2nd Squadron and the remainder of Machine Gun Troop were committed that afternoon. Soon after I reached the 1st Platoon's position, there was a high-pitched cracking sound overhead. The sound was repeated in staccato rapidity. At first, I could not figure it out. One of the 1st Platoon's light machine guns was moving back toward me. The men were crouching low. Then it dawned on me that the cracking sound was the same as that heard in the rifle pits during rifle practice. Jap machine guns were firing high. The crack was the sound of their bullets passing overhead. For the first time, we were under direct fire from Japanese troops.

Getting back to my position, I found that our platoon was also beginning to receive small arms fire. The fire appeared to be coming from a ridge some 300 yards to our front. With binoculars, I could pick out helmets and occasionally the head and shoulders of a Jap along the crest.

Our heavy machine guns soon got the range. The strike of tracers told us their fire was on target, however, the intensity of the Jap fire continued to increase. The air was soon filled with the cracking sound of bullets.

The firing had started at about 1400 hours. It was nearly 1500 when our position came under artillery fire. We assumed it to be from 75mm guns in the valley to the west. From the plain below, a ragged line of small enemy tanks, supported by infantry, had started to move toward the 1st Platoon's position. For the moment, they were out of range.

The machine guns on my position had kept up an incessant fire for the past hour. Steam was hissing from their water jackets. Despite the fact that our fire appeared to be taking a heavy toll of the Japs infiltrating over the ridge to our front, they continued coming. Those who got across dropped out of sight into a depression, which gave them cover.

The Jap tanks approached the 1st Platoon; they stopped when their supporting infantry came within effective range of fire from the 1st Platoon. Their main guns started to fire in our direction. As the enemy fire increased, keeping the rifle squad firing became a problem. The men preferred lying behind the crest of the ridge that was giving them protection. I had to physically force the corporal to get his men forward into firing positions.

Watching the fire of the heavy machine guns was engrossing. The Japs now were presenting only fleeting targets as they dashed over the ridge to our front. The gunner, assistant gunner, and ammunition bearer of each gun were searching for targets. When a Jap was spotted, the gunner traversed as quickly as possible onto the new target to fire a burst before it disappeared. There was only a moment to act.

About 1530 hours, I first heard, and then could see, bursts of artillery fire to our right. It was in the area to which the mounted squad had been sent, but there had been no word from them. I looked around for my messenger, whose job it was to be with me all the time; he could not be found, anywhere. A rifleman had to be taken off the line to contact the mounted squad.

Two riflemen had received slight nicks from either shrapnel or flying debris. One of the machine gunners went into shock. He was firing on the Zeros overhead, which was against orders, and kept mumbling that the smoke from our tracers was gas being dropped by the planes. It was necessary to pull him away from the gun and send him down to the horses. The increasing pressure from the Japs was having an impact.

I was becoming apprehensive about the lack of any contact with the squad protecting our right flank. At 1600 hours, I first noticed Japanese infantry to our right and rear. They could be seen for just a few moments at a time as they passed in squad columns over high ground.

I made my way to the troop command post to advise the troop commander. Not long thereafter, Major Ketchum, the squadron commander, strode up from the rear. I felt very exposed in a kneeling position. The air was filled with the crack of rifle and machine-gun fire, the swish of artillery shells overhead, with an occasional nearby burst, and the methodical, periodic, single crack of a rifle bullet that was undoubtedly that of a sniper.

Major Ketchum stood beside me. I warned him that he was unduly exposing himself. He paid no attention, remaining standing, while I explained the situation. (The thought went through my mind that he had forgotten that the accuracy of weapons had improved considerably since the Civil War.)

Calmly, almost as if read from the field manual, he said, "In a delaying action when the enemy has developed superiority of fire, and is outflanking your position, it is time to fall back." I could not have agreed with him more.

The horses were in the valley to our rear. South of this valley was more high ground overlooking our present position. I was ordered to occupy this hill to cover the withdrawal of the rest of the troop.

One heavy machine gun was immediately withdrawn from action. I carefully explained to the crew the route to, and the exact location on the hill to our rear, where they were to employ the gun in its new position. After the gun crew had been dispatched, I instructed the corporal of the rifle squad to stay where he was for ten minutes after the second machine gun pulled out, then to withdraw his squad and join the machine guns. The two machine guns would cover the withdrawal of his rifle squad. The new position was less than a quarter of a mile away and in plain view.

When the first gun had ample time to get into position, yet still could not be seen, I started back with the second gun. On the way we picked up ammunition and water, and had the horse-holders move the animals to the rear of our new position.

The first gun and its crew could not be located. I later learned that on seeing the bulk of Troop A pulling out, disregarding his orders, the squad leader had taken it upon himself to move to the rear with them.

The rifle squad also never got to the second position. Later, the corporal told me he had believed it was necessary to get the horses out at the time, or they might have been lost. I had explicitly told him to move his horses behind our second position. Instead, he had followed the bulk of Troop A to the rear.

The one machine gun left in action had too much area to cover. After firing on one target, it was sometimes necessary to change direction as much as 90 degrees to fire on some other enemy movement. To do this, the gunner used a loose traverse, firing by observing the strike of the tracers.*

Toward the end of the withdrawal, the Japs had worked up onto positions overlooking our movements and were putting a good amount of small-arms fire on us. It was mostly ineffective, however, either because they could not shoot, or the fire from our machine gun was suppressing them, forcing them to keep their heads down.

On a signal from the troop commander, I pulled the last machine gun out of action. We dropped back over the hill and down into a wash, where my orderly had my horse, but the pack horses for the gun and the mounts of the crew were gone. The gun had to be carried on foot to a scout car on the road.

Troop A marched back to the Apangat River, a distance of about three miles. A Japanese plane observed us as we marched back, but did not attempt to strafe or dive-bomb. Reportedly, the company of light tanks was still between us and the enemy.

After watering the horses in the Apangat River, the troop marched back a half-mile or so toward the enemy, where we took cover along the road. The horses had

---

*The most accurate way to traverse a machine gun of this type was to employ the "traversing and elevating" (T&E) mechanism, a device which raised, lowered, or pivoted the gun by precise increments, and held it on target as it was being fired. By disengaging the T&E mechanism, the machine gun could be much more rapidly aimed, but the accuracy of its fire was then diminished by the considerable vibration of the gun during firing, as well as the natural flinching of the gunner. [Ed.]

been fed the last of the oats during the afternoon. Much of Troop A was missing, and most of our ammunition had been expended.

Somehow, my platoon sergeant had found his way back to the troop. His face was caked with blood from a shell wound. He was the only one of that mounted detachment to return. He reported that the squad had met a considerable force of Japs. Although it had held the enemy up for some time, it was finally overpowered by fire from their mortars and mountain artillery. No one from that detachment was ever sent to notify the troop that contact with the enemy had been made. I never heard what happened to the man sent to contact the detachment, nor did I ever find out what happened to my messenger.

There had been bravery displayed during the afternoon's action, however. The gunner and assistant gunner of one of the light machine guns supporting the 1st Platoon were cousins. In the course of the afternoon the gunner was hit. He fell away from the gun. The assistant gunner, calmly, without giving his cousin a glance, immediately got into position behind the gun and continued to fire without an assistant.

Lieutenant Allen, who commanded the heavy machine gun platoon attached to the 1st Squadron, was missing. Lieutenant George, Headquarters and Service Troop, was reported killed by a bomb landing in his scout car.

The strain of hunger, fatigue, and apprehension showed on the faces of the men. The animals were restless and hungry.

About 1730 hours, Troop A was ordered into a new delaying position. Leaving the horses, we marched west a short distance, and took up a position to the right of Troop E, north of the highway. It was dark by the time we were in position; we listened intently, wondering if the Japs would push ahead in the darkness. It was not long before we counted what sounded to be the 17 light tanks that had supported the regiment throughout the afternoon, withdrawing along the highway. The clank of equipment and sound of guttural voices in the darkness ahead was reported by our listening posts.

At 1930 hours, Troop A was ordered out of position. We marched back to the horses. The troop formed on the road in a column of twos, dismounted, facing east. The order of march within the troop was 1st Platoon, 2nd Platoon, Light Machine Gun Platoon. Behind Troop A, Machine Gun Troop was also arrayed in a column of twos, but mounted. We were told that Troop E was following Machine Gun Troop as rear guard for the withdrawal.

An uneasy quietness pervaded the column of horsemen waiting in the darkness. Only the tinkle of a curb chain, or the subdued tones of a Scout speaking in his dialect, broke the silence. Mellandres, my orderly, was holding my horse at the head of the 2nd Platoon. I had walked down the column, patting a horse, saying a word now and then, assuring myself that my platoon and the Light Machine Gun Platoon were ready to move out when the order came. The apprehension stamped on the faces of some of the younger troopers conveyed the general feeling in the column. All knew that before Troop A had pulled out of its last position, listening posts had reported the sounds of equipment and Jap voices.

As I came to the end of the Light Machine Gun Platoon, the sergeant said in a hushed voice, "Sir, should we not mount and move out soon?"

I looked at my watch. We had been waiting on the road more than half and hour.

"We should receive orders soon," I answered.

Like a thunderbolt, the crash of a cannon broke the stillness, and signaled the nearness of the enemy. The crack of bullets filled the air, while projectiles from the cannon passed overhead with a swishing sound.

Machine Gun Troop, already mounted, stampeded into Troop A's column, creating havoc. The pounding of steel-shod hooves racing over the hard surface of the highway set up an ear-shattering din. In a mixture of rage and anguish, men of Troop A screamed at each other and their horses. Neighing, rearing horses made it nearly impossible to mount. When I reached my orderly, he had mounted and was frantically trying to hold his horse and mine from running away. I grabbed the reins of my horse and motioned him to go. In the *melée*, my horse had become unmanageable. As I was mounting, he bolted, dragging me for some distance with my foot in the stirrup and knocking me unconscious.

Chapter 14

When I regained consciousness, it took a few moments to come back to reality. The firing had stopped. There was an eerie silence. The movement of forms, in the direction I was sure to be that of the enemy, was barely visible in the starlight.

Jumping a fence, I dove into a nearby bamboo thicket. Out of breath and still stunned, I dropped to the ground, listening for any sound of being followed. There was no firing. From the sound of tanks, and occasional guttural shouts in an unfamiliar tongue, it was apparent that there were already Japs on the road where Troop A had been surprised.

Badly shaken from what had just happened, I was overcome with a feeling of loneliness. All I could think of was to get back with the regiment.

The back of my head and shoulders were bruised and painful. The right leg of my breeches was torn away and my leg and hip were cut and bleeding. The "mud cleats" which I had put on the soles of my boots during the rainy season probably had been the cause of my foot catching in the stirrup. My helmet was gone. It had never been anything but a nuisance and I was glad to be rid of it. My flashlight was broken.

As my head began to clear, I remembered that the Apangat River, where Troop A had watered horses earlier in the afternoon, should be only a short distance to the east. The Japs would be pushing hard to occupy any crossing. Possibly, at the moment, the 26th Cavalry was taking up positions on the far bank; the possibility got me up and going. I removed my spurs and stuffed them into a pocket.

The terrain was hilly, covered with underbrush and occasional clumps of trees and bamboo thickets. The night was pitch black. There was a good chance of Japanese patrols being in the area. I remembered that just before Troop A had pulled out of its last position, observation posts on the right flank had reported sounds of equipment and Jap voices.

To move quietly meant feeling for each step. I would walk a short distance, and then stop to listen. Progress was painfully slow. During one of these pauses, the sound of machine-gun fire came from the road, a momentary silence, then another burst, and all was quiet again. Were the Japs doing away with the prisoners they had taken?

Suddenly, a red glare filled the sky to the east, slowly becoming brighter. From the crest of a hill, the bridge across the Apangat River came into view. The center of the bridge was ablaze. Later, I heard that holes were shot in the gas tank of the regimental veterinary truck, which was then set on fire on the bridge, as the last elements of the regiment cleared it.

From the glare of the fire, I could see several low-built tanks parked along the road on the side of the bridge toward me. A group of Japs was on the bridge examining it. All of a sudden, they turned and double-timed toward the tanks.

Two of them climbed into the leading tank. It started to move forward, slowly. As it nosed into the flames, the sound of cracking timbers filled the air. The bridge started to crumble and the tank slowly eased over on its side, crashing into the water. The Jap advance was at least slowed. The river at this point was not more than a hundred feet wide, but because of its depth, it was a formidable barrier to a column of tanks.

The sound of sporadic rifle fire was coming from the near river bank, but there was no shooting from the other side. This had me both puzzled and dismayed.

Starting north, I paralleled the river with the hope of crossing it further upstream. After a short distance, I turned toward the Apangat, believing that this time there would be nothing to stop my crossing.

About to let myself down a steep embankment bordering the road by the river, the clomp of marching feet mixed with the sound of guttural jabbering came to me all too clearly. I could have reached out and touched any member of a Jap patrol that passed. As the last man went by, the front of the patrol came to a halt.

A few words were spoken, and then all was quiet. I hardly dared breathe. The Japs were so close that the shuffling of their feet sounded like my own. One Jap, probably leaning against the embankment, loosened a small landslide; it sounded like an avalanche. Carefully feeling each spot before putting my weight on it I crawled 100 feet or more back from the road. When I felt it safe to stand up and walk, my continued effort to move quietly made progress extremely slow.

At one time, there was a sound of movement in the bushes. Undoubtedly, it had to be a Jap from the nearby patrol following me. With pistol ready I knelt, waiting in the darkness. Every nerve and sense in my body was alert and ready to react to this danger which was slowly approaching. Into the far side of a clearing, only a few feet away, a shadow moved low and on all fours. I leveled my pistol at it, ready to fire if it rose up. At that moment it gave a grunt. It was a pig searching for its supper.

I slumped back. Events of the past few days, especially the past few hours, had put me into a high state of tension. The feeling of relief, followed by that of fatigue, nearly overpowered me. During the rest of the night I continued north, paralleling the Apangat. Toward morning, I crawled beneath a bush to rest, wondering how much longer I could last without a drink of water.

It was after daylight when I awoke. I lay quietly for a few moments, trying to think where I was. Everything was still. Cautiously, I looked around. There was nothing moving and no noise. What had happened to the war?

Making my way to the top of a nearby hill, once again I had a view of the great Lingayen Gulf. It stretched to the west as far as the eye could see. And it contained, as on the day before, a concentration of Japanese transports and warships. To the southeast, I could make out the winding ribbon of highway leading to Rosario. There was little traffic on it.

As I lay there, three American B-17 bombers flew out of the south toward the ships. They were flying low at an elevation of about 1,500 feet. As they passed over the Japs, I could hear their bombs exploding, but the ships appeared to escape unscathed. The sky was full of antiaircraft bursts, little black dots seemingly occurring from nowhere.

I watched the planes continue in a northerly direction until out of sight, wondering where they had come from and where they were going.

There was a lump in my throat. All was still not lost.

Leaving the hilltop, I carefully proceeded down to a stream. At last it was possible to have a drink and a wash. I lay with my head near the water, alternately drinking and ducking, reveling in its refreshing coolness.

With my thirst satiated, I sat up and took stock of my plight. The quietness and lack of activity had me puzzled. It appeared that the 26th Cavalry had fallen back much farther than I had expected. No easy way presented itself to get back with the regiment.

My field glasses and gas mask were still with me. The latter had been about as useful as the helmet. My pistol was in good shape, which was a consolation. In my shirt pocket I had a toothbrush, bottle of iodine, pencil, and message book. In my breeches was a scout knife, compass, a wallet with five or ten *pesos,* my watch, a pack of cigarettes, and a lighter. I threw the gas mask under a bush, relieved to be rid of the burden. I was ravenously hungry.

Following the stream, I came in sight of a clearing and a *nipa* shack that looked deserted. About to search it for something to eat, two men in Scout uniforms walked out. As soon as I was sure they were not Japs, I whistled.

As the Scouts approached, one called out, "Lieutenant Whitehead." We shook hands, glad to see each other. One was a recruit, but the older one had been in my platoon in Troop E, and spoke English quite well.

"It's good to see you are alive, sir," he said. "I don't think there are many left of Troop E. They came right through us, shooting at anything that moved." He seemed to explode. "It was terrible." For a moment he was unable to speak. His eyes reddened as he shook his head in disbelief.

"Slow down," I said, "tell me just what happened. You were the rear guard?"

"Yes, Sir. Troop E was the rear guard of the regiment. Jap tanks came right up to our roadblock and stopped. Someone, believing them to be American, rode up and knocked on the lead tank, signaling the crew to open the turret hatch. Recognizing the enemy, the Japs immediately stared firing. All hell broke loose. They drove right through our roadblock. Horses and men were going in every direction. Many were hit by the Jap fire. It was terrible. I don't think there are many left."

Through all this, the recruit added only a few remarks in *Tagalog,* showing by his motions his disbelief that it all could have happened.

They had walked all night, and were as hungry as I. We started off, in search of something to eat.

The countryside was completely deserted. It seemed an endless search through vacated *nipa* shacks before we found enough food to make a meal. Eventually, we found sufficient rice and eggs, cooking them in dirty pots left in a deserted shack. Fried eggs on steaming rice with a little salt proved to be wonderfully filling. What was left of the rice was wrapped in banana leaves and carried along.

By mid-afternoon, we were hiking east along a trail in the foothills bordering the great plain. To the south and west, as far as the eye could see, the plain was covered with dried-up rice paddies. Here and there, on a knoll, the monotony of the scene was broken by a *nipa* shack surrounded by banana trees.

Through this vast plain wound the highway to Rosario. Japanese tanks and trucks could now be seen moving along it. Armored cars coming from the Gulf of Lingayen were unloading cyclist troops who joined the columns moving east.

It was hard to believe that on this same road the morning before, the 26th Cavalry had marched in the opposite direction, spoiling for a fight.

No firing had been heard during the day. I wondered what had happened to my regiment.

The steep foothills forced us to keep down on the edge of the plain. Even there, the trail was poor, and progress slow. Often we had to crouch down to avoid being seen by the Japs on the highway. Soon, the trail and highway were so close that it was impossible to move any further during daylight, without the chance of being detected. We got back into a concealed area and rested the remainder of the afternoon; one standing watch while the other two slept. As long as we kept going, I felt fine, but the short rest while waiting for darkness made me realize how exhausted I was. We dared not stop, however, for fear of losing any remaining chance to get back with regiment.

The few Filipinos to whom we talked seemed stunned. They could not understand why the Americans had allowed the Japanese to enter the Philippines. They all asked the same questions, "Are American soldiers coming from the United States to help us?" I assured them that help would be arriving.

At about 0200 hours on 24 December, we came to a road along which the Japs had parked armored cars about a quarter of a mile apart, with patrols between them. From time to time, the Japs would fire into the darkness. At the time, this seemed very odd, but later we learned there had been fighting in the area the day before.

As it was obvious that it would be impossible for us to get past them, we decided to hike away from the road into the forest and rest until morning. Before finding a suitable place to camp, we needed to climb a good distance. The chill at the higher elevation made it impossible to sleep without a blanket. As a result, we spent the remainder of the night huddled around a fire.

Shortly after daybreak, a local Filipino guided more Scouts from the 26th into our camp. I wondered how he knew of our whereabouts. I am not sure whether this last group had been cut off from the Regiment near Damortis or in another action. They had with them a good supply of rice and it was not long before it was cooking. Breakfast consisted only of rice; there was not even salt to go with it. When I eaten all I could stomach, I realized there was some adjusting to be done, as far as my taste was concerned, if rice without salt was going to be my diet for a while.

After breakfast, we received word that the Japs were still on the road to the east. Our route now took us north into the mountains, hoping to get around the enemy. Our column was strung out to reduce losses if ambushed. We were armed only with pistols.

During the morning, more Scouts from the 26th Cavalry appeared. Some of them had changed into civilian clothes. I told them to get back into their uniforms and join the column.

By noon it appeared that we had gone far enough to get around the Japs. The column halted for a rest and to find something to eat. The Scouts who had joined us during the morning had disappeared. Days later, I was told by two Americans from Baguio that one of these men, whom they passed on the trail, had given them the story that a Lieutenant Whitehead had told him to put on civilian clothes and hide.

One of the Scouts sent out in search of food returned to report there were Philippine Army soldiers in a nearby hut, with enough rice to feed us all. A Philippine Army lieutenant and four of his men were found in the hut. They had been on in a beach defense position on the coast of Lingayen Gulf when the Japs landed. All but one were wounded, one quite seriously. I asked the lieutenant what had happened.

"When the Japs started to place fire on our position, many of our units pulled back," he said. "Like the others, I was very much afraid, until one of their bullets did this." Taking off his cap, he pointed to a perfect part on the top of his head, creased by a Jap bullet. "Then I got very angry at myself for being afraid and at the others for running away. I tried very hard to stop them, but they were like frightened animals. Seeing that I could not stop them, I got behind a deserted machine gun and fired at the Japs coming at us until there was no more ammunition. As I left, I found this man sitting under a tree, too dazed to move." He pointed to one of his men with a makeshift sling on his right arm. The shirt had been torn away, exposing three neat bullet holes, two in his arm, and one in his shoulder. I could see the man was in pain, but the wounds looked clean.

"These other three men joined me later. They, too, stayed on their positions until their ammunition was gone. They had been unable to find their unit." Two of these men had superficial wounds from shrapnel on their arms and legs.

Like us, the lieutenant and his men were trying to go south, to rejoin their units.

During our meal, a civilian from the mountains to the east came into camp. He reported a good trail free of Japs leading that way. Hopefully, this would get us around the enemy and we could start moving south. There were now 21 in the party.

By mid-afternoon, we came to a broad valley running north and south. Crossing this, we picked up scraps of paper with Japanese writing. Filipinos in the area told us that a large force of the enemy had passed that way, moving south toward Rosario. The Japs were using *carabao* sleds and Filipino carriers to transport their equipment. (Perhaps this was the reason why the 26th Cavalry had not made a stand west of Rosario.)

Through the afternoon, we took food from deserted huts. The trail had started to climb into the mountains. By nightfall, we had found a hidden glen by a stream. This was the first place that gave us a feeling of security. We talked aloud and whistled and forgot the war for awhile. Before supper I washed the wounds of the wounded with hot water, disinfected them with iodine, and wrapped them with the pads from first aid packets and torn-up undershirts. This was the first care any of them had received. The man with bullets in his arm and shoulder was feeling all right, but the flesh around the bullet holes was swollen and beginning to take on a darkish, ugly color. I hoped we could find a doctor before long.

We had rice and bananas for supper. Along the way the men had picked up some earthen cooking pots. Banana leaves were used as plates, our hands for eating.

That afternoon we had met a Filipino who said he had been in Rosario during the morning. He had seen a good many Japs, but had heard no firing either that morning or the night before. I wondered how the enemy was able to push south so fast, and what we had to stop him. I knew that there were not many American troops on Luzon, but there were a good many Philippine divisions. I also knew that the Philippine Army was not considered well-trained or equipped, and that there had been a question of how well it would hold up against determined Japanese assaults. It was possible that the Japs were a lot further south than I had believed. With this in mind, and having no map to tell me distances, directions, and the steepness of the mountains that we would have to cross to get around the Japs, I decided that night to head for Baguio. Surely the garrison there would be holding out. Also, the man with bullets in his arm had to be given consideration.

That night was another cold one; we spent it shivering around small fires.

At daylight, we cooked and consumed the last of the rice.

I had a compass bearing on the general direction of Baguio, but there were neither trails nor guides to help us on our way. Up and down steep ridges and through streams we plodded in the mid-day heat and into the afternoon. The exertions of the past few days, along with going without proper food and rest, were starting to tell on us. It was a tired group of men that carefully made its way into an Igorot village in the late afternoon.

These people live in tiny villages scattered here and there throughout the mountains. They live in small valleys with only enough level ground on which to build a few *nipa* shacks. The surrounding hills are terraced, forming small paddies in which to grow their rice. This was the first village we had seen all day; it was deserted. It soon became apparent, however, that people were living there and had recently left in a hurry.

The Philippine Army lieutenant spoke the Igorot dialect.

"I will find out," he said. "It is best you stay under cover until we know."

In less than an hour he returned with the headman of the village, the *barrio teniente,* an old wizened fellow; he was barefoot and clad only in a G-string and shirt.

He allowed that the villagers had watched us coming for the past several hours, and then had fled to the hills, fearing that we were Japs. After considerable talking and dickering we made a deal with the old man to sell us a pig. The villagers would kill and cook the pig and furnish rice to go with it.

Singly, and in small groups, the people of the village returned. They were of lighter complexion than the inhabitants of the valley, with high cheekbones and heavy jowls.

Soon the pig was squealing and then turning on a spit over a bed of hot coals, sizzling and spitting from the droplets of fat. The whole, or unhusked rice (*palay*), was put into *lusongs* with four persons around each, pounding it out to the tune of a rhythmic song. The Scouts joined in, joking and laughing with the young girls, forgetting the hunger and fatigue of the past few days in anticipation of the feast in preparation.

A wooden mortar, into which the cooks placed the *palay* for husking, is called a *lusong* by the Filipinos. They pound the *palay* with a pole five or six feet long and two or three inches in diameter, rounded on both ends, with the center narrowed for a handgrip. From one to four persons can pound in a single *lusong.* The more people pounding, the more difficult the timing of the strokes. Pounding the *palay* gradually knocks off the husk without destroying the grain. After the *palay* is husked, it is poured into a shallow round tray, about two and a half feet in diameter. By dexterous movements, the cooks shift the mixture in the tray and throw the contents into the air; the husks are blown off by the wind.

By nightfall, dinner was on the floor on great mats. The steaming meat of the roasted pig was piled on a slab of wood in the center; large, wooden platters of steaming, red rice were at the ends. Each place setting had a clean piece of banana leaf spread out for use as a plate. Beside it was a small wooden bowl filled with a mixture of boiled pig intestines and cooked blood. It was a wonderful sight to a hungry man.

Our party was divided into two shifts, so there would be enough bowls to go around. Sitting cross-legged on the floor, we ate with our hands. We squeezed small handfuls of rice into balls, dipped them into the bowl of savory sauce, then popped them into our mouths. After each rice ball, we immediately consumed a piece of intestine or a bit of the steaming pork. What a wonderful Christmas dinner that was. When I first saw the roasted pig and the great mounds of rice piled near it, I did not believe it possible for our party to eat it all, but by the time the second shift had finished, there was not enough left to satisfy the hungry dogs that came in afterwards to clean up.

Except for guards, we were all asleep before dark. Laid out like sardines in a can, we covered the floor of a large hut, using grass mats over and under us. We had a much needed, warm, and long sleep.

The following morning, the Igorots had rice cooked for us when we got up. After breakfast we each rolled a packet of rice in leaves and stuck it in our pockets. From the village, a trail led into Baguio over Santo Tomás Mountain, which could be hiked in a day. The headman offered to provide a guide; he could not understand why we could not keep up with him.

At one point during the morning, the trail led over a peak that overlooked Lingayen Gulf. We were again able again to see Japanese ships anchored in the bay around Damortis. We counted a total of 54 of them.

High in the mountains, we passed though a coffee plantation. I didn't even know such things existed in the Philippines.

After the middle of the morning, we started to drop down into a deep gorge. The guide pointed across it and up to a misty height that he said was Santo Tomás Mountain. Looking down into the gorge and up again to the top of the mountain, I doubted if I would ever get there.

By noon we were eating by a clear mountain stream in the bottom of the gorge. The afternoon was spent climbing the tortuous trail up Santo Tomás. As we neared the top, the air became brisk and the mountainside was covered with pine trees. Again, it was a reminiscent of the mountainous regions in the western United States. It was all beautifully scenic, but I was too tired to really appreciate it.

Several times during that climb, I remember thinking that if I ever got to Baguio, I would do nothing but eat American food and sleep for days. I had eaten all the rice I ever wanted.

By 1600 hours, we had crossed the mountaintop and reached the rest station on the Baguio side. There we were able to get cigarettes and coffee, a treat after the last few days. While drinking the coffee, the station keeper told us he had heard that the Baguio garrison had left two days before. As far as he knew there were no Japs in Baguio, but they were expected at any time.

If this were true, our hike to Baguio could prove to be a waste of time. If it proved to be true, should we try to catch up with the Baguio garrison or should we return to the valley and try to reach Bataan? More and more, I was coming to believe that the old "ORANGE" contingency plan, which called for a last stand on the Bataan Peninsula, was being put into effect. Maybe our trail cutting and mapping last May would prove worthwhile. I wondered if I would get there to find out.

I phoned Camp John Hay. The operator, whom I hoped was not a Jap, verified what the stationkeeper had said. He connected me with a colonel of the Philippine Army Medical Corps who volunteered to send a truck to the end of the Santo Tomás Road to pick us up.

It was about an hour's hike down to the place we were to meet the truck. On the way into Baguio, I stopped the truck at a building that turned out to be the offices of a local mine. As I approached the entrance, an American stepped out and asked me not to stop there but to be on my way. I insisted upon speaking with the man in charge, and barged into a large room with several scouts behind me. Sitting at the desks was a group of the most scared looking Americans I ever hope to see. The Japs were expected any moment. They had met to plan what to do, and had decided to surrender. Our arrival had not helped matters. The man in charge indicated that the Japs might kill them all should they walk in and find us there. I felt an overwhelming disgust for them. We walked out without saying a word.

Chapter 15

It was nearly dark when we entered the city of Baguio. It showed little effects of the war except for a general tenseness. Baguio had been declared an open city. According to reports, the city council had contacted the Japs, who were expected to arrive at any moment. The only bombing that had occurred was in the vicinity of Camp John Hay. There we saw a few bomb craters on the road and lawn below the mess hall of the Officers' Club, but no evidence that any buildings had been hit. I was told the bombs had been dropped early in the war, perhaps by the bombers reportedly driven away from Clark Field on the morning of 8 December.

We stopped the truck in front of the commissary. It still contained a significant supply of canned goods, cigarettes, and beer. As these supplies were being loaded onto our truck, a car drove up with two American civilians, one of whom was a doctor, and the Filipino colonel I had talked with on the phone. They had gotten themselves pretty well worked up thinking about what the Japs would do on their arrival. They offered aid and advice, but could give me no idea where the Baguio garrison had gone. They ended by taking three of the wounded men to the hospital. Later they returned with two of them, having hospitalized the man with bullets in his arm and shoulder. How, in his shape, he ever made that grueling trip to Baguio will always be a wonder to me. I hoped his exertions were rewarded with successful recovery from his wounds. The doctors also brought a hospital blanket for each of us, and a pair of trousers and a road map for me.

It appeared that to try to catch the Baguio garrison would turn out to be nothing more than a wild goose chase. Looking at the map, I decided the best option left was to go by truck to Itogon, a mining town a few miles east of Baguio, and from there, hike through the mountains to the Agno River Valley and down into the central Luzon plain. This should bring us out of the mountains at a point about 30 miles southeast of Damortis, where we hoped there still might be a chance of rejoining the Americans.

At about 2100 hours, as the party was ready to leave for Itogon, the Filipino colonel drove up again, this time followed by a truck with 20 ragged-looking Filipinos. These men had been part of a group of 500 trainees en route to Camp Murphy, near Manila, for induction and training. At the foot of the Kennon Road, going down from Baguio two days before, they had been intercepted by the Japs. Some had been killed, and the rest sent back to their homes. Most of the 20 men were barefooted, had no hats, and were dressed in rags. There were, however, rifles and ammunition to spare in the bottom of their truck. They wanted to come along with us. With some apprehension, I agreed.

An hour later we were in Itogon. The town showed signs of the hurried departure of the Baguio garrison. Along the road and off the sides were discarded civilian and military vehicles; here and there were small piles of equipment, too heavy for men traveling across the mountains to carry.

The mayor of Itogon greeted us and offered to give us supper. I warned him that it would mean feeding 40 men. He said it was little enough for him to do.

We traded the beer we brought down from the commissary for two sacks of clean rice. This, with the canned food taken from the commissary, was distributed among the men. Each man was also given a rifle and two bandoleers of ammunition.

Before leaving Itogon, we rendered inoperable our trucks and others left behind by the Baguio garrison. The mayor provided us with a wonderful supper, which we ate with a great deal of gusto. It was well past midnight by the time the feast was finished. We crossed a broad riverbed not far from town, and passed into the hills on the other side where the trail to the Agno River started. We camped there.

On 27 December 1941, the group was organized into a company of two small platoons. The newly-arrived Philippine Army soldiers were placed in squads, with the Scouts as squad and assistant squad leaders. The highest ranking of the Scouts became the acting first sergeant.

The rifles we had inherited were .30-caliber bolt-action M1917 Enfields of WWI vintage. It was the basic weapon of the Philippine Army.*

Up until the last year, the Scouts had been armed with the Springfield Model 1903 rifle, which was also a bolt-action weapon.† However, recently the Springfield had been replaced by the M-1 Garand. The Garand was the only rifle the younger Scouts knew. It was semi-automatic, quite different in construction and functioning from the bolt-action rifles.‡

First, the older Scouts who had used the Model 1903 rifle had to show the young Scouts how to load and unload the Enfields, the mechanics of firing, and a few safety measures. Then the newly-arrived Philippine Army soldiers had to

---

*At 45.5 inches long, the M1917 Enfield was much too bulky for the average Filipino soldier to handle comfortably; its nine-pound, three-ounce weight also contributed to its unwieldiness for soldiers of the Filipinos' smaller physique. With the bayonet fixed, its 61.5 inch overall length made it nearly as long as the average Filipino soldier was tall. It was, however, an accurate and fairly dependable rifle which fired the standard US .30-caliber bullet to an effective range of 600 yards. [Ed.]

†The Springfield "'03" fired the same round as the Enfield, but was of superior manufacture and reliability. At 43 inches long (57.5 inches with fixed bayonet) and nine pounds, it was not much easier for Filipino soldiers to handle than the M1917 Enfield.

‡The M-1 Garand was by far the most advanced infantry rifle in existence in 1941–42. Although it was 43 inches long (58.5 inches with the early-war bayonet) and weighed 9.5 pounds—and was therefore just as difficult for Filipinos to handle as the Springfield or Enfield. Its ability to fire eight rounds with eight squeezes of the trigger afforded its users an overwhelming advantage in firepower.

be given the same instructions. These men were supposed to have had five months training by the Philippine Army at some time or other, but apparently they had not absorbed much of it.

The Japs were due to arrive in Baguio, and possibly Itogan, at any time. I decided to set up an ambush to greet them. I had spotted some high ground that provided good positions from which to place fire on vehicles on the highway, and from which we could pull back into the hills if necessary. No one I had talked to could say when the Japs would arrive, but if this should be the night, I felt this was an excellent way to welcome them.

With their newly-acquired rifles, the Scouts took up positions as daylight was fading. At first there was a good deal of excitement and expectation, but as the night wore on uneventfully, the fatigue from the past few days' exertion set in. We rested as we could through the remainder of the night, with only a two-man listening post on the alert. At dawn we returned to camp, disappointed, but knowing we had tried. If the Japs had shown up, we would have given them a good surprise.

Filipino refugees who were evacuating the mining areas gathered in the valley where we camped. They carried the young children and whatever belongings they could manage. They were a pathetic-looking group. One could not help feeling sorry for them.

By mid-morning we were on the trail heading for the Agno River Valley. The column was long and straggly; the advance guard consisted of Scouts. The new men spoke no English and gave little evidence of ever having any military training.

Everyone carried a blanket tied into a roll and slung over a shoulder like a horseshoe, a rifle with two bandoleers of ammunition, and a small sack of rice. To my dismay, I found that all the canned food taken from the Camp John Hay commissary had been consumed. I believe the Filipinos had tried to see how much of it they could cram into themselves at one time. They were sorry for it later. Cooking and mess gear consisted of one five-gallon can with the top cut out, per platoon.

I had ordered rifles loaded and locked. This meant a round in the chamber with the rifle cocked and the safety on. I prayed no one would be shot by an accidental discharge, a problem common with incompletely trained soldiers handling live ammunition in weapons with which they were not thoroughly familiar.

I got very little sleep that night. There were two guard posts to man. I was determined to teach the new men how to stand guard before we got down into the valley, where there was sure to be Japs. Every hour I inspected the posts and consistently found the guards asleep. No matter how much I, through the interpreter, explained the importance of staying awake on guard, as soon as the interpreter and I walked away, their will to overcome their sleepiness broke down. From the standpoint of soldiering, they were a sad lot. It seemed a waste to send young men like these, with neither discipline nor training, into combat. I hated to think what would happen if we got into a scrape with the Japs.

The following morning was one of the rare times that I was not able to eat food put in front of me. Try as I would, the saltless rice would not go down. Those of us who had come up from the valley to Baguio were physically exhausted, but to stop for a day's rest might mean losing the slim chance we hoped we had of overtaking friendly troops. We were on the trail again soon after sunrise.

At the outset of the new day's march, I tried out a squad of the new men as advance guard. This task proved to be too complicated for them and I had to give the job back to the Scouts. The Scouts were showing evidence of becoming tired of taking care of these men. I did not blame them for that, but was at a loss to know the best thing to do.

At noon we came to the Agno River, which was swollen from recent rains. It was swift and chest deep in the middle, with no bridge or even a rope across it. Its banks were broad, level, and covered with small, round boulders.

More refugees from the mines were camped on our side of the river, waiting for the water level to go down. The scene reminded me of pictures of refugees the world over. These people looked tired, hungry, and bewildered. A few enterprising Igorots with horses were carrying on a brisk ferrying business, transporting some of the wealthier refugees across the river by riding them behind the saddle.

By crossing in small groups, helping each other to maintain good footing, it was not long before our entire party was on the other side of the river. We stopped to cook rice. I hit an all-time low. I was having cramps in my stomach from not being able to eat that morning; my legs felt like they were made of rubber.

Throughout the afternoon we worked our way down the mountain trail. Toward sundown, we made camp in a likely-looking spot across the river from the trail. We were about six miles from the town of Tayug; it could be seen burning. The little town was only about 30 miles southeast, as the crow flies, from Damortis. The thought of the exertions we had gone through to gain that 30 miles did little for our morale.

Filipinos coming up from the valley that afternoon told us that there had been a battle near Tayug a day or so earlier, but that the fighting was now somewhere to the south. Jap columns had been passing through the town all day. None, however, had stopped there for the night.

Shortly after we went into camp, the Philippine Army lieutenant disappeared. It was not long, however, until he returned, followed by a civilian carrying a live pig on his shoulders. The lieutenant had gotten together enough money from the soldiers to buy the pig. Everyone set to, and in no time it was dressed and turning on a spit over hot coals, its wonderful aroma filling the air.

While the pig was roasting, I took a swim in the river. It did a great deal toward physically reviving me. My appetite came back in a hurry.

When supper was ready, I took my place in the circle of soldiers around a mound of steaming rice piled on several banana leaves on the ground. The meal was much the same as we had had in the Igorot village and a very welcome change from the unsalted rice of the past two days.

When I got up from the feast, I had eaten enough to make up for the past several days. As each man finished, he went to the river to wash and drink his fill of water. I drank with the feeling that I would regret it later.

A full stomach did wonders for morale. The day had been a trying one. Those of us who had come up from the valley had been too tired to be civil, and the new men without shoes had had difficulty over the rocky trail. With all this, they maintained a good spirit throughout the day. The Filipino has a great propensity for keeping in a good humor.

After supper, two Scouts were sent to Tayug to gain whatever information was available. The camp was across the river from the trail, against the mountains, with only one approach. Just one guard post was adequate for this situation. Two men were on guard at a time, while the rest of the camp was asleep before dark.

I had slipped my boots off to rest easily and to let them dry from the day's stream crossings. About 2200 hours, we were awakened by two shots fired in the vicinity of the guards, and shortly afterwards, another. I was up on the first shot, struggling with my boots; it seemed an age before I could get them on in the darkness. When I arrived at the outpost, everything had quieted down. The two Scouts returning from Tayug had done the firing. They had used that method to locate the guard. I was not a bit happy with it, as the firing could have alerted any nearby Japs of our presence, but it did teach me to wear my boots when I slept.

The Scouts brought back the news that the 26th Cavalry Regiment had been in Tayug a few days before. There had been a battle, but the Japs were still advancing. They were now reported far to the south.

It is strange how things work out. Had we started for Baguio sooner, we probably would have joined the garrison there. Had we not gone to Baguio and continued east, we might now be back with the Regiment.

We also learned that the smoke we had seen in the afternoon was from Chinese stores set afire by the Japs.

Next morning we were on the trail again, and by noon had skirted the eastern edge of Tayug. We cooked dinner in the hills east of San Quintin, which is about five miles southeast of Tayug. There, we met remnants of a Philippine Army infantry company that reportedly was part of their 91st Division. It had fought several days before in the vicinity of Porzorrubio.

Two Americans, both from Baguio, walked into our camp while we were eating. The older, a Mr. Lupton, was in the lumber business; the other, Ted Malmsbury, was a young mining engineer. They had left Baguio on the night of 27 December, not long before the enemy arrived. They had hopes of getting to

Manila before the Japs—Mr. Lupton, to get his wife out, and Malmsbury, to join the Army.

About the middle of the afternoon, with the two Americans coming along, our party moved south a few miles to a more secure campsite. The soldiers from the 91st had been camped for the past few days where we had our noon meal. With the Japs not more than two or three miles away and the possibility of fifth columnists around, I did not want to stay there overnight.*

We finished the last of our rice on the morning of 31 December. I had a piece of ham from Malmsbury's pack that morning, which was a great treat. Also, I remember guiltily bumming a cigarette from him. After breakfast, Malmsbury and Lupton left, heading to the south. Several groups of two or three men each were sent out in search of food. They were begging, since none of us had any money.

By noon, none of the foraging parties had returned. In the afternoon, I checked on the men and found that most of those who had joined us at Baguio had disappeared; some of the Scouts were also gone. Later on, some of the groups that had been sent for food returned without anything, reporting that civilians they had seen would feed them, but would not give them rice to carry away. My first impulse was to take the food by force, but after thinking it over, I was reluctant to take the rice that the civilians had grown to feed themselves until the next harvest. Certainly, this was no time to turn the civilians against the US Army.

The mayor of San Quintin came into camp to say that he felt badly about not being able to furnish us rice. The harvest had been so bad this year that there was barely enough for the townspeople. He also begged us to move on, for the Japs had threatened to kill anyone who gave help to the soldiers in the hills.

It was becoming increasingly apparent that if our forces were to make a stand, it would have to be on the Bataan Peninsula as called for in the old defense plan. As it was growing dark, I assembled what was left of our party. There were no more than 14 of the Scouts left. We decided that we should break up into small groups to work our ways into Bataan.

*"Fifth columnists" were indigenous people who collaborated with the enemy on a clandestine basis.

Chapter 16

An American *mestizo* Scout named Michell and I headed south. Most agreed that the best chance of getting into Bataan was to stay in the foothills of the mountains bordering the eastern side of the central plain, to a point east of Manila. We hoped that from there we could find a way into Bataan.

Before dark, we ran into two of the Igorots who had made the trip south from Baguio with us. They were not returning to their *barrio* in the mountains, as were the rest of the 20 men from Baguio. The brother of one was among those killed at the foot of the Kennon Road; they were bent on revenge. The life of at least one Jap had to be taken in compensation.

Our first need, as usual, was something to eat. At the first shack, we found Lieutenant Archy Hendricks from Troop E of the 26th Cavalry. He had been cut off from the Regiment, probably in the recent fighting around Tayug. Like us, he was heading south in hopes of getting through the Japs to our own forces. He said that after being cut off, he had spent the next day trying to get through the Jap lines. One night he had chosen to sleep in a road culvert. The next morning he was awakened by firing overhead. It soon became evident that he was between two firing lines. Not knowing which direction was friendly, he started crawling toward the side the thought most likely to be American. Soon, he found himself surrounded by Japs. He had to crawl back to the culvert where he hid through the remainder of the day, with the Japs moving overhead.

This incident did not appear to annoy him as much as one that occurred the night before we met. As he was crossing a partially destroyed bridge, he had stumbled and fallen into the river below, breaking his only pipe and soaking his last remaining tobacco. He was an inveterate pipe smoker. From this time on until we parted, through every *barrio* we passed, he made an intensive search for a pipe and some decent tobacco.

The people in the *nipa* shack where we met Archy gave us a chicken and some eggs. They were afraid for us to stay long, so we continued until we came to an empty hut. There, we roasted the chicken and slept for the night.

I had a dream that night which took me bodily across the Luzon plain and let me down safely in the Zambales Mountains. It was so real that I was sure I was there, even minutes after I awoke.

We hiked most of the next day, stopping only at mid-morning and mid-afternoon for something to eat, sleeping that night in a rice field on a pile of straw.

On the following day, we ran across an American coast artillery officer from the Philippine Army 91st Division. His outfit had been scattered in the battle of Pozorrubio. He was a large man, probably of Italian extraction, hailing from Worcester, Massachusetts. I remember he still had his helmet and gas mask, which he insisted upon keeping.

There were 15 or 20 Filipino soldiers and two Filipino officers with him. They, too, were working their way south, feeding themselves by taking the drying unharvested *palay* from the rice fields and carrying it out of the neighborhood, where they dried and pounded it. They were reportedly from Leyte and expected no hospitality or help from the civilians on Luzon. The American lieutenant decided to join us; once more we were on our way, now with six in our party.

Toward mid-afternoon, the trail we were following started to lead into the open, over bare hills in sight of, and not a great distance from, the highway. With my binoculars, it was easy to discern the figures and faces of the Japs on the road. We sat down in the shade of a *nipa* shack until dark, watching the columns of tanks and motorized infantry moving south. The highway was now running closer to the mountains, which meant we had do our traveling at night.

We walked until early morning by the light of a nearly full moon, stopping before dawn at an out-of-the way shack for something to eat and to rest. At first, the family was startled, fearing that we were Japs. After they saw us, however, they could not do enough. They prepared rice and other viands for us. After eating, we were taken to a well-hidden hut to sleep.

The Japs were camped not more than a mile away. We were near the town of San José, Nueva Ecija, which reportedly had become a Japanese Army headquarters. Heavy traffic was reported on Highway #5, which ran north through San José to Balete Pass and Aparri. Sooner or later we would have to cross this highway.

It was afternoon before we awoke. Michell decided to leave us. His home was in a *barrio* near Fort Stotsenburg. He planned to cross the central plain into the Zambales Mountains, through which he could reach his home, and then to later go on into Bataan. I would have liked to have gone with him, but the chances of an American getting across the central plain seemed practically nil. He left his rifle with Archy. The Igorots decided to go with Michell.

That left three of us—tall, white, conspicuous Americans, unable to understand the local language.

Later that afternoon, we again ran into Malmsbury and Lupton. Ted Malmsbury was in his late twenties, tall, lean, and blond. He was quiet and reserved, almost overly modest. Lupton was in his late fifties or early sixties, of medium height and build, of ruddy complexion, and tough from a life spent largely outdoors.

Based on the news that Manila had fallen to the Japs on 1 January, they were considering turning back toward Baguio. Whether this news was rumor or fact, we had no way of knowing. So far we had not been able to locate a radio. I believed there still might be a chance to get into Bataan. I was now sure our forces would assemble there for a last stand. At any rate, not knowing anything better to do, Malmsbury and Lupton decided to join us.

Late in the afternoon we sighted a stray goat. Hungry, as usual, we caught it. Before long its parts were broiling on sticks suspended over a fire. The goat proved to be thin and tough, but we chewed enough nourishment out of the gristly meat to keep us going.

That night, by a late moon we moved north around San Jose and across the Balete Pass road. Daylight found us in the hills east of the road. Civilians we passed said the Japs had not yet gotten very far from the main highways, but were thick in the valley below. Rizal, a few miles to the southeast of us, was also reportedly full of the enemy. There they were training troops before sending them south to fight. One somewhat shocked Filipino told us the Japs were forcing young girls into their tanks as they passed through the towns.

Rumors were rampant. Stories of Japanese activities, their whereabouts, and how far south the Americans had retreated varied depending on who was relating the story. It was a constant search for a true picture of what was happening. We were never very sure what to expect next. This was the so-called "bamboo telegraph," which was as many times hearsay or idle rumor as it was factual.

At one point, we talked with a civilian who swore he had seen American troops entering Luzon from the Baler Bay area. I wondered if this could have been Troop G rejoining the regiment. Another time, Dutch planes were reported bombing Jap positions.

Our route was generally south, staying in or close to, the foothills of the Sierra Madre Range. Our traveling was done mostly at night, except when we were quite far from the Japanese. We rested in out-of-the-way *barrios* during the day, depending upon the *barrio* folk for food and security.

Regardless of the hour or place, most of the time these people would cook food for us and find us a place to sleep. Had it not been for this constantly hospitable reception, there would have been little chance of survival. The Filipinos' finest trait is hospitality. Sometimes when passing along, an individual would run out from his house and give us a chicken or some eggs, or bananas, or the like. They always asked me when the "aid" was coming, and when and where the Americans would land.

On the other hand, there were those of a certain element who had become informers for the Japanese. We heard stories of both Americans and Filipinos who were betrayed by these traitors. It became a constant concern to know whom to trust. As a result, we kept as much distance between ourselves and the Japs as possible. This often meant traveling deep in the hills. When we found time to sleep, we were usually too tired to stand guard. Our best security was to find a hidden spot.

The news persisted that Manila had fallen. At first we could not or would not believe it, but as the days passed, hearing the same story over and over again left little doubt that it must be so. We had no idea of what was going on in the rest of the world. Our efforts to find a radio for news constantly met with failure. Most of the information we gleaned was received in a combination of Tagalog, sign language, and broken English. A Filipino who spoke English fluently was a rare find.

As the days progressed and it became more and more obvious that the remaining American and Filipino forces had been, or were being, withdrawn into Bataan and Corregidor, the usefulness of continuing south became more and more questionable. I was more pessimistic than the others in our party about how long it would be before America's armed forces would become strong enough to retake the Philippine Islands. Estimates among us ranged from months to years.

One night, in a small *barrio*, I saw a Manila newspaper dated 26 or 27 December 1941. Covering the entire front page was a picture of Uncle Sam, wearing a World War I helmet with an Army .45-caliber automatic strapped to each hip, wading across the Pacific Ocean heading for the Philippine Islands. The caption beneath the picture read in essence, "He will not forsake us." The picture is as clear in my mind today as it was then. It brought tears to my eyes.

Ever since being cut off from the Regiment, I had turned over and over in my mind the possibility of a guerrilla movement. To date I had come up with nothing to encourage such an idea. The gloomiest factor against it had been the performance of the Philippine Army. The attitude of Filipino civilians with whom we had had contact was no more encouraging. I had not talked to a Filipino who felt he should fight for his country. It was all up to the Americans. An individual's interest or concern usually went no further than himself and his immediate family, sometimes his *barrio*. I had not yet heard any feelings of nationalism.

My conclusion at the time was that I would be most useful joining an organized unit and that my best chance lay to the south. I was bound to keep moving in that direction. Up until the time I had been cut off from the Regiment, it was unheard of to take a drink from a stream or *barrio* well, except in an emergency. However, since then we had had little choice, and so far I had had no bad effects. One morning I awoke, however, with a severe case of the "quick step." For two days, I was unable to keep anything down. I especially remember this first attack because on the second morning of my enforced diet, we stopped at a hut for breakfast. Sitting in misery, watching the others finish what then had become a hearty breakfast, the hostess brought out *flan,* a Spanish custard, for dessert. It reminded me of those I'd had at home in years past and I regretted terribly not being able to enjoy it with the others. A taste of it, though, sent me outside heaving.

Every now and then, when I met someone who seemed friendly and responsible, I would leave a note of my activities since leaving the Regiment addressed to my mother to be mailed when the war was over. None of them ever got home.

Deep in the Sierra Madres, we were far from the highways on the plain below where the Japs were. The *barrios* we passed through had been little affected by the war and we felt safe to move in the daytime.

My boots were nearly worn out. With footwear at a premium, there was little chance of finding replacements, especially since my feet were larger than the average Filipino's. So I began a foot-toughening routine. When the trail was smooth, I removed my boots and walked barefooted until my feet hurt. As the days progressed, the periods without boots lengthened. When the trail was good, it was becoming a pleasure to walk barefooted. One positive benefit was the elimination of having to remove the boots at stream crossings. Few Filipinos in the backcountry wore shoes.

At dusk one evening, we were approaching a stream down a forest trail. We could see a small group of *nipa* shacks through the trees. A thin haze of smoke from the evening fires shrouded the *barrio*, cloaking the scene with a dream-like pall. Lulled by the serenity and rustic beauty of this scene, we were startled to our senses in mid-stream by a series of loud splashes. Out of a nearby pool, struggling frantically to get away from us, was the most gruesome looking creature that I had ever seen. It looked as though it had to be from another planet. A giant lizard several feet in length, it was an iguana.

After supper in the *barrio*, we moved on to find a place suitably hidden in which to rest. This night, of all the nights, we saw them—the fireflies. They were not everywhere, but massed here and there on selected trees. A single tree, 15 or 20 feet in height, would be completely covered with the tiny creatures. These trees appeared as great beacons in the darkness, emitting an unbelievably beautiful, warm, blue glow. The individual flickering of the tiny lights, on and off, gave this nearly holy glow a shimmering effect. The sight made one pause for a moment. I could read my compass by this light.

Except for the barking dogs as we passed the little sleeping *barrios*, all seemed calm. The Japs had not gotten so far into the mountains. About midnight, we crawled into a deserted shack to rest.

We passed a civilian on the trail who recently had been near the highway, and he told us that he had seen an American sitting by the side of the road, blind from sticks stuck into his eyes by the Japs. We also heard that they had issued an ultimatum to all Americans in the hills to surrender by a specified date, which had long expired before we got the message. Those who failed to surrender would be shot on sight.

As the mountains spread west into the plain, we were forced to get closer to the highway. Again we could see Japanese truck convoys and occasionally columns of tanks moving south.

Large fires were seen nightly along the highway. In reply to our questions, the local Filipinos invariably gave the same answer: the Japs were burning their dead. Sometimes as many as 30 truckloads of dead in a day were reported being brought north to be burned. The bodies were piled into an empty *nipa* shack, saturated with gasoline, and set on fire. A small amount of ashes from these mass cremations was placed into small boxes to be sent home to relatives in Japan.

There were occasional reports of Jap brutality to the Filipinos. A show of resistance or lack of cooperation had reportedly resulted in the killing of several individuals.

Near Sibul Springs, Bulacan, Mr. Lupton decided to leave us. He had become too tired to continue. His parting remark was that he wondered why we were continuing south. He felt there was nothing to be gained by it. I still believed that there was some chance of getting to Corregidor or Bataan if we could get close to the Manila area. This was the middle of January 1942. There were four of us: Hendricks, Malmsbury, the American lieutenant from the 91st, and me.

As we proceeded south, the steepness of the mountains pushed us closer and closer to the highway. We moved mostly at night now, with a great deal more caution. The enemy seemed to be everywhere. Patrols were getting into the outlying *barrios* searching for food. Near a *barrio* of the town of San Rafael, we had a narrow escape from a Jap patrol that nearly ran into us on the trail. All that saved us was hiding behind some undergrowth by the side of the trail as they passed.

North of the town of Norzagaray we ran across a group of American civilians. They had barely gotten out of Manila before the Japs occupied it. For nearly two weeks now they had been hiding in a makeshift camp in the hills. They were like lost sheep. None of them knew what they should do. They feared the Filipinos almost as much as the Japs. Some members of the group thought they would be better off surrendering.

The main road into the Bataan Peninsula was not far to the west of us. Enemy forces from both the south and north were reported pouring into Bataan. There was little doubt that we would not get into Bataan by this route. Many Japs were reported to the south. Turning back was the question that continually plagued us.

Near the Angat Dam we ran into an American who introduced himself as an Army sergeant. He acted a little wacky and I suspected he was an impostor, but he professed to know a back trail to the hills north of the town of Montalban where there was a large group of Americans and a radio. We decided to go that far, at least, and there decide what to do next.

On 20 January, we arrived at the American camp. It was on a high plateau overlooking the town of Montalban to the south. Montalban is about 18.5 miles north and east of Manila. It had taken nearly a month to get there from Baguio. In an automobile, using the highway, it would not have taken a full day.

There were about 15 Americans in camp, including soldiers, sailors, engineers, and businessmen. The military personnel had been cut off from their units during the retreat into Bataan. Most of the civilians had been away from Manila at the outbreak of the war, their families left in Manila. Several had learned through Filipino friends that their wives and children had been interned by the Japs. Most were of the opinion that it would not be many months before the United States would retake the Philippines and were going to sit it out where they were. I still felt it could be years.

The camp seemed relatively secure. The one main trail up from the valley was watched night and day, everyone taking a turn at guard duty. To the rear of the camp was a dense jungle where a man could get lost in no time.

Getting enough to eat was a constant problem. Some of the Americans in the camp still had money. The four of us who had just arrived had nothing to offer but ravenous appetites. Food was procured by nightly excursions into the valley by both scrounging and purchasing parties.

The big event of the day was listening to the news over the radio, sometimes from San Francisco, but mostly from stations in the southern Philippines. Occasionally, we listened to the propaganda in English broadcasts by Japanese sources. The main topics of discussion among the Americans always were how long before our forces would retake the Philippines and what should we do now?

There were several Filipinos in camp, some military, some civilians. They were especially welcome as they were mostly responsible for our supply of food. I remember one, especially, for his skill in playing the guitar and singing. After supper, around a fire back in the jungle, he would play and sing for the enjoyment of the entire camp.

The hike from northern Luzon with the diet of rice and haphazard sleeping had been exhausting. The four of us now were luxuriating in the chance to rest, having enough to eat, and the feeling of some freedom from the constant threat of running into the Japs. Our basic food three times a day was still rice, but I was getting quite used to it. With a few extra dishes, such as boiled chicken and vegetables, sometimes a piece of pig or *carabao*, it went down very well.

One day I was taking a walk in back of camp and sighted a stray cow. It was not long before I was stalking her and soon placed a .45 bullet between her eyes. The sound of the shot brought most of the camp. In no time, we butchered the cow. Nothing was wasted. Even the stomach and intestines were saved. Some of the meat was hung up to dry; some went into the boiling pot. Choice bits were broiled over the coals. Bones were cracked open to extract the marrow. It did not last long, but everyone had a glorious feast, which did a great deal to improve dispositions and our outlook on the world. It made us new arrivals feel less like bums.

The guns from the Bataan Peninsula could be heard night and day, yet there seemed no chance of getting there. The Japs were everywhere, in the towns and on the highways. Several Filipinos had been sent on different routes to find a way to Corregidor or Bataan; none were ever seen or heard of again.

As I became rested, I also became restless. I wanted to have an active part in the war. This is what I was trained and paid to do. Occasionally we heard a radio station broadcasting from Cebu City. We gathered that there were American and Filipino forces still intact on that island in the central Philippines. Three of us decided to try to get there: Hendricks, Malmsbury, and I. Our fourth companion on the trip south decided against it. No one else was interested, most believing that the United States would be back soon, and that our ambitions were suicidal in any event.

The three of us were in our late twenties. Malmsbury was lean and wiry and never seemed to tire. Hendricks was as strong as a bull; his hunched-over, slouchy gait belied his powerful six feet. I was usually hard put to keep up with them.

Chapter 17

At dusk on 30 January 1942, the three of us left the Montalban camp and started south toward the Tayabas coast. A full moon made travel easier. We each carried a pistol; a rifle with extra ammunition; a blanket with a few odds and ends rolled in cast-off Philippine Army packs; and a canteen. I still had my binoculars, compass, knife, watch, and the road map given to me in Baguio. Our clothes were becoming threadbare and dirty. Ill-fitting, worn-out tennis shoes were all we could find when our boots finally fell apart.

Our first test came on the first night, crossing the main highway from Montalban into Manila. There was heavy enemy truck traffic that night. Concealment on either side of the road was almost non-existent. The moonlight, while helpful, made us very conspicuous crossing the open fields. Finally we found a drainage ditch. We used it to crawl a hundred or so yards to the road. Then, individually, we madly dashed across between trucks. Again, on the other side, we had to crawl a great distance until we reached cover.

The Filipinos continued to feed us and provide us with places to sleep. Usually, we would find someone who spoke some English in each *barrio*, and he would would guide us to the next, and, if needed, act as an interpreter. We were again traveling as much as possible in the hills, mostly at night. We were in sugar cane country and chewing on a piece of it became the mainstay of our diet.

Hearing that there was a bakery in the town of Antipolo (in Rizal Province, immediately to the west of Manila), we went there to get some bread. More than anything else, we craved bread, which was almost impossible to find. While we were dickering with the owner, two truckloads of Japanese soldiers drove into the town plaza and parked in front of the bakery. The owner quickly showed us a place to hide. Soon we could hear the enemy's voices in the bakery. We were at the complete mercy of the owner and his helpers. If they were pro-Japanese, our days were limited. Even a thoughtless slip of the tongue could give us away. Fortunately, the Japs left without incident. After dark, a guide showed us a way out of town by a devious route that led through houses filled with wide-eyed people talking in hushed tones.

That night we barely escaped another patrol, and the next day we all but walked into an ambush, had it not been for a last minute warning by a young Filipino running up the trail. The Japs seemed to be everywhere. It was hard to tell in which direction it was safe to move. We gleaned every possible bit of information from each individual that we passed on the trail. We were constantly trying to piece together a true picture of what the enemy was doing.

We continued south, knowing nothing better to do. In a *barrio* on the northern coast of the Laguna de Bay (Lake Bay), south of the town of Taytay, we were taken in with open arms. A prominent citizen invited us to his house. The Japs had not yet bothered the little out-of-the-way *barrio.* If they should come this night, though, the *barrio* police were guarding the road and trails into it. This should give us ample warning. If needed, they had already selected a hiding place for us. They had done this before for other Americans who had wandered into the *barrio.*

Waiting for dinner, we were offered American whiskey and cigarettes, but there was no pipe and tobacco for Archy. The whiskey was too strong for our poor physical condition, but the cigarettes were a great treat. At first Archy scorned them, but took one and smoked it as if it were a pipe, complaining about its taste the whole time.

Our meal was a sumptuous one of rice and fish. When our host heard we were heading south toward the Tayabas coast, he suggested we take a sailboat to the south shore of the bay. This sounded good and before we knew it, the owner of a fast outrigger was in the house, discussing the possibility of taking us that night. It was agreed we would be landed near the *barrio* of Pila in the Province of Laguna. As the wind was now favorable, we should leave as soon as possible.

"With this wind, the Jap patrol launches will be unable to overtake you," our host said. This was happy news! It was, though, the first mention of enemy patrol boats. I immediately was apprehensive about accepting the ride. We knew little about Jap naval activity and nothing of the area where we were to be put ashore.

We decided to take the chance. I got a quick glimpse of our boat as we loaded in the darkness. Its hull was shaped like a great canoe, some 25 to 30 feet in length, with a narrow beam and outriggers on both sides. The forward part was decked. There was a crew of three. As the sail was raised, the man at the tiller headed into the wind while we boarded. The owner signaled for the three of us to climb onto the windward outrigger. In a moment, the boat was brought around to fill the sail with the full force of the wind. The little boat seemed to leap ahead. Instantly, we were skimming along at breakneck speed. The prow dug deep, throwing out great sheets of water to the sides. Soon we were drenched from the spray and chilled from the wind, but it was a welcome chill after so long in the hot, humid, inland climate. This was the first time I felt the thrill and exhilaration of sailing in such a swift little craft. This one was designed for speed, and certainly had it.

We had not been long on our way when, off the right bow, a light came into view. At first, I assumed it was a light from shore and paid little attention to it. The next time I looked, it appeared larger. The crew was watching it now with some apprehension, and a lively discussion sprang up among them. Several times I picked up the word *"Japon."* We could soon hear the throbbing "thump, thump" of a motor above the noises of the water and the wind. With my field glasses, I could easily make out the outline of a launch. It appeared to be headed for us. The launch's crew could have observed us sometime before with powerful glasses.

The owner told us he planned to continue on his course. If the launch flagged us down, he would make a run for it. If the wind held, he believed he could outrun it. As the launch drew nearer, the boat owner cautioned the three of us to lie down inside the hull. Peering over the side, we could now easily discern the black hulk of the launch, high-decked and tubby. We passed within 100 yards of its bow. As it turned to follow us, a voice in the local dialect ordered us to come alongside.

The wind had been striking us from our right. A command from the boat owner and the man at the tiller brought the direction of our boat slowly to the left. The sail was let out to take the full blast of the wind. The little craft was straining at her seams, the spray from the prow fanning out in great arcs. The Filipino on the megaphone was frantically yelling at us now. We were drawing away from the launch. I caught the boat owner's eye. He smiled as he said, "I think the wind will be with us." Then, we heard gunfire. We could see flashes in the darkness, but there was no crack of bullets overhead. The distance was too great to be dangerous. The launch crew soon gave up the chase and changed its course.

"You are a good captain, Juanito," I told him. He smiled again and nodded.

It was 0200 when we reached the south shore of the Laguna de Bay. We had covered a distance of 25 to 30 miles in a very few hours. Jumping overboard, we waded ashore. The boat owner had told us that the town of Pila was not far. A main highway from the south ran through it, which the Japs surely would be using. The boat owner's last words to us were, "Make sure to cross the highway and get into the hills before daylight." Wet and tired, what we wanted most was a place to rest. We were in the middle of a swamp. Had the boat owner landed us in the wrong place? Had he lost his direction when he changed course to get away from the launch? He had spoken as though it would be easy to get across the road and into the hills before daylight.

Slogging inland through the morass in the darkness, our progress was painfully slow. After an hour or more, we came to a rice paddy that, in the dim starlight, appeared to stretch as far as one could see to the right and left and ahead. The solid ground we had sought was nowhere to be found. Only narrow, slippery dikes separated the paddies. In the darkness, it was nearly impossible to keep one's balance when walking on them.

The boatman's last words kept running through my mind. It was 0400. We had seen no sign of a road or highway, and there was no evidence of any hills ahead of us. Dawn would come shortly after five. To be caught in the open after daylight could be disastrous. We quickened our pace, not an easy thing to do on the treacherous footing.

I heard a curse behind me, followed by a solid plop like a rock falling into a deep pool of muck. Archy had lost his balance. He was neck deep in the hole, floundering frantically to free himself. He was raving as he pulled himself onto the dike, swearing like the trooper he was. I could not avoid laughing out loud, which did not help matters. What hurt him most was the condition of his rifle. He swore it would never fire again.

Waiting for Archy to pull himself together, I subconsciously checked over my equipment. To my dismay, my binoculars were missing. The strap must have snapped on one of my falls earlier in the swamp. The glasses had been very handy several times and I much regretted their loss.

As daylight arrived, we were still struggling across the level field of rice and there was still no sign of the highway. Had we been going in the wrong direction? Several times I had checked direction with my compass.

My mind went back to tactics classes at the University of Arizona, to the professor analyzing a situation that might justify taking a calculated risk to gain a tactical advantage. He defined it as one that might have only a 50 percent chance of success. Such a risk is always dangerous and only justified as a last resort. For the past month or more, this had been our way of life. Each *day* had been a calculated risk. At the moment, caught as we were in daylight in the middle of a large rice paddy, I felt the chance of success should be changed to about 10 percent, but there was nothing to do but continue. Daylight showed there was little cover or concealment anywhere, except for trees that could be seen far ahead on some rising ground.

Finally, the highway came into view. It was at the same level as the paddies, barely discernable from a distance. Not long after sighting it, we heard the sound of an approaching motor. There was nothing to do but sink into the muck of the rice paddies. The occasional sight of small green snakes, which I had been told were as poisonous as the cobra, did not make jumping in anymore pleasant.

A single truck passed. We were up again, slipping and sliding, struggling to cross the road before another passed. Then, once again, we heard the sounds of motors. We were close to the road, now: our position could not have been worse. There was a patch of long-stemmed grass growing next to the dike. I dived into it and hoped the others behind me had done the same. There was no time to look back. The convoy was passing just yards from us. Through grass in the dim light, I caught glimpses of Japanese soldiers in open trucks. I hardly dared breathe, and prayed to the Almighty to make the slant-eyes sleepy-eyed.

As the last truck disappeared, we were up and across the road. Picking a dike that looked drier and wider than the rest, we set out at a run for the hills ahead. When out of breath, we slowed down to a fast walk, watching and listening for any sign or sound of movement.

It seemed to take forever to reach the hills. Unsure if we had been seen, we zigzagged in a crouched position for some time until deep into the tree-covered hills. Our weapons were in as bad a shape as we were. There was a comparatively secure place where we could rest and clean up. The hills led to a mountain. By noon we were high up on it, a good distance from the road and, hopefully, from the Japs.

The sound of chopping led us into a camp of half a dozen woodcutters. Startled at first, they became friendly when they recognized us to be Americans. Our few words of Tagalog, mixed with some sign language, allowed some limited communication. They were obviously poor and had little food to spare, but they nevertheless offered us each a welcomed plate of rice. To go with it, they passed around a small piece of rock salt. The idea was that each of us was to scrape a little salt off and sprinkle it on the rice.

Our blankets were wet, our clothes stiff with mud, and our weapons were nearing the point of rusting solid. The afternoon was spent cleaning up.

Gathered around a campfire that night, the fare was again rice with a watery broth to pour over it; there were a few pieces of boiled greens in the broth that may have been bamboo shoots. Some joking got through to both the Filipinos and the Americans bringing laughter and a pleasant, easy atmosphere. It reminded me of the carefree night spent in the hills with the scouts last December before starting toward Baguio.

It seemed impossible to get enough to eat. No matter how much I stuffed myself with rice, I always felt hungry. My dreams were filled with visions of feasting on various American dishes. The one I missed most was breakfasts consisting of fried eggs, juicy bacon, warm toast dripping with butter, and cups of steaming coffee.

By morning, we were much refreshed and ready to hit the trail again. Early on, we skirted the mountain town of Nagcarlan. Looking down on the town from a distant trail, we could easily see Japanese soldiers roaming the street.

At one time, approaching us ahead on the trail, I noticed two Filipinos wearing armbands. As they drew closer, they started running toward us, waving their arms frantically. Their armbands were covered with Japanese ideographs.

The one in the lead gasped, "*Japon* patrol come soon," and pointed down the trail. "Better you get off the trail now. Hurry!"

We quickly complied. In a moment, we were scrambling up an embankment into the thick mountain foliage. We did not stop until we were out of breath, and then huddled down in a thicket. The sound of heavy boots clomping on the trail below became louder. Hardly daring to breathe, I carefully spread the bushes apart to have a look. Steel helmets bobbing up and down along the embankment edge came in view. Thank God the Japs were little men. The helmets passed out of view and the clomping sound became fainter and fainter.

Why had the Filipinos failed to reveal our presence to the Japs? We might not be so lucky the next time.

"No more of that trail for me," Archy said in a very positive tone. We all agreed.

We climbed ever upward, into the safety of the mountains. Several times during the afternoon we passed camps of Filipinos who had left their homes in the valley out of fear of the Japs. The Filipinos were a miserable lot, ill equipped for such living, having brought with them only the barest of necessities. They were friendly and offered to share with us what little food they had. Time and again we were warned to watch out for fifth columnists, or anti-American, pro-Japanese informers. They were reportedly members of an organization called the *Makapiles*. We had been warned earlier that they were numerous in this part of southern Luzon.

Evening found us high on the northern slope of Mt. Banahao, feeling secure in the deep forest. The country was much like that near Baguio. The trail was poor and little traveled. Again we spent the night in a woodcutter's camp. Our fare was rice and a rock of salt passed from one person to the next. The night was cold.

Two young Filipinos who had been staying in the camp were on their way to their homes on the coast of Tayabas Bay. They volunteered to guide us there by out-of-the-way trails, where, they said, there were no Japs. Their names were Mario and Bernal. Mario spoke English sparingly.

During the next morning, we looked down on the town of Lucban a few miles to the northeast, and soon after to the southeast, the town of Tayabas. Each was reportedly full of Japs. Now and then, we could see columns of trucks moving along the highway between the two towns.

On this day, we had a particularly disgusting experience. The trail led through streams, some of which were hip deep. To avoid walking in wet, soggy trousers, we removed them before fording. Emerging from the first stream, I noticed my legs covered with little brown slimy creatures squirming in every direction. The shapeless bodies of these bloodsuckers were about two inches in length and about a half an inch thick. Frantically, I began to yank them off my legs. They were more tenacious and active than those experienced on Bataan. Mario quickly put a stop to this, pointing to small brown specks left in my legs. These creatures has embedded themselves into my skin so deeply in the short time it had taken to cross the stream that a quick yank severed the body from the part embedded. If left in, they would fester and cause uncomfortable sores. The guide removed each leech by slowly increasing squeezing pressure on its body and gently pulling. Often, this removed the entire leech. When the leech would not let go, a lighted match was applied to the tail. We were finally rid of them.

"You rub soap on before going in water, will keep these worms away," our guide said.

Archy laughed, "But who the hell has any soap?"

Fortunately, Ted pulled out a small piece from his pack. At the next stream, we all tried the soap. It worked, and subsequent stream crossings were less stressful.

As the sun was setting, we were down in the valley again to the north of the town of Tayabas, close enough to make out a good bit of Japanese military activity. After dark, we crossed the highway between Lucban and Tayabas. By midnight we were again in the hills, heading east, and well away from the Japs. We slept on a level spot hidden from the trail. We had nothing to eat.

The next morning, still moving east, we were again in the lowlands. Before us spread park-like stands of coconut palms; the damp ground was carpeted with moss, soft and resilient when trod upon. The great fronds of the palm trees high above the ground met one another, allowing only a diffused light to sift to the ground. We were walking through a great natural pavilion.

I was puzzled why the guides still continued east, while our map showed Tayabas Bay to the south.

"Less people, less roads, maybe less *Japons* this way. Some people here are bad. They like *Japons* better than Americans," Mario answered. "Also we know this way. My companion and I passed this way before."

Just as our guides had warned, it was this morning that we experienced our first outward sign of inhospitality. The husband and wife who resided in the first hut we encountered refused to give us anything to eat, saying they had no rice. This was quite unlikely, and it took some forceful persuasion to get a fresh pot of rice cooking.

As usual, while waiting, we busied ourselves cleaning weapons and trying to piece our clothing together. Suddenly, I noticed that the husband was gone. I asked Mario if he had seen him go

"Yes, sir, sometime ago, down the trail."

"Where does the trail lead?"

"To the highway from the town of Antimonan."

"How far is the highway?" I asked.

Maybe one, maybe two hours, maybe more, maybe less," he responded.

This did not sound good. If so inclined, the man could have Japs here within an hour or so. From his attitude, it appeared he was so inclined.

We sent Bernal down the trail to watch. We were in an area where there was little chance of escaping if surprised. As soon as the rice was cooked, we gobbled about half, wrapping what was left in rags in our packs, and hurriedly set out east again.

By nightfall we were near the Antimonan highway, waiting in a thicket for the guides to return. They had gone ahead to make sure all was clear.

As usual, a passing Filipino spotted us. He came over and sat down to pass the time of day. He was naked, except for a pair of crudely sewn *nipa*-cloth shorts, with a long bolo hanging from his waist. His face was expressionless; he was very old. I felt we had little to fear from him. He probably desired to keep out of the way of the Japs as much as we did. Realizing we could not understand him seemed both to amaze and to embarrass him.

After a silence, Archy asked, *"Japon ditto?"* The old man shook his head, and then pointed in the direction of the highway to the south, passing his finger from east to west. This was accompanied by a long explanation in his dialect. The only words we could understand, besides *"Japon ditto,"* were "Antimonan" and "Lucena," the closest nearby towns of any size.

After another period of uncomfortable silence, Ted touched his knee to get his attention and pointed to a liter-sized bottle he was carrying.

The old man smiled and reached for the bottle. Knowing we were interested, he removed the cork with ceremony and handed the bottle to Ted. The old man made a sign of putting the bottle to his lips, then patted his stomach and nodded with a broad smile. Ted took this to mean the contents were good to drink. He took a healthy swig and choked. "Jesus Christ!" he coughed, "Its pure alcohol," Ted pointed at the bottle, looking questionably at the old man.

"*Ginebra,*" he said, pointing to some nearby coconut trees.

Ginebra meant gin. This evidently was distilled *tuba,* the mild wine from the flower of the coconut tree. Learning from Ted, I barely wet my tongue with this firewater, as did Archy. It was nearly unbearable to swallow. This was our first and, hopefully, our last experience with it.

Mario and Bernal returned, saying it looked safe to cross the highway as soon as it was dark. Natives they had questioned said the Japs had been preparing what sounded like delaying positions along the route. The work was being done only during daylight hours, with the Japs returning to the safety of their garrisons in the towns at nightfall. Our main concern would be the movement of vehicles along the highway after dark, which should not prove much of a problem

By early evening, we were across the highway and on a trail leading southeast, which looked on the map as if it would bring us to the Tayabas coast somewhere between the *barrios* of Padre Burgos and Unisan. We made our camp in an empty, ramshackle *bodega*, a hundred or so feet off the trail. Archy was starting to play out. Through the afternoon, he had complained of fever; it could be seen in his face and eyes. The big toe of his left foot, which stuck out through a hole cut in his too-small canvas shoes, had been bruised and stubbed innumerable times and was becoming infected and painful.

I awoke the next morning as the first light trickled through the doorway into the *bodega.* The sour smell of spoiled coconut meat permeated the air. We had spent the night in a *copra* shack where the meat of the dried coconut was stored prior to shipment.* The floor was dirt, uneven and dusty. The walls were made of hand-sawn planks laid one on top of the other, parallel to the ground, nailed to a series of uprights. The roof was made of the broad-leafed *nipa* palm. A fine place, I thought, to spend the night, yet not as bad as some we had slept in. At least we should be thankful that another night had passed without incident. I had made it a habit each night before I slept and each morning when I awoke to thank the Almighty for being alive and not in Jap captivity.

It was 9 February 1942, 49 days since being cut off from the Regiment. Now, God willing, by the end of this day we would dig our toes into the sands of Tayabas Bay and soon be on the open sea sailing for Cebu.

The movement of unwinding from my blanket caused small clouds of dust to rise into the torpid air, making it thicker and warmer and hazier. Still asleep, the hairy heads and faces of Achy and Ted stuck out from their blankets. Archy was breathing heavily, letting forth an occasional groan. His face was buried in the dirt as usual; he could not become accustomed to using a canteen for a pillow. The two Filipinos had no blankets and were huddled up like babies in a womb.

Ted pulled his arms from underneath his blanket, glanced around the shack and outside where the sky above the palms had become a deep blue. He sat up and lit

---

*Copra is coconut albumen, from which coconut oil is extracted.

a cigarette. Sitting Indian-fashion on his blanket, as if in a trance, he was enjoying what he called his best cigarette of the day.

Mario opened his eyes, taking in as much of the scene as possible without moving his head. Then he turned over, nudged his companion awake and they immediately started to jabber.

Archy struggled to his elbow, breathing heavily. His eyes were bloodshot from the fever that had worsened during the night. His normally large lips were swollen and dry and overly red. It was a struggle to get to his knees; every move he made was an effort.

"How are you feeling?" I asked.

"I'll make it." Archy answered, getting to his feet. I noticed his ankle was swollen from the poison in his toe. By force of habit, he pulled out his .45 and gave it a quick inspection. Then picking up his rifle, he looked to see that the muzzle was clear, checking that there was a round in the chamber and making sure the safety was on. Grabbing his blanket and pack, he made his way outside the hut, limping and half staggering. His actions left little doubt that he was determined to move on that day.

"He's staving off an attack of malaria through sheer willpower," Ted observed.

We should have stopped to rest for the day, but we had been living for this opportunity, which, with luck, would bring us to the shore of Tayabas Bay. Hopefully, we could find a boat that would take us south to the island of Cebu, where we hoped to find American and Filipino forces still intact.

Like the others, I was over-eager to see the water and feel the fresh, salt breeze. We were eager to complete this trip, which the other Americans in the hills east of Manila had believed impossible. We were fed up with ducking the Japs like so many scared rabbits, fed up with hunger and fatigue and insects and vermin that had become part of our existence, and with the stinking heat that never let up. Also, if the Japs had been warned of our presence in the area, it was not smart to stay in one place.

Our guides were sitting in a corner of the shack, continuing to jabber. I was still not sure how far they could be trusted.

"Are you ready to go?" I asked.

"Yes, sir," Mario answered as they both rose to their feet.

"Then take a look at the trail and let us know if all is clear." I wondered as they filed out the door, if I should tell them again how far up and down the trail to go, and what to look for. They had done well the past few days.

"You going to shave today?" Ted asked. I felt my beard that itched in spots and was caked in places, then looked over at the growth of silky blond beard hanging from Ted's face.

"What about you?"

With an almost imperceptible crinkling of his blue eyes, he said: "No, maybe tomorrow, if we get on that boat." None of us had a razor.

What an evil looking crew! We all had needed a shave for the past 49 days; also haircuts, baths, and clothes, but worst of all, shoes. At first, not bathing or shaving had bothered us, but by now we had become impervious to both, paying little attention to our appearances. Our thoughts were ever busy with the basic problems of survival, keeping clear of the Japs, and getting enough food and rest to keep moving.

Mario soon returned to say that the trail was clear. I hoped he knew what he was talking about. We were a motley-looking crew as we filed away from the shack. Rifles were slung as the owner saw fit and packs hung askew to miss sore spots on our backs.

"Looks like your shirt has a new tear in it," Ted said to Archy who was in front in him, struggling up the trail.

Archy stopped and turned around with a gleam of anger in his eye. His ragged shirt had been a sore point for some time. Ted was moving to defend himself when Archy turned, mumbling that Ted's pants did not look like they had been tailored for him.

The trail still led through pavilion-like groves of coconut palms, beautiful in the clear morning air. We focused our attention on the guides out ahead, the trail and its signs, and watched off the sides of the trail and to the rear for any sign of the Japs.

A single house came into view ahead of us. We were above the coconut groves now, near the edge of the jungle. The house was not the usual dwelling found in the back areas. Instead of a frame of posts held together with hemp, with walls and roof of *nipa*, the frame and walls were of hewn and smooth lumber, nicely fitted together, and topped with a tin roof. Instead of the usual filth caused by pigs and chickens overrunning the area, the ground beneath the house was clean and raked, with little flower gardens surrounding it.

A middle-aged Filipino dressed in European clothes answered the door. He was startled at seeing three Americans on his doorstep, but quickly regained his composure.

"Come in, please, and make yourselves at home," he said, using excellent English.

Our position was obvious and he at once took it for granted that we would have breakfast with him. He told us there had been little Japanese activity in the back areas, and that they had been staying near the main highways and towns. I hoped this was so and would remain so.

After talking with our guides, our host turned to us and said, "There is a shorter way to the next *barrio* than the way your guides have planned. I think this way will be much better for you. You really will do well to take it." His insistence made me suspicious. I got the feeling he knew more than he was telling.

I asked Mario what he thought. "You can take either way, whichever you please," he said.

That was a great help. Our host could be leading us into trouble, as well as out of it. There was no way to tell what we should do.

With breakfast, instead of the usual glass of water, we were served hot chocolate with coconut milk, a truly wonderful treat.

We had no trouble finding the cutoff to our host's shortcut. The trail proved to be a good one. Near the middle of the morning, we had our first sight of Tayabas Bay, off to the south through the coconut groves below. Our spirits rose. Ted and I were almost exuberant, if such a feeling was still possible, and even Archy cracked a smile through his fever and pains. Things were certainly looking up. Mario told us that at the rate we were traveling, by mid-afternoon we would be in the small *barrio* on the coast to which they were taking us. In the *barrio* there were boats large enough to make the trip to Cebu Island. We rested in a papaya grove along the trail, refreshing ourselves on the fruit as we talked over our plans for the future.

Chapter 18

An hour later we entered a small *barrio*, hot, tired, and hungry. Archy was worse. He had had difficulty keeping up during the morning.

The inhabitants of the *barrio* became overly excited upon seeing us. The *barrio teniente,* an older man, spoke enough English to make himself understood. He spoke excitedly and urgently, "many *Makapiles* here. *Japon* soldiers here, too," motioning across the countryside.

"There are informers and Japan's soldiers not far away," Mario repeated. "He says it is very dangerous for you here. You must go right away."

This was certainly different news than we had heard that morning at breakfast. On questioning the *teniente,* he was very vague about his source of information, or the exact whereabouts of the Japs or informers. We had heard so many such warnings without anything ever coming of them that we gave little weight to this one. It was conceivable that informers could be anywhere. Anyone could start a rumor that Jap soldiers were nearby.

When we asked for something to eat, the old *teniente* told us there was little food in the *barrio* and that it was better we go on. It is almost a code with the Filipinos to never refuse a stranger food or a place to rest, so the *teniente's* refusal to provide us something to eat was like a slap in the face.

"You get us something to eat in a hurry," I told the old man in no uncertain terms. I remember the look of anguish on his face when I said it, but he went off to see that the food was prepared.

Archy had gone to a nearby *bodega* and was removing his belt and pack. Ted and I followed. The *barrio*-folk were talking in small groups, occasionally glancing at us and shaking their heads. Our guides followed us into the *bodega*. Mario started to speak, almost imploringly:

"You should not wait here any longer. It is very dangerous. The *barrio* people are afraid for you. They say they know Japan's soldiers have come this way from the Antimonan highway, but they don't know where they are now. We should leave at once."

I knew he was sincere in his warning, but felt he had become overly frightened by the talk in the *barrio*. This was similar to all the fearful rumors with which we had been plagued down the entire length of Luzon. If we had heeded all of them, we would have been constantly on the run.

I said to Mario, "We will wait for our meal and then go." Mario and Bernal walked away, shaking their heads.

While waiting for the meal to be cooked, I took a walk, and as a matter of habit looked around for an escape route in case of a surprise. To the north of the *barrio*, I noticed a thick forest not too far distant that we could reach in a hurry if necessary.

We had our lunch in the *bodega*; Archy's consisted of a soft, rice gruel called *lugao*. His face was becoming even more flushed with fever. After eating what he could, Archy lay down and started to groan and shiver. He was having a malaria attack. With all the warning and nervousness of the *barrio*-folk, I was beginning to feel we should get moving as soon as possible, but there was nothing to do but let Archy rest a little.

Ted was sitting in the doorway of the *bodega*, watching. I was inside, sitting beside Archy, dozing.

"Myrone Japon ditto." All of a sudden the dreaded alert came from the area where the trail entered the *barrio*. Soon the cry was everywhere. People were running past the *bodega* in utter confusion.

Ted yelled at us to get going. Grabbing his rifle and pack, he disappeared. Archy was struggling to get his equipment together. Pushing his rifle into his hand, I helped him to his feet and out the door. My rifle was in the far corner of the building. By the time I had grabbed my gear and weapons, Ted and Archy had disappeared. The *barrio* was in complete confusion. Women were screaming for their children; chickens were flying in every direction; dogs were barking and fighting over unwatched food.

People were streaming past me, yelling *"Japon!"* and pointing in back of them. I joined them at a dead run, hoping to overtake Archy and Ted.

Before I had gone far, I could hear gunfire. Bullets cracked overhead and ricocheted through the trees. I recognized the now familiar high-pitched crack of the Japanese .25 caliber rifle.* The almost simultaneous crack-boom coming from behind left little doubt about the nearness of the enemy.

I followed the stream of Filipinos over a hill into a small hollow, and then cut to the north, by myself, toward the forest in an effort to throw the Japs off my trail. Over a fence, across a field, I zigzagged into the forest as I ran, not once looking back. By a tree at the wood's edge, I dropped my pack, hoping to return for it later. I then proceeded into the forest's depths as fast as my legs and breath and the undergrowth would allow. It was an hour before I stopped to rest. The Japs would have had to be pretty good trackers, as I had come a good ways through streambeds. I hoped I had thrown the Japs off my trail.

I lay down in a hole left by the roots of a tree that had blown over, out of breath and exhausted. Soon after the first shots had been fired in my direction, a large number of rifles commenced firing from another part of the *barrio*. This firing had continued at a rapid rate for several minutes, and I kept trying to imagine what the Japs had found to shoot at.

---

*The Japanese Type 38 rifle fired a 6.5mm (.25-caliber) round. Introduced in 1905, as the war in China war continued during the 1930s, the Japanese Army's leadership realized that this bullet and cartridge were inadequate. Beginning in 1940, the Type 99 rifle was introduced; it fired a 7.7mm round that was comparable to the .30-caliber ammunition fired by the Americans and the .303-caliber ammunition used by British and Commonwealth forces.

The question uppermost in my mind was the whereabouts of Ted and Archy. We had been together so long that I felt completely lost without them. How would we find each other in all this jungle? Maybe the Filipinos would help. On the other hand, maybe they would help the Japs find me. The three of us had the understanding that if we were scattered, we would look for each other at the next *barrio* on our route. One of the others had our only map, but I still had my compass and knew that the next *barrio* was almost directly south. I prayed we would meet there.

Then I began to wonder where the Japs were and how thoroughly they would comb the area searching for us. What should I do?

The hole I was in was deep enough to keep my head below ground level when sitting up. I decided to sit tight until dark, then work south, with the hope of running into Ted and Archy on the way, or at least meeting them in the next *barrio*. Unable to tell a friendly native from an informer, I knew I must keep clear of everyone until well away from this area.

The trees around me were large and close together and the foliage dense, giving me a feeling of security. A hawk circled toward me and perched on the top of a nearby tree and looked down at me. I always liked hawks and his presence gave me hope. I was mentally ready to hold on to anything that would buoy my spirits. I watched him for some time, developing a sort of friendly feeling for him. I almost felt he was watching over me.

Settling down in the hole, I started to mull over the events of the day. Before today we had had several close calls with the Japs, but they had all appeared to be accidental. Today the affair appeared to be pre-planned, based on information that we were passing through the area. Otherwise, what were they doing in this isolated mountainous area, when up until now all reports indicated they were staying close to their lines of communications, paying little attention to the remote areas? The more I thought about it, the more I was convinced that the Japs had been waiting for us on the trail we had originally planned to take that morning. Then, when we were seen in the *barrio*, an informer slipped out to tell them.

If this was the case, how did the information of our presence in the area get to them? We had seen very few natives the past few days. Did the husband, who disappeared while rice was being cooked in the coconut grove, tell the Japs of our presence? Or had our guides inadvertently or purposely told him of our planned route? Had they perhaps told others we had previously passed on the trail? I did not suspect our host at breakfast that morning because of the time element, but did wonder if possibly he did know of the enemy's whereabouts. If he had known, why had he not told us? I also believed the *barrio teniente* knew much more than he would tell us, but again, why had he not come out and told us instead of acting as he did? I had seen others act like this before, and was beginning to believe it was a Filipino trait that must be accepted.

Suddenly, the hawk flew away, as though startled by something. I squeezed more deeply into my hole and listened. Sure enough, there was a sound of distant voices. In a few moments, it became obvious they were coming toward me, but I could not yet make out who they were. The voices were not coming from the same direction from which I had come. This made me certain no one was on my trail.

The voices were coming closer. They were deep and rasping and guttural, accompanied by the heavy tread of boots. There was little doubt of the source: it was the Japs again. I removed my pistol from its holster, clicked the safety off and laid it in front of me. Beside it I laid out an extra magazine and an extra clip of rifle ammunition. We had long since agreed that we would never be captured alive. We would save the last .45-caliber round for ourselves. I kept saying to myself, "I must not forget this. I must not forget this. I must do this."

The sound of heavy boots on the trail came to me more distinctly as the moments passed. There were several pairs of feet approaching, but there were no voices. This worried me. Then a voice spoke out in Japanese almost directly in front of me. It was answered by a few curt words. The voices were so close it seemed that I should be able to reach out and touch the speakers.

My heart was pounding madly. This was probably it. At least I would get as many of them as possible. I was ready, praying to God to steady me at the first sight of a head that peered into my hiding place.

The *clomp, clomp, clomp* of heavy boots continued. Their dreaded sound was going past, going on, and now dying out. It seemed an age before I could no longer hear the steady tromping. I believed the sound lingered in my imagination long after it had gone. It took a while to realize the Japs had passed by. I was so sure they would find me that I had made up my mind that this was the end. It was several moments before the realization took hold that I was *not* going to die in this hole. I slumped back, breathing deeply.

The fireflies and stars were coming out when I started south. The forest was "pitch black" and my progress was slow. I had an old compass with a non-luminous face that was difficult to read in the dark, so it was necessary to stop to check it often. The going was rough through the swampy jungle. At one point, I had to wade knee-deep in water through a marsh for an hour to stay on course. I avoided any trails for fear they were being patrolled.

After midnight, the level, swampy forest gave way to a gentle slope toward the sea. Soon, to my relief, the forest gave way to a growth of short underbrush, which improved the light and allowed me to pick a star to guide me. As I proceeded, however, the underbrush became increasingly dense until, eventually, I was forced to stay on a trail. There were marks of hob-nailed boots on the trail. I moved ahead by walking a short distance, stopping, listening, and proceeding again.

Rounding a bend in the trail, not long after getting onto it, the clank of metal hitting metal stopped me dead in my tracks. After a moment's listening, I heard the clanking sound again and could faintly hear the tread of heavy boots. I turned and ran back up the trail toward a ford in a creek through which I had waded moments before. In passing, I had noticed that the small creek provided a dark, tree-covered, cavernous tunnel in which I now hoped I could hide.

I stumbled up the creek bed, bending low to avoid the overhanging foliage that made an archway. I must have gone 30 or 40 feet before stopping and was still trying to regain my breath when the form of the first Jap came into sight. There was enough starlight at the mouth of the tunnel to see his outline. He uttered a few words and dropped to the ground. The remaining four or five men in the patrol successively came up and dropped down beside the first one. They were breathing heavily and seemed quite tired. I was not nearly far enough up the creek for my peace of mind, but to try to move any further over the rocks in the streambed might reveal my presence. The best thing I could think of was to stand there and hope the Japs were too exhausted to explore the creek. The seconds dragged into minutes and the minutes into a long period of suspense. I began to wonder if the Japs had decided to spend the remainder of the night there, but finally, with a few words from their leader, they all got up and walked off.

At dawn I was nearly down to the coastal plane. There was no sign of the sea. I knocked on the door of the first *nipa* shack I reached, where a man and his wife and son were preparing breakfast. They were startled to see me and it was necessary to invite myself inside. Only the boy spoke a little English. I told him that I was hungry and would like breakfast. He relayed this to his folks who were standing across the room from me in an attitude that appeared to be none too friendly. With what seemed a grudging consent, they turned their backs and busied themselves around the hearth. On questioning the boy about any other Americans in the area, he said that he had neither seen nor heard of any. He said that there were no Japanese close by, but that there were many staying in a railroad station named "Yawe" (adjacent to Padre Burgos) which was several miles down the trail.

When breakfast was ready, instead of everyone sitting down at the table, which was customary, the man laid a plateful of rice and fish before me without saying a word, and returned to the fire. I believe they were afraid of what the Japs would do if I were caught in their home; but possibly they just disliked Americans. I ate with my pistol on the table, all the while keeping a sharp watch out the window overlooking the trail. Halfway through my plate of rice, the boy started to leave the house. He said he was going to a neighbor's on an errand. I was sure he was going to inform the Japs at the "Yawe" Station of my whereabouts and I made him sit down.

On leaving the house, the boy insisted that he walk with me. This was the last thing I wanted, but felt that it was better for him to be alongside than following me. I finally shook him by going down the opposite fork of the trail, after having him commit himself to the other. As soon as he was out of sight, I hot-footed it toward a large hill with banana trees at its top.

The banana grove turned out to be exceedingly dense; in some places it was necessary to squeeze sideways past the trees, as I worked toward the center. Soon I came to a small clearing where I planned to hide for the day and rest.

Try as I might, it was impossible to relax enough to go to sleep. Could it be that the strain was getting to me? In a similar situation a month ago, I had been able to sleep soundly.

There were plenty of bananas, but I soon reached my capacity for them. As the day wore on, I became hungry, but felt as though I would retch if I ate another banana.

Although plagued by the possibility that the Japs were close by, I was so anxious to find Archy and Ted that, against my better judgment, I started walking south about an hour and a half before sunset.

The coastal plain was a great field of rice paddies broken into small patches by innumerable small tree-covered hillocks that appeared like so many tiny islands. It was through these little islands of trees that I traveled, running from one hillock to the next across the level stretches of rice paddies. It was a little before dusk when I sighted in the distance what looked to be a well-made house. After watching it for a few minutes and seeing no activity, I started toward it across an open rice field. I was hoping to be able to get something to eat.

About halfway across the field, a railroad track came into view. I flopped on my stomach. A closer look at the house showed a signal light sticking up above one end of it and painted on the side facing me was the name "Yawe." What a predicament! The nearest cover was 75 yards away. I looked back at the station. At the moment, there was no activity around it. I got up and walked hunched over, like the field workers, toward the nearest hillock of trees, hiding my rifle alongside my body. I expected at any moment to hear a shot, but the Lord was certainly with me. Arriving under the trees, I had another careful look at the station. Still no one could be seen around it. The Japs had missed a good chance. I had no intention of giving them another. But where were they? I walked back into the trees and sat down. I knew I would not get many more breaks like that.

It was dusk before I started south again, moving more cautiously now. I had little idea of where I was. The *barrio* where I might meet Ted and Archy was as unknown to me as the distance to the shore of the bay. The only thing to do was to continue moving south, with the hope of finding a friendly person who spoke English. The first house I came to was deserted except for a lone pig. The fire in the hearth was still smoking. There was an unnatural look to things. It reminded me of the early days in northern Luzon, when the Filipinos were leaving their homes to take to the hills because of the fighting.

What was going on? The next house I came to was also deserted.

I blindly walked into the yard of a third house, too tired to know what I was doing. The last of the daylight was fading. All of a sudden in the dim light, I barely discerned a man who stood watching me approach. I quickly knelt, with my rifle at the ready. He didn't move. He had seen something, as I had, and was trying to discern its identity. I looked to the right and left. There was no sound or movement of anyone else in the area. As my eyes adjusted to the dimming light, I could vaguely make out a man dressed in shorts and loose, sleeveless shirt. He was bareheaded and barefooted, undoubtedly an unarmed Filipino. Suddenly, he recognized me as an American and came running towards me. He was extremely excited, talking and gesturing frantically. When he discovered that I could not understand him, he motioned me to follow him to a nearby bamboo thicket. There, he soon made it clear to me that a Japanese patrol had just passed that way and might return any moment. He wanted me to stay hidden where I was, and he would bring me food.

I did not know whether to trust him. It would have been as easy for him to bring the Japs to my place of hiding as it would some food. It was not long, however, until he returned with a bowl of rice and another Filipino who spoke English. The name of the man who hid me, fed me, and brought the interpreter, was Miguel. I shall never forget him as long as I live. More than anyone else, I owe him my life.

As I gulped the rice, squatting there in the darkness, the man who spoke English told me in hushed tones the top news story of the past two days. He said that early that morning, 50-odd Japanese soldiers had unloaded at the "Yawe" station and had been searching the area all day for an American. The Japs were still everywhere, in small patrols. He said that the day before, a patrol of Japs had surrounded two Americans in a *barrio* to the north, killing one, and wounding and capturing the other. A third American had gotten away. He added with a great deal of satisfaction that during the scrap, two Japs had been killed and one wounded. The news of my friends was devastating.

Miguel then made a proposal that I had hardly expected. In a hushed tone, he explained to me through the interpreter that there was a *banca* (a native boat) hidden about a kilometer away, down in a lagoon that led to the sea. He knew of two men he thought would paddle me across the strait to Marinduque Island where there were no Japs as yet. He said it was the only chance I had of escaping the enemy. If I stayed, they would surely find me on the morrow.

We started out, feeling our way down a steep trail in the deep blackness of the forest. The Filipinos talked in whispers and grunted disapprovingly each time I set a stone rolling. After a half-hour of slow progress, we reached the lagoon. They showed me the *banca* made out of a log about 15 feet long and 2 feet wide. So far, so good. They hid me beside the trail, while they sought the boatmen.

Things were going too well. It was not long before the boatmen arrived. Instead of suggesting that we get moving at once, which would have been my preference, they squatted in front of me and started to haggle about the price of the ride. This can become very frustrating for anyone in a hurry, especially when a delay of only a few minutes could cause a disaster. Not only was it important to leave ahead of the Japanese patrols, but I wanted to make the trip to the island under cover of darkness.

The boatmen wanted to be as well paid as possible, which was understandable. Although I had learned it was a mistake to be in a hurry to open negotiations, I stated what I thought to be a fair price for the ride. The boatmen immediately threw up their hands and started enumerating the dangers and fatigue involved. They finally stated their price. While exorbitant, I was in no position to argue and after a few moments of countering to show good faith, I agreed to pay what they asked. I had not one *centavo* on me, but hoped my credit would be good on Marinduque.

Throughout the negotiations, I had been skeptical about whether the deal would ever be carried through. Now, as the last-minute preparations were being completed, I had my fingers crossed, hoping that the boatmen would not change their minds and that a Japanese patrol would not stumble onto us.

We were going to make our trip in a river *banca*. This type of boat is long and narrow, without outriggers, and is comparatively difficult to balance. The bank of the lagoon fell off sharply into the water, which made it possible to bring the *banca* right alongside the shore. I first noticed their respect for the delicacy of their craft when, with a man holding each end, they motioned me aboard. I sat down in the center of the boat. The rear boatman and I steadied the craft while the man at the stem boarded. The man at the stern got in while the two of us aboard held onto the shore.

We pushed off, gliding down a narrow inlet overgrown with thick foliage on the banks. It was impossible to see more than a few feet ahead. The Filipinos were on their knees. They neither talked nor smoked. They were handling their paddles with great care, being careful that they neither splashed, nor hit the side of the *banca*. We slid out of the inlet into the main flow of the lagoon, keeping to the middle. The boatmen were constantly watching the banks, carefully listening for any strange sound. I was crouched in the bottom of the boat, barely daring to breathe. The only light was the phosphorescent glow in the water stirred up by the motion of the paddles; the only noise was the trickle of the water off the blades as they were lifted out to take a new bite into the oily, limpid lagoon.

On we glided toward the sea suspended in an eerie world, wondering at each paddle stroke if the Japs had gotten word of our plan and were in a position ahead to spray us with bullets.

Holding to the middle of the lagoon as it broadened, our chances of being discovered from shore diminished. Tirelessly, the boatmen kept their paddles swinging, never breaking their rhythmic strokes. Now that we no longer had the swamp trees overhead, the starlight illuminated the world around us with a dull brilliance that allowed us to see quite far ahead. No words were spoken. We were concentrating on watching and listening. Thus, we passed the mouth of the lagoon and became engulfed in the broadness of the open sea, skimming away from the dangerous area where my two companions had been snared. I wondered why I was being allowed to continue. Exhausted, I fell asleep in the bottom of the *banca*, covered with some old *buri* mats.*

---

*Leaves of the buri plant are fibrous and tough, ideal for weaving into mats which can be colored with a variety of natural dyes.

When I awoke, around daybreak, the *banca* was heading into shore. The boatmen were still holding to their same rhythmic, driving strokes which were pushing the *banca* through the calm seat at a rapid clip. Apparently they had kept up the same pace throughout the night. I marveled at their stamina and examined their faces for signs of fatigue, but found little. From a combination of sign language and Tagalog, I found that the mouth of the lagoon we had passed through the night before was far to the northwest. We had spent the night following the southern coat of Luzon, and were now heading into a deserted-looking beach, still part of Luzon. It surprised me to find that we were not approaching Marinduque Island, which could be plainly seen to the south. I had thought that we would proceed directly across Tayabas Bay to the island, but the boatmen shook their heads. It was much better to continue on the way we were, making the crossing to Marinduque at the narrowest place during darkness. Getting this information had been a struggle, and was acquired mostly through the use of sign language.

It was good to get onto the beach to stretch and unbend. We were on a sandy spit covered with driftwood and fringed by fields of waving *cogan* grass, with clumps of wild banana trees growing here and there. There was no sign of animate life anywhere. The distant hills were covered with dense, green jungle. The sky was overcast, giving a gloomy aspect to the surroundings. A slight roll gave the gray water of the bay a breathing motion, like a living being.

One of the boatmen had a fire started. I busied myself gathering driftwood for him. The other boatman had pulled a cylindrical package rolled in banana leaves out of the boat and brought it over to the fire. I had taken it for granted that we would eat the normal meal of boiled rice. Instead, the boatmen pulled out of the package several handfuls of short, squatty bananas. They were thrown onto the fire as soon as a few coals had formed. He then pulled out several round cakes of native brown sugar.

The bananas, when cooked, became mealy and quite tasteless, but when eaten with a nibble of sugar cake, they were quite palatable. This was my first experience with such a breakfast and I felt well satisfied when finished. It seemed to provide a good deal of energy.

After eating, the boatmen wasted no time getting on our way again. We proceeded southeast following the shoreline, about a mile and a half out. The only sign of Japs throughout the day was their planes, which paid little attention to us. I marveled at the strength of the boatmen, both appearing well past middle age, who all through the day continued to work their paddles with practically no time taken to rest.

In the late afternoon we veered toward the shore again, where an old pier and warehouse, overgrown with tropical vines, came into view. As we drew closer, the pier and warehouse proved to be quite picturesque, with their uprights of unfinished tree trunks and sides of roughly hand-hewn boards turned white from long exposure to the elements. Where the foundation of the building or pilings of the short pier had given away, the boards sagged, somehow adding to the place's charm. They were obviously used to store and load *copra* on the small inter-island boats that plied the protected waters of the islands. We glided past the old structures, up a small lagoon, and beached near a *nipa* shack that had been hidden by the dense growth of mangroves. The shack was built on a high spit of ground. It appeared to be in the same state of decay and disrepair as the pier and warehouse.

The boatmen quickly beached the *banca*. They jumped out and beckoned me to follow. What were we doing here? Why were we stopping? My inability to communicate had kept me in a state of puzzlement throughout the trip. I had no idea of what the boatmen had on their minds. I was at their mercy, except that I was armed.

One of the boatmen called out. The door of the shack opened and two men appeared. There was an exchange of greetings as we entered. They were old friends who were happy to see each other.

Inside there was a crudely put-together table and a few gimpy chairs. Mats were spread on the wooden floor where the two men had been sleeping.

Our hosts turned out to be father and son. The son had studied English in school and spoke it well enough to let me know what was happening.

We were still on the island of Luzon, just across the Mompog Pass from the island of Marinduque. He said we were near a small *barrio* named Lobo. The boatmen had stopped for a rest and something to eat. No, there were no Japs on Marinduque, by the last report, which was no more than a day old.

The group started a fire. The stove was a sandbox with a few stones to support a pot above the fire. While the boy and I talked, the three men kept up a constant, staccato exchange of words. For all their exertions, the boatmen were in good humor, helping with the fire and rice. They were telling of my escape.

"You are lucky," the boy told me. "That area where the Japs found you, are many people who call themselves *Makapiles.* They are not loyal to the Americans. They could have been the ones who told the Japs that you were in the *barrio* of Antimonan."

We spent the rest of the day and part of the night there, eating, resting, and talking about the war. I was told that it was a comparatively short distance from where we were to Marinduque Island. The boatmen wanted to cross this stretch of deep water during darkness, to diminish the chance of being picked up by a Japanese launch.

Shortly before midnight we pushed off again, this time on our last leg to an island that, as far as any of my companions or their friends knew was not occupied by the Japs. This was hard for me to believe.

At dawn we were entering the small harbor of the town of Santa Cruz, located on the northeast coast of Marinduque Island. Along the shoreline, the townspeople could be seen performing the normal early morning chores that go on around a small fishing village. I was scanning the coastline for any sign that might disclose the presence of Japanese. Closer in, we passed a *banca* full of fishermen.

"*Myron Japon ditto?*" we asked.

"*Voila,*" was the answer. "There are no Japanese here."

Chapter 19

I had a strange feeling as we stepped ashore. Here was a tiny area that had been practically unchanged by the now more than two-month-old war that had caused so much anguish, terror, and suffering throughout other parts of the islands.

I had noticed that the majority of Filipinos with whom I had come in contact seldom worried about anything that did not have a direct affect on them at that moment. This impressed me again as I saw the carefree, happy faces of the group gathered around to have a look at the strange-looking American. There was a bit of good-natured fun being poked at me, which I did not understand until I started to take an account of my appearance. I had not had a haircut or shave for two months, which I'm sure gave me the appearance of a shaggy dog. I was barefooted and my shirt and trousers were ill-fitting and ragged.

The boatmen and I started out for the municipal building to find the mayor, the chattering crowd falling in behind. The eternal grapevine had warned the mayor of our arrival, and he came down from his office to greet me on the street.

After he had notified the Philippine Constabulary in the town of Boac on the western coast of my presence and ordered something to eat, we started talking about Luzon and the Japs. He felt that the enemy might come to Marinduque at any time; he couldn't say why they had not come long before. He hoped he would do the right thing when they arrived. We talked on and on while I gorged myself on hot coffee and an enormous egg sandwich prepared to my specifications: a half-dozen fried eggs stuffed between two halves of a loaf of bread. After that I was given a bottle of beer, some Filipino cigarettes, and a pair of sneakers. The mayor agreed to pay the boatmen the amount I had bargained for, though he said it was far too much. I signed a chit for the amount.

A lieutenant of the Constabulary arrived from Boac around noon. He was tall for a Filipino, nice looking, and spoke English well. He wanted me to go with him to Boac, where I could stay in their barracks. After seeing that the boatmen were paid and saying goodbye to the mayor, we took the road for Boac in an old, beat-up station wagon. It was great to ride through the beautiful countryside, relaxed, and not wondering at each turn in the road if someone was going to shoot at us. The lieutenant drove and I sat next to him in the front. Like the mayor, he wanted to know all about Luzon and the Japs. He was obviously worried how the small detachment of Philippine Constabulary at Boac could prevent the Japs from landing. He went on to tell me their plans, with their limited means. He ended by saying, "but we must fight." And then he went into a long silence. His face took on a worried, strained look as he appeared to be mulling over the problem for the hundredth time, anticipating the final outcome. I did not envy him.

Most of the area that we were driving through was covered with ripening sugar cane. At intervals, along the road, were small mills grinding the juice from the cane stalks and boiling it down to make brown sugar cakes.

Each little mill we passed made my mouth water. Soon, I had developed a craving for one of those sugar cakes and a bite of juicy cane. The lieutenant, sensing this, said he thought we ought to stop to have a look at one of the mills.

The method was crude, but interesting. The grinding mill was made of two large stones, one on top of the other. The top stone, the smaller of the two, was formed convexly to fit into the cavity of the lower stone. The top stone had a heavy pole set vertically out of its center. To this vertical pole was attached a stout horizontal one that, fastened to the neck of a *carabao* (water buffalo) with a yoke, supplied the power for the mill. The *carabao*'s job was to walk around and around the mill in a circle of not more than ten feet in radius, thus rotating the top stone. It was a truly monotonous job, but the beasts were well suited to it. The stalks of cane were forced between the stones and were almost immediately ground to shreds. The juice of the cane drained off the side of the lower stone into a basin. From this basin, the juice flowed a short distance downhill, by way of a bamboo tube buried beneath the path of the *carabao*, into a large, metal holding vat. Below this vat, raised off the ground by three or four stones, was another metal container filled with boiling juice, with a fire roaring beneath it. Next to this vat were a series of shelves holding circular molds, into which the hot juice, boiled down to the proper consistency, was hand-poured by ladle to harden. Each factory was covered by a shelter of *nipa* leaves which the women laborers from the sun of the hot season.

I ate three of the hard sugar cakes that were each about three inches in diameter and a half-inch thick, and got into the car chewing on a long stalk of cane. I felt a bit squeamish, but the satisfaction of getting enough palatable food to eat compensated for the discomfort.

Boac, the capitol of Marinduque Province, turned out to be a good-sized town with its fair share of western-type buildings. The Philippine Constabulary barracks were built on a small hill overlooking the town. They were the same tropical, wooden type we had at Fort Stotsenburg for the Scouts. The area and buildings were well kept and the few men we passed looked smart and alert.

The commanding officer, an elderly captain, was a bit startled at my appearance. He was not a very communicative soul and seemed quite depressed. As we talked, I learned why. He had about 40 soldiers to protect the whole island of Marinduque and no artillery or tanks. There wasn't much ammunition for the small arms his men did have, either. He had lost contact with his commanding officer who was on the island of Luzon and who was his sole source of supply. Nor had he money with which to pay and feed his command. His main concern, however, was how to comply with the last orders he had received, which were to repel Japanese Imperial Army landings on Marinduque.

He had the usual questions about the war on Luzon and the Japs, but we did talk a little about the 26th Cavalry Regiment. We had mutual friends at Stotsenburg. He told me I was welcome to stay as long as I pleased. He arranged a bed for me in the apartment of the lieutenant who had picked me up at Santa Cruz. I bathed, shaved, and had a haircut.

I spent five days on Marinduque, luxuriating in my freedom from the constant threat of running into Japs. The town tailor volunteered to make me a suit of clothes. The cloth was of the texture and pattern used to dress convicts in our better prisons and of about the same cut. Although I felt conspicuous and uncomfortable wearing it, the thought kept going through my mind, "beggars could not be choosers."

The people of Marinduque treated me royally. I attended gatherings and parties given by the townsfolk. Everyone seemed to attempt to be especially friendly. While I stuffed myself every time I was exposed to food, I could not seem to get enough to eat. I suspected I had been starving on rice and boiled vegetables. Also, I was so wound up from being on the alert for so long that it seemed impossible to relax, even though I knew there was no danger on the island.

Although the garrison had lost contact with its higher headquarters on Luzon, which had probably been overrun by the Japs, it still had radio communication with Corregidor. Several messages were sent there reporting my presence on Marinduque and requesting orders for me. While receipt of the messages was acknowledged, there was never a reply.

It was rumored that inter-island boats were stopping at towns along the eastern coast of Mindoro Island, picking up supplies to be taken to Corregidor. I decided to try to catch a ride with one of these boats.

The commander of the Marinduque garrison was not pleased to hear of my leaving. He insisted that I remain on the island. I sensed that he wanted to have someone, later on, to help explain his problems and his actions when a Jap landing on Marinduque occurred. I told him that my staying would probably do him more harm than good in the long run, as Americans were considered as the common enemy of all Asians. They might accuse him of giving aid and comfort to the enemy. With that in mind, he agreed that I should leave.

I left with only one regret—the loss of my watch. I had managed to hold onto it and keep it running all the way down Luzon. It had become part of me during the struggle to survive. One morning, I left it on a dresser in my room, where I had placed it the night before. When I returned, it was gone. The incident stayed with me because of my attachment to the watch and the fact that I had known of no thievery among the Scouts.

Before dawn on 17 February 1942, I boarded a small *batile* (a native sailing boat) bound for the town of Pinamilaya, on the eastern coast of Mindoro Island. Pinamilaya is about 35 miles from the city of Boac over open water, which I hoped would be free of Japanese launches or patrol craft.

The only incident of interest on this trip had to do with a *carabao*. In the hold of the boat was a lone *carabao* that must have weighed 900 or 1,000 pounds. The hatch into the hold was too small for the animal to get through. Even if that had been possible, it would have taken an enormous hoist to lower it without injury. I was sure no such equipment existed in the islands, outside the docks of Manila Bay. There was no one on board who could give a viable explanation for the *carabao*'s presence. To this day, it is a mystery why and how that *carabao* got where it was. My conclusion was that it was lowered into the hold when very young, and it was easier to leave it there than to remove it.

On arrival in Pinamilaya, I went to the Philippine Constabulary headquarters where I was welcomed by its commander, Major Ruffi. His attitude was altogether different from that of the Marinduque commander. Major Ruffi had a definite plan, which was to fall back into the mountains when the Japs appeared, and from there to carry on a guerrilla campaign until help from the States arrived. He had packed food and ammunition back to his alternate headquarters. He hoped that a network of guards, who watched the beaches night and day, would give him sufficient warning to evacuate his present garrison and get back to his new positions in good order.

He spoke of the *Bukidnons,* the wild tribes in the mountains, who sometimes stole his food. These people had lighter complexions and higher cheekbones than the Malays of the valleys. He also spoke of the little wild and vicious buffalo called *tamarau* that existed only on the island of Mindoro.

According to reports, the only Japs on Mindoro Island at the time were on its southern tip, near the town of San Jose. They had occupied an American airfield near the town.

I was not able to verify the rumor that the inter-island boats were sailing for Corregidor from Mindoro. I concluded that either it was not happening, or it was a very closely-held secret. According to Major Ruffi, however, there was a Philippine Army division commanded by Americans on the island of Panay. As far as he knew, that island had not yet been invaded by the Japs. With chances of getting to Corregidor or Bataan seeming to dwindle, I decided to try to get to Panay.

After three days with the Constabulary in Pinamilaya, I hopped a truck going south to the town of Bongabong. There I caught a sailing boat bound for Panay.

Filipino boatmen had periodically sighted Japanese launches off the eastern coast of Mindoro. I was assured, however, that they would not bother to stop us. We sailed early in the morning and by noon were becalmed in the strait between Mindoro and Tablas Islands. The sea looked like a great piece of glass. The tropical sun was beating down with all its force. I was hot and uncomfortable, sweating like a horse, very much tempted to jump overboard to cool off, but the occasional sighting of a shark made me change my mind.

This was one of the few times I had a good look at a giant ray. It seemed to be playing, surfacing occasionally near our boat, its blackish, bat-like wings flapping and splashing on top of the water. It looked to measure 10 to 12 feet between wing tips and was probably 8 feet long.

The wind finally picked up out of the north. By early afternoon we were entering the little bay of the *barrio* of Baruanga on the northwestern tip of the island of Panay. It was 22 February 1942, Washington's birthday. As we drew near the shoreline, the scene made a lasting impression on my mind. The deep blue, calm of the sea, the pale blue sky, the long white beach strewn with small fishing boats and fringed with tall, waving, coconut palms was a picture of serenity. There were people walking along the shore, but none in Jap uniforms. The crew had lowered the sail as we glided toward a dilapidated bamboo and plank pier.

Chapter 20

Several Filipinos, wearing cotton shorts and loosely-fitting, sleeveless palm-fiber shirts, were congregated on the broken-down pier as we came alongside. They were bareheaded, barefooted, and dirty. Each carried a large bolo, sheathed in a wooden scabbard, tied to his waist with a twisted fiber chord.

These men were part of the Home Guard of the island of Panay. Their job included watching the shores. They questioned the crew and passengers for some time before we were allowed to go ashore. The Home Guard reported that there were no Japanese on Panay. There were, however, American and Filipino soldiers on the island, which I had hoped for and really expected. I soon found, however, that there were no soldiers in the *barrio* of Baruanga and no telephone.

Baruanga was typical fishing *barrio*: there was a plaza with its statue, a marketplace, and its share of *nipa* huts scattered about. Its few roads or lanes were unpaved, dry at this time of year, and full of ruts, a holdover from the rainy season. Pigs, dogs, chickens, and naked children ran free. A few adults were in evidence on the streets or hanging out of the windows of their huts. The men wore nothing but shorts. As on Luzon, the women were dressed in long, colorful skirts and pretty *pina*-cloth blouses with puffed sleeves. Their hair was usually worn long and twisted into a roll on top of their heads.

The *barrio* had a bus terminal, but no bus was scheduled to leave for the interior until early the next morning. There was no place to sleep, no place to eat, not even a store.

The chief of police came to my rescue. Wearing a non-descript uniform, he was middle-aged and wore a shifty look on his face. I could tell he was of the bureaucracy, as he wore shoes and a hat. He took me to his home, where we had a drink of *tuba* (the mild alcoholic drink made from the flower of the coconut palm) and a fine lunch.

With the afternoon free, I took a nap on the chief's floor, cleaned my pistol, and took a stroll through the *barrio* and along the waterfront. Except for the Home Guard and some of the *barrio* officials, few persons seemed aware that there was a war.

Early in the evening, the chief returned from his office with a large bamboo tube of *tuba* and two friends. I had been sitting at the table in his parlor, watching the sunset. After a few glasses of *tuba,* the chief and his friends started an ever-increasing volume of probing questions about my past. What was I doing in the Philippines? How long had I been here? Why had I come to Panay? Where was my home in the States?

It slowly dawned on me that I was under suspicion of being a German spy. There had been a few instances of Germans being picked up on Luzon, but I never imagined I would be suspected of being one. The situation seemed preposterous. So for the fun of it, I played along with my host and friends, bringing them slowly to the belief that I was suspect.

By the time dinner was over, my companions had concluded that something must be done about me. The three men excused themselves, and I could hear rumblings of their drunken council being held in the next room. They were voting on my ancestry.

Nothing positive came from the council meeting and I went to bed early. The chief promised to wake me in time to catch the bus into the interior.

The next morning I awoke with a start. I was past 0600 and too late for the bus. The chief of police greeted me with a sheepish "good morning." He appeared to have been up for some time. Why had he not awakened me?

He was very sorry, he said; he had not understood that I wanted to be on the morning bus. I knew he was lying. He asked if I would not stay another day. It was apparent that he wanted to take credit for capturing a German spy. As far as I was concerned, the joke had gone far enough. I cursed him for being a stupid fool and stormed from his hut without breakfast, a meal I hated to miss.

Pandan, the nearest good-sized town, was about 25 miles to the southeast. I decided that it was better to start out on foot than to wait another 24 hours for the bus. I picked up a bunch of bananas along the way to stave off hunger. By late morning I had hitched a ride and arrived in Pandan before noon.

Pandan was not much more than a *barrio,* but there were stores open. The main street, while unpaved, had a few solid front stores. There were also several houses built of hard wood with corrugated tin roofs, which was a sign of wealth and prosperity. With money from the Marinduque Constabulary, for which I had signed, I bought a razor and toothbrush, as well as a meal of rice, fish, and beer. I had relished the thought of a cold beer, but the first sip of the lukewarm liquid killed the desire.

A Filipino lieutenant drove through town in a sedan during the afternoon. After some coaxing, he agreed to give me a ride to the headquarters of the division that commanded the troops on the island. He was skeptical at first when he saw my street cleaner's suit and learned that I had no identification.

The division headquarters was on the opposite side of the island, through two provinces at a distance of nearly 93 miles. We took the road around the north end of the island. Every 6 to 10 miles we were slowed by roadblocks. They were primitive, but effective. They consisted of 15 to 20 large logs laid 20 feet apart, perpendicular to the flow of traffic, and firmly secured to the roadway. They alternately protruded across two-thirds of the road, forcing vehicles to slow to a crawl while they zigzagged around the end of each log.

Most of the road around the north end of the island was on the coastal plain close to the sea, winding through coconut groves. Soldiers were occasionally seen working on bridges along the way. The lieutenant told me they were preparing them for demolition. At one point, we passed a unit motor pool that looked more like a junkyard than a military installation.

The troops we passed were not an impressive lot. They brought back memories of experiences on Luzon. The more I spoke with the lieutenant, the more it became evident that he cared little for God, country, or anything else. I wondered what I was getting into.

As we went south into Iloilo Province, the mountainous Aklan area of Capiz Province gave way to plains covered with rice paddies interspersed with banana groves.

We arrived at the Philippine Army 61st Division Headquarters in late afternoon. It was located near the small *barrio* of Misi on the eastern side of the main mountain range at about the center of the island. It was well concealed in a bamboo thicket that covered a large hill. Soldiers of the division had done an excellent job of camouflage and dispersion within the headquarters area. Small bamboo shacks roofed with *nipa* housed the various elements of division headquarters. Tall bamboos, meeting at the top, concealed the shacks and pathways connecting them. The uncontrolled activity outside the headquarters area, however, undoubtedly gave its location away.

Brigadier General Bradford G. Chynoweth, formerly the commander of the unit, was in command of the division; Colonel Albert Christie was second in command. The division G-1 (Personnel), G-3 (Plans and Operations), and I believe the G-4 (Logistics), were Filipino officers. The G-2 (Intelligence) was an American. The preponderance of division headquarters personnel was Filipino.

I was given a royal welcome, including dinner with the division commander and members of his staff. It was a pleasant experience. We had drinks, an excellent chicken dinner, and American cigarettes.

I also caught up on the news. The Russians were barely holding their own. The United States was now engaged in total mobilization, including conscription and mass manufacture of military materiel. It appeared the Pacific might come second to Europe in priority, which would mean a long wait before we could expect help in the Philippines. The Japs had occupied the islands to the north of Australia, and Australia could be next. The fall of Bataan and Corregidor was only a matter of time.

There was a good bit of interest in my experiences since leaving Fort Stotsenburg. The talk went far into the night. I made only one *faux pas* during the evening. As was our habit, I made reference to white officers, in contrast to those of Filipino blood. I was later informed that this was now taboo. We were all now clearly equal members on a single team.

The following morning, I attended a briefing on the division and the situation on Panay. Panay Island is shaped like a triangle, its base is to the west, its apex to the east. Running parallel to the base, on a north-south axis along the western coast of the island is a high, rugged, heavily-wooded mountain range. Almost throughout, these mountains are inaccessible to anything except a man on foot. On the eastern side of this range, the country consists largely of plains that become hilly in the northern part. The island is divided into three provinces: Antique Province takes in nearly the entire western coast; Capiz, the northern coast; and Iloilo, the eastern and southern coasts. All of these provinces have a share of the mountain range.

The 61st Division, with the mission to defend the island of Panay, consisted of three infantry regiments, plus division special troops. Two of these regiments were provisional: the 64th and 65th, which had been activated after the loss of the two original regiments. The original 61st and 62nd Regiments had been sent to Mindanao, and with them, the 61st Field Artillery Regiment. An infantry regiment defended each of the three provinces. The 64th and the 65th did not have enough rifles to arm its men. In the entire division, there were probably no more than 30 machine guns and no mortars. The division possessed an extremely limited amount of small arms ammunition. Hand grenades were being manufactured in local foundries.

Artillery, mortars, machine guns, and rifles, plus ammunition and other needed equipment scheduled for Panay had reportedly gone down with a ship sunk in Manila Bay. Because of this serious lack of equipment and ammunition, the division commander had decided that it would be impossible to repel landings on the island, but he believed that by falling back into the mountains when the Japs arrived, it would be practicable to carry on guerrilla operations. If and when the Japs invaded the island, each of the regiments was to destroy everything that might be useful to the enemy. They would then fight delaying actions back into the mountains and carry on an insurgency until American forces could retake the island.

Division, regimental, battalion, and company alternate command posts were established in the mountains, with six months' supply of food, medicine, and some ammunition. *Bodegas* (storehouses) had been built of logs, bamboo, and *nipa* to hold the supplies. They were hidden, the paths into them camouflaged and guarded night and day. These supplies were to remain untouched until absolutely needed. They had been packed to the *bodegas* at night to reduce the chances of their being discovered by enemy planes, which were often overhead.

Even though the civilian Home Guard patrolled the coastline, it was necessary for the army to man observation posts at critical points and operate a system of telephones to report information to regimental and division headquarters.

Seven airfields were under construction. A few were large enough for B-17 bombers to land and take off. They were located primarily in Iloilo Province. American engineers from the Masbate gold mines, who had been inducted into the army, were in charge of the airfield construction.

Filipino civilians of service age, not yet inducted, were being trained in the hope there would be arms for them if reinforcements should arrive from the United States.

There was also the work of improving defensive positions, roadblocks, and the placement of demolitions to aid in the delaying actions planned while withdrawing to the mountains. It was a continuous job that never seemed completed. All these activities required a lot of manpower and left little time for training.

The briefing left me with the impression that everyone was striving to picture the 61st as a viable division despite terrific inadequacies in training and equipment. Underneath, there was really very little optimism for the future of Panay.

Chapter 21

I was assigned to the 63rd Infantry Regiment, the only original regiment of the division left on Panay. It was headquartered near the *barrio* of Janiuay, between Misi and Iloilo City to the south.

Lieutenant Colonel Fitzpatrick, regimental commander of the 63rd, was of medium build and sandy complexion, with a pleasant face, and an affable manner. He had recently been called to active duty and, in his words, "Shanghaied" to the Philippines. His demeanor was that of a man resigned to his fate, but not happily so.

Regimental headquarters was in the local school building augmented by several small bamboo shacks covered with *nipa*. Except for Colonel Fitzpatrick, his executive officer (a pleasant, slow-moving fellow from New Orleans), and one or two other American staff officers, personnel of regimental headquarters consisted of Filipinos, none of whom were very impressive. An air of hopelessness seemed to pervade the headquarters.

I had arrived, looking and feeling like a scarecrow, dressed in my street cleaner's suit. Primarily to get me out of his sight, and secondly, to get some uniforms, Colonel Fitz sent me to Iloilo City for a few days. Iloilo City was dusty, rundown, and hot. Before the war the city had been considered one of the most beautiful spots in the Visayan Islands. Now, with most of its important people evacuated into the hills, many of its stores and other activities had closed down. There was little incentive for what was left of the city government to keep things up.

I was to stay at the headquarters of one of the three infantry battalions of the 63rd which was stationed in the vicinity of Iloilo City. Major Bickerton commanded the battalion. I had known him as a second lieutenant a few months before at Fort Stotsenburg. He had been sent to Panay on Philippine Army duty in October or November of 1941. His headquarters was in an old two-story, brick school building on the northern outskirts of the city. Bickerton was the only American officer in the battalion. Living with him were two English civilians, whose reasons for being there, or usefulness, I was unable to determine.

It took a few days to finish my uniforms. In the meantime, I was able to locate a pair of sneakers that fit, and had a pair of boots made of *carabao* hide by the "best cobbler in town." I planned to save the boots for use in the mountains after the Japs invaded the island.

The first thing I did after receiving my new uniforms was to burn the street cleaner's suit. Colonel Fitzpatrick had loaned me some scrip to pay for the uniforms. Scrip, like paper money, was a temporary promissory note printed by authorized representatives of the US government. Practically all payments and transactions were then being made in scrip.

There were two things I especially remember about my short stay in Iloilo City. The first was the shower maintained by the division. I found an excuse to use it on a daily basis. The second was the gift of a steel helmet and a .45 caliber revolver from a Navy captain waiting to catch a plane for Australia. I met him in the shower. He thought I might have more use for these items than he.

I left the Iloilo headquarters with a vivid impression of the deplorable state of discipline in the 3rd Battalion. I was happy to be returning north.

American officers of the 63rd lived in a series of rooms constructed of bamboo and *nipa*, hidden in a large growth of bamboo; platforms of bamboo strips, which had some flexibility, served as beds. The mess, with a place to wash, was in a nearby shack. The latrine was an outhouse, some distance away.

Colonel Fitzpatrick assigned me as the Regimental S-3 (Operations Officer). He and his staff provided me a very comprehensive briefing on the status of the regiment. In essence, it was much the same as that received at division headquarters. Iloilo Province, being the least mountainous and most populated, would be the Japs' most likely initial target. The regiment had nearly all its authorized rifles, Browning Automatic Rifles, and water-cooled heavy machine guns. All the .30-caliber ammunition allocated for training had been fired prior to my arrival. As with the rest of the Philippine Army, the issue rifle was the WWI-vintage M1917 Enfield. There was still a great deal of .45-caliber ammunition available, but the only weapon on the island that fired it was the pistol carried only by the officers and a few non-commissioned officers.

With personnel requirements for coast watching, preparation of delaying positions, and the completion of alternate command post and supply bases in the mountains, there had been little time for training. Colonel Fitzpatrick recognized the need to accomplish these various tasks, yet was quite concerned about the lack of training, especially discipline. Would the young soldiers and officers hold up under the stress of combat? They had not on Luzon.

It was made clear to me that the American officers, while responsible for the success or failure of those under them, actually had no authority or command status over any Filipino. They were there as instructors only.

My first job was to set up a series of squad, platoon, and company tests. To turn out a squad for testing was a major effort, sometimes an impossibility. There were too many other activities going on which took precedence. When a squad turned out to be tested, it was usually made up of men from several different squads who had never trained together. The same held for platoons and companies. The testing soon died a natural death, but the effort told us clearly where we stood. The weaknesses were a lack of cohesion, pride, and training within units, and a terrible lack of discipline. The meaning of the terms "morale" and *esprit de corps* were practically unknown.

Prior to mobilization, the troops were supposed to have had a five-month period of basic training. Some received it, some did not. For those who had received the training, there was little evidence of its effectiveness. (I was reminded of the

Igorots who had joined us in Baguio.) How the non-commissioned officers were selected and trained prior to mobilization, I could never determine, but whatever the system, the product was not the best. The majority of junior officers had earned commissions through the Philippine Reserve Officers Training Corps Program; they were intelligent, well educated, and spoke English, but they had little military training or interest in being soldiers. Many lacked a feeling of nationalism and pride in their country.

MacArthur's organizations and concept of the Philippine Army looked good on paper, but even he could not wave a wand and say the magic word—"Mobilize"—and have a combat-ready army.

In June 1941, plans were getting underway to mobilize the Philippine Army, an army that up until then existed mostly on paper. Part of the army was mobilized in September and October 1941, another part in November, and still another in December. Most of the remainder was mobilized after the war started.

The Philippine Army consisted essentially of untrained civilians, partially equipped with WWI-vintage equipment. To compound the problem, leadership and experience in the higher echelons of command were badly wanting. Unit cohesion and *esprit de corps* in the 61st Division were gravely deficient.

There is little wonder that many of these units, thrown into combat soon after mobilization to meet the full force of the Japanese attacks on Luzon, performed as they did.

Soon after my arrival in the 63rd Infantry Regiment, I went to the pistol range to observe the firing. My pistol had not been fired since shooting the cow in the hills to the north of Montalban, and I thought it might be well to see how it functioned. At 25 yards, slow fire, I put six rounds into the bulls-eye. This surprised me as much as those standing around. The argument that the Army .45-caliber automatic was not dependable and accurate lost a lot of ground that day.

I had little use for the heavy, cumbersome Enfield that I had carried all the way down Luzon. I was well acquainted with the Springfield '03, but was unable to find one on the island. During my search, however, I found a .300 Savage, a light, handy, bolt-action rifle which I quickly adopted.

As time wore on, Japanese activity in the offshore waters gradually increased. Regimental headquarters was on the alert day and night with reports from the coast-watchers. While as yet there was no report of any attempted landing, it was obvious that the Japs were making preparations. We assumed that when the landings did come, they would be in force as on Luzon, and there would be little chance of stopping them. We did not have one piece of artillery on the island.

Japanese bombing and strafing on various parts of the island were becoming almost daily occurrences. Anticipation of the landings, which from day to day never came, was causing a chronic case of jitters in many. Anyone who left headquarters, even temporarily, did so with his weapons and field equipment. No one thought of going to sleep without his baggage ready to grab upon awakening.

Despite all this, much was being accomplished. There was still the faint hope that Uncle Sam would get help to the islands before the Japs had seized everything.

We believed that our business-like and confident show of preparedness kept the Japs out of the Visayan Islands until they could spare a force large enough to conduct a successful invasion.

One day, during the hot season, a British subject who was a long-time resident of Iloilo City hiked with me out of the mountains into the hot, dusty town. The humidity was such that our clothes were drenched with perspiration. I remarked to my friend that I would give anything for a refreshing drink. He said he had just the thing as soon as we got to his house.

"We would have a gin and bitters, a most refreshing drink."

I visualized the tall, cool, quinine-water drink served at the Fort Stotsenburg Officers' Mess. When we arrived at his house, we entered a very uninteresting, hot, stuffy room where I sat while he went to the rear to prepare our drinks. After an overly long wait, he came forth with a tall glass in each hand, passing me one. In the bottom was about a half-inch of warm gin to which a few drops of Angostura bitters had been added. The concoction, though seemingly relished by my host, went a long way from refreshing me.

I also became acquainted with Hank Meider, an American civilian pilot who lived in Iloilo City. When the war broke out, he applied to the Army for a job. He was accepted and became chief of the 61st Division's one-man air force. His plane was an old, totally outdated biplane. Despite that, his reconnaissance capability proved to be very useful to us.

During the entire spring, while Americans and Filipinos held the southern islands, our ports and air bases were used to push supplies into Bataan and Corregidor, and to take out the wounded. I often wondered how this activity had completely escaped me while on Mindoro Island.

One day I learned that some wounded had been brought down from Bataan and that among them were a few Scouts out of the 26th Cavalry Regiment. I went to see them. They were a pathetic looking sight. Only men who had no chance of being useful for service again had been evacuated—those with sight gone, limbs missing, or minds deeply affected by battle fatigue.

There was one man from Troop A of the 26th whom I had known well. He did not remember me or what had happened to him during the past months or how he had gotten where he was. He had a look in his eyes like that of a severely-punished animal.

Another Scout of the 26th, from Machine Gun Troop, had lost a leg, but he did not seem to be at all bothered by it. He was in a fine state of mind. I questioned him about the Regiment and officers in it, but he knew very little that had happened outside his own troop. He said that there had not been time to do anything other than take care of his gun, his horses, and himself from northern Luzon down to Bataan. Upon reaching Bataan, he was wounded and taken to a hospital and after that saw no more of his troop.

Chapter 22

Early in March, the division commander issued orders for each regiment to activate horse units. As I was the only cavalry officer available, I inherited the job in addition to my S-3 duties.

Due to the widely varying terrain in each regiment's area of operations, each regimental commander was allowed to decide exactly how to organize the new units. The terrain of Iloilo Province was flat or rolling up to the mountains, with very few roads. It was ideal country for the use of horses. In some places, there was a distance of 12 to 18 miles from the alternate command posts in the mountains to the main roads and towns, which were considered likely to be occupied by the enemy. Units that could conduct reconnaissance over these distances would be useful. There would also be requirements for units that could conduct ambushes. Thus, mobility and firepower were key characteristics for units that would be able to get into place quickly, hit their targets, and get out just as fast. These are classic cavalry missions.

In addition, there was a need for pack animals to assist foot units in transporting supplies and equipment when operating in the rugged foothill country.

Once it was determined that the horse could assist in these missions, it became my job to create the units that could execute them. Lieutenant Trujillo, a veterinary officer, and Lieutenant Suarez, who had some cavalry training, were assigned to help me.

The native pony averages 12 to 13 hands. He is usually short-coupled, heavy-barreled, and has endurance beyond belief, considering the feed he gets. With a moderate amount of grass and a little rice bran, he can carry a 150-pound man over hilly terrain day after day. Few native ponies were gelded, and it appeared that the stallion had much more endurance than the mare. The drawback was that the stallions would fight each other, and usually went crazy when a mare was around. Despite this, Colonel Fitzpatrick decided to use stallions in the 63rd Infantry Regiment. A location was selected for stables and their construction started. They were made of bamboo frame covered with *nipa*. Each stallion had to have a separate stall that had to be strong enough to withstand his habitual, rambunctious pulling and kicking.

Volunteers from the three battalions, who could ride and wanted to be cavalrymen, were assigned to the unit. While Suarez and the recruits worked on the stables, Trujillo and I started to scour the countryside for suitable mounts. Sine the army had taken most of the automobiles and had a monopoly on the alcohol that fueled them, most of the civilian population had become largely dependent on ponies for transportation. As a result, there were only enough suitable animals available in the regiment's sector on Panay to mount one platoon of cavalry and provide a few pack animals.

A platoon of cavalry was organized and started to train in both extended and close-order drill. Native saddles, bridles, and packs were used initially to get things moving.

Feed for the ponies consisted of a native grass that was trucked in daily. Each pony had his fill three times a day. Hulls from the rice mills made a nourishing bran. The troopers fed a double handful to each pony morning and night after flavoring the bran with sugar or syrup, a pinch of salt, and a tablespoon of coconut meal mixed with enough water to make a firm mash. The ponies seemed to thrive on the diet.

As experience with the stallions increased, the decision to use them became more and more questionable. When they weren't kicking and biting each other, they turned on the men, causing disagreeable wounds and eventual sores. Stables were often kicked asunder and a loose stallion was a danger to anything in its path.

Ready-made shoes, small enough for the native ponies, were purchased, and a farrier located. Only the front hooves were shod.

Curb bits to fit the ponies' mouths were available. Native leather workers were hired to complete the bridle.

The native riding saddle was constructed on the order of the American McClellan, with a wooden tree that was usually uncovered and splintery. Stirrup straps and cinches were made of hemp rope, rougher than sandpaper. Stirrups were made of wood. We covered the saddles with *carabao* hide and replaced the hemp stirrup straps and cinches with the same leather. Burlap sacks were the best we could come up with for saddle blankets and, surprisingly enough, proved quite satisfactory.

The big problem was to come up with a workable packsaddle. Native packsaddles were useless for our purpose and there was no information available on the Phillips packsaddle that was in general use in the US Army.

With the help of foundry men, I undertook to make from memory, a small version of the Phillips Packsaddle that would fit the native pony. With steel, one-eighth by one-half inch, a frame was made to duplicate the form of the Phillips saddle. Then, 12-by-14-inch pads were screwed onto the insides of the frame. The base of the pad was made of stout leather with a canvas pocket sewn onto it. Native *kapok* (a mass of silky fibers from the *ceiba* tree used as padding) was stuffed into the pocket and held in place by quilting. When stuffed, the pad was three inches thick, with leather against the steel frame and canvas toward the pony's back. The pad could be detached from the frame by releasing six screws. There was an opening in the leather back, through which kapok could be added or removed, to make the saddle fit. Two cinches, a breast strap, and a crupper (loop behind the horse's tail) completed the harness. The frame was rigged so that loads could either be lashed or hooked onto it. Again burlap sacks were used as saddle blankets.

Each cavalryman carried a rifle over his shoulder, a long bolo on his belt, and a light blanket with uncooked rice and a mess kit around his middle. A small sack of dry mash was carried on the cantle of the saddle. In the field, the mash was fed off the saddle blanket; the pony foraged his own grass.

To increase the cavalry rifle squads' firepower, carriers for Browning Automatic Rifles were constructed for the lead horses. Besides the rifle on the center of the pack saddle, six magazines of .30-caliber ammunition were carried on each side.

Carriers were also constructed for lead horses for the dismounted heavy machine gunners. The animals packed a gun, tripod, water can, and a box of ammunition. When loaded, the pony could walk for as long as a man could lead him. Another type of carrier was constructed to carry three boxes of linked .30-caliber ammunition for the heavy machine-guns on each side. Each machine-gun squad had, in addition to the two lead horses, a pack pony that carried extra food and fodder. This arrangement, which caused a slight reorganization in the machine-gun squads, made them self-sustaining for two to three days.

By the end of March, the horse platoon was shaping up. Enough native saddles and bridles had been modified to go around. The men were handling their mounts better, the stallions were calming down, and basic drills were becoming second nature to both. Several of the packsaddles had been completed and were in service.

Colonel Fitzpatrick wanted to activate a horse platoon for each battalion. He also wanted a good many more pack animals than we now had. Since no more ponies were available on Panay, the island of Negros was selected as the best nearby source.

Necessary arrangements were made with the commander of the Negros. Trujillo and I left Iloilo City after dark one evening during the last days of March. We sailed on a small launch that had been fitted with stalls. The trip was made at night to avoid the ever-increasing enemy planes and warships that were now seen regularly in Visayan waters.

Just before we sailed, I was handed orders promoting me to captain. Colonel Fitzpatrick had recommended my promotion to major a month before, but the division commander refused to approve two promotions at once. Ironically, I learned later that some months before, I had already been promoted to captain by the War Department.

Landing near the town of Bacolod, on the western coast of Negros, we spent the remainder of the night in the quarters of some quartermaster officers.

The next day we went inland to contact the commanding officer of the forces of the Negros. He had fewer troops and fewer arms and ammunition that we did on Panay. Many of his men were armed with .22-caliber rifles, shotguns, and *palteks* (a native homemade shotgun with a length of plumbing pipe for a barrel). Some of his companies were armed only with bolos. Like the Panay garrison, there was no artillery or mortars. His most prized weapons consisted of a few scout cars with machine guns mounted on them. They had been made bulletproof, according to the commander, by adding an additional plate of iron six inches out from the frame. The space between was stuffed with *begas* (the crushed fibrous stalks of sugar cane). The armored scout cars on shore patrols had reportedly driven off Japanese launches attempting to land.

The plan for the Negros defense was much the same as that for Panay. When the Japs landed, the commander intended to fall back into the mountains and from there would carry on guerrilla warfare. He felt that Negros would be invaded any day; already Japanese warships had been shelling the eastern coastal towns.

The farms had been warned of our coming. They were ready and prepared for us. The ponies shown were usually the culls. When I refused to purchase them, I was usually asked to return the following day. The owner would have better-looking animals to show me that were now in pasture. Sometimes I would be presented with the same "crow baits" the second day, but sometimes there would be good stock. This procedure of going back and forth and finally haggling over prices was very time consuming, however.

The last farm on my list was halfway down the eastern coast. Arriving there one afternoon, unable to raise anyone at the main house, I drove down to what looked to be the stables. Finding no one there, I had just started to look around when a black sedan raced up, coming to a skidding stop in a cloud of dust.

From the car stepped an apparition, a most beautiful Filipina. She was dressed in a lavender silk pantsuit that subtly enhanced her attractiveness. She strode toward me with a firm, self-possessed walk.

"We've been expecting you," she said, after introducing herself. "You have come to maybe take some of our ponies."

"Yes," I answered and extended my hand to grasp hers. "I'm Captain Whitehead."

I was spellbound. She had the fine features of the Spanish aristocracy, the creamy complexion of the *mestiza*, with dark eyes, black hair, and a tinge of rouge on her full lips.

"Before we look at the ponies," she said, "let's go to the house for a refreshment. You must be tired."

I went along with this thinking, "Here we go again. We'll sit in the house while she hides her best animals."

The afternoon was spent looking at the ponies she wanted to sell paraded around in a ring. I rode some of them, thinking none of them could compare to my little sorrel mare that had been killed at Fort Stotsenburg, seemingly a lifetime ago.

It was nearly dark when we finished. My hostess asked me to stay for dinner and, as it would be late, to spend the night.

In the twilight before dinner, we took a long stroll along the beach. We talked about anything that came to mind with the exuberance of two young people trying to find out all about each other. The thoughts of the war disappeared. For a while, I was in another world.

The next morning I awoke, barely able to breathe; an attack of bronchitis had come on during the night.

After a couple of days in a small hospital at the north end of the island, I was up and going again. The last of the ponies reached Bacolod before I did. In Bacolod, I heard the Japs had attempted landings on the island of Cebu, but had been driven off. Before my arrival in Bacolod, a series of explosions reportedly had been heard one night, south of the town of Dumaguete on the southeast coast of Negros. These were followed by a tremendous red glare in the heavens. Later, reports came in from fishermen near the scene, saying that an American submarine had sunk a Japanese destroyer. True or not, rumors or this sort certainly helped morale.

I returned to Panay with the last load of ponies on the night of 9 April 1942. As I was leaving the launch, the captain drew me aside and said in an apprehensive tone that he had just heard by radio that American and Filipino forces on Bataan had surrendered.

By this time, the platoon of cavalry that had been activated in early March was considered combat-ready. Modification of saddles and bridles for two more platoons of cavalry had been completed and several more packsaddles were finished. Additional soldiers from the infantry units, who had ridden and worked around ponies, had been selected to make up the new units. With the arrival of the Negros ponies, two new cavalry platoons and additional pack units were formed and equipped.

A few days after my return to Panay, we received the report that Cebu Island had been invaded. Sightings of Jap warships and transports off the coast of Panay were increasing daily. Late in the afternoon of 15 April, four enemy transports, closer than usual, were reported moving slowly off the southwestern tip of the island. It was just a matter of time now, perhaps hours, before the invasion of Panay would begin.

Chapter 23

Sometime before daylight on 16 April 1942, Japanese landing parties managed to get ashore in the vicinity of Oton, a small town west of Iloilo City.

Bickerton, the commander of the battalion garrisoned in the city, was first notified of the landing at 0600 hours. By that time, a fairly large force of enemy troops was ashore and approaching the city. A flanking movement by the Japs into the town of Jaro, a few miles north of Iloilo City, nearly succeeded in cutting off the battalion's route of withdrawal into the mountains.

At 0700 hours, our regimental staff received word of the landing. The Japanese reconnaissance planes that were already overhead and the sounds of explosions coming from the south tended to confirm the invasion report. We hoped some of the explosions signaled the destruction of highway bridges between us and Iloilo City, some 22 miles to the south of Janiuay.

We ate breakfast, dismantled camp, and turned our baggage over to the regimental supply officer for transportation into the mountains. The movement of our regimental headquarters into the mountains had been rehearsed and seemed to have gone well.

I went directly to the stables where things were not going so smoothly. Fighter planes had started strafing and dive-bombing our movements. There had been a few passes at the stables, which excited the men and, in turn, the animals. The evacuation plan called for all animals to at least carry their own equipment, but some of the more feisty stallions refused to be saddled. By overloading some animals and the trucks we had, the cavalry unit was able to get its animals, equipment, and fodder back into the mountains by nightfall.

The next morning, a few of us rode back the 9.3 miles to the stables to see if anything of value had been left behind. They were then burned, a difficult thing to do after all the work that had been put into building them. Janiuay had not yet been occupied and the roadblocks to the east and south were reportedly still intact.

I rode into Janiuay for a last look. The civilians had completely stripped the regimental headquarters, barracks, and quarters of everything they could manage to carry away. Our soldiers, resting in their trenches that covered the roadblocks outside of town, appeared to be calm and in good spirits. I had no word of what the Japs were doing. Telephone communications had been out since early the day before, and there had been no radio contact with the 3rd Battalion since the invasion. There were observation posts beyond the roadblocks, but no communications other than by runner. No thought had yet been given to employing the cavalry platoon except as a cadre to help train the newly-activated units.

Late in the afternoon, a runner from the outpost to the south of town reported dismounted Japs a little over six miles south of Janiuay, moving north. As I had been instrumental in the establishment of this roadblock, I decided to stick around and see how it worked. Where the road passed through a cut, a series of logs were strewn in a way to cause traffic to slow to a crawl. A squad of infantry with Enfields and a Browning Automatic Rifle was entrenched 100 yards to the north on the brow of the next hill. Their fire could cover the roadblock, its flanks, and the road between. I ate canned rice and fish with the soldiers and rolled up beside them for the night. I felt our security was somewhat precarious. Experience had shown that the young Filipino with a bellyful of rice had a propensity to fall asleep on guard at night. I prayed that I would not be awakened by a Jap glaring down at me.

Before daylight, the men on outpost duty came to our position, excited and out of breath, reporting the sounds of metal on metal on the road not far to the south. Everyone was awakened and put in readiness. There was to be no noise, no smoking, just listening and observing.

An hour passed. We could observe the beginning of morning dawn in the east. We could discern the logs and the crest of the hill ahead. The tension was starting to get to the young soldiers; they were nervous and jumpy.

If the Japs were coming, they should soon show. Obviously, they were not rushing headlong, taking losses as they had on Luzon.

Suddenly a bobbing head appeared through the road cut, then a pair of shoulders. Behind the first man, a second came into view. They were riding bicycles. The sergeant next to me cautioned his men to hold their fire; just over the brow of hill, the two Japs jumped off their bikes and un-slung their rifles to kneel by the side of the road. It looked as though they had only spotted the roadblock, not us in the trench. At the blink of an eye, the Japs turned and were gone back over the brow of the hill.

Not a shot had been fired. It had all happened too quickly. Now came more waiting. The soldiers were surprisingly calm, listening and watching. One said a few words in Visayan dialect to the sergeant. The man thought he had seen a movement in the bushes on the crest of the hill ahead. The sergeant alerted his automatic rifleman.

A shell exploded behind us, then another. The men were looking around, wild-eyed. They were mystified by the suddenness of the attack, apparently coming from nowhere. Soon there were two explosions in front of us. I was sure the next ones would be close, and they were. The fire was undoubtedly from a small mortar. At first we were unable to locate the observer who was directing the fire, but before long, movement could be discerned through the bushes behind the crest of the hill ahead. Our fire kept the enemy pinned down, but mortar fire was still coming in along with an occasional crack of an overhead bullet that told us their riflemen were getting into position.

The sight of Japs off to our left was the first sign of the flanking movement we had been expecting. I thought of Major Ketchum reciting withdrawal instructions at Linguyan Gulf.

We had delayed the enemy and our job was done. One by one we dropped back behind the crest of the hill, leaving two men hidden behind the crest as rear guard. A messenger was dispatched to advise the element guarding the roadblock to the east of Janiuay. The rest of us headed north and then west toward the mountains where another delaying position had been prepared.

The next day I rode and then hiked over the foothills into the mountains to the regimental command post, arriving after dark. During the day I had to wade in a stream for some distance. To my surprise, disgust, and then disappointment, my new boots made in Iloilo City were coming apart. They had been held together primarily with glue and it wasn't long before I was completely without soles.

Since early on the morning of 16 April, no word from the 3rd Battalion in Iloilo City had been received at regimental headquarters. The 2nd Battalion in the center had become badly disorganized while withdrawing to the mountains. The whereabouts of battalion headquarters and its companies were unknown. I found it hard to believe because withdrawal rehearsals had gone so well. The northernmost 1st Battalion was the only one in contact and apparently still intact. On top of all this, our personal luggage had either been lost or stolen, so my wardrobe now consisted of what I had on my back.

On 20 April, four days after the invasion, I started back to the cavalry bivouac with orders to send squads of the cavalry platoon that had been activated in early March to each of the three rifle battalions. I arrived on the afternoon of the second day to find the camp in utter chaos. My two lieutenants had disappeared, as had the new men recently received as cavalry recruits. Only a small number of the Negros stallions remained and many of them were running loose. Those remaining, still tethered, were nearly crazy with hunger and thirst.

Most of the newly-finished riding and packsaddles were gone, taken by civilians, I was told. The pack and cavalry units that had been activated the first part of March were still intact, however. They had taken over the remainder of the fodder for their own animals, but had felt no responsibility for the care of the new ponies. The exodus of Suarez and Trujillo had left the cavalry and pack training unit in turmoil. Fodder for the animals and food for the men were nearly exhausted.

Moreover, what was left of one company of the 2nd Battalion had moved into the cavalry camp; many of them had already deserted. Of those left a good number had put on civilian clothes, stashing their uniforms and weapons in the forest. The only remaining officer was the company commander who had completely lost control. The report or rumor that Japanese infantry, supported by artillery, were only a few miles away had everyone in a frenzy. There were no patrols out, no local security, and no attempt to establish a defense, nor was there any order or organization within the company.

I called the company commander into a nearby shack and told him in no uncertain terms all the things that needed to be done immediately. He sat wild-eyed before me, hearing every word I said, nodding agreement, but I was sure he remembered nothing. At the end, I told him to get out and get going.

He had not been gone more than a few minutes when a shot was fired. I never saw an area clear so quickly. Most of the soldiers made for the forest. The company commander was kneeling over a soldier who was prostrate on the ground. Beside him lay one of our ponies that appeared to be making its last kick. The commander had shot the pony because it had kicked the soldier, who happened to be his brother.

The others started filtering back from the forest. I suspected these would happen, as there was an object in the center of the area which I was sure would, at least temporarily, act as a magnet on the men. It was a giant rice cauldron, three and a half feet in diameter and three feet deep. Full, it would feed the entire company. It was now half full and would more than feed those who were left. The aroma of freshly-cooked rice permeated the entire area, enough to drive a hungry Filipino mad.

I found a soldier in camp who could speak English, a real godsend as usually only the officers spoke the language.

The squad of cavalry that would be assigned to the 2nd Battalion was sent to scout the area where it was rumored there was a Japanese force approaching. Another of the cavalry squads was sent north with the remaining Negros ponies to the 1st Battalion, along with the rest of the pack animals. I sent them because that unit seemed the most certain to be able to put them to good use. The third squad was sent south where we hoped it would be able to locate the 3rd Battalion in its prepared alternate command post in the mountains.

After the infantry company was fed, it cleared the area, heading for a prepared camp a short distance away, followed by the great cauldron riding on a litter. At dusk the squad of cavalry sent on the reconnaissance mission returned. They had seen no sign of the enemy, but were informed by local Filipinos that an enemy patrol had been in the area earlier and had returned to the lowlands.

So far I had found no sign of the 2nd Battalion commander or his staff, or of the other two companies of the battalion. The cavalry squad of the 2nd Battalion would use the cavalry camp as its headquarters, drawing rations from the nearby infantry company *bodega*.

Early the next morning, a newly-arrived American engineer from Masbate Island, my interpreter, and I left to return to regimental headquarters.

The trail led west up the deep valley of the Suague River, then turned north over a broad, rocky streambed. We had not gone far when we ran into a group of Filipino soldiers hurrying in our direction. Through my interpreter they said they were from the 2nd Battalion. They had no idea where their company was, or their battalion headquarters. They had spotted Japs on the trail ahead and were now trying to put as much distance as possible between them. I told them to report to the company that had been in the cavalry camp the night before, which was now down the valley. From these men's report, it was questionable where the Japs were, if, in truth, they had come into the mountains at all.

I knew the trail we were on would get us to regimental headquarters by dark, but wondered if we should continue on it. I considered looking for another trail, but from past experiences, knew this might prove disastrous. We decided to continue on the trail we were on, moving more cautiously now.

Ahead at a distance two figures were approaching. They had rifles slung over their shoulders and at first resembled Japs. Maybe our imaginations had something to do with it. We ducked behind some nearby boulders, ready to fire. We had almost decided they could be Japs when one removed his cap to scratch his head. His features were unmistakably Filipino. They reported many Japs ahead, some mounted on horses, moving into the mountains.

The same story from two different parties convinced me that there must something to it. As much as I disliked the thought, we decided to detour west. Regimental headquarters was to the north. Hopefully, we could find a trail further west paralleling the one we were on, which would lead to the regimental area. We struck out west, up a steep mountain, through dense jungle growth. The going was slow and tiring. By nightfall we were in the next valley, tired and somewhat bewildered regarding what our next move should be. I had a compass, but no map. Our food was nearly gone, so that night we ate snails from the creek and bamboo shoots boiled in our mess kits.

The next morning we decided to continue west, still hoping to find a north-south trail. Up and up we climbed over incredibly steep mountains covered with the lush growth of the rain forest. This was a land of almost constant rain or fog, a land of beautiful ferns of many shapes and colors, variegated mosses covering the rocks and carpeting the forest floor. To my surprise, we found wild bananas growing at this altitude. The fruit was a welcome find, as we had finished the last of our canned rations that morning.

We came to the camp of a native who was cutting *bahuka* (rattan) that afternoon. He gave us a meal of rice from his limited supply. To my surprise, he was a native of Antique Province. It was hard to believe that we had traveled so far west. Hopefully, we were nearing the 61st Division Headquarters, located on Mount Baloy. By nightfall we had found the trail and a group of soldiers patrolling it. They shared their food with us and, to my delight, made me a bed of banana tree trunks pressed together, which lifted me off the soggy ground.

We arrived at division headquarters at noon on 25 April. General Christie was startled to see us. He had considered the route we had traveled impassable. I assured him he was almost right and that the chance of Japanese forces using it was nearly zero.

The presence of the Japs reported by the soldiers we had met on the trail two days earlier was correct. The Japs had begun to pull back to the lowland on the previous day. They had quickly discovered that they could not find us in the mountains, which were extremely rugged and densely forested. When they attacked in force, we dispersed. When they resorted to small patrols, we sniped at them. The more extended they became, the worse their logistical challenges became. During the confusion of retreating before the advancing Japs, however, many *bodegas* had been burned to deny their use to the enemy. Some of the *bodegas* had been burned in areas where the Japs never reached.

We arrived at regimental headquarters on the following day. Of the regiment's three rifle battalions, we could account for only one. No contact had been made with the other two, except for the company stationed near the cavalry camp.

With favorable terrain and threats of death to deserters, the 1st Battalion commander had held his companies together during the initial onset of the Japs. At his last prepared delaying position, he had stopped the Japs, making them pull back with considerable casualties.

Those at regimental headquarters had also had some trying times during the past few days. In addition to the loss of personal baggage, office supplies and some records had disappeared during the confusion of retreating to the mountains. This was all difficult to reconcile, as withdrawal rehearsals had gone well. There had been desertions and an almost complete breakdown in passing information.

In desperation, Colonel Fitzpatrick had sent a Filipino captain from his staff to determine the validity of a certain report. It required a personal reconnaissance of a specific area in the foothills. Within three days the captain returned, reporting that the area in question contained no Japs. About the same time another report came, which verified the initial report that a Japanese buildup of forces was taking place in the area in question. Upon investigation, it was learned that the captain had spent his three-day absence with a friend in a *nipa* shack in the next valley.

After a day's rest at regimental headquarters, I again started south to locate what we could of the two missing battalions. If I could not locate the commander of the 2nd Battalion, I was to assume command. In addition to my interpreter, I had two American corporals with me. One of them, Cotheran, had been assigned to the US 31st Infantry Regiment. He and a sergeant had fought on Bataan, refused to surrender, and worked their way down southern Luzon much the same way as I had, eventually landing on Panay and joining the Philippine 61st Division. Glew, the other corporal, and a Sergeant Mackey had been assigned to the 48th Materiel Squadron, 27th Bomber Group, stationed on an airfield near the town of San Jose in southern Mindoro. Soon after the beginning of the war, the squadron was driven off. There Glew and Mackey left the squadron and made their way to Panay. It was wonderful to associate with two energetic, straightforward Americans.

Back at the cavalry camp, we found the single squad of cavalry was still intact. Most of their time had been spent procuring food and fodder. Their biggest problem was finding enough grass to feed the ponies, for it only grew in abundance in the lowlands.

By now the Japs were back in the lowlands occupying major towns along the main highways. There was little aerial activity. Parts of companies of the 2nd Battalion were located at their prescribed alternate command post areas, but there was still no sign of the battalion commander or his staff, so I took command, as ordered.

Corporals Glew and Cotheran went south to contact Bickerton's 1st Battalion. They found Bickerton, but his battalion was not in much better shape than the 2nd. He and his staff had a hair-raising time getting to the mountains past the enemy flanking movement on Jaro. His radio had been lost, but a system of foot messengers was now established between him and the regimental command post (CP).

Colonel Fitzpatrick sent out orders to his battalions to harass the Japs as much as possible by raids and ambushes. The first priorities were to establish some idea of the pattern of Japanese activities in our area. The cavalry squad proved extremely useful for distant missions. The men had learned the necessity of taking care of their ponies and most of them, being residents of the province, could go from one place to another, day or night, without aid of a map or compass. They usually worked in pairs. Close-in reconnaissance was accomplished dismounted, but the cavalry could cover two to three times the distance possible for a man on foot.

Corporals Glew and Cotheran were gone from camp most of the time, leading small patrols in the lowlands. They had managed a few ambushes with moderate success. The Japs, however, instead of coming into the hills after us, took reprisals against the civilians in the town or *barrio* nearest any such incident. They made it a policy to kill ten people—men, women, or children—for every Jap injured. The ambushes continued, but an effort was made to warn the civilians in time for them to evacuate an area.*

The two young corporals became the mainstay of our harassment missions. There was no one else I could depend upon to carry them out. When sent out, I knew they could control their men and would make every effort to complete their

*As long as the American and Filipino forces on Corregidor held out, the author and his men were conducting legitimate military operations; the Japanese reprisals against Filipino civilians were simply mass murder. However, after General Wainwright surrendered all Fil-American forces throughout the Philippines, under the law of land warfare then in effect in accordance with the provisions of the Hague Conventions of 1907, the author and his men became "war rebels." This meant that, as a last resort, proportionate reprisals against civilians in the area of the guerrilla operations became legitimate. As the author documents here—and as so many have documented elsewhere—for many Japanese commanders, murdering civilians was a "first resort." (See, for example, Iris Chang's *The Rape of Nanking*, Penguin, 1998) In any case, reprisals against a disproportionate number of civilians, that is, the 10–1 rule, was never appropriate and always considered a crime. See US Army Field Manual 27-10, Rules of Land Warfare (US War Department, 1 October 1940), 89–90. [Ed.]

mission. Eventually, I recommended both of them to Colonel Fitzpatrick for battlefield appointments as second lieutenants.

Our camp was made up of a few crudely-built shelters on the south bank of the Suague River, back from the foothills, into the mountains. The river was about 15 feet wide, clear, shallow, and fast, running over a rocky bottom. It flowed from the west, making a bend to the north just below camp. It was a comfortable camp and relatively secure.

The remnants of the 2nd Battalion's rifle companies were encamped short distances to the north and south. They were our source of manpower for patrol activities and the main source of our food supply, which was rice from their *bodegas.* The procurement of fresh viands, which could only be found in the lowlands, kept two men busy most of the time. Chickens, eggs fruit, greens, and occasionally *carabao*, horse, or pig meat were our staples.

Our cook knew only how to boil. Our normal diet was over-boiled chopped-up chicken with greens. This, poured over a plate of rice three times a day, was monotonous. Sometimes we would have fried eggs, which were a real treat. From time to time, a piece of pork, *carabao,* or horse would get into camp. Invariably, they went into the boiling pot. One day when the foragers returned, I noticed some slabs of meat that looked like steaks. The cook and I did have some trouble communicating, but he knew well the words fry and boil. I called him over and pointed to the meat.

"Tonight fry with coconut oil," I said, pointing to a container of oil.

He nodded that he understood and said, "Fry."

"With coconut oil," I repeated.

He nodded again.

"No boil," I said, and shook my head.

"No boil," he repeated and nodded.

My mouth watered at the thought of fried steak for supper. Suppertime came. A plate of rice was at each place and, as usual, a pot of boiled meat and greens was in the center, from which we helped ourselves. I yelled to the cook to bring the steaks. This was going to be a surprise for everyone. The cook did not seem to understand me.

"Tell Cookie we're ready for the steaks," I told the interpreter. After a long conversation, the interpreter returned.

"The steaks are in the pot," he said.

Sure enough, there in the pot before me were my steaks, cut up into small pieces and boiled to tastelessness. I could have shot the cook. Forever after, boiled food is spoiled food, as far as I'm concerned.

Corporal Glew came in one morning with a Japanese prisoner. He was barefooted and nearly naked, stripped of his uniform, with his hands tied behind him. He was frantic with fear that he was going to be killed. Our camp had no facilities to take care of a prisoner and no one to interrogate him. So we fed him and tied his hands and feet for the night, with a guard sitting near him. The next morning he was sent to the regimental CP.

On another occasion, Corporal Glew returned earlier than expected from a patrol. Asking him how this happened, he said that he had commandeered an automobile.

"How did you pay for it?" I asked.

"With a chit signed 'G.I. Blanket'," he replied. I could only imagine what the finance officer of some future liberating American unit would say when presented with *that.*

One morning after breakfast, those left in camp were performing morning chores when rifle shots rang out, high on the hill above us. The Americans ran for their rifles and soon had a line formed to meet anything coming down the hill. As the minutes passed, the noise of the shooting increased until it sounded like a full-scale firefight. There was, however, no sign of the enemy or the familiar crack of rifle fire overhead. I looked back into camp to see what was going on. The Filipinos seemed unconcerned about the whole thing. I caught the cook's eye. He said one word in Visayan and pointed toward the noise.

"What does that mean?" I yelled to the interpreter.

"The noise is from burning the bamboo. The mountain people do this so they can more easily get to the young shoots."

These were the mountain people I had seen occasionally on the trails nearby. Their dwellings were high on the hillsides. They were like the mountain people of Luzon and Mindoro, and of lighter complexion than the valley Malays: they were shorter, stockier, and with facial features revealing a mongoloid ancestry. They were strangers to the valley Malays, having little contact with them. When met on the trail, which seldom happened, they were shy, acting like surprised animals. Their language was different from the Visayans; neither could understand the other. The men usually carried a bolo of their own design at their side and often a long spear or lance.

They lived frugally. Their small huts, made of logs and palm leaves, clung to the steep hillsides. Water came from the streams below. Usually, a *camote* patch was in evidence. This sweet potato appeared to be the mainstay of their diet, augmented by anything else they could glean from the forest.

Division headquarters had radio contact with the other islands and on 8 May word came that Corregidor had surrendered. The news was a shock, although we all had realized it would happen eventually. Until then we had held onto the dim hope that help might get through from the United States.

Our harassing patrols continued operating to the last, however. We were becoming quite adept at setting up night ambushes. A network of civilian informers kept us apprised of enemy activities. When a pattern started to develop in an area we considered suitable for an ambush, our own reconnaissance verified such reports, on which detailed plans were based. We seldom undertook a plan that did not give us the odds for success. Our efforts were not always successful, but it was certain that we kept the Japs in a constant state of suspense.

About the middle of May, the promotions for Corporals Glew and Cotheran came through. They were now second lieutenants. We made a trip to regiment for Colonel Fitzpatrick to pin on their newly-won gold bars.

Chapter 24

In the third week of May, a messenger from the regimental CP came into camp. I was to report immediately to regimental headquarters. There was little doubt in my mind what it was about.

When I arrived at the CP, it did not take long to verify my fears. Orders to surrender had been received. We all had hoped that General Christie would win out in his efforts to disregard General Wainwright's order to surrender the entire Philippine Archipelago. (General Christie had taken command of Panay on General Chynoweth's transfer to Cebu Island.) Many felt that Wainwright, by then a prisoner of war, had no authority to order the forces in the southern islands to surrender. The Panay garrison still had food and some ammunition, the health of the command was generally good, and the will to resist was stronger than the desire to surrender. We believed we could hold out until the United States returned to the Philippines and, in the meanwhile, cause the Japs a good deal of unpleasantness.

We were informed that as a last resort staff officers from both the American and Japanese commands of the Southern Islands had been flown to Panay to persuade our commanding general to surrender. The American commander of the southern islands had questioned his authority, but finally gave in.

Fitzpatrick read General Christie's surrender order to his staff and battalion commanders. Following is a copy of the surrender order given to me at the time, which I carried out of the Philippines:

Headquarters, 61st Division
In the Field
May 19 1942
Subject: Surrender

To: All Unit Commanders

To put a stop to further useless sacrifices of human lives, Lieut. General J. M. Wainwright surrendered at midnight, 6-7 May 1942, to the senior Japanese general on Corregidor, the formal surrender of all American and Philippine Army troops in the Philippines. You will therefore be guided accordingly, and will, repeat, will surrender all troops under your command to the proper Japanese officer.

This message has just been received by me. I know that General Wainwright would not have surrendered without good and sufficient cause. There is no doubt that it was done to save further unnecessary large loss of life. So, regardless of our personal feelings in the matter, as good soldiers who obey commands, we must comply.

Therefore: All regimental commanders and officers of this division will prepare to carry out the following instructions:

All land mines and other explosives of any description will be immediately removed from any place where they might cause damage to Japanese troops particularly. They will be removed within twenty-four hours. Where it is unpracticable to remove such obstructions without destroying structures or highways, they will be clearly marked "Danger" in the presence thereof. No destruction of property, military or civilian, will be countenanced. All officers are enjoined to carefully instruct those under them and any with whom they may come in contact to strictly observe the above provisions. Any violations of this order will be dealt with summarily. All members of the armed forces failing to report to places designated in this order by date specified will be considered deserters and will be reported to the Japanese authorities. The Japanese Army will treat the officers and enlisted men according to international law. Their orders are absolutely necessary.

A. The 1st Bn, 2nd Bn, and HQ & Hq. Bn of the 64th Inf Regt will turn their arms and ammunition at Tapaz, and then proceed to the intersection of the Tapaz-Calinog-Capiz Road where they will report to the Japanese.

B. 3rd Bn, 64th Inf Regt will turn its arms and ammunition to Libacao and proceed to Balete to report to the Japanese representative.

C. 2nd Bn, 63rd Inf Regt and attached troops will turn its arms and ammunition at Daja, and then report to the Japanese representative at Maasin.

D. 3rd Bn, 63rd Inf Regt will turn in its arms and ammunition to barrio Tambal and report to the Japanese at Maniuay.

E. The 65th Infantry Regiment and attached troops will turn in its arms and ammunition to Valderama and proceed to Bogtasan to report to the Japanese.

F. 1st Bn, 63rd Infantry Regiment and attached troops will turn in its arms and ammunition at Alibunan School and proceed to Calinog to report.

G. HQ & HQ Bn, 63rd Regt Provisional Regiment and Division HQ and attached troops will turn in their arms and ammunition at Misi, and proceed to Lambunao.

(3) All units will report to specified location noted above on or before May 30, 1942.

(4) All units must carry a white flag when reporting to position where depositing equipment and also to final location when reporting.

(5) Units will march during daylight only.

(6) All units will carry sufficient rations for trip to place where they are reporting and further sufficient rations for three additional days.

(7) All units will release to the local Japanese commander where they report any prisoner of war which they may have.

(8) It is absolutely prohibited that arms, ammunitions and other equipment, military establishment or food caches be destroyed or dispersed.

(Sgd) Albert F. Christie
Brigadier General
Commanding

A True Copy

The reason given for the surrender was that the Japs, having taken Corregidor, were still holding the prisoners there and demanding that either all American and Filipino forces still active in the Philippines be surrendered immediately or the prisoners on Corregidor would be murdered.

As General Christie's order specified that any officer or enlisted man not surrendering would be considered a deserter to the United States Army, it left little choice.

Battalions of the 63rd Regiment were assembled near designated contact points, where white flags were raised. Records and paper money were burned. About 21 May, two officers from division headquarters gained contact with the Japanese commander on Panay. Division and regimental headquarters of the 63rd were ordered to assemble at the barrio of Misi on 24 May in preparation for surrender the following day.

It was a glum, quiet group of officers and men that hiked out of the mountains on the 24th. The division finance officer and I had gotten well ahead of the main group and when we came to a spring along the trail, we sat down to wait for the others. The finance officer set about building a small fire, which puzzled me at first. He then pulled out a sheaf of genuine 100 *peso* bank notes and, without saying a word, began to burn them one by one. I offered to help and he handed men a handful. As I watched one after the other shrivel in the fire, my Yankee soul cried out. I asked him if I might not put a few bills into my wallet. I crammed in quite a few.

That night most of us slept in the *barrio* schoolhouse of Misi. We were ordered to shave our beards and look as presentable as possible for the surrender. The morning of 25 May 1942, most of us had a bath and shave in the nearby river. The noon meal was over and we were sitting around discussing what the future might hold for us. General Christie had already surrendered. We were awaiting instructions from him.

No one was very talkative. It was a good time for a nap, but the nagging thought of the surrender kept me awake. From the standpoint of the garrison on Panay Island, the surrender made little sense, but we had no choice.

Over the past months, the hope that aid would arrive from the United States in time to prevent the surrender of the Philippines had been the key to morale. As time wore on, this hope had become ever-diminishing and with it, morale. The order to surrender had killed all hope.

That war would break out between Japan and the United States was no great surprise. It had been expected months before it came. It took a while to realize how ill-prepared we were, however, and that it might be years before our forces would return to the islands.

Little did I know at the time that this was the end of an era, that the order of human existence would never be the same, at least not in my lifetime.

Chapter 25

A Filipino soldier entered the schoolhouse with a message for Colonel Fitzpatrick from General Christie. We all stopped talking and watched the colonel read the message. He read it through twice, then slowly looked up and said, "General Christie has instructed me to select four of you to accompany me to the Calinog municipal building; we're to meet him there. The rest of you will follow later. The Japs will be waiting for us on the far side of the Misi River."

I was one to go with Fitzpatrick. My rifle and revolver were left in the schoolhouse, hoping they would get into good hands. We put on our packs and filed off through the bamboos toward the river. Our guide had disappeared.

The Misi River was 15 to 20 feet wide at the place where we were to cross. It was a clear, shallow river running over a clean, stony bottom. On each side of the river, green meadows, fringed by thick clumps of bamboo, sloped down to the water's edge. A narrow, rickety, bamboo bridge provided a precarious crossing.

On the far side, a Japanese officer and several soldiers were waiting. Between 75 and 100 yards beyond, more of the enemy soldiers could be seen deploying in a line of skirmishers, in the bamboo bordering the edge of the meadow.

Colonel Fitzpatrick remarked that we ought to show a white flag. I pulled out a rag of a handkerchief and tied it to a twig. We filed toward the bridge, all of us tense, and all of us hoping contact would be made without an incident. As we neared the Japs, the officer motioned us to follow him. The soldiers, bayonets fixed on their rifles and holding them ready, marched on each side.

Crossing the meadow, the trail circled a hill and brought us to a clearing where several civilian sedans and two or three Japanese Imperial Army trucks were parked. There were 15 to 20 Japanese officers and enlisted men gathered in this area. There were also several other individuals, not in uniform, who appeared to be representatives of their press or public information service, clicking off pictures like mad.

This was the first chance I had for a close-up look at live Japs in uniform. They were of medium height, broad-shouldered, barrel-chested, long-bodied, and short-legged, with alert faces. Their hair was closely cropped and they were clean-shaven. They wore visored wool caps with strips of tan cotton cloth hanging from the back. Their khaki shirts had short sleeves, no collar, and fit very loosely. Breeches, made of the same khaki material, hung like pantaloons. Their footwear was either a heavy brown suede leather shoe, or a black rubber-canvas sneaker that had a special compartment for the big toe. Below the knee to the top of their shoes, their legs were covered with wraparound leggings.

The enlisted men were armed with either a long or short-barreled Type 38 6.5mm rifle. In front on their belts they wore two leather cartridge boxes; on one side hung a bayonet scabbard.

The officers were dressed much the same as their men with the exception that some wore dress boots. Instead of the cartridge boxes and bayonet scabbard, a pistol hung from the right side of their belts; a katana, or "samurai sword" hung from a frog on the left. A strap over the right shoulder supported the belt.

Their long bodies and comparatively short legs, which were most often bowed, gave the impression of great strength and endurance. They had a somewhat simian walk.

The Japanese officer whom we had followed into the area told us in English to hand over our side arms and open our packs for inspection. My pistol, bolo, first aid packet, and extra ammunition were taken. The Jap allowed me my canteen and cup.

My pack, which contained a blanket, mess kit, spoon, a pair of socks, razor, toothbrush, some old rags I used as handkerchiefs, and the helmet given me by the Navy captain were untouched. I do not remember why I held onto that helmet; there must have been a sentimental reason.

The Jap did not ask to see anything in my pockets. This was strange, as two other Americans standing close-by, were having money removed from their wallets. Hearing Fitzpatrick swearing under his breath, I turned to see a Jap taking his last good cigarettes.

The group of Americans surrendering at this time consisted of Lieutenant Colonel Fitzpatrick, Captains Horney and Hay, and me. After the inspection, we loaded into two civilian cars. As we entered the town of Calinog, the Japanese soldiers we passed came to attention and saluted. I felt this was a ploy to win our cooperation.

On the second floor of the Calinog municipal building, in a large, square, bare-walled room, General Christie with his chief of staff and two Japs were seated around a large table in the center of the room. Several young Jap officers, who appeared to be aides, were standing.

General Christie bade us to be seated. He then explained that the officer seated at the head of the table was the executive officer of the unit that had invaded Panay Island. This unit, reportedly a regiment in strength, had its headquarters in Iloilo City. The Japs had come to Calinog to arrange the surrender of the 61st Division. Those of us who had just arrived were to assist in contacting the more isolated units of the division.

As General Christie was talking, I glanced over at the Jap colonel. He was sitting erect on the edge of his chair, reading over a page of notes that lay on the table in front of him. He was of medium height, broad, lean, with short-cropped, graying hair. His clean-shaven face was round, intelligent, masked to some extent by a pair of thick-rimmed spectacles. He wore a loosely-fitted, greenish cotton uniform which had no frills. His attitude was serious and he appeared impatient to finish the job at hand and be on his way.

I particularly remember one of the young officers standing behind the Jap colonel's chair because of the contrast in his appearance to the others. He wore a well-tailored, light-green uniform; a single belt around his waist supported his sword. I guessed that his father was European, perhaps German.

General Christie had previously submitted lists of the number of our troops remaining in the mountains and their whereabouts. The Japanese colonel spoke in a slow, even tone, through his interpreter sitting beside him. As he designated a unit he wanted one of us to assist in contacting, General Christie, after consulting Fritzpatrick, named one of us for the job. As our names were given, the Japanese colonel wrote them down with slow exactness. I was to go the north, to contact units of the 64th Infantry Regiment.

The meeting ended as abruptly as it had begun. The Japs took their leave and left us alone, except for a sentry at the door.

We waited for we knew not what. The work on Panay was finished without glory and with a very unsatisfactory ending.

By mid-afternoon, the remainder of the Americans from Misi began to arrive, along with four or five senior Filipino officers. General Christie seemed somewhat alarmed at the absence of the remainder of his Filipino staff. Colonel Fitzpatrick's Filipino staff was also absent.

Among some of the Americans there was a feeling of complacency, of relief, knowing that, at least for them, the struggle had ended. At this time, General Christie remarked that now that we had surrendered, we had obeyed our orders. He continued that if we could escape, we were free to do so.*

About 1600 hours, a platter of steaming rice was brought into the room and placed on the table, followed by bowls of broth which contained remnants of boiled chicken and greens. Also, enough plates for all of us were brought in and, as I recall, spoons. We piled our plates high with rice and poured a little broth over it. We then sat down on the floor along the wall to eat. We all could have eaten more when the food was gone. After finishing, we were told to stack our plates by the door.

Suddenly, there was a great crashing of dishes over by the door. The Jap guard, appearing to be in a rage, was smashing dishes with his feet and gun butt. After a few minutes of this, he ran downstairs, quickly returning with an American flag. With the flag, he proceeded to clean up the mess he had made. Suddenly, he stopped and with his rifle at the ready, bayonet fixed, glared individually at each one of us in the room, with an expression on his face as much as to say, "Which one of you wants to make something of this?" After a few moments, he stomped out and back downstairs. We saw no more of him that afternoon.

---

*This was a clever move. Under the Hague Convention of 1907, a prisoner caught after escaping was subject to punishment, but was still a soldier protected by the Hague and Geneva Conventions, whereas a soldier who refused a lawful order to surrender was classified a "war rebel." If apprehended, war rebels were subject to punishment by death. Further, a prisoner who regained contact with friendly forces and went back to fighting before being captured again, was completely protected as a prisoner of war. See Article 50 of the Geneva Convention of 1929.

That night, we slept on the floor, jammed together like so many sardines in a can. It was just before the time for the monsoon to break; the moisture hung heavily in the still air. The ever-present mosquitoes were there in hoards. Some of us had blankets to use. No one had a mosquito bar. There was little rest for anyone that night.

The next morning we had breakfast at about 1000 hours, eating rice and broth from a lot fewer dishes. We were informed that we were on a two-meal-a-day regimen.

Through the morning, we were taken individually down into a small room and questioned by an English-speaking Japanese officer. His English sounded American with an accent, and we learned that he had spent many years in the United States, having graduated from one of our more prominent universities. He started by making a few sugary remarks about how well the surrender of the 61st Division was going.

Then, "What are the major units of the division? What are their strengths? What weapons are they armed with? How much ammunition did the division have? How many American officers are there in the division? I would like you to answer these questions for me," he said. "We will take them one at a time."

I sat across the table, looking at him.

He repeated the first question. I continued to say nothing.

"Why don't you answer my question?"

"What unit were you assigned to?"

I just shook my head.

"You should be able to answer that, at least."

I continued to look at him and said nothing.

He was getting red in the face. "You are a hard-headed lot. There are ways to find these things out," he said. He then motioned me to get out.*

---

*Under the provisions of Article 5 of the Geneva Convention of 1929, prisoners were obliged only to render name and rank and, if available, service number. The same article also specified that, "No pressure shall be exercised on prisoners to obtain information regarding the situation in their armed forces or their country. Prisoners who refuse to reply may not be threatened, insulted, or exposed to unpleasantness or disadvantages of any kind whatsoever."

Chapter 26

Shortly after noon, I laid down to take a nap, believing the trip to the north had been called off. No sooner had I gotten to sleep, though, when the Japanese guard awakened me. He motioned me to get up, grab my pack, and follow him. As I walked from the room, I told "Buck" Layton, the regimental executive officer of the 63rd, that I would see him later, sure that I would be back in the next day or so.

Downstairs, I was turned over to a Japanese lieutenant who spoke English. He was dressed like all the rest, nearly six feet tall, a little stooped, with a bandage around his right wrist. His expression took on a snarl as he looked me up and down and told me to follow him. Outside the municipal building, a Filipino lieutenant named Perez joined us. We walked around the town plaza to the highway. The Jap told me what we were going to do, which amounted to the same as told us the day before. He ended by saying that if I did a good job, I would come back alive. That was the reward for good behavior.

He said his father was a German and gave me a superior look. Inquiring about the bandage on his wrist, he told me that he had been shot by a Filipino a few days before in the town of Mambusao, to the north. I regretted that the bullet hadn't gotten him between the eyes.

While we were talking, two civilian sedans drove up. The Jap motioned one of the drivers to follow him into a nearby shack. Soon, both came out loaded with baggage. The lieutenant had half a dozen leather bags draped around his neck, a briefcase in one hand, and a number of packages in the other. He got into the back seat and motioned Lieutenant Perez and me to do the same. We headed north, preceded by the other car, which was full of soldiers.

After driving for half an hour, we came to a destroyed bridge. On the north side were about 20 Japanese soldiers, stripped to the waist, trying to assemble a footbridge across the stream. Demolition details from the 64th Infantry Regiment had blown the bridge on 17 or 18 April. The Japs were trying to move the heavy timbers by brute force and were not doing too well. It took a lot of yelling and grunting before the footbridge was completed and then all it amounted to was a couple of 8-by-8s suspended just above the water. A couple of privates came across to greet the Japanese lieutenant, who apparently belonged to their unit. During the greeting, there was a good deal of saluting and bowing, but not much talking.

We then crossed the river and I witnessed another greeting ceremony. Nearly every soldier came up to the lieutenant, saluted, bowed, and said a few words, then backed off, saluting and bowing. The lieutenant spoke to each one of the men individually, seeming pleased with it all, saluting and bowing right back.

Another driver with a sedan waited for the lieutenant on the north side of the river. The enlisted men, Perez, and I climbed into a truck.

We drove north on Highway #3, arriving a little before dark in the town of Dao in Capiz Province. The Japanese camp was just west of the tracks in the town marketplace. It was surrounded with trenches and manned by sentinels with emplaced machine guns. Perez and I were shown our beds. We were to sleep on part of the covered platforms on which the farmers placed their wares on market day, part of which now was draped with a large, green, platoon-sized mosquito bar. We sat for awhile, wondering what would come next, as we watched a few Japanese soldiers, stripped to their loin clothes, showering under a nearby water hydrant. They were acting like a bunch of kids playing with a water sprinkler on the lawn. The Filipino remarked that to his surprise, our people acted very much the same at such times.

Before long, each of us was brought a heaping plate of rice, with a captured can of American corned beef to share between us. My mouth watered at the sight of the corned beef. It was hard to beat a can of good salty beef with a plate of rice when you are hungry. I wiped the can clean, then holding it over my friend's plate, I carefully opened it, letting the juice run out onto his rice. When the top was twisted off I gave it to the lieutenant to clean out, then took my spoon and gave him half the meat. The rest I put onto my own plate, turning the can upside down. In doing so, I got more of the juice than he. There was nothing said at the time, but I knew from experience that he had noticed it. It was a fine meal we had that night.

While sitting around talking after supper, two Japanese soldiers came over and politely introduced themselves in English. One of them spoke English very well and we had quite a conversation. According to his story, he had been a telephone operator in Tokyo before being taken into the Imperial Army. He had spent nearly two years in China before his regiment had arrived in Manila. They had staged in Manila for several weeks before embarking for the Panay invasion. He told us he had a wife and two children in Japan whom he wished to see very much. He said he was sick of the war, and that he wanted to get home and back to his old life. He had brought an American magazine with him and after talking a while, opened it to an article and asked me to read. I think he wanted to hear how I pronounced the words. At any rate, I read. From time to time he would stop me to ask the meaning of some word. When the article was finished, they both seemed very pleased and we talked of the war and Japanese victories.

"We control all of Asia now," he said. "Soon, we will turn west toward your country. Nothing can stop us. We have already proven this," he continued, seemingly repeating something he had been told. "Before many months, the Japanese Army will be in your capital of Washington. Nothing can stop it."

I looked at him, thinking he might be joking, but the look on his face was cold and serious. And I thought, "You really believe that, don't you?"

I was awakened next morning by a tugging at my feet. Looking out, I saw a soldier beckoning to me. Stretching and putting on my sneakers, I got out from under the mosquito bar, waking my companion in the process. The Jap led us to a nearby clearing where the soldiers of the little garrison were assembling with their rifles. It appeared to be a reveille formation. We were given a place behind the last rank. This was the first chance I had to get an idea of the size of the garrison.

There were three different groups lined up in double rank, each about the size of a platoon, with an officer in front of each group. Forward of these was another officer, facing the groups, who appeared to be the company commander. The platoons were facing the east. They were called to attention and after a short speech, the company commander barked a command and all came to present arms. The captain saluted the right end of his unit. Then like a robot, he stiffly and slowly shifted position to his right, by slight, shuffling movements of his feet, all the while holding his body stiff and remaining at the salute. He ended up facing the opposite flank of the company. By another command, the company returned to the position of "Attention." He uttered a few more words, removed his hat, and about-faced to the east. The entire unit removed their hats at the same time. The sun was just showing itself above the mountains. The Japs bowed to the east and, as if by a signal, repeated aloud in unison what I assumed to be a short prayer. At the beginning of the prayer, our guard motioned us to remove our hats and also bow towards the east. The captain then said a few more words and dismissed his company. Perez and I returned to our beds, rolled up our packs, and washed.

A short while after dismissal from the morning formation, one of the kitchen boys brought us two plates of rice with another can of corned beef. It looked as good as the night before. In dividing it, I made sure Perez got a little more of the juice than I did.

After breakfast, we readied ourselves to move, believing we would leave early, but the morning passed away while watching the Japs bathe, cut each other's hair, and exercise. The soldiers who had talked with us the night before came back for awhile and I read to them again. We could get no information about when we were going into the hills.

That afternoon I had the chance to watch the officers practice their sword drill on upright, wooden posts. They gripped the sword with both hands; the majority of the strokes they made were diagonal slashes from the right or left shoulder, with variations. Occasionally, a jab was made similar to a bayonet thrust. The officers seemed to take a great delight in the practice and went at it very seriously. It was not too impressive, but looked to be good exercise.

As the afternoon wore away, it became apparent we were not leaving that day. Just before sundown, I managed a bath and shave. I remember how wonderfully refreshing it was, after the past few days and nights of sticky humidity.

For dinner, we had rice and corned beef again.

The routine on the next morning was a different story. We were up at the same time, stood prayers, and had breakfast, but from the activity and preparation, it was evident that this day we were going to move. Lieutenant Perez and I received white cloth armbands with Japanese lettering. The party we were to join consisted of two truckloads of Japanese soldiers and three officers riding in a civilian sedan. Perez and I climbed onto the front truck.

The Japs were dressed a little differently today. The enlisted men, instead of their billed caps, were wearing steel helmets. Around their waists they had wrapped a piece of water-proofed cloth which looked similar to our shelter half, but was lighter and more finely woven. In this roll, the weight resting on the buttocks was a mess kit and small bag of hulled rice. Instead of wearing boots, the officers wore legging and shoes, like their men. Besides their swords, they carried pistols, binoculars, and one or two leather cases about the size and shape of our dispatch cases.

The party moved west along the highway to the town of Sison, then north along the Capiz highway. As we passed civilians, they respectfully removed their hats and bowed. I remember thinking at the time that it had not taken the Japs long to get them to do this. Or was it just a holdover from the days of the Spanish? We continued north until we came to the town of Ivisan where the road turned west leading into the Aklan area of Capiz Province. There was only one main road that led into this area and it was a sort of a defile. I had known that the 64th Regiment was supposed to blow the bridges along this road when Panay was invaded, but up to this time, did not know it had been done.

We had not driven far, however, when we were stopped because of a completely demolished bridge that had crossed a good-sized river. I dismounted with the Japs in the front truck to examine the bridge. The men of the 64th could not have done a better job. It was apparent at first glance that no vehicle would pass that way for a while. After a good bit of examining and jabbering, the Japs came to the same conclusion. A few of them looked around at me, glaring. I felt they thought that I had been personally responsible. With their fixed bayonets and knowing what they were capable of doing, I had a few moments of apprehension. In a few minutes, though, it became apparent that they had decided it would be better to keep me going a while longer, to help them get the Filipino soldiers in from the hills.

Before long, we were on a side road looking for another way. I knew there was a bridge on this road, too. With one bridge gone, I felt the chances of another remaining serviceable were slim. I was not sure how much it would take to get the Japs into a bayonet-jabbing mood. When we came to the bridge, or what was left of it, Perez and I were very nonchalant, concentrating our gaze on objects in the opposite direction. I was not until we were traveling south again that I breathed more easily.

About noon, we drove into the town of Mambusao, 10 or 12 miles west of Dao, where we had started from that morning. The Japs had been forced to change their plan with the road into northwestern Panay impassable. I wondered what would be their next move.

In Mambusao, we parked by the side of the road and ate lunch. My companion and I were both given a can of milk and a small cheesecloth bag of hard, small biscuits. In the bag with biscuits were a few small pieces of hard candy. This bag of biscuits and candy was a type of Jap emergency ration. It was quite a palatable lunch.

While Perez and I sat by ourselves eating, he told me of the killing that had taken place in Mambusao on a Sunday, a week or so earlier. A civilian of the locality had just told him about it. The story goes—and I later verified it many times—one afternoon, two Japs in a sedan drove into Mambusao. A soldier from the 64th, returning from a scouting mission and seeing the car approach, hid in some bushes by the side of the road. As it passed, noticing there were Japs in it, he fired two rounds wounding both of the occupants. Two or three days later on a Sunday morning, while the townspeople were in church, a truckload of Japs drove into the town plaza and dismounted. Armed with rifles and machine guns they formed in front of the church. As the people came out after the service, the Japs fired on them killing or wounding nearly the entire congregation, men, women, and children alike. After wreaking havoc in the town, the Japs moved into the countryside shooting civilians as they found them in their fields or in their homes. We had heard of similar incidents prior to the surrender, but never like this.

After eating, we hiked to the northwest side of the town. For a while, there was much ado amongst the Japs. Soon it became evident they were preparing to proceed on foot. As the roads were out, we were going to hike into the Aklan area.

For the first time, I had a glance at a Jap map of Panay Island. It was clearer and gave much more detail than ours. Many trails and some roads that I knew existed but were not shown on our maps were clearly defined on the Japs'. The reason for my patrol on the South China Sea coast a little over a year before came back to me.

I was standing next to Perez, waiting for the party to move out, when I noticed him looking at me, shaking his head in a sorrowful manner. He had been talking in Visayan to a man dressed in civilian clothes who looked to me like a Filipino. The lieutenant told me he had just learned that this man was a Jap from southern Japan who several years before had come to the Philippines to live. He had learned the Visayan dialect and at present was an interpreter for the Jap captain. Last January (1942), he had been sent from Manila to Panay to gain information. He told Perez that last February he had been in division headquarters at Misi.

Chapter 27

The march started at about 1400 hours, the hottest time of day. The extreme humidity made any physical exertion an effort. It was not long before our clothes were soaked through from perspiration. In the party, there were two platoons of men with three officers; the company commander had come along. Perez and I marched at the head of the column with the platoon leader of the forward platoon. This Jap officer wore a full, black beard. He was a young and cocky individual, and we were given to understand he was of noble birth and should be treated as such. The soldiers did actually treat him with a great deal of deference. In fact, I noticed the men showed more respect for him than they did for the company commander.

We marched in two groups, about 50 yards apart. There was no front, rear, or flank security and there was little effort to control the men. Each platoon looked like a mad scramble forward.

After about an hour's hiking, we arrived at the top of our first big hill, the Japs as tired and thirsty as Perez and I. An old man was caught trying to duck out of the back of his hut, and was sent up a coconut tree. The water and soft white meat of the fresh green coconuts were very refreshing for the moment, but seemed to make one sweat more and feel greater fatigue after starting to hike again.

While we were resting near the old man's shack, some of his chickens wandered out to pick up the coconut scraps. One was caught by a Jap who proceeded to tie its legs together before tying it onto his belt. The bearded lieutenant nearby told the soldiers to let it go. This he did, but not without an amazed look coming over his face. And I noticed several other surprised looks in the group. I suspected the Jap did this to impress Perez and me. It was a normal Japanese practice to live off the land.

We marched on in the same disorganized fashion, moving generally north over a section of mountains, coming to the highways into the Aklan area by mid-afternoon. Before sunset, we stopped to make camp in a small *barrio* southeast of the town of Altabas. It took ten minutes, from the time the head of the column stopped for the last men from the trail platoon to close up. They straggled in by twos and threes.

The company commander lined up his men and gave them a long harangue. When dismissed, they broke up into small groups, to occupy *nipa* shacks around a nearby school building. The officers, their orderlies, two radiomen, Perez, and I occupied the school building. On arriving in the schoolyard, the radiomen started to put their set into operation. I watched them with curiosity. The radio had been carried in two watertight packs about a foot square. It was put into operation in no time. The workmanship in the set appeared to be of a very high quality; not at all like many of the second-rate items with which the Japanese had been flooding foreign markets. Within minutes, they were in contact with another station, either Dao or Calinog, I guessed.

While watching the radio operators, I heard a few shots on a hill across the road. Soon afterward, a group of Jap soldiers came down carrying a young pig and goat they had shot. Evidently the company commander had not seen eye to eye with the lieutenant who had made one of his men release the chicken earlier in the afternoon. As far as I could determine, it was customary for these troops to carry only rice, tea, and sugar in the field, depending upon the countryside for their food.

We were given a handful of rice that we set about cooking in an old can Perez found. To go with the rice, we had a can of asparagus. I especially remember this night for its discomfort. The schoolhouse was built in a swamp. The place was overrun with mosquitoes and the atmosphere so humid that even without exertion, one would sweat profusely. On top of this, a type of flying ant swarmed about the area in clouds. When you opened your mouth, they flew in; when you breathed, they went up your nose. They even got into one's eyes and beneath one's clothing. It was impossible to take a mouthful of rice without taking in the same amount of ants.

After eating, a Jap signaled for us to follow him inside the schoolhouse where a corner was allocated for us to sleep. I unrolled my blanket and lay down. Added to the discomfort of the flying ants and mosquitoes, the place was like an oven. Without mosquito bars, there would be little sleep. The smoke from a cigarette was the only thing that diminished the activity of the insects . . . and that only temporarily.

Perez and I were reviewing the events of the day when one of the Japanese lieutenants walked in and sat down beside us. With him was the interpreter who spoke Visayan. Perez talked with the Japs for several minutes before he turned to me and said the Jap wanted to know if we had enough to eat and if we thought we would be comfortable for the night. We talked such nonsense for some time. I spoke English to the Filipino, he Visayan to the interpreter, who in turn relayed my words to the Jap. The Jap then reversed the procedure back to me. The substance of the Jap's message was to assure us that we would receive as good treatment from them as we were accustomed to in our own home towns. The Japs wanted to be nothing but friendly with the Americans and Filipinos. I nodded and smiled at this last and told him I appreciated it. This was apparently the point he had come to get across.

I think the Jap left convinced that we believed his every word. If so, we had gained more from the conversation than he. They were obviously making an effort to win our confidence.

That night was as miserable a one as I can remember. If you covered yourself completely, which was necessary to keep out the myriad mosquitoes and ants, the heat was unbearable. Without covering up meant being incessantly perforated by the insatiable insects. Either way, it proved impossible to rest. Evidently the Japs had the same trouble, for, about 0300 hours that morning, 29 May 1942, the interpreter advised us that we would resume the march.

The company formed on the road, received a short speech from its commander, and took off in the same unorganized fashion as the day before. Security and control of troops apparently were of no concern. This was a result of either ignorance or overconfidence.

Perez and I again marched at the head of the column. We halted after about an hour's march and all laid down in the middle of the road for a nap. I do not know how long we stayed, but I fell asleep for the first time that night and when awakened felt greatly refreshed. We had lain down in a high place where the breeze swept away the insects. I inwardly cursed the Japs for not having sense to pick such a place to camp the night before.

After daylight, still marching on the road, I had a chance to evaluate the state of training in the Japanese unit. On a hill, about a half-mile off the road, a native "hallooed." From farther up the road came another "halloo." The Japs knew it was possible for a significant number of Filipino soldiers to be in this area. The Japanese lieutenant at the head of the column immediately signaled his platoon to halt and take cover. He went down on his knee and started scanning the countryside with his field glasses. In a moment, his whole platoon was crowded around him like a flock of sheep, jabbering and even getting in his way. They made a beautiful target. However, this did not seem to bother the lieutenant. Five minutes passed before he decided it was a false alarm and gave the signal to continue the march, again without any security to the front, or flanks, or rear.

We entered the town of Altabas at about 0800 hours. A few civilians were caught by surprise in the streets and questioned by the interpreter, but were soon released.

On reaching the center of town, the lead platoon waited for the rest of the company to close up. Then small patrols reconnoitered the town. While this was going on, Perez and I were sitting on the steps of a shack near the company commander's group, resting and observing the general progress of the operation. The townsfolk were shyly wandering into town to have a look at the strange soldiers. An old woman came up the road and offered to sell us bananas. As she approached, one of the Japanese officers went over to her, handed her two or three *pesos*, and selected a bunch out of her basket. The old vendor made motions to return the change. The Jap motioned that she could keep it and gave her a bow and friendly smile. This was certainly a different approach than had been used on Luzon. A little later a soldier brought a few bananas over for us. Their kindness was killing me.

When the patrols had returned, the captain assembled his unit, and, astonishingly, put his men through about 20 minutes of strenuous calisthenics. Given the tactical situation—even with the town seemingly clear—this seemed completely inappropriate. Moreover, from a training point of view, given the hike the troops had just finished, this did not seem like a very good idea. Nevertheless, the

Japanese troops went at it as if they enjoyed it. Stripped to the waist, the men before us were barrel-chested, sinewy individuals, undoubtedly the result of some effective system of physical training.

After dismissal from this formation around 0900, a soldier motioned to us to follow and we straggled along with the rest of the company down the road to the town schoolhouse. There, we were again allotted a corner of a room. Immediately on arrival at the schoolhouse, the majority of the Japs stripped off their sweaty uniforms down to their loin clothes and around a nearby pump, washed themselves and their clothes.

At about 1000 hours we were given a little rice, which Perez immediately started cooking. As I was taking care of the fire under the rice pot, I watched the Japs around the pump. They were acting like a bunch of schoolboys on an outing—joking, laughing, and playing tricks on one another. It was a source of wonderment to me, watching them, knowing it would take only a moment to turn them into sadistic fiends.

After eating, we went inside to lie down. A first aid station had been set up in the room; an enlisted man was treating sore feet and other minor complaints. A soldier entered the room, carrying a steaming mess kit, and invited us to drink from it. At first sight I thought it was tea, but on tasting, found it to be only sugar and hot water. The color was brownish due to the native sugar. On inquiring why this mixture was being drunk, I was told it was a substitute for tea. However, the mixture of sugar and hot water was exceedingly refreshing and I remember, after drinking it, I had no trouble dozing off.

Around noon, I was awakened by a soldier pulling my foot. The Jap motioned for Perez and me to follow him. The soldier led us into another room in the schoolhouse. An obvious air of formality prevailed. There was a guard at the door. Seated inside, behind a long table, were the three Japanese officers of the party, the company commander in the center. They had on fresh uniforms and were sitting very stiffly, watching us as we entered. On the table in front of the Japanese captain was a piece of paper covered with Japanese ideographs. Near the officers stood the soldier who had spoken English with us the first night in Dao. He directed us to remove our hats and be seated in front of the officers.

The English-speaking soldier started out by asking me my rank, which he already knew. When I told him I was a captain, he replied that the company commander was a major, which I knew he was not. He then told us we were to be sent on a special, important mission and that it was our duty to perform well. He asked us if we understood this. We nodded that we did. There was then a conversation with the company commander who soon began reading what was on the paper before him. He would jabber a few words in Japanese, then the translator would explain in English. When the piece was finished, the gist of the instruction was that with a Filipino guide, Perez and I were to start immediately for Belete, a town about 14 miles into the mountains from Altabas. At Belete, we were to contact the commanding officer of a battalion of the 64th Infantry Regiment, the headquarters of which was nearby. We were to give him General Christie's surrender order plus written stipulations added by the Japs. Then we were to return to Altabas the following day, with as many Filipino soldiers as could be rounded up. The remainder of the battalion was to surrender in Altabas on 31 May; they should make sure to have a white flag flying at the head of their column when returning to approaching Altabas.

General Christie's order of surrender given us by the Jap captain was a copy of the general's original order. The added stipulations were only a copy of those contained in the original order restating the amount of food and clothing to be carried by each surrendering individual, how arms would be carried, what would be done with stores in the hills, and so on.

I called to the attention of the Jap commander the near impossibility of hiking the distance to Balete, contacting the Filipinos there, and returning the next day. He answered through the interpreter he did not believe it was impossible and that we would return the next day. After a little more talk, I asked for a carrier for our packs. To my surprise, this was granted. I almost asked for a gun, but thought that was going too far.

After a little more chattering, the Japs were confident that we understood the mission. The Japanese commander then handed us a few pieces of hard candy and a package of cigarettes apiece, both of which were unheard of luxuries. We thanked him and he smiled back, seemingly very pleased with himself. He grew serious again and rose. The officers at his side did the same; one of them motioned us to get up. The Japanese captain sounded off with quite a *spiel,* looking at us while giving it. Translated, he told us we were being entrusted with an important mission; that it was our duty as good soldiers to successfully to complete it; and he wished us good luck. On finishing, he bowed very low; we walked out. The whole thing had been somewhat dramatic. Why? First of all, I suspect it was their custom. It did seem they were making a lot over a simple matter. Also, they probably figured the extra attention might make us do a better job.

While we were putting our packs together, a soldier brought us more hot water and sugar. I downed my share with a relish. My craving for sweets was still terrific. Three men from the town were brought in, one to guide us, the others to carry our packs.

As we left the town, the Jap who spoke English waved goodbye wishing us a good trip. He said we must return tomorrow; it was our duty.

A mile or so out of town, we stopped in a coconut grove while our guide knocked down some green coconuts. We sat around for half an hour eating these, smoking, and resting. After the past couple of days, the thought of hiking 14 miles made me tired. It was hard to believe the Japs would send us out alone as they had, but there we were. In the back of my mind I felt there was some trick, but could not quite figure what. I could not talk to Perez for fear he would misinterpret the remark or mention it to the others. We were still duty-bound by General Christie's instructions to deliver the papers to the battalion commander.

That would fulfill my obligation, but what I should do after that was the problem. General Christie's words that we were then free to escape kept echoing through my mind.

We followed the winding country road from Altabas to Balete throughout the afternoon. Several times, we had to cross streams with blown-out bridges. These always caused delay, as it was necessary to hunt up someone with a *banca* to take us across. The afternoon was steamy hot. We stopped often in the shade of the coconut trees along the road to eat green nuts. Those we met along the way were few and wary. News that we had come from the Japs in Altabas had traveled ahead of us. The bamboo telegraph was at work.

It was a little after sunset when we arrived in the town of Balete. The majority of the public buildings in the town and the bridge across the Balete River had been destroyed by the soldiers as they withdrew into the hills. The few residents left in the town treated us with suspicion. It was some time before we could find anyone who would have anything to do with us. I knew it was felt that the soldiers in the hills would take it out on a civilian harboring anyone connected with the Japs. Finally, the mayor came into the town and dutifully offered to take us in for the night. There were only two things I wanted that night: something to eat, and a place to sleep. Before going to sleep, I sent a messenger to contact the major who commanded the Balete battalion of the 64th Infantry Regiment, asking him to come to see me the next morning.

According to available information, Altabas was the western limit of the Japs' advance in the Aklan district of Capiz Province. There apparently had been no landings on the northern coast, west of the town of Capiz.

For the past few days I had a cold, but it had not seemed bad enough to bother about. When I woke up on the morning of 30 May, however, I could hardly breathe and ached all over. The exertion and lack of rest during the past few days had taken more out of me than I realized. I decided not to move out of the mayor's house that day.

The major came in toward the middle of the morning. He was a short, good-natured officer who had been a teacher before the emergency. He was planning to get married soon and that was all he could talk about. I asked him about his battalion. He told me there were only a few men and officers left in it, waiting in the hills for his return. They were undecided whether or not to surrender. The bulk of his command had already gone to their homes.

He took the papers I had for him, scanned them and put them in his pocket. He did not ask any questions or say what he planned to do. After a glass of *tuba* and a few well wishes, he departed, Perez with him. I did not see either of them again.

On the next morning, I still did not feel well enough to travel, and decided to spend another day with the mayor. He was wonderfully hospitable, scurrying around the neighborhood to find the best food for me; he had even gone and gotten his wife out of their hideout in the mangroves to take care of me. During the day, a civilian coming from Altabas reported that the Japs were still waiting there and getting angrier by the hour at the American they had sent out. I knew the Japs thought there was a battalion near Balete and they would not dare to extend themselves so far, with the possibility of being attacked by it. They did not know it had practically melted away.

Chapter 28

On the morning of 1 June, I asked the mayor to make arrangements for me to be taken by *banca* through the mangroves from Balete to Altabas. I was feeling well again and was anxious to get going.

A boatman came at about 1500 hours and told the mayor he was ready. I gathered my gear, thanked the mayor and his wife for their hospitality, and took my leave. I disliked leaving so suddenly, especially after all the trouble the mayor had gone to bringing his wife into town and storing up food, but the Japs certainly would not give me much more grace. The boatman led the way down a narrow trail, across a dry paddy, and into the mangroves for several hundred yards, to a place where a small *banca* was pulled up onto the shore. Another fellow squatted by the boat, chewing *betelnut,* as contented as a cow chewing her cud.*

The boat was the usual native *banca*, hewn from a log, about 15 feet long, and two feet wide, pointed at each end; not too steady, but fast and fairly easy to maneuver. The situation and setting reminded me of my departure from Luzon months earlier.

I asked the one who had guided me down from the mayor's house if he was ready. He understood enough English to comprehend what I said, and nodded with a smile. The man chewing the betelnut got up with a grunt and the two of them pushed the *banca* into the water. The guide eased himself into the prow. I threw my pack on the bottom and carefully sat down in the middle of the boat. The other carefully eased himself into the stern and pushed the *banca* away from shore with his paddle.

We glided down a narrow trail of water bordered by the roots and overhanging branches of the mangrove trees. The trees were amazingly grotesque. The base of the trunk, instead of being even with the ground as is usual with trees, is four or five feet above. What would normally be the roots, under ground, extended from the base of the trunk above ground, spreading in all directions, like the legs of a giant spider, to the soil below.

The tide was just beginning to ebb. We were 10 or 15 miles inland, but by keeping the *banca* upright and in the right direction, the tide from the sea would have us over that distance in just a few hours.

In places where the water ran swiftly, the men had their hands full, keeping the *banca* on course. In places where the water flowed slowly, they paddled in a leisurely fashion, to keep us moving. At first, we had to duck continually, to avoid overhanging branches. Fortunately, as we proceeded, the way became broader. How the boatmen found their way out of the maze of little streams I will never

---

**Betelnut* is the fruit of a palm tree common in the Philippines. It is a refreshing, mild stimulant with an effect similar to caffeine. [Ed.].

know, but they did, and apparently did so without giving it a thought. Once, we stopped on an island among the mangroves to eat young coconuts.

The tiny inlet to the mangrove swamp soon became a great stream of salt water 100 yards in width. The mangroves spread from each bank as far back as the eye could see, their grotesque roots reaching out into the water. The sun was still well up, but had lost its noonday intensity. The sky was a clear blue, broken here and there with little puffs of white clouds. We were gliding with the ebbing tide at a very fast rate, in a northeasterly direction toward the sea. The boatmen held the *banca* in the middle of the stream with an occasional stroke of the paddle. The cool breeze coming from the sea was wonderfully refreshing after the stale closeness and humidity of the swamp.

The boatman at the bow of the *banca* turned.

"Altabas," he said, motioning toward the east.

Ahead, a long line of trees was beginning to take shape above the water. Channels were visible this side of the tree line, leading off to both east and west.

I pointed to the east. "To Altabas?" He nodded.

I questioned. "New Washington?"

He pointed west.

I gestured to turn west. They smiled and nodded.

I believe they suspected all along that I would not return to the Japs.

The decision completely changed my situation. I was once again the hunted. On the other hand, I was not a prisoner. I was free. Breathing in the cool air which now had a fresher smell, I sat back in the *banca*, enjoying the landscape, feeling thankful I was not back at Calinog in that stuffy room with only two meals a day and no future.

I had one qualm about not returning. Would my escape have any repercussions on the rest of the Americans left in Calinog? I had argued it to myself, *pro* and *con*, for two days. I wondered if Captains Horney and Hay, and Lieutenant Cotheran had been sent out as I had, and if so, where they were. Also, General Christie's words kept going through my mind, "If you can escape, you are free to do so."

I had obeyed my orders from Colonel Fitzpatrick and General Christie by delivering the documents to the battalion commander of the 64th Infantry Regiment. I had no further obligation.

I wondered if I would be smart enough, and lucky enough, to avoid being captured again. If not, I would not have much to worry about. There was little doubt about what the Japs would do to a prisoner who had tried to escape. The feeling of being free again, however, gave me a whole new outlook on life.

In the back of my mind, I was beginning to consider the possibility of getting to Australia. While waiting in the municipal building in Calinog I had picked up an old geography book in which there was a map of Asia and the Oceanic Pacific. It looked possible to island-hop all the way to Australia by following Palawan Island down to Borneo, through the Makassar Strait, across the small islands to the west of Java and then a short hop to the northwest coast of Australia. I reasoned that it had been possible to get from Baguio down to Panay, then why should it not be possible, in a like manner, to get to Australia from Panay?

At the moment, however, there was the more pressing problem of getting as much distance as possible between the Japs and me. I had no idea what towns in the north of Panay were occupied. A short distance to the northwest was the small town of New Washington, which was as far as the boatmen were willing to take me. From there, I should be able to find a way to get to a more remote part of western Panay Island.

The Filipinos had consistently reported that there were no Japs in the vicinity of New Washington. I was not certain this was so, even though I had seen several bridges leading into the area destroyed. There was nothing to prevent the Japs from landing anywhere along the coast, but there was also nothing to prevent them getting a launch to where we were at the moment.

Near sundown, New Washington came into view. The bay was a quiet body of water, deep and narrow. A few large coastal sailing ships were at anchor. American warships had reportedly visited this harbor in the past.

We pulled ashore across the bay from the town to question a group of fishermen. I had no desire to land in the middle of a Japanese camp. Again, the report was that there were no Japs in New Washington. We then took the time to stretch and eat the food offered us by the fishermen.

It was dark when the *banca* grounded on the south shore of the town. The boatmen led me through a maze of dark, narrow streets to a dimly-lit wooden house. The owner was the mayor of the town. As he spoke little English, the boatmen explained my situation, and that I wanted to sail that night for Baruanga. He understood and offered to help.

My first objective was to get the Japs completely off my trail. After that I could determine my next move. The barrio of Baruanga, located on the northwest coast of Panay, isolated and near the mountains, was where I chose to go first. That was where I had first landed on Panay Island in February. If I still thought that going south was the right move, Baruanga would be a good starting point.

Before long, the owner of a sailboat appeared. After a discussion in Visayan, English and sign language, the boat owner offered to make the trip for 70 *pesos*. I threw up my hands. Although not in a position to bargain, I did. Finally, 50 *pesos* was agreed upon. This was more than twice the normal peacetime charge.

We pushed off from the north shore of New Washington at about 2200. A light wind blew from the northeast. The sailboat was called a *parau*, a narrow-hulled outrigger built for speed. It was 35 to 40 feet in length, had an outrigger on each side, and a triangular mainsail and jib, which appeared too large for the size of the hull. It was much the same as the one in which we crossed the Laguna de Bay. It took only a slight breeze to send the boat racing through the water.

In a short time, the shoreline of Panay was no more than a thin black line in the clear starlight. The cool sea air was a welcome change from the humid heat in which I had lived for so long. I had learned that in the tropics, the place to be is on the sea.

I was fascinated watching the men manage their native craft. As the wind's intensity changed, instead of reefing or letting out the sail, they deftly shifted positions on the windward outrigger supports to counter wind's force. To counter a strengthening breeze which drove the off outrigger deeper into the water, the crew slid further out on the inward one, setting the boat on a more even keel.

With much satisfaction, I watched the phosphorescent waves bounce off the bow of the boat as it cut through the dark sea, taking me further and further from the Japs. I lay on the deck, feeling grateful, and soon fell asleep.

At daylight, barely a breath of air was stirring; the sea was glassy. A heavy swell moved toward the Panay shore. Here and there, gray-black patches of clouds were streaming water into the sea. We were about seven miles out from shore and more than halfway to Baruanga. I prayed there would be no Jap launches.

A pot of rice was cooking on the deck near the stern. Rice cooking has a clean smell. The stove was a good example of Filipino ingenuity. It consisted of a square five-gallon can from which an opening on the top and on one side had been cut, and the bottom was filled with sand. A black earthen pot was placed on the open top suspended on wires. A fire was built on the sand and was fed through the side opening which also provided the draft.

Breakfast consisted of a large plateful of steaming red rice with a viand called *ginamus*. This was my first experience with *ginamus*, a heavily-salted, fishy-tasting paste made by fermenting salted shrimp for several months in an earthen jar. As the shrimp disintegrated, they acquired a highly repellent odor and a musty, fishy, yet savorous taste. A pinch of *ginamus* with each mouthful of rice made a tasty morsel once one became accustomed to the odor.

By early afternoon, the *parau* was skimming through the shallows of the channel between Panay Island and the small island of Borocay to the north. The sky had cleared. Brilliant white sand covered the bottom of the channel, giving the clear seawater a greenish hue. Schools of vividly-colored fish could be seen swimming about aimlessly. The sunlight glistened like a million diamonds on the rippled surface of the channel. Along the beaches on each side, native fishermen, nearly black from the sun, dressed in shorts and wearing great *buri* hats, were casting their round hand-nets into the shallows. Back from the far edges of the beaches, stands of coco palms covered the land as far as the eye could see, their great green crowns swaying in the breeze. The beauty and tranquility of this spot appeared untouched by the war.

Leaving the narrows, we sailed into an expanse of calm water resembling a great bay. Far to the southwest, the island of Caluya was a tiny speck on the shimmering sea. To the northwest, rose the blue mass of Mindoro Island.

Standing on the bow of the *parau*, looking over the horizon to the southwest, I tried to visualize the island of Palawan. It would be the first objective of my projected route south. I knew nothing about this island, but pictured it populated and developed much the same as Panay and Luzon. Before landing that afternoon, I made the owner of the *parau* a handsome offer to take me to Palawan. He refused. He had never been there and thought of Palawan as in another world.

There was no Home Guard this time to board us as we dropped anchor in Baruanga harbor. A small crowd gathered around me on the beach as I waded ashore. The gathering was worried about the Panay forces. Had they really surrendered? I assured them they had, at least some of them, and explained the circumstances on Corregidor that had brought it about. Their reaction was one of disbelief and bewilderment. I did not try to answer their questions about the return of American forces.

Other Americans were reported in the area. They were staying in a valley behind Baruanga. None of their names were familiar, but I wanted to meet them. A young Filipino going in their direction offered to guide me. Before leaving, I learned that the chief of police, who had tried to prove me a German spy last February, had been kicked out of office. I had planned to pay him a visit.

A half-hour's walk beyond Baruanga brought me to a *nipa* shack where one of the Americans was staying. Inside was a young man barely 20 years of age, tall, broad, and blond, clothed in ragged Army Air Corps fatigues. He was in the middle of a tall tale of his war experiences. His mannerisms, with his mild southern drawl, held his audience spellbound. An interpreter was backing him up, but most of his words seemed to be understood by his audience. He appeared, as did the enthralled group surrounding him, half-full of *tuba*, the mild alcoholic drink made from the flower of the coconut palm. I expected at any moment to see him pull out a bottle of patent medicine to sell to his näive audience at an unheard-of bargain.

When he noticed me standing by the door, he came over and introduced himself as Private Dunham of the United States Army Air Corps.

Dunham, a member of the 27th Bomb Group's 48th Materiel Squadron had been one of a group of 50 men and one officer, shipped from Manila a week after the war started, to reactivate an old airfield near San Jose, Mindoro. According to Dunham, theirs was the third detachment sent. The first two had been sunk enroute by Japanese aircraft.

The Japs had invaded southern Mindoro in April, driving Dunham's group into the mountains. They had remained there, living with the *Bukidnons,* a mountain people, until the middle of May. At that time, General Christie had sent a Filipino officer to bring them to Panay. They had arrived to find the 61st Division in the process of surrendering. The group had remained near Baruanga for a time, outfitting boats with the intention of sailing to Australia. A few days prior to my arrival, most of them had departed. Dunham and four others had elected to sit it out in Baruanga.

A short hike further inland, I found another of these Americans, Hank Linblom, who called himself a mining engineer and speculator. With a twinkle in his eyes and a slightly surprised look, he greeted me in a high, rather squeaky voice. Linblom, in his early thirties, was a tall, skinny man, loosely-hung together. Like Dunham, he was dressed in worn Army Air Corps fatigues. The trousers were torn off above the knees. The sneakers on his feet looked large enough to be snowshoes.

At the outbreak of the war, Linblom had been on Mindanao, prospecting for gold. He had started immediately for Manila where most of his belongings were stored. Mark Hubbard, also an American mining engineer living in Mindanao, had left with him. Hubbard was concerned about his wife and two sons, who had gone to Manila on 1 December to do their Christmas shopping.

Arriving in Cebu City, they found that transportation by inter-island steamer was no longer available, so they proceeded by native sailboat. From Cebu Island they sailed to the island of Masbate, then to Tablas Island. The two of them hiked across Tablas and took sail for Mindoro. At this point, they learned that the Japs had entered Manila. This was a terrible shock, especially to Hubbard.

Hearing that there was a detachment of the US Air Corps on the southern part of Mindoro, Linblom and Hubbard joined them. They found the Americans at an airfield near San Jose. They had no more than gotten settled when the Japs drove them off the airfield. Linblom and Hubbard accompanied the Air Corps detachment into the mountains to the north, where they made out until recently brought to Panay. Linblom thought that American forces would be back in the Philippines within a few months and had flatly refused to leave for Australia with the group from Mindoro. For the present, he was considering going to Tablas Island with a Captain Raval, the Filipino officer General Christie had sent to bring the group to Panay.

That evening I walked back to the seashore, looking for a boat bound for Palawan Island. Not only was I unable to find anyone who was planning to go there, but I found no one who had ever *been* there. I started to wonder what kind of a place it was. When I spoke about wanting to go to Palawan, the locals looked at me as though I was crazy. This was the same reaction I had gotten from the captain of the *parau* that had brought me from New Washington.

The next morning, Linblom and I hiked north over a ridge of hills to the *barrio* of Caticlan. Caticlan faced the narrows that separated the islands of Panay and Borocay, the same through which I had sailed the previous day. The *barrio* is made up largely of coconut groves interspersed with rice paddies. Instead of being bunched together, most of the houses were scattered throughout the area.

We came to a large green wooden house, raised high on stilts, with a silvery tin roof. It was about a kilometer back from the shore. This was the house of the *barrio teniente,* where three of the Americans from Mindoro Island were staying.

Privates Palmer and Oakley were members of the Air Corps; both were in their early twenties. Oakley was having an attack of the malaria that he had contracted in the mountains of Mindoro. No one admitted having any quinine, which Oakley needed badly.

The third American was Hubbard. He was sitting apart from the other two, whiling away the time, seemingly having a spell of grouchiness by himself. As we approached, he looked up, squinting through his crudely-mended spectacles. He acknowledged our greetings with a grunt. Hubbard was middle-aged, of medium height, slightly overweight, and prematurely gray. In his cast-off, weather-beaten and ragged Army Air Corps fatigue uniform, he gave the appearance of a hairy and healthy-looking beachcomber. According to Linblom, Hubbard's hair had turned gray during the past few months in the mountains of Mindoro.

The remainder of the day was spent discussing plans for the future, with little result. It did become clear, however, that none of the other four Americans were in the least interested in going to Australia. They were unanimous in the opinion that the war would be over in a matter of months and felt that taking the chances entailed in sailing to Australia was utterly crazy.

Toward evening, Captain Raval, who had brought the Mindoro group to Panay, returned from a trip into the mountains. Raval, between 30 and 35 years old, of medium height, was a slim, erect, square-shouldered man with sharp, hawk-like features. He walked with a swagger and had a presumptuous way of speaking.

Raval brought back the story that an American bomber might land on a nearby airfield, either that evening or the next. The story reportedly came from Captain Meider, the pilot and chief of the 61st Division's one-man air force up until the time of surrender. In spite of the fact that there were no airfields in the area large enough to accommodate a bomber, and that it was illogical to believe that a lone bomber would be sent into the Philippines at this point, the story was given some credence by both Americans and Filipinos and generated a fair amount of excitement. Needless to say, the story soon died, and with it most of the little remaining hope. This was typical of the frustration that dominated the minds of those who were left in the Philippines, Americans and Filipinos alike.

Few had yet arrived at the full realization that the United States had been defeated in the Philippine Islands. It was nearly six months since the Japanese invasion. Although it seemed like yesterday, it was hard to believe so much had happened in such a short time. It had started calmly, then slowly built to a crescendo, which ended in the fall of Corregidor. Those left had to fend for themselves as best they could.

The following day, I crossed to the island of Borocay, where a large sailing vessel could be seen anchored off the southern shore. I was still in the hope of finding a boat bound for Palawan. There was still the possibility of finding the Americans who had sailed from Baruanga a few days before my arrival.

The vessel was a two-master, built for inter-island travel. From one of her masts flew a small black flag, designating her as a leper ship. She was homeward bound for Culion Island, to the west and not far off the coast of Palawan. She had just completed a voyage through the Visayas, returning lepers to their homes. The leper colony in Culion was no longer capable of taking care them.

The captain of the ship offered to take me with him, but made it clear that Culion was a small island and was occupied by a large garrison of Japs. Even though Culion was practically where I wanted to go, my chances of getting any farther seemed slim. Reluctantly, I refused the offer.

I was beginning to believe that it was not meant that I should go south, at least for the time being.

Linblom, Hubbard, and Palmer decided to go north with Raval to Tablas Island. Palmer had been there with Raval during the past week. The residents of the little town of Santa Fe, near the southern tip of the island, had offered the Americans refuge for the duration. I was welcome to accompany them. With little choice left, I decided to go.

Oakley, still weak from his malaria attack, stayed on Panay, joining Dunham in Baruanga.

As we were preparing to leave, one of Raval's boat crew died of malaria. They hastily constructed a crude wooden coffin. In the afternoon, a solemn procession wound through the coconut groves to the local cemetery. The coffin was carried by a motley group of half-uniformed soldiers, their rifles strapped to their backs. A band of three or four screeching wind instruments led the way, each playing his interpretation of the same jazz tune in a different key. Following the coffin were Raval and his remaining soldiers, the Americans, and several of the *barrio*-folk.

A local padre said a few words and the coffin was lowered. Raval had some of his men line up beside the grave to fire a parting volley. That firing turned out to be an individual affair, hazardous to the onlookers. The soldiers were firing live ammunition, some, I suspected, for the first time.

We had returned to the house of the *barrio teniente* when a series of shots were heard from the direction of the shore. I was sure the Japs had surprised us. For a few moments, there was great confusion. Then word came that the shots had been fired by Raval's men. After the burial, they had returned to the house where the man had died. At the request of the owner, the soldiers had discharged their rifles in the air, to drive away evil spirits that were surely hovering around after a death.

The sun was setting by the time we were ready to sail. A slight breeze coming from the southwest barely rippled the sea. Raval's boat was a pretty little craft, a *parau*, a small version of the one that had brought me to Baruanga. We waded out to it and climbed aboard. A few minutes at the oars put the *parau* in position to catch the offshore breeze. The sails filled gently. A little singing sound came from the prow as it cut through the smooth water.

As usual, the coolness and openness of the sea were very welcome after the past few days in the steamy coconut groves. I was trying to persuade myself that sailing to Tablas was the right thing to do. I had come only for lack of a better plan.

As we sailed north, close to the eastern shore of Borocay Island, our mood was pleasant. Linblom had brought a bamboo tube of *tuba* aboard and *hunguts* of the golden liquid were being freely passed around.* Linblom and Palmer were exchanging jokes. Even old Hubbard threw off some of his moodiness. We were momentarily free of the trials of our existence.

*A hungut is a small bowl made from a half of a coconut shell. [Auth.]

Part Three
DERELICTS

Chapter 29

It was after dark when we beached at Santa Fe. There was no wharf in the little bay. As we waded ashore, the waves from the now-strong southwest wind soaked us to the mid-section. Palmer led us along a dark street to a house that he singled out as being "the one." We knocked, then heard a voice from inside.

"Who is it?" The words came in a crackly, nasal tone with an accent that obviously had been acquired in the United States. A middle-aged Filipino stood in the doorway. He had a kindly, pleasant face.

Juanito Sanchez, bare-footed, dressed in an undershirt and a pair of old trousers, wearing horn-rimmed glasses, asked us into his home. He greeted us as old friends. In his nasal voice, he made it clear that we were welcome in his home as long as we wished to stay.

As soon as we were all seated, and he had made what he considered to be proper apologies for the poor accommodations he had to offer, Señor Sanchez started to tell of his experiences in the United States. We were to learn that this was his favorite topic of conversation. He had spent nine years in America as a young man and looked back upon those years as the best of his life.

Señor Sanchez's recital was interrupted, somewhat to his annoyance, by the entry of his family from the back area. *Señora* Sanchez was a fine looking lady, a refined Spanish *mestiza*; her daughter, Aida, was 20 and beautiful; and there were three boys: a fat 16-year-old, a slim 10-year-old and a baby. The children were dressed in shorts and shirts, much the same as American children would dress in a warm climate. *Señora* Sanchez wore the blouse and long skirt of the Filipina.

Señor Sanchez hurriedly introduced his family, then immediately continued his "Experiences in the United States." His storytelling, much to our relief, was gradually brought to a halt by the noise and confusion of the townsfolk crowding into the Sanchez house for a look at the newly-arrived Americans. They were on the floor, crowded in the corners, even hanging in the windows. It was midnight before we went to our beds, which were mats and blankets on the wooden floor.

Santa Fe was a small town of about 200 souls located on the southern shore of Tablas, a small island in the center of the Philippine Archipelago. Up to the time of our arrival, it had not been visited by the Japs. The nearest towns of any consequence were Looc and Odiongan to the north, on the western coast. Looc was a little over 9 miles by trail; Odiongan was another 12.5 miles beyond that, by a cart road.

There were no roads into Santa Fe and few trails other than the main one to Looc. The small horseshoe-shaped bay provided the main means of communication with the outside world. Being shallow and without landing facilities, seagoing traffic was restricted to small boats, and at low tide even these had to anchor far from shore. For the moment, I welcomed this isolation.

The houses in Santa Fe were crowded together in square blocks that were separated by wide dirt streets. Their construction varied between the bamboo-*nipa* and the wooden with galvanized iron roofs. Inside, there was usually a living room, maybe two bedrooms and a kitchen, and practically no furniture. The kitchen stove was an open fire made on a sandbox. The houses fronted right on the street. When the great bamboo and *nipa* windows were open, which was most of the time, anyone in the street could see what was going on in the entire house. Sanitary facilities were either down the beach or in the forest. The chickens and pigs made up the sanitary corps. A nearby well provided water. Life was uncomplicated and relaxed. The war had had little affect on the people of Santa Fe.

A mayor, a secretary, a treasurer, a few clerks, and a police force of three or four men still functioned as the government.

The majority of townsfolk were Spanish *mestizos,* landowners, whose livelihood came from growing rice and *copra.* Their land had been owned by their respective families for generations. In most cases, it had been passed down from their Spanish forefathers. As a rule, they were well educated. During the Spanish occupation, their children were usually sent to schools in Spain. Since being taken over by the United States, many attended universities there, returning afterwards to their towns or *barrios* to live out their lives quietly.

In contrast was the life of the *Tao,* or peasant who made his living as a sharecropper. He lived in a one- or two-room *nipa* shack on the land he cultivated or in a nearby *barrio.* His life was grim, being one of ignorance, poverty, and hard work. Most of them with whom I came in contact, however, seemed happy and contented.

Señor Sanchez had outlined a plan for evacuation into the hills in the event the Japs decided to make a visit. I had been on the go for so long that it seemed unnatural to slow down. I was tense and nervous and tired. This was a wonderful opportunity to relax.

None of us knew the best thing to do. I felt sure it would be years before the Allies would be able to drive the Japs out of the Philippines. The idea of starting a guerrilla movement did not seem plausible in light of the poor performance of the Philippine soldiers I had seen to date. The best move at the moment seemed to be to head for Australia, but I was at a loss regarding how to go about it. No one with whom I spoke provided any hope of even getting as far as Palawan

Island, especially at this time of year, with the southwest monsoon coming on. It never occurred to me that the islands to the south were not as well settled as Luzon, or that the inhabitants would not be as friendly. Additionally, I knew very little about the weather, the sea, or sailing a boat. In my ignorance, all these things were discounted, along with disease, and the physical and mental strain entailed in such an undertaking.

The alternative was to stay a while in Santa Fe. I decided to stay.

At first it was difficult to adjust to the comparative security and slow pace of Santa Fe, but, as the days passed, the constant feeling of tenseness began to subside. I gradually started to relax and slowly came to enjoy the simple routine of life there.

My diet consisted of rice with a watery viand three times a day—greens, fish, chicken, or meat were usually the ingredients boiled and served in the watery broth. Occasionally, fresh or dried fish would be fried in coconut oil. When available, eggs were soft-boiled or sometimes fried. Once in a while, *Señora* Sanchez served fried rice with little chips of meat and onions. I could eat two heaping plates of this combination at one sitting.

I had never really gotten over the hunger with which I left Luzon months before. Fill myself as I would with rice and the soupy concoctions, I never felt completely satisfied. I still often literally dreamt of feasts consisting of various American dishes and meals. The one I still seemed to miss most was breakfast—fried eggs with loads of bacon, stacks of warm toast soaked with butter, and cups of steaming, real coffee.

After breakfast I usually spent a short while listening to Juanito's continuing story of his "Life in America." Always, as memories of the days of his youth came back to him, his eyes would sparkle and the languid manner that usually engulfed him changed to one of vivaciousness.

One of the few activities in the town that happened with any regularity was the morning bath of Juanito's fighting cocks. To him, this was a ritual of love. Staked out individually in his front yard, he poured a little water over each one. Then, wetting his hand, he would massage each bird, all the time speaking with him by name. The owlish-eyed birds would gurgle back at him as though understanding every word.

To me, with their powerful bodies, stunted wings, and oversized thighs plucked nearly bare of feathers, these creatures resembled an ugly caricature of a handsome barnyard rooster. Their fiery red combs and wattles, heavy beaks and beady eyes added to their fierce appearance.

If there was any good in these birds, I was sure Juanito brought it out. The reason for the daily bath and massage was to give the cocks endurance in a fight, but as long as I knew Juanito, I never knew him to fight any of his birds. He thought too much of them.

After the ritual of the roosters, I sometimes accompanied him in his daily search for food. This was probably his most important duty and often took not only the remainder of the morning, but sometimes the entire day and even into the night. At such times, in the late afternoon, tiring of our unsuccessful search, we would stop to sample the local *tuba* at a nearby *barrio*. These were the days we would arrive home late, exhausted, and would have only salt with our rice.

On days when I stayed in town, *Señora* Sanchez would serve parched corn coffee with sugar-topped rice cakes in the middle of the morning, to suppress my hunger until lunch.

After a good lunch, it was the custom to have a *siesta*. After that came the *merienda* hour, or snack time. This was typically followed by another walk, and by sunset we were ready to test the day's batch of *tuba*. This usually ended in a few songs, accompanied with a guitar. Supper was served late, lit by dim, coconut-oil lamps and made lively by the *tuba*.

A good number of the townsfolk spoke English and were well educated. Many pleasant hours were spent with them. Their questions about America never seemed to end. Many times there was an expression of appreciation for the way America had treated the Filipinos during its 40 years of presence in the islands. I was becoming a firm believer that the establishment of first-aid stations and elementary schools in the small towns and *barrios* did more to influence the culture and thinking of the Filipinos than anything else done by the United States.

There were a few books in English scattered around the town, which I read. Often, I was content to just sit in the living room, gazing down the main road of Santa Fe toward the bay. At this time of year, with the change of the monsoons, it was calm and green, and restful to watch. Beyond, to the south, across a broad channel was tiny Carabao Island.

There were no American cigarettes, but there was plenty of native tobacco, grown both on Tablas and Carabao Island. It needed processing before it made a tolerable cigarette tobacco. After selection, a good sheath of leaves was washed. To wash it too much took away the flavor; to wash it too little made it taste too strong. After removing the spines, the leaves were shredded and soaked in a sweet, spicy mixture. Lastly, the tobacco was fried or dried in a *wok,* to a soft moistness. This process created a good smoking tobacco, but it was just as important to find a good paper. After much searching and testing, a varicolored drawing paper found in the schoolhouse was the best. This paper became precious trade material.

On days when the tide was low, the bottom of the shallow harbor was free of water and nearly everyone, with their baskets, would be out digging for snails. The variegated shells were oval in shape and ranged from the size of one's thumb to an inch or more in diameter. The snails were found just below the surface of the sand. Probing with a stick easily located them. Usually, these outings were turned into a game, to see who could fill his basket first or who could find the largest snail.

The snails were dumped live into boiling water with a handful of salt. They were served steaming hot, poured along the center of the bamboo dining table, where they could drain through onto the floor. To eat the snails, you sucked them out of their shells. Perhaps they did not compare to the *escargot* of France, but rice with snails in Santa Fe made a fine meal.

For special occasions, a *lechon* would be prepared. This could be a suckling pig or a chicken, barbecued over hot coals, and then eaten as a *hors d'oeuvre* with *tuba* while waiting to start the main meal.

I especially remembered one dish that was served at a wedding feast. A compliment to my host brought an odd smile. After dinner he explained its preparation. A pig was killed by sticking, letting all its blood drain into a pan. The heart, liver, kidneys and intestines were washed and chopped into small pieces. They were then boiled in a *court-bouillon,* until the liquid was nearly evaporated and the meat was tender. Then the blood, mixed with a little rice flour, was added to make a rich, brown sauce for the cooked innards. Served all together on rice, it was wonderfully tasty.

About the second week after our arrival, Linblom and Raval left Santa Fe for the town of Looc. Some people in Looc reportedly had a radio hidden in the nearby hills.

What news we had been getting in Santa Fe came second or third hand from visitors coming overland from Looc or arriving by sailboat. We had little idea of what was going on in the rest of the Philippines or how the war was progressing around the world. Linblom was firmly convinced that the war would be over soon and wanted to be in position to get into Manila as quickly as possible.

After several days with no news from Linblom or Raval, Hubbard and Palmer decided to follow. Hubbard was also still of the opinion that the war would not last long, and being constantly concerned about his family, wanted to be near a source of news, so he might get to Manila as soon as it was reported cleared of Japs.

Not long afterward, I followed.

In Santa Fe, I had acquired a rectangular-shaped basket that I now used as my pack. It was 12 by 14 inches on the sides and four inches deep. It swung over one shoulder, comfortably supported under the arm. In it, I stuffed my belongings—a cotton blanket, mess kit and spoon, a toothbrush and razor. The helmet had been discarded. My sneakers had nearly disintegrated. One of my reasons for going to Looc was to look for shoes.

The trail to Looc wound north and west across a hilly peninsula covered with *cogan* grass, rice fields, and clumps of papaya and banana trees. It entered coconut groves as it wound down toward the shore of Looc Bay, continuing northward around the shore to the town of Looc. It took nearly a half a day to make that hike.

The business section of Looc was in disrepair. Few shops were open. Most were crudely boarded up for the duration, making the area look like a shantytown. It reminded me of Iloilo City, but on a smaller scale. The town plaza was overrun with weeds, partially hiding a few unkempt statues. The market place was probably the best-maintained and most active part of the town. There, the country folk displayed their produce for sale or barter.

There were some nice homes of wooden construction with tin roofs, however. These were occupied by well-to-do Filipino families.

I went to the house of Erbacio, a relative of Señor Sanchez. He was on his porch, deeply absorbed in a game of *mah-jongg*. The tenseness and deep concentration of the players and onlookers made me think the stakes must be high. I was later to learn that this game went on day after day, sometimes far into the night, the year around.

At the end of the round, Erbacio excused himself and came to greet me. He was very cordial and asked me to stay with him while in Looc. Linblom was staying across the bay in the *barrio* of Agaho with a man named Marianito and his family. Hubbard and Palmer had moved into an empty shack outside of town. Raval and his soldiers had taken over a vacated building in town. With his rank and a few armed soldiers under him, Raval had been throwing his weight around, which, according to Erbacio, the townspeople resented. The radio was hidden one to two miles out of town. The news from San Francisco came on late in the afternoon. Erbacio offered to furnish me a guide to the radio site.

After lunch I had a visit with Raval. He and a half-dozen of his soldiers were lolling around doing nothing. I asked him what he had on his mind. He said nothing. Looking back, I believe this is the only time I ever suspected Raval of telling the truth. The townspeople were feeding them.

Raval did tell me he had talked with a trader from Baruanga, who reported that the Japs had come into the *barrio* searching for a Captain Whitehead. They had offered 10,000 *pesos* for his capture. Raval assured me he had said nothing of my whereabouts.

I wondered.

I met Hubbard and Palmer at the radio site that afternoon. They had decided not to return to Santa Fe. Hubbard was grumpy as usual. Palmer had a sore on his leg that looked bad.

The news on the radio was not encouraging, but it was current and from a reliable source. It was the first I had since the surrender. The news reported the Japs were still moving south. They had occupied Port Morseby, New Guinea, just north of Australia, and several islands to the east. It seemed we had nothing to stop them. I wondered if Australia would be next. The thought came to me that we must really have taken quite a shellacking at Pearl Harbor. I never had brought myself to believe the losses reported by the Japs, but was beginning to realize that Pearl Harbor may have been as disastrous as Clark Field.

The next day, I sailed across the bay to visit Linblom. He had lost none of his optimism. He believed it impossible for the war to last much longer. He also had decided not to return to Santa Fe. Linblom's host, Marianito, asked me to stay with him, too. I was tempted, as I enjoyed their company, but could see no reason to forsake Señor Sanchez and his tales of America.

The next day, I took the trail back to Santa Fe. The mayor of Santa Fe, who had moved onto his farm in Agmanic, was in town that night. I met *Señor* Gomez for the first time at a *tuba* gathering. After a few *hunguts,* he asked me to stay with him in the country. Next morning, he asked me again and I accepted. This was the latter part of June 1942.

Chapter 30

Agmanic was four or five miles southeast of Santa Fe around the southern tip of Tablas Island.

It was late afternoon when we arrived. I was sweaty and tired from the walk. The not-too-distant beach and the glisten of the calm, green water beyond were too much to resist. I had a good, refreshing swim before *tuba* time.

The mayor believed in a generous amount of *tuba* before dinner. After dinner, there was little time wasted in getting to bed. The entire Gomez family slept on the floor in the one small sleeping room of the house. I was given a mat on the floor in the living room.

The mayor had a house full of children and a pretty wife who was a little the worse for wear. For the duration, they were living in a small *nipa* shack, back a few hundred yards from the sea, in the center of a coconut grove.

Señor Gomez was a *mestizo* and had inherited his land from his Spanish ancestors. He was a tall, well-built man, with black hair and a little black mustache. His looks and bearing reminded me of what I pictured as a "Spanish Dandy." He was intelligent and well educated, yet seemed perfectly content to live out his life with his family and friends in this isolated little community. This had been the custom of his forebears for generations.

Señora Gomez was also of Spanish descent, a lovely, kind woman, devoted to making life as comfortable and pleasant as possible for her husband and their brood.

It did not take long to get into a routine. Usually, I was up before daylight and out on the beach for a walk and a bath in the sea.

Señora Gomez served excellent meals, but how she did it with her limited means, I never understood. Her kitchen was a cubicle off the dining room. Her stove was a sandbox with stones placed around to support her pots. She had a frying pan or *wok,* a rice pot, a few kettles, and some ladles made of coconut shells with bamboo handles.

She did not believe that food had to be boiled to be good. While rice was the mainstay of every meal, there was often fried fish, chicken, or pork to go with it.

After breakfast I usually tried to help, sometimes chopping wood for the kitchen, cleaning fish, plucking a chicken, or hauling water from the well.

When time allowed, I had a short nap before lunch. There was usually a *hungut* or two of *tuba* left over from the night before, which, from the standpoint of economy, should not be wasted. This gave one's appetite a good edge for lunch. These new practices were the result of association with the mayor. We seldom drank *tuba* before breakfast.

After lunch, of course, we had a *siesta* that lasted an hour or two. After *siesta*, we had *merienda* with corn coffee and sweets such as rice flour cookies sprinkled with sugar. Then the mayor and I took our daily walk looking over his farm and coconut plantation. His farm was sharecropped with a *Tao* who lived in a nearby *barrio*. The father of the *Tao* had worked for the mayor's father and the son of the *Tao* someday would probably work for Ernesto, the son of the mayor.

One time walking through his coconut groves, taking stock of the condition of his trees and the coming crop, he lamented his lack of industry. He pointed out spaces where new trees could be planted or should have been years past. If only he could make himself plant just one tree a month, or even one a year, before long his groves would be full-bearing again, but he never could quite bring himself to do it. And the old *Tao* refused to plant coconut trees, as it was definitely not his job. The mayor agreed with that.

Planting a coconut tree amounted to digging a hole, selecting a sprouting coconut, with which the ground was littered, placing it in the hole and covering it over with earth. I told the mayor that one day I would plant one for him.

Due to our position just north of the equator, the sun set the year around at about 1800 hours. *Tuba* call was one hour before sundown.

Whatever our afternoon activities, the mayor and I assembled on the little porch in front of his house, in our appointed chairs, with *hunguts,* ready to taste and discuss the day's *tuba*. Each day it was different in flavor, color, smell, and alcoholic content.

Tuba comes from the flower of the coconut palm. Right after the flower opens, before it starts to spread and while still a light green color, it is bound together and its ends clipped off. The clipped end is tied into a bamboo tube, "tubo" in Spanish, thus its name. The sap from the flower, which normally would develop young coconuts, instead, flows into the tube. The sugar in this sap is sufficient to ferment it to an alcoholic content of five or six percent, over a 24-hour period. The movement of the palm caused by the wind and the temperature has a decided influence on the fermentation process.

The *tuba* from each palm is different. And the *tuba* from the same tree varies throughout the year, even from day to day, under changing weather conditions. After the *tuba* had been strained, ground tanbark usually was mixed with it to give it a golden, brown color and to improve its taste. There is an odor to *tuba* not unlike the smell of sour coconut meat. Its taste is sweetish with a little nip, like mild applejack.

To the right of the Gomez' front yard grew an old coconut tree, its lower trunk forming a great bow. This deformity had resulted from a storm that had nearly destroyed it when quite young. The mayor, himself, was a boy at the time and nursed the tree back to life. Now it was rewarding him.

"The finest *tuba* in the islands comes from this old tree." The mayor would repeat this belief nearly every evening.

The *Tao* who sharecropped *Señor* Gomez's nearby rice fields, was also the *menengeti,* the harvester of the *tuba*. Each evening, dressed in the same discolored pair of cotton shorts, with a bolo at his side and a bamboo tube over his shoulder, the *menengeti* shinnied to the top of the old palm. After carefully filling the tube on his shoulder from the one in the tree, he re-clipped the tips of the flower, placed it back in its tube, and shinnied back down. The old tree gave him a precarious ride when there was a strong wind.

After straining and adding the tanbark, the *Tao* would always have a *hungut* with us. Then he and the mayor would have a serious discussion over its quality. My opinion of it was always asked. I was by now becoming a connoisseur of the golden liquid.

This daily event was a pleasant time. We discussed the happenings of the day, plans for the morrow, and philosophized on life in general. Sometimes, these discussions ended with a few songs accompanied by the mayor on his guitar. I look back on those evenings with a great deal of pleasure.

Dinner was after dark by lamplight, around a big bamboo table with the whole family. Usually it lasted an hour or so. It was a happy time, with the children talking and laughing at the stories and jokes of their father, who liked to make his family laugh. Dinner usually finished with songs and the mayor playing his guitar some more.

After dinner, everyone turned in. I usually slept with my clothes on because of the mosquitoes.

For the first time in a long while I was becoming relaxed, thoroughly enjoying doing nothing and eating my fill. One day the mayor even remarked that I was getting fat.

On 4 July, Linblom made a visit to Agmanic. He liked the mayor as much as I did, and the three of us spent a few very enjoyable days together.

Linblom had recent news from San Francisco. The allies were starting to build up their forces in Australia. The Japs had not landed there yet. The United States had tried some landings on islands occupied by the Japs east of New Guinea.*

Linblom was still his carefree, optimistic self. His theme was to sit tight; the war would be over soon. I never understood the basis for his optimism.

Occasionally, I accompanied the mayor on his official trips into Santa Fe. One of these was on a Sunday, when an important cockfight had been scheduled. Santa Fe did not have a specially constructed pit in which to hold such fights. According to the mayor, one was badly needed, but these were poor times and money was scarce. So the big fights, when birds were brought in from the surrounding *barrios*, had to be held in the main street, which was dirt.

The crowd formed around a circle drawn in the street. An individual was appointed to act as "Master of Ceremonies," and several judges were appointed. These individuals stayed in the ring the whole time. Entries had been made and the cocks paired off beforehand. A blackboard displayed the order of upcoming fights. The procedure for each fight was the same.

---

*The main American combat landings east of New Guinea began in early August 1942, on the island of Guadalcanal.

A fight is called. The owners carry their participants into the circle. A steel spur is lashed to one leg of each bird. The razor-sharp spurs are about two inches long and a quarter of an inch wide. Thin, double-edged and pointed, they curve slightly upward. Each bird is then inspected by a judge. Lastly, the "Master of Ceremonies" explains the rules of the fight.

The officials allow a few minutes for bets to be laid. Individuals bet between each other on the sidelines, raising, calling, and laying their paper notes and coins on the ground as they commit their money. When any given bet is made and agreed upon, a rock is placed on top of the money. Only the winner of the bet can touch the rock. Some enterprising individuals were giving odds and taking bets.

Finally all is ready. There is an air of excitement in the crowd, much the same as at the big tracks. The owners of the birds have a good deal at stake. Besides their reputation, there is the money and the time spent in selecting, raising and training a cock. And besides, usually a fair amount of money is bet on their darlings.

The fighting cocks face each other in the center of the ring, their eyes ablaze straining to get at one another. Held by their owners in such a way as to prevent their wings from flapping and the spur from doing damage, the cocks are being pushed toward each other, nearly touching beaks. Each moment their rage becomes greater.

At a word from the judge, the cocks are thrown together. There is a flurry of feathers as they jump into the air, each trying to spur his adversary.

The crowd goes wild, yelling for their favorite. There is a combination of groans and shrieks as one bird sinks a spur into his opponent. After the initial flurry, each bird has felt the spur. If evenly matched, they will usually back off at this point. Seemingly taking measure of each other, heads close to the ground and barely separated neck feathers ruffled, poised to jump. Then, together in the air again, feathers flying, the steel on their legs flashing.

One cock puts his spur deep into the vitals of his opponent. The doomed cock feels little, yet is still full of fight. At the next flurry, the wounded cock sinks his spur into the vitals of his opponent. The first doomed cock is about bled out now, and slowly folds up on the ground. The other cock is on him like a tiger, tearing him apart. Blood is coming from the beak of the victor. He slowly sinks to the ground. In moments, both are dead.

Now it is time for the next fight. The fights continued like this until all are resolved, and bets paid off.

As enjoyable as the early evenings on the porch were, there was one annoyance: the mosquitoes, which chose that time of day to feed. My ankles became a mass of small sores. One of these became infected and soon looked like the sore I had seen on Palmer's leg. It was a tropical ulcer. The mayor called it *bococong*. It gradually grew, causing no end of annoyance and some pain.

One morning I heard the mayor venting his anger on something on the edge of the coconut grove outside the house.

"*Hisus, Maria, Hosep, Hindut, Yaput, Yut,* Son-of-a-Beech."

As I approached him and asked what the trouble was, he pointed to a hole in front of him where a few days before I had planted a coconut.

"Those goddamn pigs. You know, I always thought there wasn't much use to do this planting."

Another morning early, walking along the beach, I noticed a wriggling fish rising out of the sea not far from shore. It was suspended on a thin shaft that had pierced it through the middle. Following it, a brown hand and arm and head rose out of the water. Gasping for air, the fisherman swam to a nearby rock to catch his breath. He had pulled his goggles down around his neck.

I waved to him and yelled, "*Marami pescau*" (plenty of fish). He nodded and smiled.

A deft blow on the head of the fish stopped its wiggling. The boy removed the arrow and attached the fish to his waist with a string through the gills.

Rested, he started floating face down searching below the surface, propelling himself by slight movements of his legs. Then down he went, out of sight. Several moments passed before he came up for air to try again.

On mornings when the sea was calm, there would often be several fishermen diving among the rocks and coral, bobbing up for air and going down again like so many seals. Dressed in scanty shorts, they wore goggles and carried a short gun-shaped stick. Like a kid seeing a new toy, I wanted to try it.

It did not take long to induce one of them to let me try his goggles and spear gun. Face down, cruising slowly over the corral and rock formations, it was possible to see a good distance below the surface of the clear water. There were always schools of small fish in the crevices and little channels, but it took searching to find a fish worthy of a stalk. One, eight inches or more in length, was acceptable. A 12-"incher" was trophy class.

The spear fishing did not turn out to be as easy as it looked, but a few tries with borrowed goggles and gun sold me; I wanted a set of goggles and spear gun of my own. I assembled the materials with the help of the mayor and one of the fishermen.

Goggles were whittled from two pieces of soft wood, oblong-shaped to fit the eye, hollowed out leaving only a rim. One side of the rim was cut to fit the contour of the eye; the opposite beveled, to insert a piece of glass. The glass was held in place by a native waterproof gum applied around the edges. The eyepieces were held together by a light cord threaded through tiny holes on the inside of each piece, and the cord rested on the bridge of the nose. The goggles were held in place by another cord threaded through tiny holes on the outside of each piece, which was slipped over the back of the head. Properly fitted and adjusted, the eyes were kept perfectly dry.

The handle of the spear gun was made of wood, whittled into the shape of a small gunstock. It had a trigger, a rubber band from an old tire tube as a propellant, and a 12- to 14-inch barrel. A hole through the barrel was sufficiently large to insert a wire arrow. The arrow was generally an eighth to three-sixteenths of an inch in diameter and 18 to 20 inches in length. At one end, the arrow had a barbed head, at the other a notch, and close to the notch a small hole.

The ends of the rubber bands were attached well forward on each side of the barrel; opposite ends were connected with a piece of cord that was placed in the notch of the arrow.

The cocking and releasing mechanisms consisted of a wire trigger pivoted inside the hollowed-out center of the handle. The trigger was connected to a wire pin that protruded through a hole, out the top of the handle, behind the barrel. The arrow, pulled through the barrel to the rear under tension of the rubber bands, was secured by this pin inserted into the hole in the arrow.

Pulling the trigger to the rear pulled the pin downward and released the arrow. The arrow was driven through the water a short distance with sufficient force to penetrate the body of a small fish.

With my new goggles and gun, I spent part of each day learning their use. The best place for this type of fishing was among the rocks and coral formations in the shallows not far from shore. I found it took practice to stay down below the surface of the water with lungs full of air. It also took finesse to approach the fish without scaring it off. A certain amount of skill was required to properly launch the arrow.

I watched the others closely and tried to copy them. When a desirable fish was located, the fisherman took a gulp of air and dived, fast at first, slowing as he approached his prey and occasionally releasing streams of bubbles to reduce his buoyancy. With arm outstretched holding the cocked spear gun, barely moving now toward the fish, he fired the arrow. A twitch of the fish, a slight jerk on release of the arrow, the action of an unseen current: all these could throw the arrow off its target. I learned that, ironically, these also could cause a mis-aimed arrow to find its mark.

Getting fish within shooting distance often became a game of hide-and-seek. The fish uncannily seemed to know the range of the gun, moving just as one was ready to shoot. Sometimes, I would find myself in deep water, where an encounter with a shark or one of the big eels was not unlikely.

The trick, never easy, was to get the head of the arrow nearly touching the broadside of the unsuspecting fish, and then releasing it without a jerk.

My efforts at first were neither skillful nor very successful, but I enjoyed it. I also felt it quite worthwhile when I could present *Señora* Gomez with a fish or two for her table.

I knew the fish trap out from the shore in front of the mayor's house was his and that his *Tao* occasionally walked in with a string of fish taken from it. Other than that, however, I had given it little thought. Several times the mayor had offered to show me his trap and one day, I had agreed.

We arose before the dawn. Nothing was offered as breakfast except the suggestion of freshly-caught fish if we were lucky.

I stumbled along the coconut-strewn path towards the shore, wondering why I had ever volunteered to be a party to such an excursion. As we neared the shore in the darkness, the *Tao* greeted *Señor* Gomez. The sea and the sky were murky. A chill breeze made a choppy sea, and caused me to shiver.

On the shore was our transport, a *banca*. The *Tao* eased himself into the stern and began to paddle frantically. The mayor was in the stem, also paddling hard. I was on my knees amidships. Soon, the spray from the waves breaking against the side of the boat had us drenched and the boat was filling with water. In no time, I was in four or five inches of water, a coconut shell in each hand, bailing madly. With the load of three of us, there was practically no freeboard. The water came in over the sides faster than I could bail it out. The odds seemed good that we would be in the drink before the morning was over.

The fish trap was a half-mile out from shore. It was on a sandy shallow over which schools of fish feeding up and down the coastline usually passed. The trap was made in the shape of a figure 6, placed so that the schools of fish coming from up coast would be guided by the long stem of the 6 toward the small opening at the base of the 6, which trapped them. The trap was made of saplings driven into the sandy bottom three or four feet apart. Between these saplings, roots from the forest were woven to form a nearly impenetrable wall, even to small fish.

The length of the trap from one end to the other was close to 200 feet. The base of the figure 6 was 20 feet in diameter with an entrance 12 inches in width. In theory, a school of fish feeding down the coast would run into the barrier formed by the concave stem of the figure 6. In an effort to swim around the obstacle, they would follow the stem through the narrow opening into the trap. Few were smart enough to find their way back out.

"*Marami pescau*" (many fish), the old *Tao* said as we drew near the trap. Two to three dozen fish could be seen swimming above the sandy bottom.

The *banca* was secured to the uprights of the trap, which protruded several feet above the water. The old man with diving glasses and spear gun climbed into the trap and lowered himself into the water. With a gulp of air, he was below the surface, gliding toward the fish. The water was about eight feet deep. In a minute he was back on top, blowing and filling his lungs, a fish wriggling on his wire arrow, pierced through the middle.

The old man tired after a while, so the mayor put on the goggles and went after the fish. He was as adept as the old man. Then it was my turn.

My limited practice in this type of fishing along the shore was helpful but left a few gaps in preparing for this first fish trap experience. By the time I had struggled to the bottom with a lung full of air, I was ready to return to the surface. Also, my struggles had scared the fish out of reach. Each time up I received advice. Each time down I came a little closer to my quarry. At long last, my arrow pierced a fish. I climbed back into the *banca*, near exhaustion and shivering.

We beached with a load of fish sloshing about in the bottom of the *banca*. The mayor selected a few of the most choice, said a few words to the old *Tao* and we headed for breakfast.

The old *Tao* would take what fish he wanted, some to be eaten this day, some to be dried and eaten on days when the catch was poor. The rest would be given to his neighbors, whose traps had not produced that day.

Word came to Agmanic that an American had landed in Santa Fe. I walked in to meet him. His name was Hansen. We had become casually acquainted on Panay. After the surrender of the Philippine Army's 61st Division, he had sailed to the small island of Silbay off the west coat of Panay, where he had been ever since. He had hoped eventually to get to Australia, but with the southwest monsoon, had been unable to find anything sailing south of his little island. He came to Santa Fe on the news that there were Americans on Tablas.

It was difficult to talk to him. He seemed to have his mind on something other than the present. I did learn that he was a mining engineer like Hubbard and Linblom. He thought he had known Hubbard on Masbate Island before the war. He planned to go to Looc to see him. Hansen appeared to have lost the ability to laugh or even smile. I felt sorry for him.

I had put on weight and become relaxed and healthy on Tablas. Life was almost idyllic at Agmanic. The only annoyance was the occasional sightings of Jap launches, but they were always far out in the channel and never seemed to show any special interest in Tablas.

I was growing restless and—despite Hansen's reasoned inability to move south, and warnings by many, of the near impossibility to sail south during the southwest monsoon—I felt that I should be making an effort. I fully believed that it would be years before American forces would be back in the Philippines. I had no desire to spend the duration sitting under a coconut tree. I wanted to get back with our forces and get back in the war. Getting to Australia seemed like the best way to do it.

Time after time, I had pondered the idea of attempting to start a guerrilla movement. However, experience with Philippine Army troops on Panay and Luzon made me skeptical of their ever being effective and reactions from the locals indicated little chance for support.

One day, some traders passed through Agmanic on their way from Santa Fe to a *barrio* where they were staying, on the other side of the island. They were sailing to Borocay in a few days and offered to give me a ride.

The mayor was opposed to my departure. There was not a chance to find a boat going even as far as Palawan this time of year. There was no end to the mayor's hospitality. I did not feel, though, that I had any right to stay with him much longer.

The day before I was to meet the crew of the boat sailing for Borocay, I was sitting in the backyard watching the chickens and weighing in my mind the pros and cons of leaving Agmanic. Since arriving there, I had not seen a hawk. Obviously, they were strangers to the area. On that morning, however, one suddenly flew in, seemingly from nowhere. Right in front of me, the hawk snatched a black chick from a brood of black, brown, and red ones. I had come to believe that the actions of a hawk in my presence had some connection with my balance of luck. This last episode could only be interpreted as an ill omen.

I decided right then, that omen or no omen, for better or for worse, I was going to make a try at going south.

Chapter 31

In the *barrio* of Tabugan, a short hike from Agmanic over the southern tip of Tablas Island, I came to the hut where I was to meet the crew to the boat sailing for Borocay. No one was there except an old woman weaving *abacá* cloth on a crude loom.*

The crew had gone fishing. The plan had been to sail in the late afternoon. Already the afternoon was nearly gone. I sat down on the floor of the *nipa* hut to wait.

For the hundredth time, the reasons for leaving vice those for staying in Agmanic were turning over in my mind. Why leave the friendly people, shelter, food, and security of Agmanic, especially when all had advised that it would be nearly impossible to find a boat going any distance south, during this time of the southwest monsoon? All these factors, however, were dimmed by my desire to make an effort to get back with friendly forces and again have an active part in the war. It was well past the middle of July 1942. I was determined to waste no more time starting for Australia.

After dark, two of the five-man crew came back to the hut to start supper. The others were down by the shore, cleaning fish. The day's catch had been good, too good to be ignored.

Ignacio, the owner of the boat, with the other crewmembers, wandered into the hut about 2100 hours. A plate of rice with boiled fish was the evening meal. While eating, Ignacio announced that he thought it would be better to wait until the next day for starting.

After breakfast the next morning, Ignacio casually announced that he thought they should try fishing again. "It had been so good the day before," he reasoned.

So I went fishing.

After the noon meal, Ignacio asked if I was ready to leave. He said he thought the wind was right for Borocay. Sailing down a lagoon on an ebbing tide, we rowed our craft out into the open sea until the sails caught the offshore breeze.

The appearance of Japanese launches off the southern coast of Tablas had followed no pattern. It was impossible to predict when or where they would show up. I did not relish the thought of spending the afternoon on the water with these patrols around.

The delay of a day in starting proved to be to our advantage, however. A freak blow of the north wind came up shortly after noon. It grabbed hold of our sail and pushed us south at a greater speed than a Japanese launch. We raced around the southern tip of Tablas, across the channel to the eastern side of Carabao Island

---

*The fiber from the abacá plant is used to make Manila hemp, from which both a rough cloth and rope are manufactured.

and on to the *barrio* of Manoc-manoc at the southern tip of Borocay Island, arriving before dark. We had not even heard a Japanese launch.

The *barrio*-folk of Manoc-manoc took me in with open arms. I was welcome to stay with them for the duration, but they could not help me in my search for a boat sailing south. There had been none sailing west or south since the leper ship in June.

Finally, I had a boatman paddle me across the narrow channel to Panay. The channel had lost none of its beauty or serenity since I had passed through it on my way from New Washington. These tiny oases of tropical beauty I occasionally came upon never ceased to stir me. They brought short moments of rapture that were a welcome relief from the routine of daily existence.

The boatman landed me at the *barrio* of Caticlan, the same *barrio* where I had stayed before sailing for Tablas Island in early June.

After a few days in Caticlan, I walked down the beach to the *barrio* of Malay, where the *teniente* assured me there would be a better chance of catching a boat. He had been trying to get me to leave since my arrival.

My plan was to sail to the eastern coast of Palawan Island; hitch rides either by land or water down its coast; cross to the northeast coast of Borneo; again hitch rides by land or water down the Makassar Strait; go through the Dutch East Indies and on to the northwest coast of Australia. This would be a journey of roughly 2,500 to 3,000 miles. It seemed simple enough. Already, I had come from Baguio in northern Luzon Island, to Panay by the same method.

After several days of waiting in Malay, I decided to take a boat around the cape of northwest Panay, to the *barrio* of Baruanga. This took two attempts. On the first, we had to turn back and anchor in a protected cove, waiting out a *chubasco*, a severe local storm that can reach a great fury. This one came from the southwest. It nearly took our mast down and almost put us on the rocks before we were able to escape its fury. The second attempt turned out to be a grim, all-night struggle against the elements. I was beginning to realize what the southwest monsoon could be like and why everyone had been so pessimistic about finding a boat to sail against it.

The Japs had not visited Baruanga for some time. Even so, I picked a place to sleep far back in the hills. During the day I was careful to keep a good distance from the town square, where the Japs would probably first stop, should they decide to visit the *barrio.*

After several days of waiting in Baruanga, with the southwest wind strengthening and the rain persisting, I was open to compromise. It came when an old man and his son from the island of Caluya offered me a ride. Caluya is one of the Semirara group of islands 25 to 30 miles west of Baruanga.

The old man's boat, called a *buri,* was double-ended, like a canoe, nearly 20 feet in length, with a beam of 8 feet and a freeboard, when loaded, of 12 to 14 inches. It was made of crude unpainted timbers and held together with wooden pegs. It was a tub, but a seaworthy one. The sail was made of *buri* palm, from which the boat got its name. It was a rectangle, 12 by 16 feet, supported on the long sides by pieces of bamboo. It hung from the mast on the bias, controlled from the tiller man's position in the stern by four lines coming down from the four corners of the sail. The *buri* palm is tough, durable, and comparatively light. The sail is woven from strands of the palm fronds.

We sailed in the morning, much to my dislike, because of the ever-present danger of Japanese launches. The sea was rough. The wind was shifty, changing throughout the day from southwest to southeast. The little boat showed good speed when the wind was from the southeast, but moved more slowly as the wind shifted.

Between sign language and the little Visayan I had acquired, the three of us managed to understand each other. At my request, the old man let me take the tiller most of the day.

As the sun dropped behind the cone-shaped top of Caluya Island, we entered the coral shallows off its eastern shore. The glare and heat of the sun during the day had been intense. Suddenly, I could open my eyes and a cool breeze fanned my face and body. I felt I was in another world.

The crew lowered the sail. The old man's son poled the *buri* into shore. I sat in the stern, occasionally glancing down to catch glimpses of the multifarious coral formations. As often as I had seen the coral, I never tired of looking at it. Always to me, each piece resembled some plant or flower that grows above the water. It was a game to try to relate each formation with its likeness growing on land.

The shoreline was a grass-covered embankment dropping off sharply into the sea. Behind the embankment was a dense fringe of tropical growth. Further inland, the tops of coconut palms were visible. Above these, far to the rear, were the green slopes of mountains, dotted here and there with grazing cattle.

The old man produced a large seashell and blew several vibrating blasts on it. The sound resembled that of a foghorn; almost immediately, as if by magic, naked children appeared out of the jungle onto the grassy strip of the shore. They were followed by a woman dressed in a red cotton skirt and *abaca* blouse, carrying a baby on her hip.

The keel of the *buri* ground to a stop. The old man's son jumped overboard with the anchor and waded ashore. I followed.

I went with the family along a trail leading inland to a small shack in the jungle. There, the old man motioned me to go with another of his sons. He pointed to a trail leading inland and then to his house, making a gesture that inferred a larger house.

"*Marami Salamat*" ("Thank you very much") I said, as I waved goodbye, following the boy up the trail. It was nearly dark when we came to a large house located in a beautiful setting among the coconut palms. The house was made of wood with a galvanized iron roof, undoubtedly the home of a well-to-do landowner. The boy called and an elderly woman came to the door. She spoke no

English, but after listening to the boy, beckoned me to enter. She led me through the house to a porch and bade me sit in a comfortable wicker chair. To my surprise, the house was furnished in western style with chairs, tables, beds, and even pictures on the walls. Soon, she brought a coconut oil lamp, a pitcher of *tuba*, and a small plate of home-rolled cigarettes. Then she disappeared.

It was quite a while before she returned. I must have dozed, as she startled me when I first noticed her again. On the table were a plate of steaming rice, eggs, and salt, and I ate it almost without taking a breath. Exhausted, I rolled up on the floor and slept.

The next morning, the owner of the house had returned. He spoke English fluently. His home was in Manila. Only recently had he come to Caluya to get away from the Japs. He had decided to stay for the duration, spending the time improving his plantation.

I told him that I wanted to go to Palawan. He believed it was a bad time of year to sail south, but that I might be able to get a boat from Sibay Island. He would provide me a guide to the western coast of Caluya, where boats sailed regularly for Sibay.

A good rest, a full belly, and the feeling I was making progress put me in good spirits the following morning. Again, I had a young man for a guide. At first, the trail led through the cool coconut groves. Then it began slowly to ascend the grass-covered hills that rise in the middle of the island. A fresh breeze was blowing and there were enough clouds in the sky to break the intense heat of the sun, yet it was not long before my clothes were soaked with sweat. As many times before, it did not take long for my skin to take on the puckered appearance similar to that which comes from soaking in warm water.

The trail wound around pastures and along dikes bordering the patchwork of rice fields. To the east loomed the mountains of Panay like a blue mist over the sea. Beyond Semirara Island to the north, the mountains of Mindoro were barely visible. Just below us to the southwest was the small, flat island of Sibay.

Early in the afternoon, we entered the *barrio* of Caluya on the western coast of the island. My guide took me to the home of a Chinese man whose business was trading on the islands of the Semirara group. His boat was sailing for the island of Sibay later that afternoon, God willing and weather permitting. He offered to take me to the home of Janiero, the family with whom Hansen had stayed.

The Chinese served a very good supper. It passed 2100 hours before the weather was considered favorable to sail. The boat was another *buri*, though larger than the old man's. Unpainted, 30 to 40 feet in length, it had two masts rigged with large, rectangular *buri* sails. The shape of the hull was the same crude canoe type with a broad beam and plenty of freeboard. Over the deck amidships, between the masts, was a *nipa* shelter.

When we departed, Sibay looked to be no more than a stone's throw away, but we were unable to land on the island until mid-morning of the next day. All night it stormed, blowing every which way. When the wind finally settled down, it was from the southwest, directly away from the island. As we tacked back and forth, progress toward the shore was hardly perceptible.

Finally, the boat was in a position to be poled into a protected cove. Rain was coming down in sheets. The *nipa* shelter on the deck of the boat leaked like a sieve. Wading ashore, soaked to the skin, we scrambled up a steep embankment to a fisherman's dilapidated hut. To our dismay, the roof was a little better than the *nipa* shelter aboard, but after several tries, a fire was started. The wind had chilled us to the marrow. We hugged the fire through the rest of the morning, brewing tea from a tea cake carried by the Chinese.

Sibay Island is a rolling, grass-covered plateau, high above the sea. According to the Chinese, whose English was quite tolerable, mostly traders and fishermen lived in the few *barrios* scattered around the shoreline. Little rice was grown on the island, the natives depending on trade for this commodity. Most of the island was owned by the Janiero family. The land was used primarily for cattle raising.

The trader and I walked over the top of the island to the Janiero ranch. The buildings were on a hill overlooking a large pond, with a number of native ponies and *carabao* grazing on its banks. Steep stairs led up to the main house. It was built of wood, painted green, and roofed with galvanized iron. Several small *bodegas* made of crudely-hewn, unpainted timbers were scattered about the main house.

As we approached, Janiero came outside and invited us into his home. He looked like a Spanish *mestizo*. After a short discussion, the Chinese and I were invited to lunch.

I told Janiero I wanted to get to Palawan Island. As expected, he said there were few boats traveling that way during the southwest monsoon. He advised against waiting for one.

Hansen had stayed with him for several weeks after the Panay surrender. It was immediately obvious that Janiero was not fascinated with having another American around. Aside from the consideration of providing food and shelter, there was the possible danger of Japanese retaliation. I could not blame him for his concern, but at the same time, I had no intention to turning back. Possibly, his lack of enthusiasm for my presence would spur him to help find a boat bound for Palawan.

After discussing his business, the Chinese left by mid-afternoon and I was grudgingly offered supper and a place to sleep that night.

The next morning, Jella, the brother-in-law of Janiero, came to fetch me to his house. Jella was in his early thirties, tall and slim with finely-cut features. Unlike Janiero, he was constantly smiling and trying to be congenial. He wore shoes, trousers, and a shirt that surely must have been purchased in Iloilo City or Manila.

He could not have been more hospitable. The first thing he said after leaving the Janiero ranch was that I was welcome to stay with him and his family as long as I pleased.

Jella's household included his young wife, their seven children, and the older Janieros, the mother and father of *Señora* Jella. Their home was large, made of wood with a tin roof, luxurious in comparison to the *nipa*-bamboo combinations in which I was used to staying. This looked like luxury, until my bedroom turned out to be a straw mat in the corner of the dining room on the hard wooden floor.

My *bococong* was not healing. The ulcer was more than a half inch in diameter now, a reddish-white, open sore constantly excreting matter. Its location between the ankle bone and Achilles tendon was starting to cripple the muscles and nerves of my left foot. It gave me a great deal of pain at night.

A weed that grew on the seashore was suggested as a cure. The smooth round leaf, pealed to expose its center, was used as a poultice at night. It drew out a great deal of stuff, but seemed to make the ulcer worse. I soon gave it up.

Jella was no more optimistic about finding a boat going to Palawan than was his brother-in-law. The weeks that followed were spent walking to the different *barrios*, in search of a boat bound for Palawan. It was becoming a futile search. Occasionally to break the monotony, I would swim or go fishing.

I vividly remember one particular fishing expedition. Usually two or three of us in a *banca* would paddle along off the lee side of the island, until we located a school of fish in a shallow cove fairly well protected from sharks. We would catch them either using nets or diving with glasses and spear gun. This time, however, after anchoring in a quiet lagoon swarming with fish, my companion pulled out a small package of dynamite sticks tightly bound together with a fuse. Lighting the fuse, he tossed the package overboard. A geyser of water erupted as it exploded. In a moment the surface was covered with stunned fish. Hastily, we netted the fish into the *banca*. We had 30 or 40 before they regained consciousness.

While the older children and adults in Jella's household usually used utensils while eating, at these feasts of fresh fish, all were allowed to use their fingers. I was quite agreeable to this, and enjoyed as much as any Filipino, deftly probing the succulent meat from around the eyes and jaws of a fish head.

A trader arriving from the north reported two Moros living on a small island off the southern tip of Mindoro. The Moros were from Jolo to the south and were planning to return soon. I wanted to get in touch with them. This could be the chance for which I had been looking.

From the outset, Jella was opposed to my going to Mindoro to look for them. He considered that making a long trip on the sea alone with two Moros being akin to suicide. They would not think twice about throwing me overboard if I had anything they wanted. He cited actual cases of this happening. Like most Christian Filipinos, he had an ingrained distrust of the Muslim Moro. But I was so obsessed with the idea of sailing south that I paid little attention to his advice.

It was past the middle of August when I joined two fishermen going to Mindoro in their *buri* to buy rice. A day's easy sailing took us to the island where the two Moros were staying.

Both were powerfully built, lean, and muscular—one tall, one short. Each had a hard, tough look about him and a fearless, go-to-hell manner. Their sole attire was a pair of dirty cotton shorts. At his side, each carried a *borong*, a meat cleaver-type of bolo, sharpened to a razor's edge. They brought to mind two wild beasts of prey. This was the breed that reputedly made good fighting men. I could not help a feeling of admiration for them.

They had occupied a deserted *nipa* shack and were living in absolute squalor. Their sleeping mats were dirty, their rice pot a mess, and the shack stank from filth. Aside from their shaven heads, the two Moros presented an appearance that left the impression they had never been exposed to the civilized niceties of bathing and grooming.

The shorter of the two spoke a little English and we both spoke some Tagalog. With the added aid of makeshift sign language, we managed to converse.

The Moros were not overly friendly. They were planning to return to Jolo soon and would be willing to take me with them, but their price was more than I would pay. No amount of haggling could get the price down.

At noon of the second day, the fishermen from Sibay stopped for me on their return trip. I left the Moros with no agreement in price, but with the understanding that they would stop at Sibay on their way south. We could try then to come to an agreement.

By mid-afternoon on the return trip, a *chubasco* forced us to take shelter on a nearby island. It was necessary to remain overnight and we went ashore to sleep. The inhabitants were having a bad time with malaria. They blamed it on a shortage of rice that forced them to eat cracked corn in its place. They complained that the cracked corn overheated their bodies and did not provide the nourishment they received from rice. As a consequence, the malaria—which the majority of the islanders had but kept dormant when their vitality was high—was taking its toll.

On the next morning, we started again for Sibay. The day passed, weathering another storm out of the southwest. It was not until late night that we reached Sibay. Soaked to the skin, the remaining hours of darkness were spent in an abandoned shack with only a mat for cover. That night I came the nearest to freezing of any time I can remember in the Philippines. Realization of the folly of trying to sail any distance south at this time of year was being driven home forcibly.

Two weeks went by, waiting for the arrival of the Moros. Some days I would walk out to the northernmost edge of the island and for hours watch the sea toward Mindoro, hoping to see the great rectangular sail of their *kumpit* (a long, narrow boat used for trading or smuggling). After my meeting with the Moros, I had developed reservations about the trip to Jolo, but did still want to discuss it further.

Finally, in the first part of September the Moros arrived. Their attitude had changed. They were anxious for me to go with them now and quickly agreed to my original offer. This made me suspicious.

My suspicions grew as they questioned me about my belongings, especially about a pistol. To pass up this opportunity I had been waiting for so long was not easy. It would be several months before the northeast monsoon would blow steadily. It probably would be at least that long before I would find another boat sailing south. Yet I was becoming convinced that to sail with the Moros would be extremely imprudent. They sailed without me.

I had just about given up the idea of trying to get to Australia.

A Catholic padre, sailing alone from Panay, arrived on the island in the second week of September. He had come to visit some friends, say some prayers, and trade some wares. He was not making a living selling the gospel so decided to turn merchant until times became better for his ordained calling. He was brought news that a guerrilla movement was starting on Panay.

This interested me. The padre was reluctant at first to let me return with him, for fear of Japanese retaliation if caught. According to him, the Japs had been increasing their motor launch patrols off the northwest coast of Panay. With a little persuasion, however, by reminding him of his priestly vows, he consented. I suggested that we approach the coast of Panay after sundown to avoid these patrols.

The period spent on Sibay had been one of anxious waiting and a certain amount of boredom, yet nowhere could I have received more courteous treatment than I did while staying with the Jellas. I had become fond of the entire family. It was a sad day when I took my leave.

We had a beautiful day for sailing. The padre let me sail his boat most of the way to Panay. My skill in sailing had been steadily improving, as had my knowledge of the weather and the sea. We had rigged a mat above the keel of the boat, under which I would crawl if approached by a Jap launch. A little past nightfall we landed near the *barrio* of Malay.

In July I had left this *barrio* to sail to Baruanga. It was now the middle of September. During that time, I had neither heard a radio nor talked to anyone who had current news of the islands or the world. The padre had been surprisingly out of touch.

The *barrio*-folk of Malay gave me a friendly welcome. No Americans had been there since my departure in July. They expected me to have some word about the arrival of American aid and were quite disappointed when they heard I had none. Through the evening, I gleaned the latest rumors of world news and Japanese activities in the islands, especially Panay. There was no cause for optimism.

On Panay, reportedly the Japs had garrisons in the three main cities: Iloilo, Capiz, and San Jose. They patrolled extensively to towns and *barrios* where there were roads. In some instances, they had marched into *barrios* not accessible by road. One time they had visited Caticlan, a little over six miles to the northeast. Patrols by launch had increased recently. There was no knowledge, however, of landing parties from these launches going ashore. The Home Guard had been disbanded. I hoped I would not wake next morning looking into the face of a Jap.

There was talk in the *barrio* that the ex-soldiers of the 61st Division were being assembled. A lieutenant living in Caticlan was said to be working with the newly-formed organization.

The next morning, I started up the beach toward Caticlan. I wanted to know what was behind the rumored assembly of the 61st Division.

Things were about the same with the old *barrio teniente* of Caticlan. Grudgingly, he offered me a bed and a place at his table. The *palay* promised by Raval still had not been received. The officer who was assembling the ex-soldiers in the areas was a friend of the *barrio teniente.* He offered to find the lieutenant for me.

In the afternoon, the lieutenant arrived. We recognized each other at once. He also had been an officer in the 63rd Regiment. Instead of his usual friendly manner, his attitude was hostile. It puzzled me. I was at a loss for a reason. He provided little information about the rumored guerrilla movement. He would admit only that he knew that Peralta, operations officer of the 61st Division prior to surrender, had established a small headquarters in the mountains, some three or four days away. Peralta was in the process of assembling the officers and men of the 61st Division who had not surrendered.

Peralta had slipped away at the last moment before the surrender, which, aside from being in direct disobedience of orders and making him a deserter, had let General Christie down. I could well remember General Christie's concern over this at Calinog. It had caused him a great deal of embarrassment and difficulty in making arrangements for surrender with the Japanese.

As operations officer of the 63rd Regiment, I had become acquainted with Peralta. He had been somewhat overbearing in association with Americans in the 61st Division. This was not an unusual attitude of many young Manila-educated Filipinos of the time, however. The resentment of western domination of Asians had become an open issue. In the Philippines, Americans had become the focal point of this resentment.

When the lieutenant offered to deliver a letter from me to Peralta these thoughts passed through my mind. In my letter I offered my assistance in any way he could use me. I stated that I would wait in Caticlan for two weeks for an answer. The lieutenant was returning to Peralta's headquarters the next day.

It was still raining, raining, raining. The tropical ulcer on my foot was becoming so large that I was having difficulty walking. I tried the local cure in each new area I visited. Nothing seemed to have any affect. I was beginning to wonder if I would lose my foot.

With a good book on American history, I settled down to wait for an answer in the *barrio teniente*'s living room. Every day I watched the rain, had a swim, did some reading, and listened to the *teniente* bemoan the shortage of rice in his household. It was not the shortage of rice that was bothering him, as I knew he had plenty, but probably fear of reprisals from the Japs who had once visited the *barrio,* looking for Americans in general and me in particular. Ten thousand *pesos* were still being offered as a reward for my capture. Each day he asked when I would leave.

I felt fairly secure in Caticlan, as there were no roads leading into it. If the Japs approached by trail, there would be adequate warning. I knew the Filipinos well enough for that.

For two weeks I waited for an answer to my message. There was no reason to doubt that Peralta had received it. He knew me well enough to know I could be of help. Maybe he wanted the show to be purely Filipino. This would be in character. There was also the stigma resulting from the fact that he and all other members of the 61st Division who had not surrendered were, by official military orders, deserters. For whatever reason, it did not appear I would hear from Peralta.

There was a *batile* (a large sailboat without outriggers) leaving for Santa Fe, Tablas. Maybe it was time to get back in touch with the Americans there. They would know the latest developments in the war and the general situation in the islands. I had not seen an American since leaving Tablas in July, more than two months ago. I decided to return to Santa Fe.

The *batile* was loaded with several families on their way to Santa Fe for a visit. Everyone was in a holiday spirit, enhanced to some degree by the flow of *tuba.* We sailed close to the eastern shores of Borocay and Carabao Islands, to avoid Japanese patrol launches. The wind was favorable and we made a fast trip.

Chapter 32

It was dusk when the anchor was heaved overboard in Santa Fe harbor. I was glad to be back again. Barefooted and hatless, I strode up the main street waving to the happy faces as happy as a runaway boy returning home.

Entering the Sanchez house, I found them all at dinner. Without a word, Señor Sanchez sat me down at the table as though I had never been away.

I spent a week in Santa Fe and Agmanic, renewing acquaintances and catching up on the local news. Nothing seemed to have changed since my departure in July. Linblom, Hubbard, Hansen, and Palmer were still in the Looc area.

At the end of the week, I left for Looc. As usual, Erbacio, the relative of Señor Sanchez, was very hospitable. I could stay with him as long as I pleased. Also as usual, the game of *mah-jongg* was in full swing on his porch.

Raval and his soldiers were occupying the municipal building in the town, doing nothing to justify their existence. I suggested he start establishing a system of observation posts around the island, eventually to provide information on Japanese air and sea activities in the area. This would have to be tied in with Panay, which should eventually have radio communications with either Australia or the western coast of the United States. This idea did not interest him. He seemed to have other things on his mind. I wondered what they were.

There was nothing encouraging in the radio news. The Japs and the Germans were still having things their way.

Palmer was living out of town with a family, spending most of his time in bed. His *bococong*, or tropical ulcer, was now the size of a silver dollar. It was consuming his leg, which had shrunk to little more than bone. He could barely get around on it, even with the help of a cane. I asked him what he planned to do if the Japs landed on Tablas. "I'll stay right here and shoot it out with them. I'm sure I can get a few before they get me." He showed me his rusty Enfield rifle and the few clips of ammunition he had for it.

Several days spent across the bay in Agaho with Linblom and Marianito were refreshing. Linblom had lost none of his optimism. In spite of the news, he was sure the war would be over soon. We joked, walked on the beach, fished a little, and in the evenings listened to Marianito singing Spanish and Filipino songs, accompanied by his guitar. This was the best tonic I had for months.

Back in Looc, I went up with Hubbard and Hansen to spend a night or so in their shack on a hill outside of town. The first night, I came down with a severe attack of bronchitis. My face turned purple with the struggle for a breath of air. I was obviously allergic to some growth on the mountain and needed to get away from it, but had not the strength. Hubbard sent a messenger to Raval asking for help. Raval responded quickly. With four of his soldiers, he came up with a chair tied to two poles, like a litter. The four men carried me down to the town, to the house of Doctor Baredo, the town physician. The doctor kept me going for the next few days with shots of adrenaline and inhalation of the smoke from a powder he burned. The treatment shrank my tubes. I could breathe comfortably again. Doctor Baredo verified my suspicion that the cause of my attack was pollen of some plant to which I was allergic. To treat my *bococong,* Dr. Baredo concocted a combination of potassium permanganate and zinc oxide powder. This eventually proved effective.

It was a week before I felt strong enough to walk and another before I could get around on my own. During this time, I stayed in the home of the doctor. I had access to the doctor's excellent library and, above all, I enjoyed listening to members of his family play classical music on their piano.

It was nearing the time of the northeast monsoon. During my stay with the doctor, a typhoon blew over the island, taking off roofs, blowing down trees, and in general raising havoc. It was impossible to walk outside during this time. For several days, the blasts of wind stopped all activity in the town. This was the only typhoon I experienced during my stay in the Philippines.

During my sickness, Raval and his soldiers had started to go haywire. Raval had commandeered a sedan and truck in the name of the United States Armed Forces Far East (USAFFE). He had entered several towns with his soldiers and was demanding a certain percentage of the merchants' goods, especially from the Chinese. The goods were taken allegedly to provide for the basic needs of the soldiers, but many items, such as women's lingerie, had little to do with the soldier's needs. Many such items were being sold at reduced prices for personal gain. Also, the soldiers were taking food from the market places without giving vouchers for it. Most civilians had come to accept vouchers signed by an officer for services and purchases, in the hope of eventual reimbursement by their government. Raval's armed soldiers would arrive, help themselves, and then threaten anyone who dared complain.

Every day, complaints were coming to me with the hope I could do something to stop these activities, which amounted to nothing more than banditry.

Some time before this, a major named Jurado had come onto the island with his wife and child, seeking refuge. According to Jurado, the Japs had been hot on his trail in Luzon. He said he was a graduate of Annapolis and had commanded the PT boats of the Philippine Navy based in Manila Bay up to the time of the surrender. On his arrival on Tablas, Raval had him imprisoned on the pretense that he was a fifth columnist. Jurado had gotten a temporary release under guard, from Odiongan, to see me. He claimed he had been imprisoned because he had refused to take any guff from Raval's men.

The following day, I persuaded Raval to release Jurado and a few others he had jailed, against whom there were really no substantial charges.

Raval was carrying an Army .45-caliber pistol that he had recently acquired. I asked him where he got it. He answered that they were available if one knew how to go about it. I told him to get me one and also warned him to stop his soldiers' banditry.

As the days passed, ever-increasing reports of Raval's men's depredations arrived from different parts of the island. Raval started to drop derogatory remarks about the Americans on Tablas. One morning in the first week of November, he drove into town with the pomp of an oriental potentate. Something had to be done to slow him down.

I walked into his headquarters and went upstairs, where he had an office. Several of his men were standing around him when I entered. All conversation stopped as they turned to look at me. They were dressed in dirty Philippine Army uniforms, a slovenly, dirty, unkempt lot. The sight of them enraged me. All were armed. It was not hard to tell that I was not welcome and I wondered if they would have the nerve to try something.

I stepped over and pulled the end stick off a folding Army cot. It was a stout piece of oak and wonderfully handy. I pointed it at Raval and in no uncertain words, told him his acts of banditry were a disgrace to his uniform, to the name of USAFFE, and to his country. He bristled and started to turn red in the face, but had nothing to say. I told him that if he did not stop the banditry by his men that I would.

His actions indicated that he was contemplating using his gun. I stepped closer so as to be able to hit him before he could get his pistol out of its holster. He understood as fast as did his henchmen. I wondered how long my bluff would last. I ended by telling him I wanted a pistol right away or I would take his.

After mulling that over, he said he had a pistol in a nearby *barrio* and if I would drive out with him we could get it.

I said, "Let's go."

As we went out through the building, several of his men, standing around with their rifles, eyed me belligerently.

How long would my luck last? A big *mestizo* followed Raval and me out of the building. Like Raval, he was armed with a pistol. Raval motioned me to get in the front seat beside the driver. He and the *mestizo* started to get in the back. I pointed the stick at the *mestizo* and told him to get in front. Then, I poked Raval to move over and got in back with him.

"Let's go," I said.

Raval gave the driver instructions in Visayan and then started to talk to the *mestizo*. I stopped him and told him to speak only in English. We drove out into the country. Nothing was said except occasional instructions to the driver. We turned off the main road onto a little-used lane and stopped in front of an old, ramshackle, wooden house. Raval did not move.

"Let's get out and get that pistol, Raval," I said. He seemed at a loss as to what to do, but he got out of the car and started for the house. I told the *mestizo* to stay beside Raval and both to walk ahead of me. The house was unoccupied and rundown. Raval and his henchman sauntered aimlessly from room to room. Raval started to speak to the *mestizo* in Visayan.

"Speak only in English, and loud enough so I can hear," I barked ostentatiously, partly to give myself assurance.

There was little doubt in my mind that I had been brought there to be killed. Neither of them had the guts. For the moment, it was obvious they were looking for an opening.

"Let's find that pistol and get out of here," I said, raising my voice.

"It seems to have been taken," Raval answered.

I tapped the *mestizo* on the shoulder and said, "Stop where you are and don't move. Raval, turned around." They both did what they were told. Before Raval could get over his surprise, I grabbed his pistol. In an instant I had worked the slide and watched a round slip into the chamber.

"Get your hands over your head." I tapped the *mestizo* on the shoulder. "You, too." He put his hands up. "Turn around." I took his pistol.

"Now get into the car." The two of them filed out of the house.

"Tell the driver to get back to Looc." I was sitting on the right side of the rear seat with two pistols. Raval's was loaded, cocked, and the safety off, and everyone in the car knew this.

The car stopped in front of Erbacio's house. The porch was crowded and the market across the street was full of people. Again I warned Raval to stop the banditry. And as I got out, as a last thought, handed him the stick from the Army cot and asked him to please replace it.

As I had no idea what Raval's reaction might be, I thought it prudent to move across the bay to Agaho, with Linblom and Marianito, for the time being.

Raval left town the next day. As far as I could tell, he had made no move to avenge himself.

A fairly effective intelligence system began to develop. Those friendly to me in the town had someone hanging around Raval's headquarters all the time. When any of them heard of anything against me, or plans to harass the civilians, they reported to individuals in the town who immediately sent the information by messenger to Marianito.

News was coming in daily that Raval was still committing acts of banditry in other parts of the island.

About the middle of November, Raval and his henchmen returned to Looc. His first act was to demand a certain amount of food or goods from each merchant in the town.

The morning after receiving this news, I arose, determined to stop this process, permanently. If allowed to continue as he was, Raval could become a danger to everyone. I had little desire to meddle in affairs that the Filipinos should take care of themselves. I felt justified and somewhat obligated to take this action for the general safety of the Americans on the island, however, and as a show of gratitude for the hospitality shown us. Also, the fact these depredations were being committed in the name of USAFFE made me feel that I should do something.

At breakfast, I told Linblom and Marianito I was going to put Raval in jail. To my surprise, Linblom offered to help. He had the second pistol and knew how to use it.

Walking the distance around the bay, we discussed how best to arrest our adversary. We entered the town still undecided.

Approaching Raval's headquarters, I noticed his car parked outside. I told Linblom to walk three or four paces behind me when we entered the headquarters and to yell if he noticed anything untoward.

There were no guards at the entrance, no challenge, and no warning inside of our approach. Several young Filipinos in dirty uniforms, some with rifles, were lolling around. We strode in and upstairs to Raval's office. He was there, alone. As we walked in, he stood up. He was unarmed.

"Come with me, Raval." He looked at me, puzzled.

"Are you going to walk out, or do you prefer another way?" He walked slowly from behind his desk.

"Follow me and don't say a word to anyone." I told him. "Hank, follow Raval."

His men made no move to do anything as we marched out of the headquarters and down the street to the office of the chief of police.

I knew the chief. He was friendly, but afraid of his shadow. I told him to open the jail door.

Raval was taken care of for the moment, but I had no idea what his men might do. I considered two of Raval's men dangerous. The *mestizo* was one of them. I had seen neither that morning. I asked Raval their whereabouts. He replied that they had been up late the night before and were sleeping in one of the rooms upstairs.

I took the keys to the jail and asked Hank to watch the place, then returned to the headquarters. The two men were upstairs, as Raval had said. They awoke as I walked into their room.

"Captain Raval is down the street a ways and would like to talk with both of you." I told them in as casual a tone as I could muster. "I'll take you to him."

Neither questioned but got up, put on their caps, and picked up their rifles.

"No need for the guns." I could see they wondered what was going on. When he saw I meant it, the *mestizo* shrugged and threw his rifle onto his cot. The other one followed suit. Again we filed out of the headquarters and again, passed the men lolling about. I did not look back until we were out on the street. To my relief, things looked calm.

My two prisoners were walking beside me, still unsuspecting, I hoped. I opened the door for them into the police chief's office. When they saw Raval behind bars, they were startled. Raval started to talk to them in Visayan.

"Shut up." I bellowed. "No talking."

I pulled my pistol out of its holster.

"Stand over there against the wall."

The two moved slowly, but they moved, and all was silence.

I threw the jail keys to the chief and pointed for him to open cells apart from Raval's.

With the three of them in separate cells, we had a good start, but the chief and his police could not be relied upon to keep them there. If left with them, I had little doubt that Raval could talk his way out of jail in short order.

Hank stayed, with his pistol ready.

With the police chief as interpreter, I went back to Raval's headquarters to tell his remaining men what had happened. As far as I had been able to determine, those remaining were comparatively docile. I made it clear that there would be no more banditry. I was in command and I held each one of them personally responsible to me for his actions.

Jurado was staying a short distance away outside of town. I sent him a note telling him to come to Looc. It was late afternoon when he arrived. I explained what had happened and offered him command of the island. He thought it a fine idea. I had the feeling he thought that at last his abilities were being recognized. He could do as he saw fit except I made two stipulations: first, that the banditry would be stopped; second, that Raval and his two henchmen would remain in jail until I agreed to release them.

Linblom and I had made arrangements to sleep in the jail that first night.

Jurado took a hold of things in a hurry and it was not many days before the game of *mah-jongg* was the only excitement left in town.

I returned to Santa Fe and Agmanic. I thoroughly enjoyed the company of Señor Sanchez and the mayor. It was not long before I was back in the old routine. I swore I would stay there this time until the return of American forces and wondered why I had ever left in the first place.

Rumors were starting to come from Panay that submarines had been observed surfacing at night off different parts of the island.

A few weeks after taking over, Jurado suggested the release of Raval and his two men from jail if they would agree to leave the island and not return. I agreed, hoping it could be enforced.

Chapter 33

In early December, a Filipino lieutenant arrived in Santa Fe from Panay. Allegedly, he was on a reconnaissance mission from Peralta's headquarters. He painted a grand picture of the guerrilla movement. To hear him talk, it was a wonder there were any Japs left on Panay. He offered to guide me to Peralta's headquarters, which was near the town of Sara, in the northeastern part of the island. I took him up on his offer.

Our first stop after leaving Santa Fe was the town of Gibon on the north coast of Panay, not far to the east of Caticlan. From there we sailed by easy stages southeast along the Panay coast. Reportedly, the town of Capiz was heavily garrisoned by the Japs. I took leave of the lieutenant and his crew near the small *barrio* of Batan, his last landing before passing Capiz.

A cart road led inland to the town of Altabas where I had said goodbye to the Japs last May. The thought went through my mind that a criminal always returns to the scene of his crime. I walked through the town gingerly, expecting the Japanese commander who had made the impressive speech in the schoolhouse to jump out at me at any moment. From Altabas, I hiked southeast through the mountains, stopping at *nipa* shacks along thc way for meals and a place to sleep.

One incident that happened on the way to Sara stands out in my mind. I had been warned that there was a Japanese patrol in the area searching for a group of guerrillas. Passing through woods that appeared safe and devoid of any life, the sound of firing came to me from behind. It was rifle fire from at least a squad of men, with an occasional burst of automatic fire. As I listened, it seemed to be coming closer. Bullets were ricocheting through the trees and cracking overhead. There was little doubt that it was the high-pitched crack of a Japanese .25-caliber rifle. Then the sound of more firing came from my left.

I dived into a dense thicket, wondering how I was going to get out of this fix. The firing continued for a few more minutes, then stopped. I must have stayed hidden for at least a half an hour, peering out, expecting any moment to see a Japanese skirmish line approaching, but I neither saw nor heard any more of the Japs. The rest of the day I traveled very slowly and carefully. By nightfall, I was in a mountainous area where there were few roads. I never did find out the reason for the firing that morning, but concluded it was a scare tactic to clear the area of suspected guerrillas.

When I was still several hours' hikc from thc guerrilla headquarters, I was challenged by a guard at an outpost. After some delay in proving my identity, I was escorted to the headquarters. Peralta was living in a *nipa* shack, on top of a hill on the edge of the forest. With him were his wife; a young aide and his wife; and a few houseboys.

I spent the afternoon talking with Peralta. The majority of Filipino officers and men in the 61st Division who had not surrendered had been assembled into their old units. The headquarters of the 63rd Regiment was nearby, that of the 64th was to the west in the Aklan area (northwest Panay) and the 65th Regiment was somewhere in Antique Province. Guerrilla headquarters was dispersed over an area of a square mile, to the east of Peralta's command post. The different sections of the headquarters were in *nipa* shacks atop widely separated hills. During our discussion, we were interrupted frequently by messengers coming and going.

He wanted me to organize a cavalry unit for him, much as I had done for the 63rd prior to the surrender. I hesitated to agree to this because I was reluctant to become too closely involved with Peralta. Before the surrender, his attitude had been consistently anti-American. I doubted if he had changed very much since then. I also wanted to find out how he was running the newly-assembled division before committing myself. I told him that I would think about it, but would first return to Tablas. This did not seem to please him.

I told him of my experiences with Raval and Jurado, and voiced my disapproval of banditry, or any action for the personal benefit of individuals. Half-heartedly, he agreed with this. He mentioned the fact that he knew the Japs had a price on my head. This bothered me, as I did not put it past him or any of the others around him to attempt to turn me in for the reward.

While we were talking, suddenly the sound of planes was heard. In a moment there was a flight of Zeros overhead. Everyone made a dash for the trenches outside. It brought back memories of the game of musical chairs we had played on Luzon on the early days of the war.

The planes systematically began to strafe and dive bomb all the shacks and anything that moved within the area directly to the east of us. It lasted only a matter of minutes. Our hilltop position had been a vantage point from which to see most of the show. I saw no direct hits on the *nipa* shacks by bombs, but the strafing had appeared to damage some of them. There was little doubt that there had been trained informers in the camp who had provided the Japs with the detailed information they needed to pinpoint targets. They had not missed shooting at any of the staff shacks, but had not bothered us.

Peralta was shaking noticeably as we left the slit trenches. He was showing signs of the strain, under which he must have been. In the valley below, litters with men on them were being carried away from the areas that had been attacked.

The subject of refusal to surrender was never brought up. I asked about radio communications with any American headquarters. Peralta said he was working on it; that the radio from the 61st Division headquarters had been salvaged. Also, he expressed no knowledge of any submarine activity.

Peralta mentioned his plan to place all the Visayas under his command, plus Palawan, Mindoro, and Marinduque.

The next day was spent visiting Peralta's staff. My first shock was to find a less than brilliant lieutenant, whom I had known in the 63rd, wearing major's leaves and acting as Peralta's G-1. Then, I visited the remaining staff sections throughout the rest of the day. Again, I ran into several of the officers whom I had known before the surrender. Many were inflated with self-importance, having jumped two or three ranks since the surrender and were filling positions far above their professional capabilities. Talking to may of them, I found little thought was being given to killing Japs, but much to pretty uniforms and women. Their food was being commandeered from the civilian population.

During the day, I received a message to report back to the G-1. On arrival there, the G-1 handed me a typewritten order. It directed me to activate a cavalry unit at a certain place by a specified time. It came as a surprise as I had not accepted the job. I was not under Peralta and at the moment had no intention of so becoming. The order promoted me to the rank of major. I wondered how Peralta got his authority, not being in contact with any American headquarters. I passed the order back to the G-1 with no intention of complying with it, at least until I had a chance to look around.

Late that evening I arrived at the headquarters of the 63rd Regiment. It was located in a nearby *barrio* in the schoolhouse. There, I met a good many officers and men with whom I had previously been acquainted. One was the cavalry lieutenant who had deserted long before the surrender. I did not ask him why he had left. The next day I spent talking with the commander and various individuals of his staff. They were trying, but as yet hadn't established a functioning regimental headquarters. They all had been promoted one, two, or three ranks since the surrender, and did not have the training or experience for the jobs they were trying to perform.

In the afternoon, the headquarters was put into a flurry when a messenger reported a Japanese motor column of undetermined strength somewhere in the vicinity, approaching the regimental area. Later reports received from scouts were just as vague. By nightfall, the nervousness had increased. Imaginations had the Japs approaching from all directions in a night attack. Until then, the Japs had not bothered the regiment. That is why the commander had been so bold as to have his headquarters in the *barrio*. Now he was starting to regret it.

The guards around the perimeter of the headquarters were strengthened. Two scouts returned after dark and reported seeing nothing. I recalled the Filipino captain sent out by Colonel Fitz to scout a certain area that had gone over the next hill and spent the time in a nearby shack with some friends. I wondered if the guards coming in that night had done the same.

After supper, I found a place to sleep outside the schoolhouse and away from the road. Before going to sleep I had a look at the security set-up around the regimental headquarters. I awoke before daylight the next morning and decided to have a look at the perimeter guards. The starlight was bright enough to make out objects several yards away. I approached the first post very carefully, being aware of the danger of startling a man on guard under the circumstances. I need not have been so careful. When I reached the guard he was asleep. I shook him.

He drowsily raised his head, blinked his eyes a few times, and lay back down. Then I shook harder. This time he awoke with a start. Seeing me startled him more. He knew he was doing wrong and quickly crawled back to his post where his rifle was. He spoke a little English. I tried to make him understand that he should stay awake on guard. He had seen no one since then. I asked him where his corporal was. He did not know.

I looked at several more guard positions and found more sleepers. Returning to the first post visited, I found the guard had gone back to sleep. By now, it was getting daylight. Searching for the units that were supposed to be in support of the perimeter of outposts, I found groups of men strewn around, all in a deep sleep. Inside the schoolhouse, things were the same. Men and officers were spread around the floor, asleep. No guards, no one awake.

At breakfast, I told the regimental commander what I had found earlier. He shrugged and remarked that the men were young and inexperienced. Apparently, having men sleep on guard was not unusual.

The scare the night before had been a false alarm. A scout had seen a column of Japanese trucks moving up the coast highway several miles to the east. When a truck moved out of the column toward the west, the scout assumed the whole column would follow, and immediately left to advise his lieutenant. As the message passed through the many echelons to regiment, it became a large column of Japs approaching the regimental area. A message received the following morning advised that the Japanese column had moved on north.

In the afternoon, a guide took me to the headquarters of one of the regiment's battalions. There, I met more acquaintances from the 63rd. I was starting to realize that very few of the Filipinos in the 63rd had surrendered. For that matter, very few in the 61st Division had surrendered either. I had the same impression from looking over the battalion as I had at regiment. It did not seem to be working as a team under one head. There was, however, an effort being made to harass the Japs.

Japanese motor convoys were observed regularly moving along the coast highway several miles to the east, sometimes during the day, sometimes at night. It was one of these that had caused the scare in regimental headquarters the night before. There was no explanation why the Japs were moving convoys at night.

The battalion was making preparations to ambush one of these convoys. "We tried this once before," the battalion commander told me, "but without much success. The convoy we were after was led by an armored car, well ahead of the main body. My men fired on the armored car, which stopped and started spraying our position with machine-gun fire. Our position was above the road, so my men could get away without being hit, but as they were running toward the forest, they were fired on from a position away from the road, near where the main body of the convoy had stopped. The Japanese tactic was to pin us down by fire from the road, while a force from the main body dismounted and tried to circle us. This time, we will not fire until the main body is in front of us."

I asked if I could join in the platoon in the ambush.

"Yes, if you will be very careful not to give the position away." A position had been selected days earlier by the platoon setting the ambush.

The next afternoon, I was marching with the platoon toward the ambush site. The area was hilly and overgrown with tall bushes, which gave good concealment. As the platoon neared the highway, it stopped in a ravine. There, it put on camouflage, which amounted to sticking fresh cut branches into hats and packs and belts. Not to be outdone, I did the same.

The platoon commander, who had gone ahead, soon returned. He told me he had been to a nearby observation post. He had been told that there had been no convoys passing that day. And there was no sign of Japs within miles. He got his platoon together and went over the plan of action. Afterwards, he explained his plan to me in English. It was as the battalion commander had said. They would only fire on the main body of the convoy. A blast of his whistle would be the signal to fire; another to cease fire and get out. A place to assemble afterwards had been selected.

The plan seemed simple and workable. I wondered how it would turn out. It was late afternoon by the time everyone was in position. Now, to wait. I thought of the time near Baguio, when I had waited all night with the Scouts from the 26th, and the times on Panay, before the surrender, which had been nothing but waiting.

It was pitch dark before the sound of motors came to us. Then came the glimmer of lights. I crawled forward where I could get a better view of the highway. Off to the right, maybe a mile away, was a whole column of lights. They were moving toward us very slowly. The muffled sound of motors was barely audible. The man on my left was getting nervous. Beyond him I could see nothing. To my right, I had last seen the lieutenant, prone, on the other side of a bush. Looking now, I could see or hear no one there.

The column of lights continued slowly towards us; searchlights were being used to light up the side of the road. As the column neared the hilly area where we were positioned, it stopped and covered the sides of the road with searchlights. Then, moving forward again, the convoy was nearly on us. The man on my left was fit to be tied.

Would the column never get to us? I could feel the excitement that the men along the position must be feeling. I was completely engrossed in watching it approach. It stopped nearly upon us then, its searchlights covering the right of our position.

I glanced over at the man on my left. He had disappeared. I crawled over to where he had been and beyond—no one. I wondered what was going on. I had heard no change of orders. Crouching, I returned to my original position, and beyond to locate the lieutenant. He was not where I had last seen him. Then I heard muffled voices somewhere behind our line. I felt my way back to the voices. Two men saw me coming and disappeared to the rear.

I was at a loss. I moved back to some high ground, about a hundred feet from the highway, to watch and listen. The sound of the motors was loud now. The column was moving again. The reflection of lights showed it was passing our position. Not a shot was fired. Soon, the column had passed, using their searchlights beyond us. There was no one around. I slowly worked my way back toward where I thought the assembly area was. Searching for some time, I failed to find it nor did I run across anyone. There was little chance of any Japs being in the immediate area, but I was apprehensive about wandering around in the dark with the nervous young soldiers about. So I found a bush, crawled under it, and went to sleep.

By noon, I had gotten through the battalion perimeter in time for lunch. Late that afternoon, I was again at regimental headquarters. It was in a greater flurry than ever, undergoing another scare. Regimental headquarters was moving back into the hills this time. No one I had spoken with had any information as to the whereabouts of the 2nd Battalion commander, the same who had disappeared when his battalion moved back into the mountains when the Japs invaded Panay.

I had seen all I wanted to see. Early the next morning I started west, heading back for Tablas.

The following day, I ran into the two Englishmen who had been with Bickerton in Iloilo. They had not surrendered. They said that at the present time they were working for Peralta. We were headed in the same direction, so I joined them.

The next day, walking over a flat area of dried rice paddies, suddenly we were brought up sharply by the sound of planes behind us. Looking back, a Japanese fighter was coming directly for us. Instantly, running away from its line of flight saved us in the first round. The strike of bullets could be seen pounding the ground where we had been a moment before, followed by the stuttering rattle of the plane's machine guns. We had run in different directions. A second plane went after one of the Englishman on the other side of the paddy. The Englishman was zigzagging like a scared jackrabbit. The pilot of the plane was doing his best to follow, shooting short bursts whenever he thought he was on target. In a moment the Englishmen disappeared into a bamboo thicket.

The first plane had regained altitude by now and was circling above me. I had lain down behind a dike that I thought hid me, but in a moment the plane started to dive and was coming in my direction. In an instant I was up and running toward the nearest thicket. This pilot was not very good with running targets, either.

The following day was Christmas 1942. The two Englishmen and I had dinner in a deserted sugar central. For a drink, we drained the bottom of an old vat. The leavings had fermented into a strong alcoholic brew similar to rum. I remember this particularly because each sip caused me a bad case of heartburn.

On 26 December, I started west again, alone, into the mountains of the Aklan area. Days later in the town of Balete, I looked for the mayor and his wife who had given me such good care last May, but they had gone. The headquarters of the re-formed 64th Regiment was located deep in the mountains, far from any roads and farther from any Japs.

The headquarters was in a large *nipa* shack. When I walked in, I found it swarming with officers, most of them doing nothing. I walked into the regimental commander's office. He was a former Philippine Constabulary officer, a lieutenant colonel. His headgear was a red fez, which was customary with Constabulary officers who had served in Moro country. We talked for an hour or so about our experiences since the start of the war, the guerrilla movement, and his regiment in particular.

Very few of the officers and men of the 64th had surrendered. Most were now back with the regiment. The regimental commander was a professional officer. He knew that his regiment was lacking in combat readiness, but was at a loss to know where to start to improve it. Neither his junior officers, which were about all he had, nor his non-commissioned officers had had much military training.

I stayed with the regiment several days, visiting various units and talking with a good many officers. Until then, there had been no attempt to kill Japs and no one I talked to mentioned the subject unless I brought it up. Few had heard a shot fired in anger. I wondered what the mission of the regiment was.

There were two topics of discussion that dominated most of the conversations. One was women. The other was the newly-arrived news from division headquarters that all personnel in the reformed units on Panay were drawing pay from Uncle Sam. It was curious why Peralta had not mentioned this to me. He had given me to understand that he had not yet gained radio contact with Americans.

There was little evidence of discipline anywhere. Nowhere was there any evidence of training. Most of the enlisted personnel were lolling around in dirty uniforms, doing nothing. And the officers were little better.

The civilians in the lowlands were the source of supply for the regiment. Foraging parties would enter a friendly *barrio* and commandeer food, clothing, household items for their comfort, and even luxuries. They would sometimes stay for days, often mistreating the young women. The Japs would eventually come into the *barrio* and punish the *barrio*-folk for helping the soldiers. I heard complaints about these incidents both before visiting the regiment and after leaving it. Such actions could drive the population to start cooperating with the Japs. Several civilians with whom I spoke commented that they would not mind supporting these units if only the soldiers were fighting the Japs.

The whole show reminded me of Raval's gang of bandits. I left thoroughly disillusioned and disgusted with what I had seen of the Panay guerrillas—often referred to by the civilians as the "banditos guerrillas." They were being paid by Uncle Sam for this!?

I well remember one of the nights on my way back to Tablas as an enriching experience. I was staying in the house of the padre of the *barrio* of Burrocan. We spent the night by the light of a tiny coconut oil lamp, sitting around a table sipping *tuba,* discussing religion. He was a Catholic priest, and I, a Universalist, both professed Christians, but with different concepts of Christianity. The evening was spent trying to convert one another. It was a thoroughly stimulating evening that ended in neither of us changing his original concepts.

In the *barrio* of Union on the northern coast of Panay, I decided to wait a few days to look for a boat sailing north. The *barrio* padre kindly asked me to stay with him. Soon after I arrived, an officer with a group of men, reportedly from Peralta's camp, came into town looking for me. The lieutenant accosted me in the main street.

"Where do you think you're going?" he asked in an ugly tone.

"Why does it concern you?" I replied.

"We want to know."

"Who is we?"

"Peralta wants you to return to his headquarters," he said.

"You tell Peralta I want to assist in the guerrilla movement, but from what I have seen, there is little being done to justify your existence. At present you are acting like a bunch of bandits, taking from the civilians and giving nothing in return."

The lieutenant took on a threatening attitude. I told him he should be careful not to do something he might regret and casually put my hand on my pistol. Glaring, he stalked way.

This was one of the very few outward acts of hostility from the Filipinos that I experienced. Why was Peralta doing this? Was it because I had disregarded his order or was he considering turning me over to the Japs?

Chapter 34

It was past the middle of January 1943. It had become evident that there would be no boats sailing north until the change of the northeast monsoon, which could be months. A *buri* boat, much the same as the one I had sailed to Caluya in last July, had been on the beach, unattended, since my arrival in Union. The owner had not been seen for weeks. I commandeered it in the name of USAFFE and gave a receipt to the padre to be delivered to the owner. Within a week, a local sail maker had designed, cut and hung cloth sails to my specifications. It now had a sloop rig (a triangular main sail and jib, called a *batile* rig in the islands). It was much less clumsy to manage than the *buri* sail.

I was not too confident of my skill as a sailor. As it was canoe-ended, about 20 feet in length, with an 8-foot beam and ample freeboard, however, the chances of capsizing the little craft were pretty slim.

A Filipino from Tablas, looking for a way home, was going with me. We pushed off one morning against the north wind. Tacking northwest along the coast did not prove too successful; most of the time it was necessary to resort to the oars. By nightfall of the first day, we were no further along than Manoc-manoc on Borocay Island, only a few miles from Union on the northwestern tip of Panay. The second and third days were little better. While crossing the channel between Carabao Island and Tablas, the wind shifted from the northeast to east-by-northeast. It took us easily out into the strait between Tablas and Mindoro, allowing good progress to the north while it lasted, but it caused us to bypass Santa Fe. On the first of February, we entered Looc harbor, exhausted and nearly starved. It had taken a week to sail 25 to 30 miles from Union to Looc.

Hubbard, on first sight of my new boat sitting low in the water, dubbed it the *Ruptured Duck*. This became its name as long as I had it. That night, instead of returning to his shack on the hill, Hubbard stayed with me at Erbacio's house. For the first time since I had known him, he showed he could be congenial. He had the floor most of the evening, talking of his experiences as a miner in the islands.

One was about a cobra in the wild Igorot country of northern Luzon. Hiking along a trail one evening, alone, he had the feeling he was being followed. Never knowing when a young Igorot might get the urge to take a white man's head, he felt a little nervous. Looking around, he saw a large cobra following him on the trail. When he stopped, the cobra stopped and raised its head. When he proceeded, the cobra followed. If he increased his gait, the cobra increased its. If the slowed down, the cobra slowed down. Never did the cobra get closer than 25 or 30 yards. Unarmed, Hubbard was not sure what was best to do. The *barrio* where he was headed was still quite distant; it was too far to run, so he kept walking at a normal pace. One time when he stopped to look around, the cobra was gone. He saw no more of it. Hubbard also said that he had talked with others who experienced the same thing. The consensus on the reason for this behavior was that the cobra was just plain curious about the two-legged beings in its territory.

He spoke of occasional visits of cobras to his house, while working on the island of Masbate. One of these occasions happened while he was taking a shower. Nearly through with his shower, Hubbard looked up and, there, not two feet away on the window sill, was a large cobra, staring down at him. How long the cobra had been there, or how it got inside, Hubbard never knew. They eyeballed each other for several minutes. Then, as the cobra showed no signs of moving, Hubbard slowly backed off, never losing eye contact, until a safe distance away. This time he had a gun to settle the issue.

Also that evening, I was told a story that had come from Mindoro in the past month. The Japs had caught an American there, tied him to a pole, cut off his genitals, ripped his belly open and left him in the sun to die. The Filipino who had brought the story swore he had seen the mutilated body of the American. My guess was that this was the act of a young Japanese officer who had a burning desire to emulate his Samurai ancestors.

I visited Jurado who was still in Looc, maintaining law and order on the island with a few soldiers. The main thing we discussed was Peralta's interest in tying in with Tablas. Jurado liked the idea. I wondered what would come of it.

The *mah-jongg* game on Erbacio's porch was going strong.

For the first time, I had a good look at the Looc marketplace in full swing. Tropical produce of all kinds brought in by the *barrio*-folk was displayed on stands for sale or trade. There was some money available, but most business was transacted on a barter basis.

Rice was the most important commodity. Next in importance were the meat and fish. Fruits and vegetables grew everywhere, were plentiful, and were not in such great demand. There were two commodities completely absent: refrigeration and sanitation. The fruits and vegetables were laid out in the open, with nothing to keep them from wilting, and covered with sweet-seeking insects. The rice was sacked and tolerably well covered. On the other hand, the slabs of *carabao*, horse, and pig meat—with piles of intestines and other innards—and fish of different kinds and sizes—some cleaned and partially cut up, and some just partially cleaned—were all strewn about on boards covered with slime and blood. To add to its repulsiveness, the whole display was covered with hoards of crawling flies, and stank. It seemed all would be too spoiled to eat, but the wives of Looc were choosing pieces that would be eaten that night. The thought that, unknowingly, I had eaten many meals of such stuff gave me a squeamish feeling.

After a few days, Jurado loaned me two soldiers who would help sail my boat to Santa Fe.

Following a brief reunion with the Sanchez family, I left again, this time for Odiongan, north of Looc. Before leaving Looc, I had received a note from the mayor of Odiongan, asking me to attend a meeting of the mayors of the larger towns on the island.

My first mistake was accepting the invitation to attend the meeting. The second was to volunteer to return a native stallion to a friend of Señor Sanchez in Odiongan.

The ride to Odiongan was nothing but misery. The animal had two gaits—a jig and a fast gallop. The saddle was of wood, splintery in places, and much too small. It was precariously held in place by a piece of hemp rope. The stirrup straps were pieces of the same material, which removed a portion of skin from my bare legs at every jig. The bridle was also of rope, loosely holding a rusty, ineffective bit in the animal's mouth. Each time I pulled on the reins I feared the bit would come free. I arrived in Odiongan worn out and raw from the hips down.

The meeting had been called to prepare a plan for a possible Japanese occupation of Tablas. The officials were concerned about the presence of Americans in Looc and Santa Fe, and Jurado's soldiers in several of the towns. They thought this might be a cause for the Japs to come to the island.

What would I advise? Instead of telling them I would try to get both elements to move to another island, which had been their hope, I advised that our countries were at war with the Japs and we should do everything in our power to annoy and slow them down. I also advised that they should continue helping the Americans on the island and to cooperate as much as possible with Jurado unless they preferred someone like Raval in his place. This little speech was not too well received. I sat through the remainder of the meeting feeling like an outcast. This, with the soreness from my ride, made me wish I had never left Santa Fe.

Back in Looc, I spent an afternoon at Judge Baredo's radio. The allies were still fighting in North Africa. I then visited Linblom and Marianito in Agaho for a few days. Marianito and Linblom wanted me to settle down there for the duration.

Marianito went so far as to offer to provide my food, a separate *nipa* shack, and a pretty girl—an offer difficult to turn down.

By the middle of February I was back in Agmanic with the mayor. It did not take long to get back into the enjoyable and healthy routine of the place: a swim before breakfast; walks with mayor; fishing with my gun and goggles that the mayor had kept for me; and our enjoyable talks in the evenings over *tuba,* followed by the fun dinners by lamplight, with the mayor's jokes and guitar playing.

I brought the *Duck* to Agmanic and each day did some work on it. There was always plenty to keep me occupied.

The channel off the south coast of Tablas Island seldom showed much fury during my stays in Agmanic. Most of the time the sea was calm, a bluish-green, sparkling in the intense sunlight, its surface rippled here and there by passing breezes. Sometimes there would be a short, strong blow from the south followed by a similar blow from the north, clearing the heavens.

On our daily walks, the mayor usually had some remark about the weather. As a farmer and fisherman, living close to the land and the sea, it was vital to him. I found, however, that in general he knew as little about it as I, yet his daily observations through the years allowed him to predict with some accuracy what the next day or so would bring. This proved to be true with most islanders if their predictions were limited to the area where they lived.

I was especially interested in the monsoons because of their affect on sailing. I knew that on Luzon Island, in the central Plain, the northeast monsoon brought clear weather from November through April, and the monsoon from the southwest brought rains starting in May and lasting into October. This pattern had not held in the Visayas. It was becoming evident that the changing of the monsoons was gradual and not predictable from year to year, affecting different localities in the islands differently.

In addition to the weather, sailboats, sailing, and the ways of the sea were taking on a new meaning for me. These all affected the only available means of transport between islands. They were especially significant if I should again decide to start for Australia.

No matter the time of day, there seemed always to be a sail in sight off Agmanic's coast, but seldom were the sails of the same shape or size, or the hulls of the boats alike. I was becoming conscious of the many different types of boats, their names, and what they were designed to do. Cargo vessels were built like tubs with wide beams and a good deal of freeboard, slow but seaworthy. Island-hoppers, built for the transport of passengers and illegal goods, were slim-hulled with outrigger and usually with excessively large sails, fast, but not too seaworthy. From the *banca* made from a hollowed log, to the two-masted, inter-island boats, there were myriad types, all designed for a specific purpose.

On days when the sea seemed its calmest and when larger boats were barely able to move, I often noticed a small sailing craft, skimming back and forth, a short distance off shore. It had a long, thin, white hull with outriggers on each side. Its mast was as long as the hull, supporting and oversized mainsail and jib. It was sailed by a single person.

Watching his maneuverings it soon became evident that the man at the helm was doing more than just sailing for pleasure. And when I saw him pull aboard a good-sized fish, I could stand it no longer. The mayor knew the owner and where he lived.

One day I made an excursion some distance down the coast to his house. I was waiting on the beach when he came in to land. With sails dropped, the boy paddled the boat into shore and without much effort dragged it out of the water up onto the sandy beach.

This little craft, the only one of its kind I had seen, was constructed solely for the purpose of trolling for a tuna-like fishing on a calm sea in a light wind. The boat apparently fulfilled its mission admirably, as the boy brought in several large fish.

The hull was about 20 feet long, with a beam of not more than 18 inches at its widest point. It was canoe-shaped, the gunwales sloping upwards from the center toward each end. The hull was slim and streamlined, resembling the blade and point of a skinning knife. Its depth at the midsections was between 20 and 25 inches.

The bottom of the hull was made from a log of light wood, hewn out, leaving only a thin shell. To secure the planking that extended upward from the top of the hewn log, extensions were attached to each end of the log, to form the canoe-like stem and stern, and ribs were extended upward from its sides. Except for a small cockpit at the stern, the hull was decked with a half-dozen light, removable panels.

The rudder was conventionally shaped, controlled by lines running forward from horizontal side arms. It pivoted on two "L"-shaped iron pins secured to the base of the rudder and dropped into metal eyes extending out from the stern.

The outriggers extended out eight to ten feet from each side of the hull. Each was made of a single huge piece of bamboo held in place by three, springy, wooden supports secured to the top of the hull. The bamboo outriggers were nearly the length of the hull, curved slightly upward on the fore-ends, which were fitted with sharpened wooden plugs to reduce water resistance. The cross supports were bowed downward at the ends where they were secured to the bamboo.

The mast was made of a light, springy timber. Set well forward, its base rested on the keel. Guy lines secured it to the hull and the outriggers.

The triangular jib was run on a bowline extending from the top of the mast to the end of a long bowsprit. Little hand-carved wood rings secured the jib to the bowline. The jib was controlled by two lines running from its free vertex through guides along each side of the hull back to the cockpit.

The mainsail had a gaff and boom rig, its surface was large in proportion to the size of the hull. The boom extended slightly beyond the tiller and slanted upward from the mast to provide clearance for the helmsman. There were two sets of tie-lines on the sail running parallel to and above the boom for reefing.

The mainsail was controlled by lines running from the end of the boom to the cockpit through brackets that provided leverage for adjustments and a tiedown.

The sail cloth was of light cotton, pale blue in color.

The depth of the draft resulting from its narrow knife-like hull reduced slippage to a minimum, thus eliminating the requirement for a centerboard or extended keel.

Native glue, wooden pegs, strips of rattan and cord made of native fiber held the boat together. The sail was secured to the mast by rings made of woven roots. There were no pulleys; instead the lines were run through highly-polished holes in hardwood. The surface of the outside of the hull was as smooth as glass, polished by scraping and rubbing with coconut husks.

This little craft was truly and example of native ingenuity and artistry. It was indeed a thing of grace and beauty.

Several times, the boy took me with him, sometimes staying out for as long as the whole day. As much as I liked to fish, sailing in this little craft was my real reason for going. I soon learned to handle it with a moderate amount of skill. The best sailing was after "a calm"—when a wind was building up, but before it had caused the sea to become rough. I shall never forget the sensation at such times, sitting far out on the outrigger supports, gliding through the nearly motionless water, balanced as though running on a narrow, level rail, the spray from the prow shooting by the sails, the lines taut and straining, and the woodwork creaking from the stresses of the wind and sea. A slight shifting of weight in the boat or a change in the wind would upset this perfect balance. At such times, this boat was at its best. This was the greatest thrill I had yet experienced in sailing.

It was at these speeds that the fish would strike the lure. The lure was a hook-shaped piece of light steel, pointed, but without a barb, a handful of white chicken feathers tied high on the shank covered the entire hook.

There were certain places where the boy knew the schools of fish fed. As we approached one of these, skimming along at a great pace, the lure was thrown overboard and 30 to 40 feet of line paid out. Then we would wait in suspense for a strike. When it came, the line tightened with a jolt, spraying little feathers of seawater in all directions. The boat was quickly turned into the wind.

At first it was not possible to hold the line, but a certain amount of tension had to be maintained to keep the fish from throwing the hook. To do this without burning one's hands took practice. The trick was to take a turn with the line around a peg of wood protruding from the deck especially made for this purpose. This saved one's hands but made it difficult to maintain the proper tension; too loose would let the fish throw the hook, too tight could tear the hook out of its mouth. As the fish tired, it was played toward the boat. Alongside, usually too heavy to lift by the line, there was the job of gaffing. This did not always turn out as hoped. Sometimes, the fish wriggled off the barbless hook before being gaffed; sometimes they wriggled off the gaff. Once in the boat, a deft blow on the head of the fish ended the game.

One day in the middle of March, on a visit to Santa Fe, three young Filipinos came up to me wanting to inquire about my boat. The oldest and biggest was the spokesman. His English was good. His companions were quite young.

"Is the boat for sale?'

"No."

"Is it true that you are thinking of sailing it to Australia?"

"Maybe, sometime, if the war didn't end soon."

"Did you need a crew?"

"Eventually."

"Where is the boat?"

"In Agmanic."

"Could we see it?"

"Why not?"

They had come to Santa Fe to visit relatives. Their homes were on the northern part of the island. Mellandres, the oldest, was in his late twenties, big for a Filipino, a good talker and maybe bit shifty. The other two, Macabato and

Malayo, were in their late teens, really no more than boys, but quite nice ones. They seemed to look to Mellandres for guidance.

The next day, they came to Agmanic. Mellandres offered to take the *Duck* to Santa Fe to finish the work on it. It would give them something to do in their spare time. I agreed to this, but made it clear I had nothing with which to pay them. That afternoon we sailed it around to Santa Fe bay and pulled it up onto the beach. I removed the sails and put them under Señor Sanchez's house. The *Duck* was not to be put in the water without me.

Work on the *Duck* progressed slowly. Mellandres hinted now and then that the three of them would like to become my crew. They were all excellent sailors, having sailed all their lives, according to him.

Jurado had been in contact with Panay for some time.

In the latter part of March, he came down to Santa Fe to discuss some instructions that he had recently received from Peralta. Jurado's instructions were to send scouting parties to Palawan, Mindoro, and Marinduque Islands, to determine what, if any, guerrilla activity there was on these islands. If there were guerrillas, he was to tie them to Panay; if there were none, he was to start a guerrilla movement. Jurado was all excited about the idea and wanted to know if I would help.

I told him I might be interested in the Palawan assignment. I could let him know in a few days, if he would come back to Santa Fe with his detailed plan.

It seemed premature to me for Peralta to be taking on more, when he could not even manage what he already had on Panay. It seemed he was having delusions of grandeur and that Jurado was right behind him with a firm grip on Peralta's coattails.

Jurado returned in two days. His plan was to send a boat with a squad of soldiers, including radios with operators, and supplies to Cuyo Island off the east coat of Palawan. Cuyo would be used as a base from which to operate. I asked Jurado where the radios were coming from. His vague answer made me suspect there might really be something to the rumors of landings from submarines surfacing off Panay. Peralta had advised Jurado that it would be two or three weeks before the operators and radios would arrive on Tablas. By that time, he would have the boat, soldiers, and supplies ready to go.

I told him I could take the job. It sounded a little far-fetched, especially the part about the radios, but I thought even if it all fell through I would be learning about the area, which could stand me in good stead, if and when I decided to start for Australia again. I also told him I would take my own boat and that I would like to leave as soon as possible, to catch the northeast wind before it changed. I would meet his boat in Cuyo in two or three weeks. Jurado would have a couple of sacks of rice for me in Santa Fe in two or three days.

I told Mellandres and the boys we were leaving for Cuyo within the week. They were elated. I was getting restless and ready to get going again.

Chapter 35

The plan was set and agreed upon. I would go to Cuyo, set up a temporary headquarters there and start gathering information on Japanese and guerrilla activities on Palawan Island. A larger boat with food, soldiers, and the radio equipment would follow within two or three weeks. They would report to me in Cuyo and all would proceed to Palawan with the idea of tying any guerrillas there in with those of Tablas, or if there were none, to initiate a guerrilla movement on the island.

Mellandres, the two boys, and I shoved off from the coast of Agmanic midmorning on 6 April 1943. I called back to the mayor that I would plant another coconut tree on my next visit. The *Ruptured Duck* had had a face lifting in the past few weeks. The sail and its rigging had been repaired, the shelter replaced, a new stove installed, and the planking caulked. The weather this time of year is mostly cloudless, with few storms and a gentle prevailing north wind.

Crossing the channel to Carabao Island took little time. Initially, we had planned to stay in close to the island until dark, to avoid the danger of being picked up by a Japanese launch, but with the wind and sea ideal for sailing, we decided to continue on our way. Shortly after noon, we headed a little south of west for Caluya Island.

By late afternoon, the *Duck* was racing south close in to Caluya's eastern coast, toward Sibay Island. At dark, we poled into a coral cove on the east shore of Sibay and threw anchor for the night.

At sunup the next morning, we were again sailing south. That afternoon, we were drawn into a game of hide-and-seek with a Japanese launch. Toward sundown a storm closed in that made it possible to shake the launch. We anchored for the night in the lee of a beautiful little island, one of the northernmost of the Quinilubin Group.

During the evening the four of us went ashore on a sandy beach to eat and stretch our legs. We had caught our first fish that afternoon. Fried and eaten with rice, it made a wonderful meal.

Morning broke cloudless with the north wind still prevailing. The dark blue sea had a deep swell to it, a comfortable sea without whitecaps or an overly strong breeze, which carried us along at an excellent rate.

A pinnacle on the north end of Cuyo Island loomed up ahead. Off to our right a low, sandy spit shot out from the pinnacle. To the south spread the island of Cuyo, its rolling hills covered with coconut palms.

We crossed a shallow, barely getting over before the ebbing tide bared its rocky bottom. In the lees of the island the sea had calmed to almost the smoothness of a pond. A few ripples shimmered brightly in the noonday sun. We were moving south at a fine clip, close in to the western coast of Cuyo.

Mellandres was sitting at the tiller, talking and laughing with his two young companions. He had visited the island many times before and appeared to be filling the two boys with tall tales of his past escapades there. The boys sat goggle-eyed, in anticipation of the good times ahead.

There was something enchanting about Cuyo. I felt it that first day as we approached the heavily-timbered, old-fashioned pier, covered with little naked brown bodies shouting, pushing, diving, swimming, splashing, climbing up onto the pier to go through the whole cycle over again. Several nice looking Filipinas were sitting on a bench near the pier-house chatting and watching the children. The outline of the town could be discerned from the shining iron roofs that were predominantly silver, but here and there, red or green. To our left, north of the pier and the town, a hundred or so yards away, was what appeared to be an old Catholic mission. With its white stucco outside and red tile roof, it was reminiscent of those I had seen up and down the California coast years ago.

As we neared the pier, two individuals came out of the palm grove. They were unmistakably Americans, dressed in worn US Army Air Corps fatigues.

"Howdy," I yelled, waving at them. "I am Captain Whitehead."

The blond, blue-eyed American replied, "I am Charles Shea."

"My name is Frank Valenzano," rejoined his dark, handsome compatriot.

I scrambled up the ladder onto the pier. "You are part of the 48th Materiel Squadron from Mindoro," I said as I gained the top.

"Yes, how do you know?" they asked.

"I ran into part of your group on Panay. What are you doing here? I thought you'd be in Australia by now," I asked.

"Come into the town where we can get out of the sun and I'll tell you what happened," Shea answered. They had been on Cuyo Island now for several months. Both Shea and Valenzano had married local girls. We sat down in Shea's house. He and his wife lived with her parents.

Shea related that, after sailing from Panay in early June 1942, heading for Australia, the group of Air Corps men had run into the same problems with the southwest monsoon as I had. Progress had become nearly impossible. When off the eastern coast of Palawan Island, a *chubasco* had driven them ashore, badly damaging their boat. They found themselves marooned in an isolated *barrio*.

It was not long before everyone came down with malaria. Between the malaria, their boat being damaged, and the monsoon against them, the group decided to delay the trip to Australia, at least until the wind changed. Then an incident occurred that changed their position.

One morning, there was a great hubbub in the *barrio* where they were staying. A raiding party of two boatloads of Moros was heading toward them. The Americans hid along the shore as the boats approached. When the Moros were within easy rifle range, the Americans opened fire. It became a one-sided slaughter, as the Moros carried no firearms. The Moros were traveling in *kumpits*, their wide-beamed cargo boats. These boats were taken over by the Americans. Now, with transportation available, they again had to decide what to do next. Some wanted to continue to Australia; others believed it more prudent to remain on the island. Shea and Valenzano were part of the group that went to Cuyo, hearing there was no malaria on the island. As far as Shea knew, the remaining Americans were still on Palawan. Shea also mentioned the presence of a guerrilla movement on Palawan.

The mission house to the north of the town was vacant, the island's padre having left months before. Mellandres, the two boys, and I moved into it. It was near the beach so we could have the boat nearby, but being near the pier made us vulnerable to a surprise Japanese landing.

We had brought a goodly supply of rice with us. At least at first, we were able to maintain ourselves without the help of the Cuyonos. The first few days were spent getting our boat and equipment cleaned up and repaired. Some of the Americans who had come to Cuyo with Shea and Valenzano were living back in small *barrios,* away from the town. Through the days that followed, one by one they would drop by the mission house to introduce themselves and talk a while.

Alfred Cobb, an American *mestizo* in his early thirties, moved in with us. His father had been among those American soldiers who had taken discharges there after the Spanish-American War. He had married a Cuyona and spent his life in the islands, eventually becoming quite prosperous. Alfred was slim, of medium height, and his appearance heavily reflected his Anglo-Saxon heritage. He had spent some years in the US Merchant Marine. His English was quite good, but often his words stuck in his throat. At such times, it was agonizing, waiting for him to finish a sentence.

Reynaldo Abadiano, also a Cuyono, and a long-time friend of Alfred, wanted to join the crew of the *Duck.* He wanted to be a soldier. He also moved in with us. I gave him his initial training as a soldier in the manual of arms and how to fire a rifle. His English was excellent.

Mellandres was a "go-getter," a sort of "con" man. Besides working on the boat, which he disliked, his job was to collect food for our meals. Often he would return to the mission house with much more than we needed. I never gave him any money and doubted if he had any of his own. When asked how he acquired all the things he brought in, I always got the same answer, accompanied by a sly smile, "They are presents to those in the mission house."

I never knew whether they were *bona fide* gifts, obtained by threats, or were outright stolen. I also never pressed the subject.

Evening was the best time of the day. We usually had visitors, both American and Filipino. Always, they brought *tuba*, and often, choice tidbits from their kitchens as *hors d'oeuvres,* or *sum-summan* as the Filipinos called it. Usually there was singing, sometimes American, but more often, Spanish or Filipino songs, sung to the accompaniment of Mellandres' guitar. Often before the evening was over, there would be dancing on the flat ground outside the mission house.

The girls in Cuyo were very pretty, of lighter complexion and with finer features than I had noticed elsewhere. They were also friendly; there was little wonder why the Americans were being charmed into taking them for their wives.

The month of May came with no sign of a boat from Jurado.

About that time, a boat came from the *barrio* where the Americans on Palawan were staying. When the boat returned, I sent a message to one of the Americans there. The message requested information on guerrilla activities and possible locations for radio stations.

The exactness of time had long since ceased to mean anything as far as the orderly progression of scheduled activities was concerned. The waiting and watching for circumstances that allowed one to accomplish something was more the way it was, than being able to say, "Tomorrow, I will do such and such." Circumstances—the weather, the way the wind blew, the activities of the Japs, the humor of the Filipinos, the availability of food and transportation—all had a controlling influence on what could be accomplished. The expenditure of a seemingly enormous amount of effort was necessary to accomplish the most minor things. I kept asking myself, "Are my efforts on Cuyo just another waste of time?"

Japanese launches were now being seen almost daily off the coast of Cuyo. It would be no trick at all for the Japs to land a group of soldiers anytime they chose.

Valenzano and another American named Vigoreaux had become sick, with pains in their stomachs. The local doctor came to see me. He had determined that they both had appendicitis. He was afraid their appendixes might burst, if not soon removed. He could perform the operations, but they must be done in his office in the town. His concern was about what would happen if the Japs landed during the operations. He had stretchers on which Valenzano and Vigoreaux could be operated. What the doctor wanted was someone responsible for carrying them into the back country if the Japs should decide to pay a visit.

The next morning, all the Americans on the island were at the doctor's office. When I walked inside, Valenzano was laying on stretcher, naked, the doctor shaving him. He was then washed with alcohol by an assistant. Alcohol was also used to sterilize the doctor's instruments and his hands and arms. The doctor and his assistant put on masks. A liquid that smelled like ether was applied to a piece of gauze and placed over Valenzano's nose. In a moment he was asleep.

The doctor made a neat incision, found what he wanted inside, removed it and sutured the incision. The area of the incision was washed with alcohol and a sterile bandage put on it. It had looked like a very neat job. There was little doubt in my mind that the doctor knew how to remove an appendix.

With a blanket thrown over him, Valenzano was carried to a nearby *barrio* to recuperate. Another group was standing by for Vigoreaux, who was soon without his appendix. My main apprehensions about the operations had been dispelled. No Japs had shown up. The doctor had appeared to know what he was doing and the chances of infection afterwards looked to be pretty slim because the doctor had taken care to keep everything clean and sterilized.

That evening the conversation turned to operations. Everyone who had had an operation was heard. After all had their say, Alfred came up with the gem of the discussion, "The circumcision of a young man." This act, part operation, part ceremony, was done without any painkiller or sympathy. It was this ceremony which passed the boy into manhood. How well he withstood the ordeal was a test of his courage and character. With male relatives and the city fathers looking on, the actual operation was usually performed by an old man. His tools were a sharp knife and a cutting board. The victim stood up to the board, placing his penis on it. He had to stand there, watching if he desired, as the painful cuts were made and as his blood slowly trickled over the board. Often, it was a month before the victim was completely healed. Alfred had gone through this years back, on this very island.

Considering the safety of Vigoreaux and Valenzano had brought home to me the vulnerability of our position. I soon concluded that living in the town or in the mission house next to the pier was foolhardy. There were no guards. During the day, there was a good chance someone would see a launch approaching, but at night, if motors were turned off, it would be simple for a Japanese force to surprise us. As a consequence, it was not long before we moved from the mission house into a *barrio* some distance from the town. We moved the *Duck* to a small, isolated cove on the far side of the island to facilitate a hurried getaway.

Sometime during the first weeks of May, more of the Americans who had remained on Palawan arrived in Cuyo. There were 10 or 12 of them. They came in the two Moro *kumpits* taken on Palawan. It was a motley crew if ever there was one—bearded, untrimmed hair in tangles, barefooted, and clothed only in ragged shorts. All were tanned by the sun to nearly the color of the islanders. They were armed to the teeth, each carrying a rifle or shotgun; a pistol or two; and a bolo. As they climbed onto the old pier, their friendly, easy-going manner and the warm greetings left little doubt that they were Americans. Malaria had been the main reason for their departure from Palawan. One or two of their number had already died of the black-water fever, a deadly type of malaria. The only ones left now on Palawan were a few of the group who were still bent on trying to get to Australia.

Singly, or in groups, the new arrivals left the pier with those who had come to Cuyo earlier. In no time, they were dispersed throughout the town and its *barrios*, some going to stay with Miss Ponce de Leon. Miss Ponce de Leon was a maiden lady who early in life had dedicated herself to helping others. Through the years, her efforts had been primarily toward salvaging young girls in trouble. Now, with the derelict Americans in need, she had included them. She had made it clear to me from the first that we were welcome to eat and sleep in her home.

The residents of Cuyo seemed to have a special liking for Americans. They did not appear a bit perturbed over the new influx. They were now supporting 19 Americans, plus my crew of three and a Filipino named Ben who had come from

Palawan with the Americans. We ate with them, worked with them, and partied with them, but we could also be the cause of Japanese reprisals against them.*

Lieutenant Errold Glew, who was among the latest arrivals, had surrendered with the 63rd Regiment on Panay. According to him, the Americans in Calinog who had surrendered were taken to an old fortress near Iloilo for internment. The fortress was located on a spit that extended a short distance out into the sea. This short distance provided no cover or concealment between the fortress and the town. Glew, Sergeant Mackey, and Lieutenant Cotheran escaped from the Iloilo fortress early one morning. At daybreak, they were discovered by the Japs in the open area between the fortress and the town. Their only chance was to make a run for it. This they did, and for several long minutes were running targets for the Japanese riflemen in pursuit. They somehow managed to get through the town and into the forest, where they hid until dark. They eventually made it to the western coast of Panay. Glew and Cotheran took a boat to Palawan Island, where they met those of the Army Air Corps group who had earlier left Panay for Australia. Mackey stayed on Panay.

Both Pryor and Swift, also among the new arrivals, had been captured on Corregidor and later transferred to a prison camp at Puerto Princess, the capital city of Palawan. Together, they managed to escape from the camp. For the next three days, the Japs and their tracking dogs had been close on Pryor and Swift's heels in a mangrove swamp. At one time, the Japs were walking beneath them as they hid in the high branches of trees above. Some days later, completely exhausted from exposure and lack of food and sleep, they were found by some Filipinos who led them to the *barrio* where the other Americans were staying. Pryor had recovered, but Swift looked like walking death, drained of his energy by the constantly recurring attacks of malaria.

My message, which had been sent earlier to this group while still on Palawan, had been duly delivered. It had been shown to and discussed with the guerrilla leader there. He had voiced displeasure with joining forces with Tablas, which eventually would have meant becoming subordinate to Panay. He felt Cuyo was part of his command, and threatened to use force, if needed, to get his point across.

The days spent waiting for some word from Tablas passed rapidly and pleasurably. Existence on Cuyo seemed idyllic. Bananas, papayas, mangoes, and casoy (cashew) fruit grew in abundance without cultivation. Pigs and chickens took little care as they roamed loose and foraged for themselves. Fish traps supplied a major part of the diet. The big grind was planting, harvesting, and pounding rice. If a man could not get around to planting rice one season, he could probably manage to borrow enough from his neighbors to get him through. The story was told that, often during the Spanish occupation, the padres had had to resort

*Appendix I contains a list of names of members of the 48th Materiel Squadron, 27th Bomber Group, which my records show were on the island of Cuyo in May 1943.]

to lashings if planting was neglected. There was still evidence that the men enjoyed their leisure, but the women were always busy, preparing food, taking care of the children, and keeping the household from falling apart. They were the mainstay of the community.

Mariendas were in order in the middle of the morning and the middle of the afternoon after *siesta*, which took place directly after lunch. Sweet rice cakes or cookies, fruit, and usually coffee made from parched corn were served. Seldom were these gatherings without a guitar player or two and often would turn into songfests or dances. Occasionally, there would be day outings to different parts of the island or to one of the tiny islands nearby.

One picnic to one of the nearby islands nearly ended in disaster. The two Moro *kumpits* and my little *Duck*, loaded to the gunwales, had started back to Cuyo. We had left the cove where the day had been spent and were heading into the channel toward Cuyo when the familiar "thump, thump, thump" of a Japanese launch came to us loud and clear. It sounded as if it were on the other side of the island that we were leaving, and not far away. The wind was hitting us directly astern; it was favorable for sailing to Cuyo, but nearly impossible for a quick return to our picnic island. Returning to the cover was our only chance. The sails were dropped and oars quickly manned, two men to an oar. Never was there a more avid, dedicated group of oarsmen. The sound of the launch was constantly becoming louder, muffled now by a palm-covered spit which shielded us from its view. Although all of the Americans were armed, a firefight was out of the question with all the young ladies aboard. I knew, though, that the Americans would not just give up. I dreaded to think of what might happen if we were spotted.

It seemed that at any moment the launch should round the spit. We were getting close to our cove.

"God give us another moment," I prayed. He did.

As the sound of the launch became clearer, the last of our three little boats glided into the cover of a cove. There were a few breathless moments as the launch passed and the sound of its motor slowly faded into the distance.

That was the last of the outings off Cuyo Island.

There turned out to be a number of ex-Filipino soldiers and officers on the island who had belonged to the 61st Division on Panay and had refused to surrender. Among these was a Lieutenant Catalbas, who had heard of the guerrilla movement on Panay and had considering joining them. He soon became interested in getting the ex-soldiers on Cuyo together and with a little push from me, formed a small company-sized unit. The thought that they might possibly become part of the Panay force that reportedly was drawing pay from Uncle Sam helped to cement his group together.

Catalbas established himself in the town schoolhouse. It was not long before drill periods and classes in basic military subjects were being held. A cache of wooden rifles used by previous military units was uncovered. These were all the weapons Catalbas and company had, but were better than nothing. It was not long before observation and listening posts were established along the main beach on a 24-hour-a-day basis. This not only provided training for the soldiers, but possibly would give some warning if the Japs should decide to land. This possibility became more and more of a concern to me as time went on, but I was reluctant to leave Cuyo until I had some word from Jurado on Tablas.

Glew, with his restless energy, had to find something to take it out on. From their first meeting, Glew took a strong dislike to the mayor of Cuyo. This was enough to get him started. He began to plague the mayor for a loan. The mayor complained to the townsfolk, and through Alfred, the complaint came to me. A few days later I walked into Cuyo to check things out. Glew and I had a long discussion, sitting on a log in the main street, with no one else around. Glew was peeved at the mayor because of his anti-American feelings. The mayor professed to be pro-Spanish, still resenting the American takeover of the Philippines at the turn of the century. A more likely reason for being anti-American was his desire to open trade relations with the Japs, so he could sell the *copra* that had been accumulating since the start of the war.

Glew told me that he and the mayor had exchanged sharp words over the mayor's refusal to loan him money. I warned Glew against becoming too antagonistic. While the mayor was not universally liked, his feeling did influence the thoughts of the townspeople. As we were living on their good will, I told him his actions would only work against all the Americans on the island. I asked him to leave the mayor alone, but I could see from his expression that he was determined to do as he pleased.

Chapter 36

Two or three days later, a nearby neighbor on the eastern side of the island asked Alfred, Mellandres, the two boys, and me to attend a noonday party. He was giving it for his daughter who was to be married soon. The boiled shrimp and *tuba* had not more than made the first rounds when Shea, obviously agitated, burst in. He wanted to see Alfred and me outside.

Several of the Americans living in Cuyo were standing under a nearby coconut tree, engrossed in serious conversation.

"What's up?" I asked Shea when we were beyond earshot of the party.

"Glew's been killed," he said.

"What?" I looked at him, not believing what he said, but his face showed he was serious.

"How do you know?" I asked.

"I saw him, lying upstairs in the municipal building. Vigoreaux was in on it, too. After the shooting we picked Vigoreaux off the floor and carried him to Miss Ponce de Leon's house. Vigoreaux is okay but Glew is dead. Killed with buckshot."

We now had joined the four others who had come over with Shea. They nodded, reaffirming Shea's statement.

"Who did it?" I asked.

"The mayor, with the help of two of his policemen," Valenzano replied.

"How did it happen?"

No one was quite sure. Vigoreaux's story had not been too coherent. Generally, the story ran that Glew and Vigoreaux had gone to the mayor's office. A heated argument developed, which culminated in the participants drawing their pistols and firing at each other. The mayor had called his policemen to help him. They had been armed with sawed-off shotguns; had cornered Glew and Vigoreaux; and had shot them down. Nobody in the party knew how badly Vigoreaux was hurt.

I did not feel we could let such an incident pass without doing something about it. I did know that Glew has been antagonizing the mayor, but at the same time, the mayor had no business killing one of us. He might try it again, hoping we would leave, so he could go ahead with his plan to sell *copra* to the Japs.

My first thought was that something must be done to stop it from happening again. Could something be done with the five Americans who had just arrived from Cuyo and Alfred and me? Mellandres and the two boys were unarmed. The mayor had about nine policemen on his force loyal to him. A few others might be persuaded to throw in with the mayor. They all would be armed with pistols and shotguns. I figured a fast and aggressive show of force might be the answer; it was worth a try.

Besides pistols, each of the Americans had brought either a rifle or shotgun. I told them that we must arrest the mayor and two policemen involved, and try them. They all agreed. Mellandres offered to ride ahead of as we walked into Cuyo. I felt this precaution necessary as the mayor might try to ambush us.

While Alfred and I got our guns, Mellandres saddled a pony, and we took off. The more I turned over the incident in my mind, the angrier I became, and more determined that the mayor would answer for this killing.

We trudged along in a formation of twos on each side of the road, sweating, alert, and talking little. Mellandres, mounted, was 75 to 100 yards ahead, riding jauntily, carefree but alert.

The town was quiet as we entered the eastern side.

The children were off the streets and the windows were down on the houses. Word had undoubtedly preceded us that we were coming into town. I wondered if the mayor would stay at his office in the municipal building. We would know before long.

Just before entering the open green that bordered the municipal building, we took up a line of skirmishers. No one was to fire unless fired upon. I hoped we could arrest the mayor and the two policemen involved and disarm and disband the remainder of the police force without any shooting.

We came into the open in a line, tense, walking slowly, watching, our weapons at the ready. Any moment we might be the target of a good many weapons, but there was nothing stirring ahead. Fifty yards from the building, still nothing. Thirty-five yards—we were walking faster now. Excitement was growing. I warned them to hold their line.

The man on the left threw his rifle to his shoulder and fired. In a second there was general firing, mostly at nothing. The two left flankers took off on their own, toward the direction they were firing. Now I saw two Filipinos who might be policemen. They were 300 to 400 yards away, running for dear life toward the shore.

I bellowed to those remaining to hold their line and watch the municipal building. Alfred and I entered the building while the others circled it. We examined each room with rifles at the ready. First downstairs, then up. In the last room on the second floor, an anteroom off the main assembly room, back in a corner where we did not see him until almost upon him, lay Glew, on his face in a pool of drying blood. The blood appeared to have come from his neck and chest. He was turning purple.

Poor Glew. We rolled him over on his back to get a better look at the wounds. He was already starting to stiffen. His face, neck, and upper chest were covered with blood. His eyes were open and teeth shown as if in a grin. It was the look I had seen on his face many times before on Panay when facing danger. I knew he had faced this trial with his same reckless abandon. "More guts than good sense." That was Glew.

A few small pellets had entered his neck and chest. How little it had taken to snuff out his life. Again the thought returned of how frail the human body is. Why had he been picked to go?

Alfred and I walked downstairs. Vigoreaux, the man with a thousand lives, had walked over from Miss Ponce de Leon's house, where he had been carried a few hours before, believed by everyone to be badly wounded. Other than a little blood on his shirt, he looked and acted no differently than ever. The rest of the Americans gathered around him, asking questions. With his big grin, he said, "Hi, Captain." I must have looked amazed as he laughed and wanted to know what the trouble was. That was the kind of big, carefree, damn fool he was. I walked up and embraced him. It was wonderful to see him on his feet, grinning. I had visualized him—at the least—as badly wounded.

"Where were you hit?" I asked.

"I wasn't." He replied.

"Well, why the blood?" And he started his story.

At about 1100 hours that morning, Glew and Vigoreaux had gone to see the mayor in his office. The mayor had taken them upstairs to the assembly room to talk. Glew was there to find out the status of his request for a loan and had casually asked Vigoreaux to come with him. The discussion with the mayor soon developed into a heated argument. All of a sudden, the mayor backed away, pulling a whistle out his pocket, and said he had taken as much from Glew as he was going to take. After blowing a few blasts on the whistle, he pulled his pistol from its holster and started firing at Glew and Vigoreaux. Seeing what was happening, the Americans ducked behind the table upon which they had been sitting. They had their pistols out almost as soon as the mayor. Glew carried two pistols and had them both out, blazing away from the hip, like a cowboy in a western movie. Vigoreaux was doing the same, and so was the mayor, as far as I could gather. In the minute or so of firing, while all three emptied their guns, no one was hit. (A later examination of the area showed that all the bullets fired had gone into the floor between the two parties).

About that time, up the stairs came two policemen carrying 12-gauge sawed-off shotguns. Off the assembly room where the shooting had taken place, in the opposite direction from the approaching policemen, was a smaller room. Seeing the policemen coming on at a run with their guns at the ready, Glew and Vigoreaux made for this side room, hurriedly reloading their pistols. They both crowded into the corner of the room to the left of the doorway. Nothing happened for a few moments. The only sound was the muffled voices of the mayor and his policemen. Then one of the policemen stuck his head through the doorway. Glew fired and the head disappeared. In a moment, Vigoreaux felt a nudge from Glew who was closest to the doorway.

"Watch it," he said.

Around the corner of the door a shotgun was being maneuvered. It was brought parallel to the wall and aimed slightly over the heads of the Americans.

Both ducked just before the gun was fired and heard the pellets spatter on the wall in back of them. This was followed by a second gun being pushed out around the corner of the door in the same manner as the first, but before either Vigoreaux or Glew could make a move, it was fired. Vigoreaux said he heard the pellets slap into Glew. Glew let out a gurgling cough and fell to the floor. Vigoreaux, realizing he was in a hopeless position, fell to the floor beside Glew, quickly wiping some of Glew's blood onto him. Then he started to groan. In a few seconds, the mayor and two policemen were hovering over the two Americans. The mayor gave both a kick, calling them "dirty American pigs." Then, apparently satisfied that the Americans were dead, the mayor walked away from the scene. So ended Vigoreaux's side of the story. Only he could have gotten away with such a thing. (As Vigoreaux told his story he was also acting it out, groaning at the end as though in the last agonies of death.)

At the sound of the shooting a crowd had gathered around the municipal building. The mayor cursorily stated to the gathering that he had been attacked by the two Americans and killed them in self-defense.

In a few minutes, the crowd was upstairs around Glew and Vigoreaux, among them Miss Ponce de Leon and some of the Americans. There was little that could be done for Glew, but Vigoreaux was picked up and carried to Miss Ponce de Leon's house, prostrate and groaning. Not until he was upstairs, being made comfortable on the guest bed, with familiar voices around him, did he open one eye. Finding Shea's worried face he opened the other eye and broke into a laugh. To the surprise of all, he sat up, looked around, and then stood up.

Beardon came down the stairs of the municipal building and out the front entrance where we were talking, his face streaming with tears.

The two men who had chased after the two Filipinos had returned without finding them.

The mayor and his policemen had completely disappeared. The story from the few townsfolk standing around was that the mayor, receiving word that we were coming into town, had taken his police and headed north along the shoreline.

It was growing dark when we started searching for the mayor and his men. We proceeded slowly, searching possible hiding places, taking care not to walk into an ambush. By the time it was dark, we had found nothing and decided any further searching was useless.

That night, we slept in the municipal building, with someone on guard all night. The next morning, word came that during the night the mayor had gotten to one of the little islands surrounding Cuyo. A boatload of Americans went after him in one of the *kumpits.*

I moved over to Miss Ponce de Leon's house, with Vigoreaux, so that I would be in town until the trouble blew over. A guard of Americans was maintained in the municipal building for the next several days, then the guard duty was turned over to Lieutenant Catalbas and his men. The search party returned, without success, having combed several different islands.

A local carpenter fashioned a coffin of rough boards for Glew's remains. A grave was prepared in the town cemetery. Eight of the Americans carried Glew's body to the graveside. In the absence of a man of the cloth, it fell upon me to say a few words. They were as follows: "Dear Glew, we will all miss you. From dust thou cometh and unto dust thou shalt return. Dear God, please take care of what there is of him besides his earthly body, as he deserves."

Someone with a bugle blew taps as the coffin was lowered into the ground. A volley was fired by four of the Americans. A wooden cross marked his grave. It read: "2nd Lt Errold Glew USAFFE."

In a week, the government of the municipality was turned back to the Filipinos, with the vice-mayor at its head. Soon afterwards, a man from a nearby island came into town to tell me that he had taken the mayor and some of his policemen to Panay a few days after Glew's death. With Glew's pointless death past and the town's leadership restored, things soon settled down again.

I shall never forget the huge *carabao* mangoes, which seemed to melt in one's mouth, and the *casoy* fruit, which I had never seen before. This fruit was about the size of a large peach. It had a rosy, pink hue when ripe. Its taste, juiciness, and texture were similar to that of a plum, but it had a pit unlike a plum, which, when roasted, tasted and looked like a cashew nut.

Young and Mageehee had located some copper tubing. With it and other odds and ends, they had built a still. With that, they distilled the local *tuba*—that was about 5 percent alcohol—to a clear, strong, evil-smelling drink that was probably close to 35 percent alcohol. It was similar to the *ginebra* the old man had given us on the trail in southern Luzon, near the town of Antimonan. On Cuyo, it was called "Magi Gin." A *hungut* of it put a man well on his way in no time. It became quite popular with the men of the island, and as unpopular with the women.

Toward the latter part of May, rumors came from Palawan that the guerrillas there had a boat and force ready to take over the island of Cuyo. The date of their sortie was identified to us, and it was not far off.

Alfred was acquainted with the individual who brought the latest word of this and considered him reliable. It was difficult to disregard this news, especially as there had been several threats like it in the past. At any rate, we thought it prudent to make preparations to link up with this force. I only wished the wooden rifles Catalbas's men had were real.

The first problem was to assure adequate warning of the guerrillas' approach. Not wanting to rely wholly on the young Filipino soldiers, we set up a listening/observation post on the pier, manned around the clock by an American.

The plan was to position eight or ten Americans, armed with rifles and shotguns, at the end of the pier toward the town. There was cover for a man in a prone position behind an incline, down from the ramp of the pier. From that position, the pier and the water to each side could be covered with fire. As the guerrilla boat approached, I was to hail it, find out who they were, what they wanted, and demand their surrender. Catalbas and his men would be hidden in the coconut grove that fringed the beach in back of the pier. On my signal, Catalbas would double-time his company out of the coconut grove and position them in a line of skirmishers, 75 yards from the pier. Hopefully, if the wooden rifles were not discovered, this might influence the guerrillas to surrender. If they refused to give themselves up, the American would open fire on them as they had on the Moros on Palawan.

For three days and nights we stood ready for this visit. Then, a report came from Palawan that when the guerrillas were only a few hours off the Palawan coast, the party was hit by a *chubasco*. Thinking the omens were bad, they turned around and gave up the project. It had proven to be only an act of bravado.

Rumors brought by visitors from Puerto Princesa that the Japs were preparing for a raid on Cuyo were increasing. Alfred maintained that these so-called rumors were brought by reliable individuals whom he had known for years. The townsfolk of Cuyo believed that the Japs were being informed by strangers who made occasional visits to the island. Strangers suspected of being informers or Fifth Columnists were being treated coolly; a marked change from the island's usual hospitality.

Feeling that I had waited long enough for word from Tablas, and with the rumor of a Japanese raid growing ever more persistent, I decided to return there. After conferring with the other Americans. I suggested that it might be prudent for all the Americans to vacate Cuyo, at least for a while. After much discussion among themselves, all decided to go to Tablas.

A day was set. The two *kumpits* and the "Duck" were not large enough to carry the entire group. A two-masted *panka* with a five-man crew was hired. About midday in the second week of June, the "migration" started.

On the way, I stopped off at one of the small islands of the Cuyo group, the island of Agutaya. Going through the schoolhouse that had not functioned since the beginning of the war, I found a small box compass and a map of the islands of Southeast Asia. I appropriated them, along with some paper for cigarettes and some medicines from a nearby first-aid station.

By nightfall, all were assembled on the island to the north of Cuyo, cooking dinner on the beach. Everyone had successfully dodged Japanese launches throughout the afternoon. The southwest monsoon had started to blow, giving the party an excellent wind for our destination to the north.

Early the next morning we left with Sibay designated as our assembly point for the night. The wind, coming from the southwest, was again favorable. The three small boats soon left the *panka* far behind.

It became a race to see which of the three would reach Sibay first. During the morning, the two *kumpits* had the advantage, but through the day, as the wind became stronger and the sea rougher, the *Duck*—which took the rough sea better—passed the *kumpits*. This was a victory for Mellandres and the two boys who spent the rest of the afternoon bragging to each other about their superior skill as sailors.

That night, we had dinner with Mr. Jella's cousin with whom I had become acquainted during my stay on Sibay Island.

Early the next morning, we were on our way again, bound for Santa Fe.

Chapter 37

The following afternoon the three small boats arrived in Santa Fe. This small town full of friendly people always seemed to be my returning point. I was beginning to look upon it as my home. It was not until late that night that the *panka,* the last of the "migration," arrived. The early blow of the southwest monsoon had persisted. Our trip had been fast and safe.

Before morning, all were fed and bedded down in the homes of the wonderfully hospitable people of Santa Fe. Counting the wives of Hogg and Shea, there were 26 of us who had made the trip from Cuyo, not counting the crew of the *panka*. This was an impossible load to put on the town.

The next day, we all assembled in the schoolhouse. I gave a briefing on what I knew of Tablas and Panay and made it clear that we could not all stay in Santa Fe. The majority of those present volunteered to leave.

With a full load, one of the *kumpits* sailed for Looc early the next morning another group started overland for Looc, while the *panka* returned to Cuyo.

Mellandres left, too. He had had enough adventuring for awhile and wanted to return home. I hated to see him leave, as I had become quite attached to him.

Jurado had moved his headquarters to Odiongan. After a few days in Santa Fe, I went there to meet with him. On arrival in his headquarters, it soon became evident that his attitude toward me had changed markedly since my April departure. His friendly, almost ingratiating manner had become one of cold belligerence. At first, I was at a loss to find a reason for this change. We did have a few words over his failure to send the boat to Cuyo, but I had accepted his explanation that he had tried and had been unable to get the whole package together—volunteers, supplies, equipment, and the boat. It slowly became evident that Jurado had been indoctrinated with Peralta's anti-American attitude. This was driven home when he related an incident that had happened to him in New York while attending the Naval Academy. It was simply that he and a taxi driver had gotten into an argument over the fare. The taxi driver made a remark to the effect, "What do you expect of these stupid brown monkeys?" And to show that he thought I had the same attitude, he asked me if I would approve of my sister marrying a Filipino. My answer did not improve our relationship. In an effort to mend relations, I spent several days at his headquarters. It became very clear that he felt he had the reins of power on Tablas in his hands and wanted no more traffic with me.*

*Born in the pre-WWII US Philippine Commonwealth, Enrique ("Hank") Lopez Jurado was a man of moral purpose, high character, and fervent patriotism. He graduated from the US Naval Academy in 1934 with a degree in engineering. Then he earned a master's degree at MIT, went to US Army flight school, and represented his country in wrestling at the 1936 Berlin Olympics.

In spite of the fact that last April I had decided to give up any thought of getting to Australia and do what I could to assist in the guerrilla movement, the more I saw and heard of the unethical ways the Panay guerrillas were operating, the less I wanted to have anything to do with them. Maybe it was just as well this difference with Jurado had occurred, before I went off on another wild goose chase.

Before leaving, I gave Jurado a complete list of Americans on Tablas, requesting that he deliver it to Peralta to be transmitted to United States authorities, and to request instructions as to what we should do. Jurado gave me his word that he would deliver the list and message to Peralta.

Then, I rolled my blanket and started south again, toward Santa Fe. Between Odiongan and Looc, several of the Americans from Cuyo had settled in some empty huts in a small *barrio*. Young and Mageehee had their still set up, producing their now famous Magi Gin. The growing demand was keeping them humping. The establishment of a second still was under discussion.

Palmer's *bococong* was no better. I showed Doc Baredo how well mine had healed and asked him to try some more with Palmer's. Hubbard had gone back into his shell. Both he and Hansen impressed me as two bitter old men. Linblom was as optimistic and carefree as ever. I stopped to pay my respects to Erbacio. The *mah-jongg* game on his porch was still flourishing. The banditry in the town had stopped—at least for the time being. Raval had not returned to the island and no one seemed to know where he was.

Judge Boredo's radio was still working. It was obvious from the news that the Pacific was taking second place to the European Theater. After the war, of course, we learned that the American strategy had been specifically to put Hitler out of action first, then Tojo.

It was a relief to return to Santa Fe and spend a good part of each day with Señor Sanchez. July came and went. I had been waiting hopefully for an answer from Jurado to my request for instructions from US authorities. I felt sure by now that my message had never been sent.

About this time, the rumor came down from Luzon that a group of Americans had fitted out a motor launch and set out for the coast of China. I had not considered this as a possible way of getting out of the Philippines, but gave it a good bit of thought now. Although a much shorter distance than to Australia, I threw out any idea of trying this because of the vast stretches of water without islands,

---

His career in the Philippine Army saw him with pre- and post-Pearl Harbor attack littoral defense units; later, he led insurgent forces against Japanese occupiers. At the start of the war, he commanded the Offshore Patrol that later became the Philippine Navy. He rose to lieutenant colonel, commanding wartime army, irregular, and partisan forces. In 1944, Colonel Jurado died in a skirmish between guerilla forces on the Island of Mindoro.

The record of his service to country is recalled by a cadet sports gymnasium (Jurado Hall) at the Philippine Military Academy, in Baguio City, Island of Luzon; on a Philippine Navy warship; on plaques in the Rizal Memorial Coliseum, an important sports venue in Manila; and at Annapolis. A hero of his time, Enrique Jurado played important roles in the service and liberation of his beloved native land.

the possibility of much Japanese shipping, and lack of information on what parts of China the Japs occupied.

The news from Panay concerning the activities of the guerrillas there became more and more disconcerting as time went on. Civilians arriving from Panay were now regularly referring them as *"banditos guerrillas."*

Word came about this time that Private Oakley and Sergeant Mackey had been killed by the guerrillas, both ambushed and shot in the back. Oakley had remained in Caticlan in June 1942 when the rest of us had left for Tablas. Mackey had escaped from prison camp in Iloilo with Glew and Cotheran months earlier.

Travelers from Panay reported that Filipino soldiers who had fought on Bataan and had been captured, then released by the Japs, were being arrested by the guerrillas there. Allegedly, these men were being confined and declared traitors to their country for allowing themselves to have been taken prisoner. The story had it that they were awaiting trial by court-martial. Word also came that Filipino soldiers from Panay had arrived on Odiongan looking for me. I put the word out that any anti-American activity would be aggressively dealt with by the Americans on the island. None of the Panay soldiers ever came to Santa Fe to get me. I wondered if they would eventually resort to shooting me in the back, too.

One day in the first week of August, as I was sitting in Señor Sanchez's parlor, mulling over what to do next, Bob Pryor appeared. He entered the house, wiped the sweat from his face, sat down, and lit a cigarette.

"What'll ya give me for my boat?" he asked.

His boat was one of the *kumpits* that had been taken from the Moros on Palawan Island. I had not thought much of it because the great sail looked so awkward to manage, but it had proven itself fast when the sea was not too rough on the trip from Cuyo to Tablas. Pryor had decided to wait the war out in Odiongan. He had a girl and a job with Jurado.

"Let's go have a look," I answered, more because I was bored, than with any thought of making a deal. The *kumpit* was out of the water, on stays, with the mast off, and the decking strewn over the beach. The crew that had been repairing it had walked off, leaving a mess.

I looked at it without much enthusiasm, but Pryor was a good horse trader and before long found myself listening to his sales pitch. He pointed out how the timbers were in prime condition. They were unpainted and had the look of mahogany. The keel, stem, stern, and ribs were heavy and well formed, held together with wooden pegs. The heavy planking, neatly fitted, was also held in place by wooden pegs. There was not a nail in the entire hull.

The *kumpit* was nearly 25 feet in length. It had a beam of eight feet. From the bow, which was as sharp as the cutting edge of a bolo, it spread gracefully out to the width of the beam, closing in again to a broad, but shallow transom. The depth of the hull was about four feet, except toward the stern where it tapered up to the transom. The rudder was conventional in shape, with a straight tiller, hung to the transom with crude, metal, hinge-like devices. The boat looked seaworthy and had good lines for speed.

The deck consisted of a series of removable wooden panels. From each side, arms protruded three to four feet out from the hull. These were covered with strips of bamboo forming a latticework that could be walked on and was useful for lashing equipment. The great rectangular sail was nearly as long as the hull and half as wide. Heavy bamboo booms were attached to its longer edges. The *kumpit* was the Moro cargo vessel, built for speed, load capacity, and seaworthiness. Maybe this was the boat I had been looking for. Maybe it would get me to Australia.

"What are you asking?" I queried.

"Your saddle and some 'genuine'." was his reply. ("Genuine" was paper money printed by the Philippine government prior to the war.)

Back in the house, I asked Pryor what his total price was. Without answering, he proceeded again to review all the fine points of the *kumpit*. He then offered me "the best possible price I can let it go for—150 *pesos*, plus your saddle." (I had acquired the saddle on Cuyo.) After more talk, I offered him the saddle and 100 *pesos*. He said that was impossible. Then, after a pause, asked if I meant 100 "genuine."

"Seventy-five 'genuine' and 25 'emergency,'" I replied. ("Emergency" paper money was another name for the wartime "scrip." I still had a little money left that was in my wallet at the time of the surrender.)

He got up and in a resigned tone asked where he could see the saddle. It was under the house in a burlap sack. After examining it, he said, "Okay, it's a deal."

I counted out the money and handed it to him. He carefully recounted it and put it into his pocket. Then throwing the saddle over his shoulder, he strode off without another word. All at once I realized that I had a seaworthy boat, which in a short time could be ready to sail.

That evening was spent planning what needed to be done to the *kumpit*. Señor Sanchez and I talked late into the night on ways to get the work parceled out.

The next morning he located a carpenter who could make oars; he made four. The mayor found a friend from an inland *barrio* to cut a new mast from the forest. The new mast was blocked and tied down and pulleys rigged. A young sail maker was found to fit what was left of the sails of my old boat to the *kumpit*. The *batile* rig had less surface area than the Moro sail, but would be easier to handle in squally weather. The *kumpit* then had two sets of sails.

We replaced missing deck boards and completed re-caulking seams and other odd jobs. Two 55-gallon drums for water were installed below deck, resting on the keel, just fore and aft of the mast, where their weight would least affect the *kumpit*'s manner of sailing. The ends were sealed and a rectangle six by eight inches was cut in the middle of the side of each drum. Wooden covers were carved to fit snugly into these holes. Two large earthen jars two feet high and one and a half feet in diameter were placed along the keel to hold rice. There was also a third one for mongo beans and two smaller ones for sugar and salt. Dried meat and fish would be kept in gunnysacks below deck, above the bilge water.

New lines were needed all around, but there were none to be had on Tablas. For some time I had been holding onto a heavy, two-inch hawser of the best Manila hemp. Malayo and Macabato suggested unraveling it, and from its strands, make the sizes of lines needed. They made a native rope-making machine to do the re-twisting. It consisted of two boards, each 8 by 24 inches, with three one-inch-diameter holes. The boards were separated by three 4-by-6-inch wooden blocks, each with two one-inch holes on three-inch centers. Secured in one of the holes of each block, a tightly-fitted wooden peg protruded through each of the three holes in the front board. Into each of the three holes of the back board, a tightly-fitted wooden peg protruded into the other hole in each of the three blocks. The front board was fastened to a tree. The pegs, used as handles, protruded out the back of the back board.

Rotation of the back board turned the three pegs protruding through the front board. Strands of rope were attached to the ends of the three front pegs. These strands were tied together at the far end and held by a man. The back board was rotated until the twist of the strands was tight enough to cause them to bind into one. We made two sets of sheets for each set of sails; new shrouds, forestays, and backstays for the mast; two long, heavy lines for each anchor; and new lines for the harpoons that came with the boat.

The galley was located in the bow. The stove, typical of the area, was fashioned from a five-gallon can. The top and part of one side was cut out. A layer of sand on which to make the fire covered the bottom. The fuel, consisting of wood or dried coconut husks, was put in through the hole cut in the side that provided the draft. An earthen pot was suspended on wires strung across the open top of the can.

We located sufficient tin plates, cups, and tablespoons to go around. Cookware consisted of several earthenware pots and a fine old iron wok that I had acquired. Utensils were coconut shell spoons, two to three inches in diameter, with stout bamboo handles, a bolo, and a coconut shredder.

The bolo was used primarily to remove the coconut husks, crack the shells, and sometimes to take the meat from the shell. Usually, however, the coconut meat was shredded. The coconut shredder is an ingeniously simple instrument peculiar to areas of the coconut culture. It was made of a three-eighth-inch iron rod approximately nine inches long, flattened at the end into the shape of a disc an inch in diameter. The edge of the disc is sharpened and teeth filed into it. The other end of this rod is inserted into the end of a small log allowing the disc to stick out about six inches. Pegs on the underside and front of the log raised the disc eight to ten inches off the floor. The shredder is steadied with one foot while a half coconut is scraped over the disc.

When the shredded coconut is squeezed, it makes creamy milk. This is a good substitute for cow's milk. On rice, with little sugar, it makes a good dessert. Also with sugar, it makes parched corn coffee quite palatable. Mrs. Sanchez often mixed it with *camote* (sweet potato) flour to make her cookie and pancake batter.

When the coconut milk is boiled it becomes oil. The oil was used for cooking, as the fuel for lamps, and for lubricating and preserving our weapons.

We constructed a shelter of bamboo and *nipa* leaves on the deck, just aft of the mast. It was ten feet long and covered the deck from rail to rail. Three and a half feet high in the center, it sloped down to the sides of the boat.

Ten days after the *kumpit* had become mine, it was afloat. After the planks had soaked, it hardly leaked. I dubbed her *"La Paloma"* ("The Dove"). I planned to take her to Australia.

By the middle of the month, a breeze started blowing sporadically from the northeast. The monsoon was not due to change until October or November, but the local Filipinos said some years it began early, blowing for short intervals from the north. I was anxious to start as soon as possible.

Some of the Americans on Tablas who had left for Palawan in mid-August in Young's *kumpit* were considering sailing to Australia. I hoped to join them on Balabac Island, south of Palawan in November. Others planned to return to Cuyo, several were returning to Panay, and a few wanted to sit it out on Tablas. Swift, as sick as he was, wanted to come with me. Hogg decided to come and made arrangements to send his wife back to her family on Cuyo. He did not want to leave her, as she was pregnant, but felt duty bound to try to get out where he could do something useful toward the war effort. Alfred and Vigoreaux were undecided. Alfred was in his glory, doing nothing but attending a *tuba* party every night. Vigoreaux was in love and considering marrying and settling down. Abadiano was going with me, as were Malayo and Macabato. The latter two, however, had gone to visit relatives on Romblom Island and their return was long overdue.

The last few days the work was rushed. Hogg pitched in with Abadiano and me to help in filling the water barrels and loading the food and equipment. The last day we managed to get a good supply of eggs and chickens. The chickens were tied on the superstructure that hung out over the sides of the boat. Except for a small area left for bailing, old, un-husked coconuts filled the empty spaces below deck. These would provide both food and fuel.

Malayo and Macabato were not back. All I could do was to leave word for them to try to catch us on Sibay Island. I felt badly going off without them, but they might have changed their minds about going. On the last day, and after all the work was done, Alfred and Vigoreaux decided to come along. There were now six of us.

Our plan was to spend the next two or three months working down to the southern end of the Philippines, waiting out unfavorable weather on land as we progressed. We would sail down the wild, unsettled, western coast of Palawan where there seemed little chance of interference from the Japs. We would then sail across the Sulu Sea to the island of Tawitawi. We wanted to be in position when the northeast monsoon came, to make a dash south through the Macassar Strait to Australia. I hoped the northeast monsoon would blow all the way from the Philippines to Australia.

Part Four
THE LONG SAIL

Chapter 38

It was past midnight, early on the morning of 21 August 1943 when we embarked on our transoceanic journey. Señor Sanchez and a few of the Americans had stayed up to say goodbye. After they bade us farewell, they gave us a push and we glided into the bay. The sails flapped gently. A slight breeze from the northeast still persisted. The tinkle of the water off the bow told us we were on our way. As we moved southward, I prayed for guidance.

It was a beautifully clear and calm night. Objects on the boat were easily visible under the bright starlight. Sleep was impossible with the excitement of getting started and talk continued through the night. Subconsciously, we were all alert for the sound of a Japanese launch.

At daybreak, the sail was lowered and we rowed the *kumpit* into a sheltered cove on the west shore of Carabao Island. An early morning swim in the clear blue-green water whetted our appetites and made our breakfast of great mounds of steaming rice and fried eggs seem like a gourmet feast.

Twenty-five nautical miles to the southwest, Caluya Island, its conical head a grayish-green in the distance, was the direction of our next run. We had planned to wait out the day on Carabao Island and sail at nightfall, to avoid the Japanese launches, but when a good breeze came up in mid-morning, we decided that it was worth the risk to take advantage of it.

By late afternoon, the *kumpit* was skimming south along the coast of Caluya with our next stop, Sibay Island, already in sight. We were suffering from the long day's exposure to the sun and frayed nerves from a narrow escape from a Japanese launch. A week before, the Japs had caught a sailboat full of guerrillas crossing this same stretch of water and had executed them.

As the sun was setting, the last breath of wind for the day pushed us into a cove on the north shore of Sibay Island. It was the same cove where I had first contracted the Moros who had wanted to take me to Jolo nearly a year before. I wondered where I would be, had I gone with them. It was good to see the little island again. Abadiano went ashore to see if there were any Japs. There were none.

The next morning, I was off to young Janiero's ranch looking for supplies. Mr. Jella came over to say hello. He had been trading with Manila and had done so well that he had bought his own boat. He needed a sail and some odd fixtures for it. We were carrying some heavy tentage I had brought from Cuyo. It would take some talking to sell it as well as a sail. Also, there was the remainder of the heavy Manila rope as well as some large pulleys and other fixtures. I had brought these along as a Yankee peddler might. By the time lunch was over, Jella wanted to see everything. After watching our newly purchased supplies weighed out, Jella and I walked to the boat, followed by the provisions on *carabao* sleds.

After dickering vigorously through the afternoon, Jella finally agreed to pay my price. I have often wondered how that heavy tent worked out as a sail. Vigoreaux went to Jella's house to pick up the money, which was badly needed as the day's purchase of food had left me almost broke. I felt a twinge of guilt taking money from Mr. Jella.

With the heavy tentage and pulleys out of the way, all the food fitted below deck. On the side arms, rolled and lashed down, rode the Moro sail, the four oars, two poles, and two harpoons. This area also had become the chicken roost where they were tied with a string around one foot. The chickens led a pitiful life while they lasted. Precariously perched, they spent most of their time barely escaping being washed or blown into the sea. The white chickens suffered an additional indignity by having their feathers plucked for the trolling jig. Under the shelter on deck were each man's mat, blanket, and few belongings. Our weapons were also there, where they could be quickly grabbed in case of an emergency. We had two .30-caliber Enfield rifles and three 12-gauge shotguns with buckshot loads.

Each of us carried a pistol. We were well armed against any trouble with the islanders, and could probably hold our own against a few guerrillas, but there would not be much chance against a Japanese launch armed with machine guns. These launches were our main concern.

A line drawn on the map from Sibay to Manamoc Island provided a compass bearing for the next run. Our tools for navigation were a box compass about four-inches square, a map of the islands of Southeast Asia taken from the schoolhouse on Agutaya, and a tracing of Palawan and its surrounding islands, done, as I recall, by Palmer. A wild guess was used for correction of wind drift, but the tides, currents, and shallow water had to be contended with, after we were into them. Fortunately, island hopping did not require precise navigation.

We made the run from Sibay to Manamoc at night to reduce the chances of being picked up by the Japs. The wind from the northeast still persisted. It was this night that I had my first experience at trying to harpoon a porpoise. Playing around the boat, they would swim deep alongside, trailing a phosphorescent stream, and jump out of the water just in front of the bow. At night, they could be seen only when they jumped. The challenge was to judge their speed, depth, and course from the phosphorescent stream, and to throw the harpoon at the spot where you thought they would leave the water. Hanging over the bow, clutching the forestay with my left hand, time and again I threw the harpoon. Each time, the porpoise managed to dodge out of the way, seeming, in their playful antics, to consider the whole thing a good sport. This was an intriguing game that we all tried, but the porpoises always came out the winners.

At dawn, fishing boats were sighted along the shores of Quiniluban Island. A choppy sea around the island indicated coral reefs. We gave it a wide berth before turning south for Manamoc, where we planned to stop. Alfred had friends there and we needed water, firewood, and more chickens.

As we approached the shore, natives came out from the coconut groves to greet us. Alfred found his friends among them. He and Abadiano went off, while the rest of us loaded wood and water. Soon, a *tuba* party was in the making. It was long past midnight before we were back on board our vessel.

When we awoke the next morning, there were black clouds to the southwest that presaged a *chubasco,* yet the wind from the northeast was still strong. Our next leg was a long one, nearly 40 miles west to the tiny island of Cabulauan. With a good wind, we could make it in less than a day. We decided to chance it, hoping we could outrun the *chubasco.*

The wind grabbed the tails and set the *kumpit* off at a fast clip. Manamoc soon disappeared. As the morning wore on, however, the wind from the north became noticeably lighter and we were sailing into a great black mass of clouds. Alfred and Abadiano, who were weather-wise to the area, said nothing, but it was obvious they were uneasy. We had all been through *chubascos* before and knew what they could do to a small boat.

The clouds to the south and west were becoming a dense, churning mass, rapidly gathering momentum in our direction. Soon, only occasional ripples on the sea were all that remained of the north wind.

I turned to Alfred. "What should we do?" He just grunted.

When I looked at Abadiano, he pretended not to see me and stared to the south. I knew both were reluctant to turn back. Finally I asked the question, "Do we turn back?"

It was a minute or so before Alfred answered, "I think we'd better." As the most experienced sailor among us, he took the tiller.

The sail was hanging loosely. From the northeast, a gently rolling sea was still coming onto us. Suddenly, Abadiano pointed and said something to Alfred in Cuyonese. Alfred made a native ejaculation and yelled in alarm, "Let's get this son-of-a-bitch turned around fast."

We were at it in an instant with the oars, one of us at the bow and two on the opposite side at the stern churning the water from the sides of the boat, causing it to revolve almost in place. There was no doubt, now, that the storm would hit us; however, with luck, we would miss its center if the direction of the wind did not change.

Far to the south, I noticed a slight ripple like an undercurrent, causing the waves to bounce and splash at their crest. It was the sea from the wind inside the *chubasco* meeting the sea from the north. This is what Abadiano had seen several minutes before. It was slower in reaching us then Alfred had thought.

The wind had stopped and the sea was dead. As the first breeze from the south touched us, the water became alive again. The sails fluttered and filled.

The first part of a *chubasco* is glorious sailing, a good wind without a heavy sea. Alfred and Abadiano pulled off their clothes, stashing them beneath the shelter. I followed suit, as did the others. This would be one of the few chances we had for a fresh-water bath.

Alfred squatted by the tiller, taking a compass reading. Abadiano stood near the mast, facing south, handsome as a bronze statue. The rest of us put ourselves where we though we would do the most good. The deck had been cleared. Everything on the sides was lashed down. The Moro sail had been shifted to the windward wing for balance.

The wind from the south had leveled the sea. We were skimming along, with the water foaming off the bow and trailing a long wake.

It was wonderfully exhilarating—the speed, the nearly motionless boat beneath us, and the cool wind momentarily overcoming the sluggish tropical heat. The black mass of clouds was creeping toward us like a great monster.

The wind built up with a fury. Great swells, now coming out of the south, were causing the boat to roll excessively. The fury of the wind attacked the sails, as though to tear them apart. All except Alfred were leaning far out over the windward side, to keep the boat as level as possible. A sudden blast caused Alfred to throw the bow into the wind to avoid capsizing. In a moment, we were speeding on again. With each dip of the boat, the sea poured over the bow.

Out of the blackness, a sheet of water was approaching; the rain was pounding the sea, its roar became audible above the wind. The *kumpit* was heeling over dangerously. Finally, Alfred gave the word to take a reef in the sail. As he nosed the boat into the wind, the flapping sail cracked like the sound of a rifle. Swiftly, we took a double reef, and in a moment were on our way again, taking the wind more easily. "Down the jib." Alfred yelled, as another gust came at us.

Then the rain descended in torrents, stinging our bodies as it hit, and making it impossible to see without shielding our eyes. Before long, we were shivering from the cold. The *kumpit* would rise on a swell, then pound down on the next, taking in enormous amounts of water. It was a wonder the mast did not snap. Vigoreaux was bailing desperately with a coconut shell in each hand, unable to keep the water down.

Alfred sat tensely by the tiller putting all his weight on it, to keep the boat on its course, alternating between watching the compass, the sea, and the sail.

Suddenly, through the bank of clouds that surrounded us, Manamoc broke into view. Alfred steered for a channel into a natural breakwater. The calmness was as if we had come into another world. Luck had been with us, but we were drenched and half-frozen. Holding our clothes over our heads, we waded ashore, to build a huge bonfire.

The next day, outside the breakwater, the sea was covered with white caps. On the island, the tops of the coconut palms were nearly touching the ground from the fury of the wind. To protect the *kumpit,* we brought it into a small inland lake bordering the town. The smallness of the lake and the density of the palms around it provided a perfect anchorage for our little craft. We occupied a vacant house near the shore. It was good to sleep on a stationary floor again.

The week spent on Manamoc, waiting out the storm, was a pleasant one. During the days, there seemed to be no end to the odd jobs that could be done on the boat, on our personal gear, or the replenishment of our food supply. The salt pot was filled from the "salt mine" in the area. This was a flat basin of rock that filled with seawater at high tides. After evaporation, the residue was almost pure salt, which easily could be scraped off. We laid in a good supply of ground parched corn (our *ersatz* coffee).

Hogg, slim, wiry, and tough, was always busy and good-natured. He seemed to never tire, being the last to bed and usually the first up in the morning to build the fire and start cooking the rice. Once in awhile he swore at himself for leaving his wife for whom he cared a great deal. One afternoon, Hogg came breezing into the house with a large metal drum under his arm. "Just what I've been looking for," he mumbled. He continued mumbling to himself apparently refining his plans for the drum. Noticing our curiosity, he said, "I'm going to butcher a pig and put it in the drum." Then he went on to explain that, as a boy, he remembered preserving cooked meat in the fat of the animal.

A change of diet while on the sea would be welcome and we all pitched in to do what turned out to be no small job. The pig was butchered and the fat rendered. The chitterlings disappeared as fast as they cooled. The meat, cut into small pieces, was fried, then cooled, and packed in the drum in warm fat. As one layer hardened, another was poured, until the container was full. When finished, we probably had 25 pounds of meat that would stay fresh for weeks.

We ate well during our stay on Manamoc. On the second day, chickens wandered to the house to pick up scraps left on the floor. I noticed Abadiano and Hogg tiptoeing from window to window, quietly closing them, and being careful not to alert the chickens. It took a few seconds to realize what was happening. Then I joined them. The house was escape-proof in a few moments and we had four chickens cooped up. It did not take long to have them on the way to the frying pan. Seldom a meal went by without chicken.

Trapping chickens became a game in which we all tried to outdo the other. It was pretty well agreed that Abadiano showed the most finesse. As an example, one early morning I notice a fine cockerel on the windowsill just above Abadiano's head. I lay there, watching that fine meal, waiting for him to hop inside, so I could start closing the window. Abadiano appeared to stir in his sleep. A second later, his arm shot out and he had the cockerel by the legs.

Malaria was never completely out of our minds. It was unpredictable and, with quinine in short supply, could be dangerous. Swift was down with it most of the time, which nearly incapacitated him. Vigoreaux had a peculiar experience with it. He had not had a malaria attack since almost dying of it on Cuyo a year before.

One afternoon, he turned pale and in minutes was shivering uncontrollably. His temperature shot up to 106 degrees before the sweating set in. Yet, within an hour, his temperature returned to normal and he had no further bad effects.

Alfred had thrown off his ragged clothes, shaved, gotten a haircut, and put on his shoes. He was in his glory as a man about town. He rarely let the sun set without arranging a party for the evening. A *lechon,* either chicken or pig, was usually served with side dishes of different kinds of raw fish, and the hosts never allowed the *hunguts* to become empty. These were gay parties with guitar music, singing, and often dancing.

Vigoreaux, too, was having the time of his life. He had put on his party clothes. They consisted of a clean, un-ironed pair of shorts and shirt, both a little ragged but far less worn than his daily garb. He never could find a pair of shoes to fit his big feet. The girls made a big fuss over him and he reciprocated with gusto, much to the disgust of the local bucks. Already, he seemed to have forgotten about his love back on Tablas.

Abadiano was the same on land or sea, in Santa Fe, Cuyo, or Manamoc: always pleasant and always willing. Up early in the morning and to bed late, he was busy all day. If there was work to be done, no matter whose turn, Abadiano was either doing it himself or giving a helping hand. We were all prone to impose on him, but tried to divide the work so everyone got his share.

Swift was too sick to be anything but mad at the world.

By 1 September, the storm had passed; the southwest monsoon prevailed. The following morning we were on our way. Cabulauan, nearly 40 miles to the west, was our next landfall. It proved to be an easy sail. We arrived off the little island in midafternoon. As fishermen on Manamoc had warned of the presence of Japanese launches between Cabulauan and the eastern coast of Palawan, we spent the rest of the day concealed in a cove.

At nightfall, we again headed west with the south wind pushing us along at a comfortable four to five knots. As the night wore on, we noticed an ominous mass of clouds gathering to the south. By midnight, another *chubasco* hit us, this one more fiercely than the last. Groping and fumbling in the darkness, the delay between Alfred's orders and their execution was, in a few instances, nearly disastrous. How we managed to keep the boat afloat was a miracle. At one time, Vigoreaux lost his balance and I was sure he was going overboard. In the blackness, and with the heavy sea, finding him would have been impossible. The strain from laboring against the shock of the waves on the port bow and the pounding on the bottom from pitching in and out of the violent sea was more than the little *kumpit* could take. The water seeping through the seams of the hull was becoming dangerously high and kept two men bailing continuously.

Despite the storm, we were able to hold our westerly course and by daybreak we stood off the tiny island of Barangonan. There, we found a secluded cove and spent the day replacing the caulking. By nightfall, we were on the way once more.

These little islands were unsurpassed in their beauty. Often, I wondered why we did not choose to stay on one of them, and stop the constant struggle.

Approaching a small island in Darocatan Bay the following morning, we saw a strange sight—on the shore stood a beautiful, almost white, Brahman cow. I could not have been more surprised had I seen an elephant, she looked so out of place. Alfred added to the surprise by saying it belonged to his family. I wondered where the influence of the Cobb family ended. For a moment, it looked as if we might eat steaks for supper, but she disappeared into the jungle.

Through the afternoon, we fished, napped, and gathered wood along the shore. That night we anchored off the island and had a good rest.

I saw very few sharks in the islands. It was a real occasion when we spotted one. I particularly remember a great one that came alongside as we approached the Palawan coast. The shark, nearly the length of the *kumpit*, was swimming effortlessly, its dorsal fin breaking through the surface of the water, leaving a miniature wake. It appeared friendly, probably looking for a handout, but we realized that if the huge fish desired, it could shatter our boat into a thousand splinters. We did nothing to irritate it. After a short while, it motionlessly glided out of sight. Despite our wonderment, we were relieved to see this awesome creature leave.

One night among these small islands, swarms of little black gnats—which Alfred and Abadiano called "nick nicks"—made our attempts at sleeping impossible and our entire night miserable. Their bite stung like the prick of a hot needle and itched a great deal afterwards. Fortunately, they never bothered us again.

Our course took us up the eastern coast of Palawan and around its northern tip. The south wind had been favorable to us since leaving Manamoc. The next several days down the western coast, however, were a different story. Tacking into the strong south wind proved useless. The only way to make any headway was to get into the protection of the shore and row. The heavy sea had loosened the caulking again and bailing had become an unending chore. We had to find a place where we could rest and repair the *kumpit*. The closest settlement was about 20 miles down the coast.

Eleven days out of Manamoc, we entered the shelter of a little harbor near Bacuit. We had nearly reached the limits of our endurance, with the pounding and battering of the wind and sea, which had been incessant since rounding the northern tip of Palawan. As we approached Bacuit, Alfred pointed to the forest covered mountains to the north. "That's where we can get a new mast."

The weather looked ugly, and we were played out, as was our boat. The struggle of the past few days had made me realize how favorable the winds had been for us until then. The *batile* rig had worked well despite the skepticism initially voiced by the others. Since leaving Tablas Island, we had sailed close to 250 miles in 24 days. It was 13 September 1943.

Bacuit was a welcome haven. Not different from other rural settlements in the Philippines, it was made up of *nipa* shacks and wooden houses crowded into a small clearing surrounded by coconut groves. Overrun with chickens, pigs, dogs, and children, it was alive and happy, seemingly out place in this isolated, forsaken jungle area. No Japs had landed in Bacuit: only occasional motor launches had been seen, and they were far out at sea.

As always, Alfred found friends and a vacant house. We unloaded the *kumpit* and pulled up onto the beach in front of the town. It was a wonder it had remained afloat. The caulking had washed out in several places, and one could see through the spaces left between the planking.

There was plenty of food in the market place. Fresh meat, fish, fruit, and vegetables were in abundance. Soon, the trials of the last few days on the sea were forgotten. We began to work on the *kumpit.*

The Filipinos here used a caulking material made locally of stringy fibers and a type of semi-sticky gum from the forest. The mixture adhered well to the seams and swelled when wet, setting the caulking. I put in a good supply to take south with us. Alfred gathered together a crew of men and went into the forest after a new mast where there grew a special wood—straight, tough, and springy—most preferred by the locals to any other wood available. He cut two masts, both longer than the one we had, which was too short for the Moro sail.

The crew blocked and tied down the new mast, and this time, rigged for both sets of sails. The extra mast was lashed to the side arms to minimize warping. Soon, the *kumpit* was back in the water. This time she was the tightest ever. We were getting better at caulking.

Hogg's pork had been so successful that we decided to prepare another pig in the same way. According to the townsfolk, a wild boar, a feral creature of enormous size, came down to feed occasionally into the nearby coconut groves. From time to time, he had attacked various individuals, and was generally feared by all. The boar was ours if we could shoot him.

One day, a boy from the town came to tell me that the boar had been seen. Deep in the shade of a nearby coconut grove, he pointed out a large, black pig, rooting and grunting. This was the renegade boar. We were within 50 yards before the boar lifted his head to squint at us. I noticed he was carrying a set of wicked-looking tusks. The boar started toward the boy and me, and as he came closer, he quickened his pace, soon disappearing into a thicket. We could follow his progress by the movement of the bushes. When his nose poked out a few yards away, I was ready for him. Before he cleared the bushes, he had a .45 bullet between the eyes. He was a big animal. It took four men to carry him. After the boar had been put away, we bought a cow and butchered it. We made jerky, or as the Filipinos called it, "tapa," with the beef.

We were ready to go, except the winds were not yet favorable. The southwest monsoon had not given up. One last, big blow came out of it and for days, the wind howled through the trees, uprooting some, blowing off roofs, and raising havoc in general. The anchors of the *kumpit* were not able to hold against the blast of the wind. We discovered this barely in time to prevent her from drifting onto a rocky shore. A collision could have been the end of our adventure. Much worse, in the midst of the storm, we all came down with malaria. Palawan was known for malaria, and Bacuit was infested with it. When we landed there, it was almost certain we would all become infected. I was the only one who had not had the dreaded disease. The chills and fever left me wracked and weak. To help fight the attacks, we injected each other in the buttocks with a solution of quinine that I had acquired from the medical stores in Cuyo. This seemed to no avail.

I wondered how the Filipinos in the area could survive this malaria without medicine. According to Alfred, they had learned to live with it since childhood. Babies unable to cope with it died early, leaving only those with the strongest natural resistance. They all carried malaria which remained dormant as long as they kept their physical resistance at a high level. At times, it appeared that some of them used this as a perennial excuse to do nothing.

Hogg had enough. He decided to leave us and return to his wife on Cuyo. I could hardly blame him, although I hated to see him go.

I knew we must get on our way soon, before our party broke up. Any day, I expected the others to tell me they also were turning back. When the storm passed, we began loading the boat. Still, the southwest monsoon persisted, and we had to wait, becoming weaker daily from the malaria attacks.

October was almost gone before the wind gave any sign of changing. The south wind, which came up in the morning, played out by about noon of each day. After about an hour of calm, a breeze from the north would start, feeble at first, then strengthening through the afternoon.

Chapter 39

We finally set sail early one afternoon. The residents of Bacuit had been hospitable and helpful, but it was good to be on the sea again. The sparkle of the sun on the water and the freshness of the ocean once again brought back our feeling of purpose and confidence, which we had nearly lost during the days of storm and sickness in Bacuit. There only were five of us now. Hogg had taken a *parau* back to the eastern coast of Palawan. We all missed him very much.

Our boat was in the best shape it had been and was crammed with food. The side arms were crowded with cackling chickens. The deck was heaped with squash, bananas, and green coconuts. As a result, there was little freeboard; the water line was only eight to ten inches below the level of the deck

Our course took us through the strait between Cadlao Island and Palawan, then southwest past Paglugaban Island and Pagananen Point. That first afternoon was a short one. Getting back into a shipboard routine was not easy.

Day after day, the good weather held, as we slowly progressed down the coast of Palawan. We sailed only in the afternoons, staying as close to the coastline as the rocks, shoals, and reefs would allow, and anchoring at night close into shore. To avoid the chance of further problems with malaria, we seldom landed. Due to the isolation of the area in which we found ourselves, we were becoming less and less cautious about Japanese launches.

Like clockwork, the south wind came up in the morning and the north wind in the afternoon. The leisurely mornings were agreeing with us. The freeboard of our little boat was increasing at a rapid rate as we consumed our provisions.

An old white rooster was designated as the feather source for the trolling jig that we had in the water most of the time. Much of our sailing was over shoals or shallow flats, which were feeding grounds for the fish. We often managed a catch, devouring it with relish.

A breeze, almost ordered, came up regularly each evening; it seemed to grab us and push us into shore. It appeared to be caused by hot air rising over the jungle, creating a vacuum filled by drawing in the cooler air from the sea.

As I took over the tiller late one afternoon, the strong wind blowing from the north shifted slightly to bring it directly onto the stern of the *kumpit*. I adjusted the mainsail, letting it out to a 90-degree angle to our direction of movement, and moved the jib, which had stared to sag, to the opposite side, also letting it out fully. This leveled the deck of the *kumpit*. The stability felt when the sail was leaning against the wind was entirely missing. We were sailing over shallows, which made for a comparatively calm sea despite the brisk wind. The *kumpit* was moving along at a speed of six to seven knots. The sensation of speed, exaggerated by our closeness to the water, was accentuated by the foam flying from the waves off the bow, and by the unusual sound of the swirling wake gurgling behind the rudder. The *kumpit* was passing through all this outward turbulence in a nearly motionless state, giving the sensation of slipping along, delicately balanced on a tight wire.

I felt that the slightest movement of the tiller would cause the boat to veer abruptly into an abyss. This lasted nearly an hour, during which time I existed in a state of suspended animation, hardly daring to breathe for fear of losing control and capsizing.

South of Ulugan Bay, it became progressively difficult to find adequate shelter for a safe anchorage. At times, this forced us to go into a lagoon for the night. Alfred warned that there were crocodiles in these lagoons and cautioned us to be careful how we hung ourselves over the side of the boat. He told the story of a sailor, who, in the process of relieving himself, hung his exposed rear far out over the water. A crocodile came up silently from the depths, grabbed him, dragging him to the water, and ate him.

One night, in pitch-black darkness, we poled our way into a shallow lagoon. The anchors were thrown overboard, and we fell soundly asleep. In the morning, the boat was aground and the tide was ebbing quickly. I feared that once the buoyancy provided by the water was gone, the weight of the cargo would spring the planking from the ribs, or even break them. There was a strenuous hour or so, gathering timbers to support the boat until the tide came in, and we had more anxious hours wondering if it would float again.

This taught us a lesson we did not forget. Thanks to the fine construction of the *kumpit,* it weathered this trial undamaged. During the timber gathering, I asked Swift why he couldn't help. A little later, I overheard him remark to Vigoreaux, "I believe the captain thinks more of his boat than he does of us." Swift almost always had a gripe, but we all somewhat sympathized with him, as we knew he was sick.

Sailing past the mouth of Malanut Bay, Alfred recalled that there was a settlement on its shores called Alfonso Trece. Palmer's sketch made no mention of the town and Alfred could not remember where in the bay the town was located.

Craving a change in menu, we decided to look for it. Our diet for days had been rice and mongo beans with pork, or *tapa*, and an occasional fish.

The bay proved to be larger than expected. There were no signs of life along the southern or eastern shores and I was beginning to doubt the existence of Alfonso Trece. As we turned west along the northern shore, the sound of a motor hit us. Through the binoculars, I could make out a high-powered motor boat heading straight for us. There was no question in my mind that it was Japanese. There was no escape; I was sure this was the end. What a fate, after all this time, to carelessly sail right into a trap! There was only one thing to do.

Abadiano got on the tiller. The others dived under the shelter for their weapons. With Hogg gone, there were two rifles and two shotguns left. Alfred, Swift, and Vigoreaux were prone on the deck with guns loaded and ready to shoot. The wind was strong and had blown up a choppy sea, making the *kumpit* bounce badly. I was standing by the mast trying to keep the glasses focused on the launch. "Don't fire until I give the word," I shouted. All three signaled back that they had heard. Remembering Cuyo, I wondered what they would do.

The approaching motor boat was about 200 yards away, tossing like a cork. I was just able to make out a machine gun mounted in the bow. Several heads peered out from behind it. The dimming light made it difficult to see, and with the violent pitching of the *kumpit,* it was impossible to hold the binoculars steady. No flag was in view, which was unusual for the Japs, and the headgear of the men did not resemble that of the Japanese Army or Navy.

"Don't shoot, they may be Flips (slang for Filipinos)," I yelled, and thought at the same time that they also could be Japs who *looked* like Flips. As they came closer, they looked more and more like Filipinos. Still standing by the mast, I waved to them. By now, they were 50 to 75 yards away. A figure in the rear of the boat stood up and waved back. He was in Philippine Army uniform. We watched them closely as they came nearer.

Alfred yelled at them in Visayan. "They're from Panay," Alfred eventually relayed.

Given what we knew about guerrillas on Panay, this was nearly as bad as if they had been Japs. I warned everyone to keep a close eye on them and be ready to shoot, if need be.

"How the devil did they get here?" I asked Alfred.

"Hiked over the trail from the eastern coast," he answered.

"What about the boat?" I added.

It had apparently been abandoned here at the beginning of the war.

The Filipino soldiers were staying in Alfonso Trece, which was just ahead. We would escort them there, and they took off.

The letdown and relief were so great, we burst out laughing. I swore then that never again would we assume there were no Japs around. I also made it clear that I did not trust the bunch from Panay.

It was dark before we were anchored and everything was secure on our boat. Alfonso Trece consisted of a few *nipa* huts. Armed, we walked into town in a group, ate supper, and returned to the boat together to sleep. I had received no satisfactory explanation about why the guerrillas were in Alfonso Trece. We took turns standing short shifts on guard that night.

After breakfast, we went ashore again to look for food. Papayas, bananas, some eggs, and a few chickens were all that were available. Somehow, a monkey got aboard. We sailed after lunch. Alfred had heard from the townsfolk that the guerrillas had been sent there to arrest us in the event we passed that way, but had not dared.

I was glad to be away from the Panay *banditos*. There were about 20 of them in Alfonso Trece, and had we stayed, it was very likely that they would have shot us from ambush, as had happened to other Americans on Panay.

As the *kumpit* crawled south, the coastline continued wild and unsettled. We passed mile after mile of brilliant white beaches back against the wild jungle, which rose with its dense greenery to mountainous heights toward the interior. There were many islands, often no larger than a football field, sand-covered, with a few coconut trees, probably grown from coconuts left by passing fishermen. Coral reefs and rocks just below the surface of the water were a constant threat. Often, it was necessary to reef the sail, and have a man on the bow as lookout. Hard and sharp as a razor, the coral could instantly rip a hole in the planking of the boat.

With the fresh air and good food, our strength had returned. The misery of the malaria attacks was almost forgotten. Many times we were tempted to land, but our fear of more problems with malaria kept us on the water. Alfred had warned us that in the jungle of southern Palawan, which we were now passing, there occurred the worst kind of malaria in the islands, the dreaded "blackwater fever," which even the natives, immune to less deadly types, seldom survived. With it, according to Alfred, "a man slowly pissed his blood away."*

Soon, we were down again to our forlorn and over-plucked white rooster. Balancing precariously on the side arms, he was a pathetic sight in his loneliness, looking more like a half-dressed scarecrow than a live rooster.

Alfred and Abadiano had as little to do with the monkey as possible. They treated it as an evil thing, and more than once, Alfred hinted that it might eventually be the cause of a dire disaster. Swift, Vigoreaux, and I, however, thoroughly enjoyed his antics. We called him "Monk" and fed him bits of the same food we ate. He could not be let loose on the boat, though, as he was into everything, especially our food.

Past the southern tip of Palawan, we sailed through myriad tiny islands that appeared to continue endlessly into the mist on the horizon. This great expanse of ocean and its islands seemed to me the most remote part of the world I had ever seen, truly the end of the earth. One might go down among those islands and be completely lost from civilization for the rest of his life. It was tempting, but the drive to return to what I knew and where I belonged was too strong.

The coral and rocks continued to make navigation difficult and dangerous, but gave us a certain amount of protection in this open area against Japanese launches. On 29 November 1943, we dropped anchor off the town of Balabac, on the island of the same name about 20 miles below Palawan. The Japs had not been there. Sailing the 250 miles down the western coast of Palawan had taken the month of November. Our next destination was the island of Tawitawi, a long sail across the Sulu Sea.

At Balabac, we cleaned and refilled our water drums, as a green slime had accumulated on top of the water. We craved fresh fruit and vegetables, which were plentiful, and soon had the deck piled high with food. We also found some

---

*Blackwater fever is a complication of malaria caused by heavy parasitization of red blood cells with the mosquito-borne *Plasmodium falciparum* protozoa. The infection causes red blood cells to burst, thus leaking their hemoglobin into the blood plasma. This free hemoglobin damages the kidneys and leaks into the urine. The hemoglobin in the urine causes a dark discoloration, making the urine appear to be black.

eggs and chickens to keep the old white rooster company for awhile. The *kumpit* was in surprisingly good shape. The caulking material obtained at Bacuit had proven excellent. There was no word of Young and his party and we never heard what happened to them.

On Balabac, a young Moro named Kahil Buangsi attached himself to us. Kahil was of medium height, stocky, and in his early twenties; he was pleasant and seemed willing enough. His dress was similar to Christian Filipinos—shorts, an old shirt, and no shoes. He was Samalese, from Tawitawi, on his way home from the Christian islands to the north, where he had spent the last several years. Although his native language was Smal, Kahil had acquired enough Visayan to be understood by Alfred and Abadiano. He claimed to have sailed the Sulu Archipelago and knew how to crew a *kumpit.* With our first long sail ahead of us, I felt lucky to have him.

The distance between Balabac Island and the island of Tawitawi is about 250 miles. I was concerned about our ability to stay on a prescribed course for any length of time, as, so far, we had islands by which to navigate. Also, occasional sightings of launches and planes had been reported by individuals on Balabac and we would be sitting ducks on the open water. There was one piece of land between Balabac and Tawitawi, however, a tiny island named Cagayan de Sulu, just a dot on our map. To hit it—with our lack of navigational aids and experience—would be dumb luck, but we would try. One factor in our favor was that during the past week, the northeast wind had blown throughout the day. If this continued, it would reduce time we would spend on the open sea.

Since leaving Alfonso Trece, Alfred had dropped ever-stronger hints that we must get rid of the monkey. If we did not, something disastrous was bound to happen. At Balabac, he strengthened his argument. Not for himself, I must understand, as he was not superstitious, but for Abadiano and Kahil. According to Alfred, as much as Kahil wanted to sail with us, he had almost refused when he learned of the monkey. As Swift and Vigoreaux and I got enjoyment from him, I decided he would stay with us as awhile longer.

Early the morning of 1 December 1943, we rowed out of Balabac Bay to catch the wind. I prayed hard that morning for guidance and a successful voyage. Our bearing was southeast. A steady northeasterly wind hit the *kumpit* abeam, driving it along at a good clip. The sea was green, a little choppy with white caps. Small, fleecy clouds floated across the sky. Kahil proved to be at home on the *kumpit.* I knew he preferred the Moro sail, but it did not take him long to get onto the *batile* rig. We had done so well with this rig that I thought we should leave well enough alone for our first long sail.

One of the injections of quinine in Bacuit had caused an infection on Abadiano's buttocks. He had trouble with it all the way down the Palawan coast. By the time we reached Balabac, it looked like a large boil, and was very painful to him when forced to sit very long at the tiller. As a result, he took over the fulltime job of cooking, which he could do comfortably squatting. The rest of us helped him, but our main tasks were regular shifts at the tiller and keeping the boat in shape. So far, there had been no sign of Japanese launches. Occasionally, a plane passed high overhead, easily identified by the great red splotches underneath the wings.

During the second night, there was some excitement when several of us thought we saw the conning tower of a submarine off the port beam. It was barely sticking out of the water and moving in the same direction as we were. Despite the darkness and the choppy sea, I was certain I saw it. When it disappeared, Kahil climbed to the top of the mast, where he remained for some time searching. The submarine had disappeared, as if there had not been one at all. The excitement was over. When Kahil came down from the mast, he staggered to the side of the boat and heaved up everything he had. This is the only case of seasickness I witnessed while in the islands. We were sailing in the trough of the sea, which caused the boat to roll excessively.

On the third morning, we sighted the island of Cagayan de Sulu far ahead. I was surprised and hopeful that it was due to my calculations, but was somewhat skeptical. Supposedly, we had followed a compass bearing taken from a line drawn on the school map between Balabac and the little island allowing a few degrees for wind drift. I had discovered, however, that some of the crew paid little attention to the compass. They based their direction on the way the wind filled the sail when their shift started. This was easy but fallacious, as the wind could shift a good many degrees in a short time without being noticed. At any rate, we seemed to have lucked out.

By mid-morning, we landed on a beautiful sandy beach. There were no inhabitants in sight, but Alfred was apprehensive about being discovered. The *Datu* who ruled the island reputedly had an inbred dislike for Christians.*

Alfred made another serious effort at getting rid of the monkey. This time I felt that he was genuinely concerned, so we took the monkey ashore and released him. I felt a definite loss, as I had grown used to greeting him and enjoyed watching his antics. Only the old white rooster remained. His companions had gone the way of all chickens aboard the *kumpit,* except for him, so far.

On the fourth day out from Balabac, we sighted land to the south. It was Borneo. Kahil, who had sailed there before, believed we were offshore from the settlement of Sandakin.

We sighted the island of Tawitawi on the morning of the fifth day out from Balabac. It was 5 December 1943. The wind had blown steadily from the north and northeast during the whole time, pushing us along at a speed of between three and four knots. It had been a good trip. We had passed our first long sail successfully and I felt confident that we knew enough to attempt the long voyage from Tawitawi to Australia.

---

*The Datu is a local chieftain considered a sort of noble in Muslim-dominated regions of the Philippines, Malaysia, and Indonesia.

Nearing the northwest coast of Tawitawi, the wind, which had blown so consistently for us during the last several days, played out. Little more than a mile offshore, we found ourselves in a dead calm. To our consternation, however, the *kumpit* was moving south at a rate of two to three knots. We were in the mainstream of a powerful current. All around us, little eddies were churning the surface of the sea like a cauldron ready to boil. At one point, objects floating on the water not fifty feet apart were noticed drifting in opposite directions. After the past few strenuous days, it was good to relax. Our proximity to land gave us a feeling of security, so we just drifted.

It was midday and heat was unusually intense. It even had an unnerving effect on the Filipinos. I came down with an attack of malaria. Despite the heat, when the chill came, I wrapped up in several sleeping mats, and shook like a leaf for more than an hour. It was late afternoon when I had finished sweating and felt strong enough to sit up.

The *kumpit* had drifted below the southwest tip of the island and was moving east along the south coast. A fishing village came into sight. We rowed in to get some news. The locals appeared calm and seemed to be going about their business in a normal fashion. That was a sure sign of no Japs around.

Before the bow anchor was well stuck in the sand, though, an old man came running up gesticulating excitedly, and told Kahil there was a camp with about 50 Japanese soldiers not more than three hundred yards away. As we paid little attention to his warning, he became more vehement, pushing us toward the boat, saying to Kahil that maybe bad people would tell the Japs of our presence. I still could not believe it, but recalling the day on southern Luzon, nearly two years ago, when Hendricks and Malmsbury were captured, made me say, "Let's go."

In the opposite direction to the Japanese camp, nearly a mile away, there was a bend in the beach toward which we headed, rowing against the current. Our progress was dreadfully slow. If there were Japs and they were warned in time, the *kumpit* would be a sitting duck. I expected them to appear at any moment. Finally, the village disappeared around the bend. We poled into the forest by way of a little inlet and threw the anchors overboard, to wait until dusk. Then I wondered if the old man had been playing a joke on us.

It was almost cool in the shade of the forest. A group of monkeys stopped overhead to have a look at us and perform a few tricks. It was good to relax in the bottom of the boat, all secure in the jungle, with a free monkey show going on. Someone knocked a bat out of a tree overhanging the boat, dressed it, and put it on the fire to broil; it did not taste bad.

Toward dusk, we could hear the noise of paddling coming up the inlet. A dugout came in sight with a single individual in it, headed straight for us, even though there was a veritable armory pointing his way.

The fellow in the boat spoke enough English for me to understand him and gave his name as "Abraham." He was like a messenger from heaven. Due to the darkness, I never did get a good look at his face. He was much concerned over our safety. According to him, the Japanese camp was just where the old man had said. He warned us not to stay where we were throughout the night. Abraham told us that we were on the island of Sanga Sanga, which was separated from Tawitawi by only a narrow channel. The only Japs in the vicinity were those in the nearby camp.

The guerrillas controlled the island of Tawitawi, with their headquarters at a town called New Batu Batu. Some of the *Datus,* the Moro leaders, were working with the Japs because of promises made to return rule of the islands in the Sulu Archipelago to them, and those who sympathized with the *Datus* might inform the Japs of our presence. Abraham told us we should leave immediately for New Batu Batu, 10 to 15 miles around the southern tip of Sanga Sanga. To get there, we would have to pass the Japanese camp.

Abraham left as quietly as he had come. I felt as though his message was a sign from God, that I should pay attention to it and do as it bid.

It was already dark. We started at once, drifting down the inlet out into the sea. There was still no wind, so we had to row. The night was clear, but moonless. The only light came from the stars. We rowed for a while, then with common consent, stopped and slept until someone awoke, and we rowed some more. During one of these sleeping periods, I awoke with a start. Alfred was shaking me. Instantly, I became conscious of the throb of a motor. The dread of being caught in such a helpless position immediately overwhelmed me.

The sound was coming from the south, each throb of the motor becoming louder. We awakened the others and reached for our weapons, while all the time the noise of the motor was getting closer. Soon, it drowned out all else and the launch came into sight. The great hulk towered up like a mountain. It was a sea-going launch; its deck and superstructure high above the *kumpit.* Swift, Vigoreaux, and I were under the shelter.

The launch came straight for us: it displayed no light and no one was visible on board. We barely breathed. Fifty yards away, the launch veered to the right. At 25 yards, there was no change in the tempo of the motor. It passed so close it seemed possible to reach out and touch it.

A Filipino said, "*Mayron banca*" (There is a boat). We froze, and then breathed more easily as the launch continued toward the Japanese camp.

"Let's get the hell out of here," Swift said. We hit the oars with a new vigor.

Daylight found us a mile offshore New Batu Batu on the island of Tawitawi. Abraham had directed us well.

The water was shallow and we had to work our way through the coral. This was the first time I had seen *nipa* shacks built over the water. Some were as far as 200 yards from shore. They were connected to the land by floating, bamboo piers, or narrow logs held above the water by wooden stakes. A few were reached only by *bancas.*

Chapter 40

As we neared the shore, we could see Filipinos in uniform. At the pier, we were met by a young lieutenant who introduced himself as a member of the local command's intelligence, or S-2 section. He wrote down our names and asked a number of questions; then took us in for breakfast. Soon afterward, a guide led us to the island's S-2, where we received a briefing on the current situation in the area. The information received from the old man and Abraham about the Japs had been correct. They had probably saved our lives.

Reportedly, during the past year, the Japs had made several raids on Tawitawi, but had been unable to land, because of the strong resistance from the local soldiers.

There were Japs on the island of Jolo and in the town of Sandakan, Borneo. The information on Sandakan had been received from a group of Australians who had escaped from there. The S-2 told us there was some guerrilla activity on Mindanao, but I was skeptical, judging from the activities on Panay.

He told us that Lieutenant Cotheran, with a native crew, had sailed for Australia several months ago. Cotheran was one of the corporals on Panay whom I had recommended for a battlefield commission prior to the surrender. His route had been down the Macassar Strait. Sailors arriving on Tawitawi from the area had reported that he had been captured and killed by the Japs in the hut of a supposedly friendly islander. The S-2 also reported that there was no word of a Marine captain who had sailed the same route at about the same time. He mentioned that US Navy submarines had landed crew members on Tawitawi from time to time and spoke of an American with a radio in the vicinity, but could not, or would not, give anything definite of his whereabouts.

The island was commanded by a Colonel Sanchez, an ex-Constabulary officer, who had organized the disbanded Philippine Constabulary and Philippine Army units—about 500 men as I recall—into a close-knit fighting force.

While in the office of the S-2, we met an American who had come to the Philippines with the US Army in 1902. He had married a Moro and had lived there ever since. We talked a long time, exchanging news and listening to him reminisce about his boyhood in America. He invited us to stay with him while on Tawitawi, an offer we gladly accepted.

Colonel Sanchez's headquarters was in the center of the island. I wanted to visit it the following morning and the S-2 offered to provide a guide.

Our boat was anchored near the landing of New Batu Batu harbor. To get to the house of the American with whom we would stay, it was necessary to go out of the harbor, around a point of land, and up the Malum River a good distance. Because of the lateness of the day, we decided to spend the night where we were.

Early the next morning, four of us were on our way to Colonel Sanchez's headquarters. Abadiano and Kahil stayed with the boat. It was a long, hot hike over narrow jungle trails. As we neared the headquarters, alert sentries along the trail challenged us. The headquarters consisted of several bamboo huts with *nipa* roofs, reminding me of the 61st Division headquarters in Misi.

Colonel Sanchez received us courteously, asking us into his office. He was a tall, slim man in his early fifties, with the features and light complexion of a Spanish *mestizo*. His bearing was erect and military. I complimented him on what I had seen of his command. The soldiers had been clean, alert, and respectful, their rifles in excellent condition.

He told us he had coast-watchers around the island 24 hours a day and small task forces deployed back from the beaches in readiness to move to reported trouble spots on a moment's notice. Other than that, we learned little beyond what the S-2 had told us. There was a marked difference between Colonel Sanchez and the Philippine Constabulary officer I had met a year before in command of Peralta's northern regiment. Colonel Sanchez and his people appeared to know what they were doing and were going about it a quiet, systematic way, a real contrast to the Panay bandits.

On our return to New Batu Batu, I noticed a detachment of soldiers near the landing, and near them, a series of foxholes forming a defensive position against the landing area. Being tired, I paid little attention and was in a hurry to get to the *kumpit* for something to eat and to rest. We planned to take the *kumpit* around to the Malum River late in the afternoon.

I was awakened by the sound of rifle fire close at hand. Startled, I crawled out from under the shelter. Two hundred yards way, a Japanese launch, with its motor off, was gliding toward the landing. It looked very much like the one we had seen the night before. It was drawing closer by the moment.

As it came alongside the landing, a machine gun opened fire into the Moro position, followed by the sound of a small mortar from the deck. It looked as if the Japs were getting ready to land. It was hard to tell if the fire from shore was having any effect.

The launch was not more than 100 yards away. We were in a devil of a fix. Undoubtedly, the Japs had seen us. We would not have a chance if the Moros broke away and let the Japs land. All at once, the crack of bullets passing close overhead was heard. It was the familiar high-pitched sound of the .25 caliber Type 38 rifle. One took a chip out of the mast. We returned the fire with our two rifles; I prayed the Moros would hold their position.

Standing to pull up the anchors was exceedingly dangerous under fire from this close range, but soon we had the boat moving. The Japanese fire was still high. It was several minutes before we were out of sight of the launch. By the noise, we could tell the Moros were holding their position. Their fire was keeping the Japs' heads down, and it seemed to have prevented their landing, at least for the moment. This could also have been the reason why the Japs were shooting high.

Overhead, two Zeros were turning and flipping like kites in the wind. I had grown used to this sight in the early days of the war. They were looking for a target either to dive bomb or strafe. Then, one came out of the sky toward the Moro position. We saw a bomb released, glide down toward the ground, and watched it explode about 100 yards away. There was stark fear on the faces of some of my companions. Our fate depended on Colonel Sanchez's Moros.

We were nearing the forest. As the bow came aground, we jumped from the boat. The Zeros were overhead. One started down in our direction. I watched it a moment, then leaped behind a large tree just as the ground on each side was splattered with a burst of machine-gun fire. As the plane came out of its dive, I moved to the other side of the tree; the heavy trunk was full of small holes oozing sap.

The motor of the launch had started up. The mortar fire had stopped and the rifle fire became sporadic. The sound of the launch was definitely growing fainter. The planes were no longer overhead.

I made my way over to the Moro soldiers to offer my congratulations. They were laughing and joking. The victory had been a tonic for them. We could not understand each other, but they knew what I was thinking and seemed very pleased. This was the first time I had seen Filipinos, other than the Scouts, hold their ground. I wondered if their religion had anything to do with it, or if their steadfastness had been a product of their training.

After dark, we rowed the *kumpit* around to the Malum River, and up to the old American's place. The next morning, we found ourselves in the midst of a busy trading center. Nearby, crews were unloading small boats laden with supplies just arrived from Borneo and the Celebes. Their cargos included staples such as rice, beans, tobacco, dried fish, and *comote* flour.

The old American was helping Colonel Sanchez feed his little army and had established this center where food coming from the islands to the south was collected. Scattered about were wooden *bodegas* for storage and small bamboo huts for the transients.

We moved into one of these huts, near the shore. The first few days were spent eating and resting. Without quinine, the only way to keep the malaria down was to build up our physical resistance.

This was my first experience in the land of the Moros. I had heard many stories about their being devious and dangerous, and was quite wary at the beginning. During my entire stay on Tawitawi, however, I had no trouble with them.

Most of the men wore baggy pantaloons of vivid blues, reds, and yellows. They were naked from the waist up and barefooted. Their heads, usually shaven, were covered with a thin, brightly-colored blanket wound around in the fashion of a turban. In the mornings and evenings, this headgear was thrown over their shoulders for warmth, and used to sleep in a night, a very practical custom. Some wore a sash around their waist, with a tiny copy of the Koran wrapped in it, worn over the navel.

All were armed with a *kris*, or *barong*, hung from their waists. The *kris* has a straight, double-edged blade, about 18 inches long. The cutting edges are wavy and honed to razor sharpness. Between the grip and the blade is a metal guard. The grip is slightly curved, made from the hardest of native woods and beautifully carved. The *barong* also has a blade of about 18 inches in length, single-edged, and curved resembling a butcher's heavy knife. It looked ideal for beheading and, reportedly, that was one of its uses.

While the Christian Filipino carried a bolo primarily as a tool, the Moro bore the *kris*, or *barong,* as a fighting weapon. To me this reflected the basic difference in their nature, possibly the results of their respective religions.

I don't remember seeing any women in the camp. Here, for the first time, we saw Dutch East Indian money. I bought some, in case of an emergency going south.

At the time, there were individuals from Java in the camp. Their boat had been wrecked and they were forced to come ashore on Tawitawi. Day after day, they sat in a circle, smoking, saying little to each other, spending most of the time looking dejectedly at the ground. I wondered if they were destined to become slaves. Several times, I tried to question them, but always to no avail. There was no one who understood their language. I often wondered what information I missed that could have been helpful to us.

I remember a school in the camp that was held daily in an old *bodega*. The class was made up of a dozen or so students not yet in their teens, sitting cross-legged in the dust in front of their old teacher. In a high-pitched, singsong voice they repeated in Arabic verse after verse from the Koran. When one verse was repeated a set number of times, the next was started, and so on throughout the day, day after day. I could not imagine American children being made to tolerate the monotony, and wondered what powers of concentration and self-control were at work to make these young Moros accept it.

To Kahil's joy, he found his uncle, Jelian Masaludin, in the camp. No emotion was shown at their meeting; a smile from Kahil, a look from Jelian, and a few words. Abadiano told me later that Kahil thought a great deal of his uncle. Jelian was 40 years old, tall, straight, and weather-beaten, with a Roman nose and innumerable gold teeth. He wore a red turban, an old pair of Japanese breeches cut off at the knees, a Koran sash, and he carried a *barong*. He was barefooted and wore nothing from the waist up. I was told that before the war, he had a reputation as a daring runner of opium from Borneo into the Philippines, and that few were his equal in sailing the native *kumpit*. Kahil wanted to sail with us to Australia, but first wanted a few days to visit his family. After the *kumpit* was unloaded, he and his uncle went off together.

Native sailors arriving on Tawitawi from the islands to the south brought discouraging news. One crew verified the report that Cotheran's party had been turned over to the Japs by the islanders and that the Marine captain's party and also been captured. Others told of the English on Borneo and the Dutch in the Indies being betrayed by the native residents.

These traders also brought with them stories of Japanese atrocities that they had either seen or heard of by first-hand account. One especially sticks in my mind—that of the Japs ripping open the bellies of pregnant women with their bayonets.*

It was becoming clear that the inhabitants of the islands to the south were anti-European, much more so than the Filipinos. Thus we agreed we should make every effort to sail all the way to Australia, without touching land. Instead of going through the Macassar Strait—the route that Cotheran and the Marine captain had taken—I was beginning to believe that to sail southeast across the Celebes Sea, to the Sea of Molucca, and thence south to Darwin, Australia, might be a better way. I spent hours poring over my simple map. I said nothing of this to the others, however. The more I thought about the incident with the Japanese launch in New Batu Batu harbor, the more I was convinced that the Japs had been informed of our presence there. If I was correct, probably by now they had word that we were going down the Macassar Strait, and I wanted to leave it that way.

The days spent on Tawitawi were busy ones, getting the *kumpit* into shape for the voyage and gathering supplies. For items we needed, we bartered or scrounged, making the few pesos we had stretch as far as possible. The hull of the *kumpit* was in as good condition as when we left Santa Fe in August. Everything not usable was either traded or discarded. We planned to start with the *batile* sail and jib. This more maneuverable sail would be used until we came to the open sea. We would then change it for the great rectangular Moro sail, which provided more speed.

The frayed *nipa* leaves on the shelter over the deck had been replaced with *buri* palm, making it tight and waterproof once more. The galley in the bow, exposed to the elements, had not been too satisfactory, but there was no other place to put it. Abadiano, with his painful buttocks, would continue to be the cook. He had found a piece of canvas about five feet square, which he planned to rig in such a way as to protect himself from the wind and sea spray.

Our stove, made on Tablas, had burned and rusted itself apart. We built a new one, fashioned after those used in the Moro camp and in Santa Fe. It was a wooden box about three feet square and six inches deep filled almost to the top with earth and sand. The fire was built in a cavity in the center. A half-dozen fist-sized stones were placed around to support the cooking pots.

The inside of the 55-gallon water drums had been scrubbed bright with sand to remove every sign of the green slime. Filling them with fresh spring water had

*Mass perpetration of exactly this sort of horrific atrocity by Japanese troops has been documented by Iris Chang in *The Rape of Nanking* (Penguin, 1998).

been a tedious job, carrying the water a jar at a time from a spring some hundred yards away.

I planned to sail with close to 30 days' supply of food. Hulled rice was measured by the native yardstick, which allowed a man a double handful for each meal. A half coconut shell of mongo beans and *comote* flour, and half a dried fish per man per meal, were measures used. These items, with sugar, salt, coconuts, and ground, parched corn would comprise our diet.

There was plenty of tobacco. The dried leaves were washed and soaked in a sweet syrup. After drying, the better ones were rolled into cigars, the rest were cut into fine strips and slightly roasted in the frying pan to be rolled into cigarettes.

Lack of matches had been a constant concern until our arrival on Tawitawi. We found a good supply there, and for the first time did not have to account for each match.

All extra space was filled with ripe coconuts, as their husks were our only source of fuel.

Time after time on the school map, I plotted the distance from Tawitawi to Darwin, by way of the eastern coast of Celebes, estimating it to be about 1,500 miles. The *kumpit* could average 100 miles a day, with luck and a favorable wind. Allowing an additional five or six days for mistakes in navigation, storms, and adverse currents, we still would have enough food. Nevertheless, three weeks would be a long time to sail without touching land. I wondered if it would be possible.

The northeast monsoon, which had taken us down the Palawan coast and across the Sulu Sea, had fizzled out on our arrival on Tawitawi. For a week there had been no wind. Not until the middle of December did the northeast monsoon blow again. Long overdue, it was coming down into the southern islands much stronger than before. Each day now, the clouds moved steadily in a southwesterly direction. I knew we should be on our way soon.

The *kumpit* had been moved downstream, near an isolated spring. From this spot, our departure might go unnoticed. The hull of the *kumpit* again sat deep in the water, loaded to its limit. We were all sleeping aboard again, never leaving the boat unguarded.

A short while before we were ready to sail, Swift and Vigoreaux disappeared. On the second day, they casually sauntered back into camp.

"We've something we want to tell you, Captain," Swift said. "We've decided not to go with you to Australia. We think our chances are better to wait here."

While this decision was not a complete surprise, coming at the last minute, it could mean a delay in sailing. Nevertheless, it was better that they left now than to create a problem after we sailed. It was just as well, as they contributed little as crewmembers. It did not take them long to gather their gear and disappear. This left Alfred's rifle and my shotgun for protection. I wondered if Alfred would also decide to leave.

Kahil had mentioned that his uncle might consider making the trip. I sent him to find Jelian. At noon of the second day, they came into camp. Jelian was carrying his mat, rolled around a few belongings.

I stood to meet them and extended my hand to Jelian. He reached for it in a hesitant manner. It was not his custom to shake hands. Jelian spoke only Samal, the dialect of his people. Kahil was also a Samalese. He had learned to speak a little Visayan while in the north, and could be understood by Alfred and Abadiano. Through Abadiano, Kahil said that Jelian would go with us.

I welcomed him and told him to put his gear under the *buri* shelter and to inspect the *kumpit.*

Late that afternoon, a procession of colorfully dressed Moros marched into camp. At first, I thought that they were traveling the trail that passed our camp, and had stopped only to rest and exchanged news, as was their custom.

Then Abadiano came over and said that one of the group was a *Datu* from the center of the island. He had come to wish us well on our voyage. I stood up to greet him and his companions. One could not help but notice their somewhat haughty and bellicose manner. With his retinue behind him, the *Datu* began to speak to me. Everyone was quiet. This was an important occasion. Unshaven, barefooted, wearing a dirty, ragged pair of shorts and shirt, I felt self-conscious.

With Kahil and Abadiano as interpreters, the *Datu* spoke of the friendship that existed between the Moros and the Americans, both in peacetime and in war. He spoke of the loyalty of the Moros to the Americans as opposed to their antagonistic attitude toward the Japanese.*

In reply, I told him how much this was appreciated at such time and would not be forgotten in the future. He presented me with a beautiful *kris* and a sack of hulled rice. These were to give us strength and to assure our safety on the long voyage ahead.

I had nothing to offer him except my gratitude, but I think he understood and accepted my apology. We parted, by wishing the Japs a short life in the Philippines, and each other a long one.

The next morning, 18 December 1943, was spent with Jelian, showing him how to use the compass, and discussing the vagaries of the *kumpit.* He did not appear to think much of the *batile* rig. I also acquainted him with the school map of Southeast Asia, pointing out the islands to the south of us, all the way to Australia. That there were so many islands in the sea was incredible to Jelian. As far as I could determine, the extent of his world was the Sulu Archipelago, the chain of islands between southern Mindanao and northeastern Borneo. I am certain that Jelian never considered the compass a viable adjunct to navigation. At night, one had the stars; in the daytime, there were the sun and land objects on

*This was a bit of selective recollection by the Datu, as the Moros and the United States had fought a series of vicious campaigns against one another during the first two decades of the 20th century.

which to bear. I am also certain that, at the time, Jelian had little faith in the existence of all the islands I had pointed out to him on the map. I suspected that he hoped to disprove their existence before the voyage was over.

By mid-afternoon, the ebbing tide was aiding the flow of the Malum River toward the sea. Since awakening from his nap, Jelian had been sitting beside the tiller of the *kumpit* as though in a trance. He grasped his tiny Koran in both hands. Now and then there was a slight movement of his lips. Soon, Jelian stood up and casually looked over the kumpit, then gazed up at the sky and out toward the sea. I was watching him out of the corner of my eye while talking to Alfred. He bent down and tied a piece of string to the rudder. To me, it looked like a plain piece of fishing line, but to Jelian it was his "*anting-anting*," his good luck fetish. This would cause the boat to steer well. Then he went forward and sent Kahil up the mast to tie another piece on top. This would protect the sail, make it serve us well, and cause the winds to be good. Kahil slid down the pole. Apparently satisfied, Jelian returned to the stern of the boat, where he squatted.

I looked over and caught his eye, then looked up at the heavens, where a few billowy clouds were drifting to the southwest past the treetops. "*Mabuti ang hangin*?" (Is the wind good?") I asked. He smiled, nodding his head, and almost inaudibly repeated the sentence back to me. He had learned its meaning that morning from Abadiano. I turned to Abadiano, asking him if Jelian thought it was time to sail. Abadiano asked Kahil in Visayan. Kahil spoke with Jelian a few moments in Samal, and then turned to Abadiano with a nod and an "*oo*" (yes), plus a few other words. Abadiano turned to me and said, "Yes, sir, the time is good for starting." We set ourselves to the oars.

Chapter 41

Jelian was on the tiller. As we got under way, Abadiano began to sing in rhythm with the stroke of the oars. We all picked up the tune. If seemed to reflect both the exhilaration and apprehension we felt. We five men were setting out on a long and highly-perilous venture, yet we could not talk freely together because no one man could be understood by the other four.

As the flow of the river carried us slowly out its mouth, the shade of the forest gave way to the glare of the open sea. The wind from the north filled our sail. We were off to the south, toward the little islands that fringe the Tawitawi.

As I knew the others were praying, I also prayed for a safe and short voyage to Australia. Once more, I turned over in my mind the many obstacles we could encounter over the 1,500 miles ahead of us. Maybe it was insane to go through with such an undertaking. Should I call it off and turn back? In another few hours it would be too late. We could go back and try again, but existence in the Philippines the past year and a half had been too fruitless to consider returning. No, the die was cast. It was Australia or die trying to get there.

At the same time, there was a feeling of elation over the thought that, at last, we were on the way, with as good a crew and equipment as we could assemble. I put the idea out of my mind that the Japs would catch us, or that we would go down in a storm. Neither would happen if we kept our wits about us and had a moderate amount of luck, the two things that had gotten us by so far.

The sight of a launch to the west caused us to take cover in a nearby cove. We anchored over a sandy bottom shallow, and all went overboard with knives to scrape the bottom of any remaining barnacles.

My school map showed Tawitawi as an irregular circle, with no detail of its nearby islands. Its scale was barely large enough to draw a line through for a rough compass bearing. To bypass the islands to the south, I had had to depend on information and advice gathered from the Moros while on Tawitawi. There were two regularly-used routes into the Celebes Sea. One was through a channel directly south of us; the other used a channel to the west, making a circle around a nearby island group. Jelian knew these routes. With the weakening wind, each was too long to assure our being out of sight of land by daylight, especially if we ran into adverse currents. This could mean detection from pro-Japanese observers from shore, or being picked up by patrolling launches. If the Japs had been informed of our departure, it seemed reasonable that these would be the two routes they would watch.

There was one other way, seldom used, across a stretch of shallows to the southeast.

I had been unable to find out if these shallows were deep enough for the kumpit to cross. Some said it was impossible; others said that it could be done at high tide. Jelian had not crossed them. The danger was to be stranded high and dry during daylight. The advantage was the shorter distance to the Celebes. With the reports of Cotheran and the Marine captain fresh in our minds, everyone was quite willing to chance it.

By the time we reached the shallows, the wind, which had looked so favorable in the afternoon, had stopped.

Even though it was high tide, we spent most of the time overboard, pushing or prying the kumpit out of the sand, rocking it when necessary, to release the keel. We struggled and strained, frantically at times, when the kumpit failed to budge. Often, we had to backtrack in search of a deeper way. Our progress was slow and grueling. A slight current was moving in our favor. This gave needed encouragement. The changing positions of distant black blotches, which were far away islands, assured us we were making headway.

It was long past midnight before the water was deeper than the length of our poles. We took to the oars. The shallow part of the sand bar had proven to be about five miles across.

During the night, Jelian had pointed out three bright stars in a line directly overhead. This was how he knew it was midnight. He said that, by sunrise, they would go below the water in the west.

As Jelian's three stars sunk in the west, we were well out in the Celebes Sea, too far away to be seen from the still-visible islands to the north. The sea was as calm as glass, the sky cloudless, and the sun a ball of fire. To be less conspicuous, we lowered the sail and slowly drifted south out of sight of the last of the islands of the Philippines.

The time had come to change to the Moro sail. The work made me forget the exhaustion and woozy feeling caused by the ground swells, the heat, and the lack of sleep. When finally rigged, the great sail on the mast was a thrilling sight. This was the rig for the open sea and the last long sail. We needed wind. Abadiano and Kahil were whistling for it. Little ripples started to appear here and there.

By mid-morning, the breeze freshened and for the first time filled our great sail. We were on a southeasterly course, moving at a good clip. Jelian was on the tiller and noticeably pleased. The kumpit seemed to know it had its own sail and a skilled sailor on the tiller, and responded like a well-trained horse to a skilled rider. It was good to be sailing on the open sea again.

In the late afternoon, we heard a launch and could see its smoke to the north, but it was too far over the horizon to spot us. At sunset, we were sailing at six to seven knots, still holding a southeasterly course. I wanted to pass the Sangihe chain of islands just north of Celebes Island. From our position, this was a distance of about 400 miles.

As long as Abadiano's buttocks were painful, he would continue as full-time cook. The rest of us took turns at the tiller. Six-hour shifts were established, changing at sunup, high noon, sundown, and midnight. The change of the midnight shift was determined by Jelian's three stars.

The wind held through the night and for the next two days. Our meals were reduced to a simple menu. For breakfast we ate camote flour pancakes with sugar. For the other two meals, we had rice, dried fish, and mongo beans. Occasionally, the rice and dried fish were fried, for the sake of variety. Shredded coconut was often added to the mongo beans, which gave them a milky flavor. To conserve our drinking water, seawater was used for cooking. The only extravagance we allowed ourselves with the drinking water was a cup of parched corn coffee, daily per person.

Eating, sleeping, taking turns at the tiller, and making repairs took most of the time. Constantly, we were scanning the sea and the sky, listening for motors and watching for any change in the weather. Several times a day we had the school map out trying to calculate our position. It was one of those first days that it came to me we might complete the voyage in 18 days. Subconsciously, I must have thought that 18 was a good figure, as that was the date our voyage began. With the Moro sail and a good wind, we could average better than 100 miles a day. At that rate, we could possibly sail the 1,500 miles in 18 days. This, of course, could be done only with great luck. At the time, the idea seemed over-optimistic and, as I recall, I never mentioned this to the rest of the crew.

On the afternoon of the third day, the Sangihe chain of islands came into view. As the afternoon wore on, we sighted what had to be the north coast of Celebes Islands. Shortly after, the sound of a motor came from the direction of the Sangihes. We immediately lowered the sail to reduce our profile against the horizon. The sound faded without incident, and we never determined whether it had been made by a launch or an airplane.

With our sail down, we tossed around on a squally sea until dark. Small thunderheads continually passed overhead; the strong winds, rain, and heavy sea they caused were separated by intervals of calm.

Our hope was to pass the Sangihe Islands during the night and be into the Molucca Sea by daylight. The northeast monsoon had blown itself out again. It looked and felt like a night of calm. We had about given up hope when at midnight a capricious breeze came up rippling the surface of the sea for a few minutes. It soon disappeared, however, leaving the sea as calm as before. Throughout the rest of the night, this shifty breeze tormented us. We made little headway.

Daylight found us close in among the islands, within plain sight of shore. They looked the same as those in the Philippines—white sandy beaches, backed by coconut groves, with rolling hills toward the interior, covered with dense green jungle. Smoke was rising from fires along the shore. We could easily pick out huts and even see people stirring about them. Hurriedly, we started rowing. There were no boats in sight and we had no way of knowing if ours was peculiar to these waters and would attract attention.

We were just barely out of sight of land when we then saw three kumpits almost identical to ours approaching us. As they neared, Kahil warned that they were in a Moro attack formation and we should prepare ourselves. We broke out our firearms, but before we were within hailing distance, the approaching kumpits changed direction. The sight of boats similar to ours made us bolder.

Around noon, we passed through a fishing fleet. The boats were small sailing dugouts, anchored near a reef, each with two or three men using fishing poles. They looked harmless, so we did not bother to change our course. As a precaution, though, Alfred and I crawled under the buri shelter. Nearing them, we noticed a Jap in one of the dugouts, complacently fishing. Abadiano wanted to shoot him. The Jap paid no attention to us. It appeared that as long as Alfred and I kept out of sight, we could sail these waters without arousing suspicion.

Before leaving the Sangihes, we were surprised to see a cone-shaped island with coconut trees growing on its steep slopes. In the Philippines, no one would think of going to the trouble of planting such steep slopes with coconut trees. It was such an oddity that Abadiano and Kahil had to examine the trees through the binoculars before they would believe it. The systematic drive of the Dutch was needed to accomplish such a feat.

The breeze strengthened through the afternoon. We held an easterly course to get out of sight of the Sangihe Islands, and to give us clearance to pass down the eastern coast of Celebes. By sundown, the Sangihe Group was over the horizon and we set a new course due south, on which, God willing, we would continue for several days, across the Molucca Sea. It was 22 December 1943.

The next morning was as fine as the night before, with a clear sky and a good wind. Nothing was in sight on the great expanse of sea about us.

Shortly before noon, I noticed Jelian and Kahil glancing and pointing at the sky. For the first time, I saw a high haze to the north, seeming to originate out of a bank of black clouds on the horizon. It startled me, as when I had looked in that direction only a few moments before, the horizon had been clear. As I watched, the cloudbank doubled in size and was obviously moving toward us. Ground swells, commonly encountered several days out on the open sea, were coming from the north. By this time, Alfred and Abadiano had their heads together. I asked Abadiano what Jelian thought of the growing cloudbank. After a lengthy discussion between Abadiano and Kahil, and Jelian and Kahil, and Kahil back to Abadiano, Abadiano replied, "Sir, maybe we will have a bad wind."

I noticed mountains looming out of the sea, far to the west. They had to be on the northeastern part of Celebes Island. The town of Manado was not far off.

To the north, the threatening wall of dark, rolling clouds was bearing down on us with ever-increasing momentum. I looked at the apprehensive faces of the others. There was little doubt that we were in for it. The sky was darkening. The wind became puffy, faltered, and finally died away. Long before it reached us, we could see and hear the wind coming from the chubasco.

Everything was made secure. Jelian took the tiller. He ordered the sail reefed to half its capacity. It was well that he did. The wind came with a blast, nearly tearing us apart with its fury. I wondered which would give way first, the sail or the mast.

Soon Jelian had us straightened out and on course. We had a glorious, wild ride. Then the rain roared down upon us, engulfing the kumpit in a wall of water, painfully stinging our bodies, and momentarily blinding us.

The wind had become a gale. White caps, blown far beyond the crests of their waves, hung momentarily in the air like foamy, white streamers. There was no break in the black cloud mass that surrounded us.

Abadiano was bailing as fast as he could. Jelian called to reef the sail down to a quarter, and then take it down altogether. As the great sail dropped to the sidearm, Jelian barked an order to Kahil, who dived under the buri. In an instant, he reappeared with Abadiano's galley canvas and attempted to tie it to the port sidearm and mast. He was putting up a jury-sail to give the tiller-man some control of the boat.

The expression on Jelian's face was a forewarning of impending disaster. Without the sail, the boat was working around into the trough of the sea, when, if once abeam to the wind, could cause us to be swamped quickly. Alfred caught what was happening and grabbed an oar to throw the stern into the wind again.

I jumped to help Kahil, holding a corner at a time, while he tied the canvas down. The piece of canvas was not more than five feet square, yet, with the terrific force of the wind, it took a gigantic effort to hold it down. It flapped and shook as though it were alive and fighting for its freedom. Finally, we got it rigged. As small as the canvas was, it pulled us along.

Unlike the chubascos that we had experienced in Philippine waters, which were usually short-lived, this storm raged through the rest of the afternoon and into the night. Jelian stayed at the tiller. When not needed by him, the rest of us took turns bailing and checking for leaks in the planking.

Massive waves loomed out of the north, threatening to sink our little craft, while the wind was making every effort to tear it apart. There was no certainty our boat would weather this storm. Our cold, fatigue, and hunger were secondary concerns compared to our anxiety for the kumpit. It was well through the night before the wind slacked off enough to let some of us sleep. Exhausted, I crawled under the buri. Without bothering to dry off, I wrapped my blanket around me, and in spite of the violent rocking of the boat, fell asleep immediately.

From habit, at the graying of dawn, I awoke and looked out. Jelian, naked and shivering, was huddling at the tiller. When he saw me, he pointed down into the bilge. I could hear the water sloshing below. I removed the boards over the bailing well. The water was up over halfway from the keel to the gunwhale. The first thing I noticed was that part of our dried fish was soaked. I started to bail. It seemed a hopeless job with the bamboo tubes. My arms were long past the aching stage when I finished.

The sea was steel gray, reflecting the color to the sky. There was not a breath of a breeze. Great swells were coming from the north. The surface of the sea was so smooth that it appeared to have a film of oil over it. Even though the swells were large and a good distance apart, from time to time they caused the boat to rock unmercifully, making the lines in the rigging crack like a whip. We were close to a small island, which from our map we judged to be the island of Tifore.

Kahil relieved Jelian who crawled under the buri to sleep for the rest of the day. He had been on the tiller for more than 18 hours. Why he had not awakened one of us through the night I'll never know. Perhaps he felt we all needed rest as much as he did; perhaps he wanted to take the boat through to the end of the storm. There was no doubt that it was Jelian's seamanship that had pulled us through.

I was stiff from the labors of the day before and from sleeping wet. We were all ravenous, but were in good spirits. We knew we had weathered the worst storm that had hit us yet. It was 24 December, the morning of Christmas Eve.

Abadiano cooked breakfast, probably one of his best, or at least most welcome. We craved fresh food. Our only chance of getting any was from the sea. The feathered jig had produced nothing since leaving the Palawan coast. That morning, while waiting for the wind, we took turns trying to harpoon a large fish resembling a dolphin, with its sharply slanting forehead. Swimming just below the oily surface of the sea, it was clearly visible, and as it neared the boat, presented a target seemingly impossible to miss. Try as we would, however, we were never able to as much as scratch it. As a breeze came up and moved us away, we had to admit defeat. The sight of the fish had only increased our craving for fresh food. Never were we able to harpoon a fish. We considered shooting it, but Alfred was sure it would sink before we could get to it.

Jelian was hardly able to move because of rheumatism, which he did not wholly get over throughout the rest of the voyage. Often Kahil, Alfred, or I would take his turn at the tiller when he was in pain.

Several of the seams in the planking had sprung leaks during the storm. We tried caulking from the inside, but finally had to go overboard to press the loosened caulking into place. The island of Tifore had given us a fix on our position. I was surprised the storm had not brought us further.

Far to the east, our map showed the legendary Spice Islands. I remembered from stories of the early sailing ships that the volcanic cones of the Isles of Ternate stood high out of the sea and were always the first to be seen. Seeing them thrilled me as much as it must have the crews of the old sailing vessels when they first sighted these romantic islands.

We crossed the equator on Christmas Day; a flight of Japanese planes passed far to the north.

On the afternoon of 26 December, land came in sight to the south. Before nightfall, it proved to be the island of Mangole. This determination was based on the shape of the island and its relation to nearby islands, compared with the school map. This was our first reckoning since Tifore Island, putting us farther west than we wanted to be. Having missed the broad channel between Lifamatola and Obi Islands, we took the riskier course between Lifamatola and Mangole.

The Molucca Sea was behind us. We were nearly halfway from Tawitawi to Australia. This was the eighth day. The figure 18 came into my mind continuously and I kept asking myself if it were possible that we were going to make it and if we would make it in that many days.

The night was one of the wildest, most beautiful boat rides I ever hope to experience. Before sundown, a stiff breeze came up from the north-northwest. Entering the Sea of Ceram, our course changed to southwest toward the channel between Sanana and Buru Islands. The breeze was hitting us just aft of starboard. Alfred was at the tiller. He pulled the sail in close and we were off. The wind hit a pitch that the fully-opened Moro sail could just take. The sea held an even choppiness that, at the time, we attributed to shallow water.

Far over on its port side, the boat skimmed along the tips of the waves as effortlessly as an eagle in its flight. Throwing great waves of foam out from the bow and trailing a roiling wake, we shot ahead at a terrific, almost dangerous rate. The clear, balmy night and the unusual brilliance of the stars were an added stimulus to the ride. Any untoward movement of the tiller could cause the kumpit to capsize, but Alfred's was an experienced hand.

We were living for the moment with a feeling of excitement and exhilaration. The sensation of the prolonged suspense felt during this ride was both wonderful and fearful. It was a time like this that relaxed and refreshed us, getting our minds away from the constant apprehension of possible disaster. We shouted and laughed, something that had not happened for a long time. It was an experience upon which one looks back, savoring it again and again, until the recollection becomes a treasured memory. Such was our ride that night. Until well past midnight, the kumpit held a nearly maximum possible speed.

No attention had been paid to landmarks on Sanana Island. It was early morning before someone noticed that little progress had been made since entering the Sea of Ceram. At daylight, when the wind slacked off, and the kumpit began to move backwards, we realized what had happened. A strong northeast current was passing through the channel between Sanana and Buru Islands. This also accounted for the choppy sea. We had been on a treadmill all night.

With sunup came "a calm." We were close enough to Sanana Island to see the shoreline and fires in the hills above. We knew we could be seen and hoped the inhabitants were accustomed to seeing boats such as ours. Hopefully, there were no Japs on Sanana. From the map, however, the southeastern coast of Buru Island looked to be a likely place for occupation and there seemed little doubt that there were Japs on the island of Ceram to the east.

Occasional puffs of wind broke the calm, which the sail caught and used to the utmost. As the sun rose into the glassy blue haze, the heat became overpowering. Our position was only a few degrees below the equator. Rowing proved fruitless against the strong current that steadily carried us back to the northeast.

Shortly after noon, three large sailboats came into sight to the south. Watching them through the glasses, it became apparent that they were heading our way. They were large, two-masted, square-sailed rigs with hulls 75 to 100 feet long unlike anything we had seen. I had heard, while in the Philippines, that the Japs were using sailboats to transport cargo.

As they slowly approached, it was apparent they must have light auxiliary motors to be able to move at all. It stood to reason they were Japs. It was nerve-wracking, sitting there helpless, watching those large boats, wondering how we would fare in a fight with them. About the time it appeared that they could not be avoided, their course changed to the west.

Finally through the night, the wind strengthened and it was possible to pull away from the current before daylight. It had taken us back nearly all the way to the passage between Mangole and Lifamotola Islands. We had been caught in that current for a day and a half.

By late afternoon of 28 December, we were heading south by east across the Banda Sea, the large mountainous island of Buru disappearing in the north.

The first morning on the Banda Sea, upon awakening, I relieved Jelian on the tiller. When I looked at the compass, I was startled. A second take was the same. The kumpit was traveling nearly 180 degrees off course. At first, I thought the compass might be broken, but checking it against a watch compass I carried proved this not so. Later, upon questioning Jelian through Kahil and Abadiano, I finally concluded that in the process of shifting the sail to the opposite side of the mast because of the changing wind in the darkness, the boat had become turned around. When he began sailing again, it was in the wrong direction. As he seldom used the compass, in the dark without any landmark, this would be quite possible.

Had we stayed on course, we should have sighted Lucipare Island on the second day. Missing it made me wonder about our position. Suspecting we were to the west of this island, our course was changed to a more easterly direction.

I was on the tiller from midnight until dawn on 31 December and clearly remember that morning for the beauty of the Southern Cross. Each night the four great stars standing out in the heavens at a slight angle had become more noticeable. It took little imagination to visualize a great cross up there.

Toward morning, a bank of low clouds engulfed us. As dawn broke, a black mass loomed ahead through the mist. Before it was recognized as land, the kumpit was alarmingly close to a small island. By checking its size and shape against the map, it had to be the island of Damar. We had crossed the Banda Sea in better time than I had figured. Taking a more easterly course from the point where we should have sighted Lucipare Island had been right. We were where we wanted to be to enter the Arafura Sea.

Three of our long reaches were over; the Celebes Sea, the Molucca Sea and the Banda. Except for Jelian's miscalculation, and seeing a Japanese bomber overhead on 29 December, the Banda gave us the best stretch of sailing to date.

There was only one more to go—the Arafura Sea. There was a bit of doing, however, before we would be in a position to cross that sea.

The line of islands running east from Timor formed a good line of defense against anything coming from the north Australian coast. We assumed most, if not all, of these islands would be occupied. The channel between Sermata and Wetan Islands was the widest. Taking it reduced our chances of being observed.

There was sufficient food and water for more than another week. Our menu, down to mongo beans, rice, and dried fish, was getting a little hard to stomach three times a day. The forward water drum was dry. Three quarters of the rear drum remained, though it had a bad smell and green slime forming on top. I daydreamed of such delights as ham and eggs, buttered toast with jelly, and real coffee.

Crossing the Banda Sea, we had changed most of the shrouds and lines on the rigging. This left us no spares, but with luck, they would last for several weeks. Most of the leaks in the hull caused by the storm of Manado had been stopped, but bailing was a periodic chore. Jelian's rheumatism stayed with him and at times he was in great pain. The rest of us had kept pretty well, though Abadiano still could not sit with comfort, and slept on his stomach.

The morning of 31 December, Kahil complained of fever. It made me notice the drawn faces and haggard eyes of the others. Luckily, we had avoided further malaria attacks. Our limited diet, lack of sleep, and constant tension were taking their toll. We could all keep going for a good while longer, though, if the fever did not hit us. I had a small amount of quinine powder that I had been hoarding. Now, if ever, was the time to use it, and after breakfast we all took some.

The storm clouds lifted in the morning. Our course was south at first, to get away from Damar Island, and later, to get around a small, grass-covered coral reef that popped up out of nowhere. By early afternoon, Sermata and Wetan Islands had come into view and we took a bearing on the channel between them. The wind became shifty. It was questionable if it would take us across the line of islands that night. It was the same situation we had experienced in the Sangihe Islands. Again we decided to chance it, but we had no luck. Before dawn, we found ourselves north of Sermata Island.

The sea was slick as glass. There was not a breath of wind. Kahil was whistling into the sail. Jelian was fingering his "*anting-anting*." A current was taking us closer to Sermata. What a cruel fate to be caught at this stage of the game! Jelian's three stars were sinking low in the west. There was only one thing to do and that was to row as hard as we could. We were all too exhausted to do much, but we had to try. Dawn caught us close to the northeastern coast of Sermata Island.

We took down the sail and removed the mast. Shifting on the oars, we crawled to and from our positions to keep as low on the horizon as possible. That is, all except Jelian. He could see no reason for it. I cursed myself many times that morning for taking such a useless chance. I was certain there were Japs on Sermata.

We had not seen any small boats since leaving the Sangihe Islands and had no idea of the type used in these waters. In the Philippines, different localities or sometimes each different island had a type of boat peculiar to itself with features easily discernable from a good distance.

I wondered if this was the case here. Also, it puzzled us why there were no boats on the water and we speculated if just the presence of a boat offshore would cause suspicion. Maybe the Japs had restricted inter-island travel, or possibly allied aircraft were sinking all boats in this area. We had heard this was being done in the Macassar Strait.

Visions of being captured and tortured, as the American on Mindoro, or being sunk on the spot, were turning over in my mind. Until we were out of sight of land, I expected any moment to see a launch chugging after us.

If there were Japs on Sermata, they missed a good chance. By the grace of God and good oars, we were in the center of the channel between Sermata and the Wetan Islands by noon. A west wind came up in the early afternoon. We raised the mast and sail and skimmed out into the Arafura Sea, the last large body of water to cross. This was the last lap of our voyage. Getting across this sea meant we would reach Australia, but a storm, a plane, a launch, a submarine, even a leak in the boat could stop us.

I told Jelian through Abadiano and Kahil that this was our last long stretch of water and we would be in Australia in a few days. Jelian had long since accepted the presence of all the islands I had pointed out to him on the school map before leaving Tawitawi. He was now looking forward to seeing the biggest of them all, Australia. Later, he had his Koran out. I prayed, too, and wondered if we would make it in 18 days.

The roar of heavy motors out of the west jolted us back to the present. It was a great, four-motored plane with a double rudder, painted olive drab with large white stars on the fuselage and wings. It was a new type and new insignia to me. The Japs were capable of producing such a craft and they used olive drab paint. The white stars meant nothing. It could be Allied insignia. It could be that the Japs were painting Allied insignia on their planes to be able to fly in these waters, unmolested.

Alfred and I ducked under the buri. The sail dropped loosely on the deck. Kahil was on the tiller, frozen. Jelian and Abadiano were by the mast watching the plane approach. We told them to try to make out what the crew looked like. The plane zoomed down on us and up again into a large circle three or four hundred feet above the water, the crew carefully looking us over. Alfred and I were peering out of the buri. It was impossible to make out the faces of the crew because of their helmets and goggles. The plane circled around and around. Guns seemed to protrude from every angle and each moment we thought the next would bring forth a hail of bullets. We had no means of identifying whether the plane was Jap or Allied. The absence of the rising sun on the underside of the wings made us lean toward believing it was Allied. I had the American flag out and my clothes off, ready to jump out on deck at the first burst of fire. After long minutes, the great plane headed back into the west.*

The incident left us shaky, then the talk started, trying to recall any evidence to prove the plane either Jap or Allied.

We tossed around with the sail down until nearly dark, hoping, if the plane returned, they would not be able to find us a second time. As the last light of day was fading, the sail was hoisted. There was a fair breeze slightly north of west.

In the Philippine Islands during this time of year, the prevailing wind was from the northeast. It was with this wind that we left Tawitawi. To the east of Manado, off the northern coast of Celebes Island, it had changed to north. Entering the Sea of Ceram, the wind had shifted to northwest. The further south we traveled the more westerly the wind had become.

Darwin was our goal. Our course lay a little west of south, allowing some drift to the east from the wind and sea. We were making between four and five knots. Toward midnight, a series of black clouds scudded by, bringing rain and a stronger wind. One man had to bail the rest of the night. None of us had much sleep.

The second day of 1944 had been full of anxiety. We expected more visits from aircraft, but none came.

Long before dawn of 3 January, a storm blew up from the south-southwest. Morning brought a sea with great waves breaking all around. Everything on board was soaked.

To make any headway, we had to change course to east of south, which put us at the right angle to the direction of the sea. One moment we would be deep down in a trough surrounded by foaming water; the next, on a crest, seeming to balance on top of all the turmoil. Each time we came out of a trough, the next wave slapped the starboard bow with the resounding "crack," causing the whole boat to shudder. The kumpit was taking a frightful beating.

We considered changing course more to the east, but from our map, the northern coast of Australia seemed to have miles of uninhabited coastline, and the great Gulf of Carpenteria was in that direction. I doubted that our food supply could last long enough to find human habitation in that desolate-looking area. Although already sailing east of our course, the kumpit was very close to the wind so as to make almost no headway against the heavy sea. Yet, it seemed necessary to continue to hold ourselves as far west as possible.

We could only hope the bow would hold up. Jelian inspected it every hour or so and each time all of us watched him intently for any sign that the ribs or planking were weakening. As the storm continued, it was our conclusion that if

*The aircraft was almost assuredly a US Army Air Forces B-24. Although the type was introduced in the summer of 1941, it did not become operational in a combat role until well into 1942, long after the author was deprived of recognition manuals.

anything were to happen, it would be caused by an unusually large wave taking out one of two planks. In that case, it would only be a matter of seconds before the boat would go down. If this happened, our plan was to cut the sidearms free to use as floats.

We reefed the sail to half to reduce the danger of the mast snapping from the terrific pitching of the boat. The Moros took great pains in the construction of their boats. They were built of the best woods available in the tropics. They were fitted together in such a way that normal swelling and stresses helped to hold the whole together. We were confident that if any boat could hold together in such a sea, the kumpit could.

The first day it became evident that this was not the usual tropical storm that passes quickly. By that night, we wondered if it would ever let up. And by the following morning, we did not give a damn, but kept going, more through habit than anything else.

By afternoon of that day, it became evident that neither the boat nor we could survive much longer. Everything on board was a mess. Because of the pitching, it had been impossible to sleep or cook. We had gotten by on coconut meat and water. Everything was wet: our weapons, the rice, fish, beans, clothing, bedding, and coconut husks. The sail was torn, lines were frayed, and the seams in the planking were nearly large enough to see through. We were numb from exposure, fatigue, and lack of food. I was starting to question my ability to reason soundly.

Miraculously, the wind started to slacken. By midnight, the sea had become calmer.

Our first order of business was to cook rice. Two men were needed to keep the boat going, one on the tiller and one bailing. The rest of us slept, relieving the other two every hour. We could all feel the fever taking hold, and double dosed with the quinine that was left.

As dawn lit the horizon on the morning of 5 January, a massive bank, either clouds or mountains, loomed high in the south. The sea was a light green, a sign that we were in shallow water. There was a fair breeze, giving the sea a gentle swell. The kumpit sailed along serenely at a good five knots; the strain of the storm was behind us.

We were mystified about what was ahead. Having seen nothing like it before, it seemed certain to be an indication of land. It gave us great hope, a sense of life reborn. While my thoughts for the past two weeks had been optimistic on the surface, deep down I had felt that any time would be the end of this hazardous venture, and that there was about as much chance of ever seeing Australia as there was of my setting foot on the moon. Seeing the wall of clouds or mountains ahead made me optimistic, since all my calculations indicated that we should be nearing land.

It was our eighteenth day out of Tawitawi. Even after the sun rose, none of us could discern what lay to the south. The school map was of little help, having no contour lines on the part of northern Australia it showed. I could not recall ever reading any description of the area. Unceasingly, we peered ahead in the hope of detecting some clue as to what we were seeing.

About noon, while finishing our rice, we heard a motor. It rapidly became stronger and it was not long before we were sure, from its high pitch, that it was a plane. The sound came closer and closer, as if heading straight for us. Out of the mass to the south, flying low and fast, it appeared, at first a dot growing rapidly into a medium-sized plane with two engines, a single wing, and a double rudder. Before we could get the sail down, it was upon us. Its color and markings were the same as the plane we had seen on 1 January. As it made its first big circle, Jelian and Kahil were sitting at the tiller, petrified. Abadiano, standing by the mast, was agog with curiosity. I do not ever recall seeing him excited and do not believe he knew the meaning of fear. I doubt that it ever entered his mind that this plane could do us harm. Alfred and I were again under the buri.

The plane circled twice. As they looked us over, we could see the crew, but not distinctly enough to make out their race. Again, I was ready to rush out on deck without clothes. After circling the second time, the plane lined up on us and dived. At any moment I expected to feel the impact of bullets.

I glanced out at Jelian and Kahil. They sat like two frozen images, looking straight to the front, with a bewildered look on their faces. Something ludicrous about the whole thing struck me, and I could not help but laugh. With a zoom, the plane passed close over us and away to the north.

It was several minutes before the tension wore off. Then came a rush of assumptions that ultimately led to the hope that the plane would not return.*

Abadiano started the fire for dinner. Jelian slumped down but did not change expression. Kahil inspected the rigging. Alfred chattered on like a monkey, and I relaxed limply on the deck. If another plane showed up, I was determined to show myself and the flag. These had to be Allied aircraft.

By noon, the heat of the sun had dispersed the clouds that had puzzled us through the morning. Again, there was only the flat far horizon ahead. I could not understand where the mistake was in my calculations. The last bearing taken from Wetan and Sermata Islands was toward Darwin. The distance had been about 350 miles, and at our estimated rate of speed, we should have nearly covered that. I thought we had made sufficient allowance for the action of the storm. Another possibility was that besides the wind and the sea, there had been a strong current pushing us eastward and now we were sailing toward the Gulf of Carpenteria, which we had hoped to avoid.

In our poor physical condition and with the short supply of food, I wondered what our chances of survival would be along those uninhabited shores. I doubted that we had the strength to make our way to any of the distant settlements inland.

---

*This aircraft seems to have been a US Army Air Forces B-25, another type adopted before the war, but only introduced in significant numbers in 1942.

These contemplations were brought to an end by Abadiano announcing dinner. I filled my belly with rice, rotten fish, and mongo beans, and fell asleep.

The afternoon wore on. The sun shone brightly in the cloudless sky. There was a brisk breeze from the west and a relatively calm sea due to the shoals below. The whole afternoon we made excellent speed with the kumpit heeled over at a sharp angle due to its lightness.

The feathered jig had been trolled the entire way from Tawitawi, without as much as a strike. Then suddenly that afternoon, there was a sharp "twang" as the cord snapped. The heavy trolling cord went limp. Our jig was gone. It had to have been an enormous fish that took it. Probably better that it did, as I doubted we had the strength left to haul in a big fish.

There was little talk. All of us were intently staring ahead, hoping to sight land. Several times I went over my calculations, but could find nothing wrong. I kept telling the others we would sight land any time. Inside, I was completely baffled.

The sun was getting red in the west when Jelian uttered a few words and pointed south. I was sitting by the tiller. Kahil climbed the mast and gazed out for a long time. Each time the boat rose, his face lit up, and he said something in Samal to Jelian. Abadiano questioned him in Visayan.

"He sees trees." Abadiano said.

It was not long before we could see a scraggly line on the horizon. Then the flat shoreline hove in sight, miles and miles of it, as flat as the plains country in the western United States. That was the reason we had not sighted land sooner. Northern Australia, in this area, is completely flat.

The trees became firs or tamarasks. The land terminated both to the east and west, and I wondered if we were approaching Melville Island, a small dot on our map.

It was dark as we neared the shore. Black masses of rock or coral jutted out from the white, sandy beach. I headed Jelian into a stretch of white beach; however, he picked a course to the east of it. I cursed him under my breath, believing he would run us onto the rocks. But the kumpit glided into quiet water without a scratch. Kahil loosened the sail. For the first time in 18 days, the anchor went overboard. For the first time in 18 days, we were within the protection of land. The shoreline was not too friendly looking, broken by outcroppings of black rocks and bordered by scrubby tamarask. There was no sign of human life, but it was land, and for the first time in two years, a land surely controlled by friendly people. It looked so remote we did not post a watch and for the first time in nearly three weeks, all of us had a full night's rest. It was good to feel the tug of the anchor rope again.

I woke with a start, and it was a few moments before I could recall where we were. Then it came to me why the boat was not rocking and why there was no sound of waves pounding the bow. I lifted the edge of the buri shelter to look out. Jelian and Kahil were squatting over the stove cooking rice. There was a sandy beach bordered by a dense growth of tamarask trees stretching in each direction as far as the eye could see. A light breeze was blowing from the west. To the north, the sea was green and calm. There was no sign of life anywhere.

I lay back on my mat and rolled a cigarette. This had to be Australia. We had made it. That much was certain. Our exact location and which way to go to find civilization presented the next problem, but it did not matter too much. We still had a little food and water and the boat was afloat. The realization that the Almighty had allowed us to complete the almost impossible voyage from the Philippines slowly came over me. I looked back at all that had happened since the war had begun. All the effort that had been expended, with so little accomplished and so much lost. I prayed the future would be better.

I rolled my blanket and went outside. It was a beautiful, cloudless morning. After breakfast we studied the school map, and with a bit of figuring, decided we had landed on Melville Island. Darwin was to the west.

Moving away from shore, I noticed our position for the first time. We had anchored in a small sandy-bottomed cove, bordered on each side by spurs of jagged rocks extending nearly half a mile out from the shore. If Jelian had followed my instructions of the night before, the kumpit would have run onto the rocks. For some reason Jelian had gone to the east of my mark. Although his action had upset me at the time, as we had entered the cove without mishap I had forgotten about it. Jelian never gave a good explanation why he went where he did. Maybe it was his *anting-anting*.

We had no more than raised the anchor when the sound of a motor launch was heard. My first reaction was that it was Jap, but it could not be possible the Japs had landed in Australia. As the launch came closer, with the help of the field glasses, I finally made out the Australian flag. The launch showed herself to be a trim sailing yacht, 50 to 60 feet long, with a small cabin. She was painted gray which took away some of her class, but nevertheless she looked to be a fine craft, and we all agreed how much easier the voyage would have been had we had such a boat.

A half mile away, the Australians lowered sail and proceeded towards us under power of their auxiliary engine. Aboard we could make out two white men and innumerable black figures, most of whom were prone on the deck or cabin looking over the sights of rifles pointed our way.

We had unfurled our American flag and it was flying in full view. An Australian naval officer hailed us as we pulled alongside. The first question asked was if we knew the password. Lieutenant Gribble, the commander of the launch, had expected us to be a group of Australians, recently escaped from a prisoner of war camp on Timor Island. He had known our approximate location for the past four days through reports from the planes that had spotted us.

All surface craft on the waters north of Australia, not recognized as Allied, were being sunk on sight. We had been spared, on the chance that we were the expected party of Australians. Although our course had been east of the sealane designated as their route, we had not been sunk because of the possibility that the strong west winds of the past few days had blown them off course.

The Australians were surprised and amazed to learn that we had been able to travel unmolested all the way from the Philippine Islands. They knew of no other parties that had come out by surface craft. This seemed to verify the story of Cotheran's capture. Also, they had no knowledge of the Marine captain and his party.

The kumpit was tied to the stern of the launch. The planes that we had seen were indeed American. It was only by a fluke that we had not been sunk. The Australians offered us whiskey, real cigarettes, bread and cheese. The whiskey was too strong and the food strange to our taste. I would have much preferred a hungut of tuba and a plate of steaming rice with some of Mrs. Gomez's fried viands. The cigarettes, however, were a real treat. I had not smoked a "tailor-made" since the Panay surrender.

The launch took us to Snake Bay on the northern coast of Melville Island where Lieutenant Gribble's headquarters was located. Anchored in the bay was an Australian warship. The captain invited us aboard. There we shaved, bathed and dined in style, barefooted and in ragged shorts and shirts.

That night we went ashore to sleep in Gribble's camp. It consisted of a group of mud-walled, thatched-roofed huts. Except for one other Caucasian his command was made up entirely of black Australians. It was his responsibility to patrol the north coast of Melville Island. Each of us was given a spring bed with mattress, blankets and pillows. They were an unfamiliar sight to us all. I had not slept in one for more than two years and I doubted if Jelian ever had. They were not standard equipment for a nipa hut.

Jelian looked his over carefully before trusting himself to lie on it. After breakfast, Gribble requested I inform Jelian it was not necessary to place one's feet on the toilet seat. In the afternoon an Australian plane came to fly us to Darwin.

Before leaving, I took one last look at the kumpit riding at anchor in the bay. She was sitting high in the water, revealing her beautiful lines. The long voyage from the Philippine Islands unquestionably qualified her as a ship. We owed our lives to her and to her builder. This was the last time I would ever see the little craft. I left her in the good care of Lieutenant Gribble.

Two days later we were flown to Brisbane in a US Army Air Forces B-24; I realized it was the same type of plane that spotted us on New Year's Day.

Epilogue

On arrival in Brisbane, Abadiano, Kahil and Jelian were inducted into the United States Army. Alfred rejoined the Merchant Marine Service in which he had served prior to the war.

At first I was hospitalized, where I was de-wormed and stuffed full of atabrine, which eventually controlled the malaria. Then there were debriefings with various staff officers and the writing of reports. I became very much perturbed over the type of person MacArthur had placed in charge of activities in the Philippines. He seemingly had little knowledge or understanding of what was going on there, particularly on the island of Panay.

Swift and Vigoreaux were eventually taken out of the Philippines by submarine.

Through correspondence after the war I learned that Tablas Island had been invaded by the Japs, who captured most of the Americans still there. Reportedly, Hubbard and Lindblom were taken to Iloilo City and executed. Palmer died as he planned, taking a Jap or two with him. Pryor was caught and executed on Tablas.

I heard nothing of what happened to the other Americans.

26th Cavalry (P.S.), Fort Stotsenburg, Philippine Islands, 1937. Note that there are more troops in formation to the left and right of what this photo shows. *American Historical Collection* (*AHC*)

Army-Navy Club, Manila (*AHC*)

My quarters at Fort Stotsenburg. Note mosquito netting over the bed.
From the author's collection (*Author*)

Philippine Scouts during Bolo drill. The Philippine scouts were armed with the traditional Philippine machete-type weapon called a Bolo. This weapon was incorporated into the official US Army arsenal. These weapons are likely M1909 Bolo or "Smatchet" knives with a 14-inch blade. It was an ideal tool for clearing a path through difficult jungle. The rifles on the ground are M2 .22-caliber training rifles. They were used in training, particularly marksmanship training, instead of the service rifle because of the inexpensive .22-caliber ammunition. (*AHC*)

Troop E in formation. Clearly visible in the picture is the rifle scabbard on the near side of the NCO's saddle. It appears that at the time of the photo the issue weapon was the M1903 Springfield, although the 26th Cavalry received M1 Garand rifles prior to the beginning of the war. (*Author*)

With the officers (I am at far left) at the Officer's Club, Fort Stotsenburg. In the years before World War II, particularly in the tropics, Army officers typically dined in formal military or civilian attire. The officer third from the left is wearing the Army Dress White formal uniform. (*Author*)

Captain Blanning (left) and me, along Duigaleu Bay, Tayabas, Luzon, June 1941. The horses here are minus field equipment. Both mounts exhibit the fine athletic thoroughbred traits that were desired by the US cavalry in the 1930s. Though troopers were equipped with the M1928 model McClellan saddle, officers were mounted on either the M1917 officer's field saddle or a similar personal saddle. (*Author*)

Camp John Hay, Baguio, Philippine Islands (*AHC*)

Ferrying horses during training, August 1941. Being able to cross water obstacles was an important task in the Philippine terrain. Horses and riders were capable of swimming rivers when necessary, but bridges or ferries were preferred. (*Author*)

Fort Stotsenburg officer's tents, November 1941 (*Author*)

26th Cavalry HHT Scout Car, 1941. Relatively heavily armed with two M1919 .30-caliber machine guns and one M2 .50-caliber machine gun, these scout cars were the main firepower of the cavalry regiment. One trooper is armed with the M1928A1 Thompson submachine gun. The troopers wear enlisted lace-up riding boots, which were issued beginning in 1931. (*AHC*)

Igorots (*AHC*)

Igorots (*AHC*)

Philippine Village near Cebu, Philippine Islands (*Author*)

Sailing boat similar to the *kumpit* that I sailed to Australia (*Author*)

Arthur Kendal Whitehead, 1944. The author wears the crossed sabers of cavalry and a major's oak leaves. His left shoulder patch designates him as assigned to the Army Replacement and School Command. (*Author*)

Reynaldo Abadiano, 1951 (*Author*)

With the monument to the 26th Cavalry, Fort Riley, Kansas. The inscription reads:
"To the memory of the
gallant dead
26th Cavalry
Philippine Scouts,
United States Army
Commemorating their
heroic actions
Lingayen–Luzon–
Bataan
1941–42"
(*Author*)

Martha B. Whitehead (left) and Arthur K. Whitehead, both in 1978 (*Author*)

Other Titles by The Aberjona Press . . .

Sledgehammers: Strengths and Flaws of Tiger Tank Battalions in World War II
by Christopher Wilbeck

"This detailed, yet readable study, enhanced by fascinating photographs and superb maps deserves to be on every tank warfare devotee's bookshelf."—*WWII History* magazine

272 pages. 35 Original Maps. 42 Photos.
Paperbound. ISBN: 0-9717650-2-2,
$19.95; plus $4.00 U.S. shipping

Slaughterhouse: The Handbook of the Eastern Front *edited by Keith E. Bonn*

"A virtual treasure trove of information and lore for all those who can't get enough of the personalities, equipment, unit histories and orders of battle related to the war in which Hitler fought Stalin. . . . *Slaughterhouse* is a 'must have'."
—*Armchair General* magazine

520 pages. 9 Maps. 88 Photos. Extensive 16-page bibliography. Paperbound. ISBN: 0-9717650-9-X,
$29.95 plus $4.50 U.S. shipping

Waffen-SS Encyclopedia:
by Marc J. Rikmenspoel

"Few units arouse such intense interest as the Waffen-SS: love them or hate them, the Waffen-SS has had more books printed about them then probably any other unit. Unfortunately, some of them are more about the 'SS cult fetish' then tangible information. Thankfully, Marc Rikmenspoel has supplied us with a one-stop reference tool worth its spot on the bookshelf."— *Broadsword Military Magazine*

300 pages. 82 Photos. Extensive 20-page bilbiography.
Paperbound. ISBN: 0-9717650-8-1,
$19.95 plus $4.00 U.S. shipping

Seven Days in January: With the 6th SS-Mountain Division in Operation NORDWIND *by Wolf T. Zoepf*

"The balanced, integrated account of American and German experiences is exemplary. . . . The evolving German perception of their American foe is fascinating. . . . The maps are perfect. . . . Anyone with any interest in the European campaign will find this a compelling, valuable read."
—*World War II* magazine

312 pages. Maps. Photos. Index.
Hardbound. ISBN: 0-9666389-5-6,
$12.95; plus $4.00 U.S. shipping
Paperbound. ISBN: 0-9666389-6-4,
$12.95 plus $4.00 U.S. shipping

Into the Mountains Dark: A WWII Odyssey from Harvard Crimson to Infantry Blue *by Frank Gurley*

"Yet another Aberjona Press classic. . . . A profound coming of age story of a young man's transition to manhood. Emotionally charged, meticulously edited, and expertly packaged, *Into the Mountains Dark* is a wonderful WWII memoir."
—*Military Heritage* magazine

256 pages. Maps. Photos.
Paperbound. ISBN: 0-9666389-4-8,
$14.95 plus $4.00 U.S. shipping

Five Years, Four Fronts:
The War Years of Georg Grossjohann, Major, German Army (Retired)
by Georg Grossjohann

"This is not an *All Quiet on the Western Front* or another *The Forgotten Soldier.* In my opinion, it is a better book."
—*The Journal of Military History*

218 pages. Maps. Photos. Index.
Paperbound. ISBN: 0-9666389-3-X,
$14.95 plus $4.00 U.S. shipping

Black Edelweiss: A Memoir of Combat and Conscience by a Soldier of the Waffen-SS
by Johann Voss

"A fascinating and unique contribution to our knowledge of the motivations of the men who comprised not only the Waffen-SS, but much of the rest of the German armed forces in the Second World War. . . . It is highly recommended."—*The Journal of Military History*

224 pages. Maps. Photos.
Paperbound. ISBN: 0-9666389-8-0,
$19.95 plus $4.00 U.S. shipping

The Final Crisis: Combat in Northern Alsace, January 1945
by Richard Engler

"Quite remarkable. . . . Superbly researched and well written. . . . What emerges is a clear sense of just how important the individual American soldier was in winning the war in Europe and just how effectively he generally performed in combat." —*Military Heritage* magazine

368 pages. Maps. Photos. Index.
Paperbound. ISBN: 0-9666389-1-3,
$29.95 plus $4.00 U.S. shipping